CRYSTAL WRIGHT'S

HAIR MAKEUP & FASHION STYLING CAREER GUIDE

THE INSIDER'S GUIDE TO A SUCCESSFUL CAREER IN PRINT, VIDEO, FILM & TV

CRYSTAL WRIGHT'S

HAIR MAKEUP & FASHION STYLING CAREER GUIDE

THE INSIDER'S GUIDE TO A SUCCESSFUL CAREER IN PRINT, VIDEO, FILM & TV

CRYSTAL WRIGHT
MOTIVATIONAL MEDIA PRODUCTIONS

Published by Motivational Media Productions, LLC.
1911 SW Campus Drive, Ste. 194, Federal Way, WA 98023

Crystal Wright's The Hair Makeup & Fashion Styling Career Guide

Motivational Media Productions books are available at special quantity discounts for bulk purchase for sales promotions, premiums, fund-raising and educational needs. Special books or book excerpts also can be created to fit specific needs. For details, write Motivational Media Productions, 1911 SW Campus Drive, Ste 194, Federal Way, WA 98023. You may also email your requests to orders@motivationalmediaproductions.com or call (323) 299-0500.

Library of Congress Cataloging-in-Publication Data

Wright, Crystal A.

Crystal Wright's The Hair Makeup & Fashion Styling Career Guide: The Insider's Guide to a Successful Freelance Career in Print, Video, Film & TV | Crystal A. Wright

ISBN 978-0-9970652-1-3

Printed in the United States of America

96 95 94 93 92   10 9 8 7 6

BOOK COVER DESIGN BY KIRYL LYSENKA AT UPWORK.COM

Choose not to be Common

I choose not to be a common [wo]man

It's my right to be uncommon if I can.

I seek opportunity, not security.

I do not wish to be a kept citizen,

humbled and dulled by having the State look after me.

I want to take the calculated risk,

to dream and to build,

to fail, and to succeed.

I refuse to live from hand to mouth.

I prefer the challenges of life to a guaranteed existence,

the thrill of fulfillment to the stale calm of utopia.

I will not trade freedom for charity,

nor my dignity for a handout.

I will not cower before any master, nor bend to any threat.

It is my heritage to stand erect, proud and unafraid,

to face the world boldly and say,

'This, I have done.'

Written by
Dean Alfange

American Statesman between 1942 and 1950

As I heard it [slightly altered] by Motivational Speaker Les Brown

VISIT

www.crystalwrightliveacademies.com/p/careerguideexclusives:

- Sign up for our mailing list
- Receive notices of updates to this book and events Crystal is hosting
- Link to and download FREE resources
- Subscribe to Crystal's Freelance Friendly Tip Advisor
- Join the exclusive PYP freelance artist community
- Register for PYP 2018 and beyond

www.YouTube.com/CrystalWrightLive to:

- Get more help with your business through Crystal's awesome videos

www.GigSalad.com/crystal_wright_live to:

- Book Crystal for your next live or online event

www.WinNowMentorshipProgram.com to:

- Register for Crystal's 10-Week Online Mentorship Program

GET IN TOUCH

To learn about Crystal's courses, consulting and training by:

- Emailing Assistant2Crystal@CrystalWrightLive.com
- Calling the office at (323) 299-0500

CONNECT

To become part of the conversation online at:

- crystal.wright
- CrystalAWright
- crystalwrightlive

Table of Contents

This 7th edition of the 'Career Guide' is dedicated to my friend, life long learner, Celebrity Hair Stylist and PYP Grad

ANTWON JACKSON

1972 – 2016

Thank You For Your Friendship,
Love & Support

You Are Missed

Credits & Contributors

Crystal Wright
Author

Bobbi Brown
Foreword

Featured Interviews

Carol Oliveto, Creative Director
Craig Brooks, Director
Daniel Chinchilla, Makeup Artist
Daven Mayeda, Beauty Director
Frank Moore, Agent
Jaleesa Jaikaran, Makeup Artist
Mary Delgado, Makeup Artist
Melissa Mangrum, Makeup Artist
Michele Gay, CEO
Mike Ruiz, Photographer
Oscar James, Hair Stylist
Reesa Mallen, Creative Director
Rose Cefalu, Photo Editor
Sir John, Makeup Artist
Titilayo Bankole, Manicurist

Contributors

Cristy Guy
David Maderich
Michael Mosher
Monifa Mortis
Reesa Mallen
Tobi Britton

Advice Contributions

Ericka Cherrie
Jeanne San Diego
Jennifer Cunningham
Jennifer Macdougall
Lisa Calderon
Monae Everett
Nicole Jay
Reesa Mallen
Tania Russell
Terria Fontaine
Titilayo Bankole

Book Cover Design

Kiryl Lysenka
at Upwork.com

Inside Book Design

Padma Senthil Kumar
at Upwork.com

Copy Editor

Susan Dimmock
at Upwork.com

Original Illustrations

Marija Smiljevska
at Upwork.com

Foreword by
Bobbi Brown

**MAKEUP ARTIST & FOUNDER
BOBBI BROWN COSMETICS**

When I began my career as a freelance makeup artist I had determination, tunnel vision and a bit of naivete. I moved to New York, opened the yellow pages and cold called everyone who I thought could lead me in a direction of success. I somehow figured it out. I have mentored many young makeup artists as I fully believe in giving back. That is exactly what Crystal has done. When I first came across her book, I was happy that someone had finally put all the information an aspiring artist needs, in one place.

What I love about the Guide is that Crystal tells it like it is. She gives the essential information and breaks it down into step-by-step instructions for anyone aspiring to have a successful career in print, video, film or TV.

As an agent for 25 years, Crystal negotiated advertising, television commercial, music video, magazine and film deals for her clients. The Crystal Agency was credited regularly in top entertainment and lifestyle magazines next to A-List clients such as Halle Berry, Alec Baldwin, Janet Jackson, Jim Carrey and Tyra Banks. When she wrote the first 'Guide' back in 1995, she took artistry to a business level never seen before in our industry.

Building a body of work that I could use to showcase my talent was the single most important task I needed to accomplish when I started out in the industry. Crystal tells artists exactly how to do it. She tells you how and where to find the right photographers to collaborate with, how to interest them in working with you and the precautions you should take to ensure that you receive the right images you need for showcasing your own work.

As a young artist, I called every agency I could and offered my assistance on shoots. I would work for free to build my portfolio. Throughout the book, Crystal calls on experts like Creative Director Reesa Mallen to share tips and tricks on how to get your foot in the door and build relationships with reputable modeling agencies.

Knowing the right way to put yourself out there can be a challenge, but Crystal makes it simple by sharing how to incorporate traditional forms of self-promotion like business cards, comp cards, your website and bio with new media vehicles such as Instagram and Facebook.

Crystal's tips for choosing and arranging images will help to take the guesswork out of laying out your online portfolio and give you the confidence to know which images should make it into your book.

One aspect of the business that is extremely important is knowing how to handle yourself on set. Unfamiliar situations pop-up regularly and, without proper guidance, it can be difficult to know how to solve a problem. To make sure you're equipped, Crystal has armed you with prepared scripted scenarios and interviews with working artists throughout the Guide.

Crystal's 24 years of experience representing celebrity stylists in Los Angeles and New York gives every reader who might be dreaming of signing with an agency the upper hand when it comes to approaching agencies for representation. Knowledge is power, and that is what Crystal is giving you with this fully revised and updated 7th edition of the Career Guide. It is packed with the Do's and Don'ts of freelancing, presentation techniques that work in the age of social media, résumé samples, a system for getting booked on jobs in all the major genres including magazines, TV commercial productions, catalogs, TV and film, music, videos and more.

This book delivers to you the information and tools you need to get booked, get noticed and be confident that you can deliver what clients, photographers, agencies and key artists want and need from you on set.

From one artist to another, if you dream of succeeding as a freelance makeup, hair, fashion stylist, or manicurist, Crystal Wright's Hair Makeup & Fashion Styling Career Guide is the definitive resource on how to break into the business and achieve star status as a beauty and fashion professional in print, video, film and TV.

BOBBI BROWN
Makeup Artist & Founder, Bobbi Brown Cosmetics

 justbobbibrown
bobbibrown

A Word from Crystal

When LA-based celebrity makeup artist, Tara Posey, asked me to be her agent, I didn't know what I was getting myself into. Heck, I didn't even know that makeup artists had agents. What I did know was that, while I had loved my sales job at Xerox, going back there to sell more copiers was not an option. My life was supposed to be fabulous—and shuttling office equipment in and out of office buildings wasn't it. So, after being coerced into negotiating Tara's day rate and overtime for an upcoming Janet Jackson video, and making her over $9,000 on that one gig—I was all in.

With her portfolio, boundless enthusiasm and a phone list in hand, I set out to gather contacts, schedule meetings, learn my new job and book her on as many high-profile gigs as possible. Word got out, and before I knew it, I was representing makeup artists, hair stylists, fashion stylists, manicurists and photographers out of my Los Angeles and New York offices.

I became inspired to write the very first 'Career Guide' after receiving a letter and phone call from an aspiring makeup artist, who, after graduating from a well-known Los Angeles makeup academy, was no closer to booking a freelance job than she was becoming the governor of California. In her letter, she asked me for suggestions on creating a portfolio. I was astounded! She had spent thousands of dollars learning how to apply makeup but hadn't been taught a thing about how to market and present herself properly as a professional freelance artist in the entertainment industry.

I wrote the Career Guide to help artists just like her and you. An associate, Elka Kovac, had taken me under her wing and taught me the most effective way of representing artists. The Guide is my way of paying it forward.

THE HAIR MAKEUP & STYLING CAREER GUIDE

ALL YOU NEED TO KNOW ABOUT

Building a Strong Portfolio
Testing with Photographers
Signing with an Agency
Working with Record Labels Magazines, & Production Companies
The Ins and Outs of Being a Hair, Makeup or Fashion Stylist in Print, Video, Film & Television

Crystal A. Wright

I love helping artists succeed. It's my passion, my reward, and my ministry. Throughout the pages of this Guide, I sow every bit of wisdom and the lessons that I've learned into you. Follow my direction, act upon my instructions and you will become a stand-out artist among your peers.

I continue to be blessed by artists that I mentor throughout this book, in my live program, online courses, and through my private one-on-one coaching sessions.

Since penning the 1st Edition in 1995, the industry is much changed. Technology is king, and an artist who is trying to succeed without an Instagram page and an online portfolio is like someone living in LA without a car—you can't get anything done! Instagram and Facebook are a must if you intend to be an artist and an influencer or just get free product for your kit. C'mon now, it's a new day, artists, and I'm here to show you the way! Whatever your choice—print, video, film, TV, catalog, e-commerce or a combination of all of them—this book is a tool. It's an oversized pocket guide with step-by-step instructions for creating a plan, locating the best resources, and setting yourself up for sustained success in your dream career.

People will tell you that the industry is saturated! Bah humbug! There is more TV, film and online content being created than ever before, and you can be part of it! Cable and network television are full of makeover and reality shows, and each day, artists become nearly as well known as the celebrities they work with. Amazon and Netflix have turned the industry on its heels, and a recording artist can find you on Instagram and book you directly for their next CD cover.

Throughout the book, I'll share the secrets I have learned and those of successful artists who have already done what you are about to do, and I provide advice from the decision-makers that you'll need to impress.

I promise that if you read this Guide, and don't skim it, but really put the steps I give you into action, the things that I prescribe for you will work. You will find yourself in the enviable position of experiencing success and getting handsomely compensated for doing work that you love.

My one request is that you implement what you learn from the Guide. It's not magic; you need to follow my instructions and put in the effort. If we ever meet, I want to know that your book is 'tore up from the floor up.' It's not meant to sit on a shelf. It's meant to be well-used, personalized, and junked up with red pens and plenty of highlights. It is the number one tool in your freelance toolkit.

Work it, use it and spill some coffee on it, and it will serve you well.

Sincerely, Your Mentor

Crystal A. Wright

I get people Unstuck!

Introduction

In 1995 when I wrote and published the first Hair Makeup & Fashion Styling Career Guide, it was a very different time. So different in fact that Apple hadn't even produced the first iPhone. Can you imagine? No, I'm sure some of you cannot.

The Career Guide, just like the iPhone, changed the game. For many artists [like you] who were searching for answers to their questions about how to build a career and make a living doing something you love—working in print, video, film, TV and YES bridal, it was the holy grail referred to by many as the "Industry Bible."

"Did she really just compare her book to the iPhone? That's ballsy," you probably thought. Yes, it is! And if you want to live as a creative entrepreneur, have some fun, make some money, and create the life of your dreams—you had better get ballsy too!

From edition #1 to the one you're holding in your hands right now, my mission was always to demystify the industry for you in a way that no one else would, with step by step instructions, specific *dos* and *don'ts*, real resources, and facts that give you confidence and make you feel self-assured.

This is not fake news.

In between these pages are the real deal. I want to teach you how to fish so you can eat for the rest of your life. Think of the Career Guide as your portable mentor. Throw it in your makeup, hair or styling kit. Just don't leave home without it!

I've put all the information you need right here in one place. I was an agent for 25 years, and during that time, I negotiated all kinds of lucrative deals for the artists I represented—and that includes photographers. They were well paid, worked on fabulous gigs, and traveled the world with their celebrity besties and commercial clients—and you can too.

But to do it, you need truthful information from experts, artists and decision-makers who are working successfully in the business TODAY! And that's what I'm giving you in the Guide.

You see, knowing what lipstick celebrity makeup artist Sir John uses on Beyoncé is good, but learning what steps he took to land an artist of that caliber is everything, because knowledge can be absorbed, learned and used. Blues legend BB King said, "The beautiful thing about learning is that no one can take it from you."

Having a producer's phone number and email address is good, but having the script of what to say on the phone or in an email and knowing when to follow up means that you can repeat the steps and win gigs over and over again.

I'm going to show you the WRIGHT way to present yourself in front of clients and celebrities who can hire you, and photographers who can help you build your portfolio with magazine-worthy models. You'll learn to combine traditional and new media tools to get noticed. Putting yourself front and center on social media works best when your brand lines up with professionalism, follow-up, and follow-thru.

The Career Guide is confidence in a box.

I'm going to take the guesswork out of how you should behave on set by arming you with set etiquette secrets that will serve you throughout your career.

And for those of you who are considering agency representation, I'm going to share my 25 years of experience running an agency on two coasts and tell you exactly what today's agents and bookers are looking for, how to approach them, what questions to ask and also how to get on the agency assistants list so you can build your résumé, experience, and confidence.

The Guide will dispel myths that you may have been carrying around for years which hinder your development and success. I'm going to provide you with the correct answers to overcome challenges that are keeping you "stuck." These shortcuts to success will shave years off your learning curve and ensure that you start each day feeling like a winner because you're confident of the next step.

Here's the truth. If you set the Career Guide down on your coffee table and never pick it up again, it won't help you. If you stick it on a shelf or put it in a drawer, it won't help you. If, on the other hand, you commit to consistently reading a little bit every day or so, it will change your career and your life forever. I know it's a big book, but you don't have to eat it all at once. Inch by inch, it's a cinch I always say. Grab a 5-page chunk, eat it, digest it and come back for more. You see, I've already given you a plan, and you haven't even started reading the good stuff yet.

> *If you set the Career Guide down on your coffee table and never pick it up again, it won't help you.*

When I was an account executive at Xerox, I learned things from my sales manager, Tom Alire, that serve me well to this day. I have incorporated them not just into my work and my life, but into my belief system. One of those things is a saying, and it goes like this: Plan to Work and Work the Plan. I'm going to give you tools, information, inspiration, and step by step instructions so that you can, "Plan to Work and Work YOUR plan."

Having a plan is essential. Chinese-American author Katherine Paterson said, "A dream without a plan is just a wish."

Everything you need is inside these pages. C'mon.
Let's do this!

> *"Foresight + Imagination + Great Attitude = Viable Candidate*
>
> *—Daven Mayeda*
>
> *Hair & Makeup Artist, Beauty Director | Splashlight Studios*

1

Getting Started

If you've ever been inside a shopping mall, you are well acquainted with the large free-standing information boards called directories. They are usually located close to the main entrance of the mall or near the escalators. The first thing most people look for when they approach one of these large directories is the brightly colored dot, and the words, YOU ARE HERE.

From that bright spot on the board, you can locate the store or stores you want to find, determine the order in which to approach them and then plot the best course for getting to each one in the time allotted. Quite simply, a PLAN!

Sir John

Celebrity Makeup Artist

Brand Ambassador, L'Oreal

A career as a freelance makeup, hair, fashion stylist or manicurist should be approached the same way—with a plan. Throughout this book, your objective will be to formulate and implement a plan for achieving your own version of creative success.

The Career Guide is your GPS, and YOU ARE HERE! I'm going to help you navigate and negotiate the opportunities right along with the potholes. Let's GO!

There is tons of work out there. In fact, there is something for everyone. Editorial, E-commerce, TV, Film, Catalog, Music Videos, Runway and the list goes on. It is a veritable candy store of opportunity. Some of you are drawn to fashion magazines and see yourselves working in New York alongside photographers like Patrick Demarchelier on the covers of Elle Magazine, Vogue and Harper's Bazaar. Others are mesmerized by the prospect of working on beauty campaigns for companies like L'Oreal and Maybelline. Yet, some put working and traveling with a big celebrity like Beyoncé or prepping Cate Blanchett for the red carpet at the top of their bucket list. These are just a few of your options.

Working for many well-known brands such as Gillette, Head & Shoulders, Nike or Coke—known as lifestyle advertising [formerly slice of life]—can be just as fun and lucrative as working with celebrities, and doesn't require that you pack up and move to a major city like New York or LA where fashion, beauty, and entertainment rule.

Bridal work is available in every market, has a pre-determined season, and can be done even when you have a full or part-time job because most weddings happen on weekends. Weddings also have a season, typically April through September, and are booked well in advance, making it possible for you to plan and project your income. In California and other warm-weather destinations where people can get married outdoors, weddings happen all year round. Weddings are a great place to start, build and grow your business.

Catalog work is as steady as the post office and often generates a high five-figure income for artists because most of it is five days a week and goes on for many weeks at a time.

E-commerce is the biggest change in the industry. Online sales increased by 9.1% between 2010 and 2017. With that a new trend has emerged wherein the photo production of various catalogs and online content is brought under one mega-studio roof that produces everything for several clients. These studios are springing up everywhere, but especially in New York, Miami, and Southern California.

Runway shows are produced in big and small cities alike, but the dream of many artists is to work backstage during New York, London, Milan or Paris fashion week. With two opportunities to jump on board in each of the cities listed above—February for Fall/Winter and September for Spring/Summer, it's never too early to start staking out your claim to get added to a team. Getting on is not as hard as you might think, but it does take persistence.

It goes without saying that the opportunities in TV and film are expanding. In the last five years, we have all witnessed new players like Netflix and Amazon get in the game. They have entered these genres not just as distributors like Hulu and Apple TV, but as content creators of television shows and feature films right alongside the big networks (ABC, NBC, CBS) and film studios (Warner Bros., Universal, Sony Pictures). I share

this to remind you that it's not overcrowded. You will hear it. Don't believe it. Just keep working your plan.

You might be asking yourself, "Well, is Crystal going to talk about being an influencer?" The answer is no. I pondered it, but it's not my forte. I would be bluffing, and you would soon figure it out. I decided to stay in my lane where I am THE expert, and that's making sure that you know how to succeed in print, video, film, and TV.

If your goal is to be an influencer, I'm pretty sure that there is someone out there who can guide you better than I. If I hear of them, or find a great book that I think is worth reading, I'll be sure to share it with you online through my social media.

Working through this chapter will open your eyes to a ton of opportunities in the industry and give you time to familiarize yourself with all of the career options at your disposal. This is where you will choose a starting place from which to build a career and achieve your goals as a freelance artist in print, video, film, and TV.

The operative word here is *start*. Who knows where you'll be in two or three years? In the past, this industry mirrored the general population going to work in a 9-5 job where you worked for 30 years, got a gold watch and went home to retire. Freelance artists who worked in TV and film worked their way up through the ranks from assistant to key artist to department head, and rarely ventured out of that genre. That was before 50 was the new 35 and orange was the new black. Now, all bets are off. Everywhere you look, there is cross-pollination. No longer do you have to spend 20 years working on films when you would also like to work on print ad campaigns and editorials or vice versa. Instagram and YouTube have leveled the playing

Sir John is a world-renowned celebrity makeup artist, visionary, and brand ambassador for L'Oréal. He is responsible for creating memorable makeup looks for Beyoncé, Naomi Campbell, Chrissy Teigen, Karlie Kloss, Liya Kebede and many others. I caught up with Sir John during a rare moment of downtime from his demanding schedule to ask if he would share some insights about his journey with aspiring artists.

You have a background in fine arts. Can you tell us how that impacted your career as a makeup artist?

Sir John: Art definitely has impacted my career. While the makeup counter taught me all the nuances of artistry and how to work with different skin tones and textures, art is what really shaped me as a makeup artist. Art is so important because we have a generation of makeup artists where it's like the blind leading the blind. We have all of these influencers and YouTubers that don't really know the art behind what they are doing.

To really know your artistry, you need to take art classes. If you can't do that, then go to museums or research online. You might want to study the different washes of color and how greats like Renoir and Rembrandt used them. Learn how colors are used in 2 dimensions and then transfer that to a 3-dimensional face. That's what will make you have an impact. People just don't understand fine art references anymore. For example, I was working with Beyoncé, and she wanted a certain look. So I suggested something from the Byzantine era. It was exactly what she wanted, but no one else was able to discern that for her. If you know art history, you become

field because Instagram gives you access to people who might never have been able to find you and YouTube provides you with the ability to learn new skills that can enhance what you're already doing and prepare you for new opportunities.

WHERE TO BEGIN

A Portfolio

In this early stage, it's important to recognize right away that the foundation of your success and longevity in the business starts with your commitment to building a body of work. That body of work begins with just one photograph, or one student film, or one music video, one TV show, or one play that showcases your talent and [over time] morphs into an online portfolio, network of relationships and experience [marketed smartly] that gets you booked, referred and re-booked on jobs.

This lifelong career pursuit is known as building your portfolio or building your book. I will use these terms interchangeably so be ready. And as long as you work, it never ends because every paid or unpaid job that you accept is done with the hope that it will return to you something that you can add to your book, résumé (credits), online reel or social media accounts that will peak the interest of a decision-maker who wants to hire you to work on his/her set.

Testing

So, how do we build this portfolio? Building your 'portfolio' typically begins with unpaid creative collaborations known as TESTING and transitions [over time] into published work (tearsheets, a.k.a tears) from paid and non-paid assignments. Yes, it was a mouthful. Let me break it down.

Testing is a collaboration between a team of artists such as a photographer, makeup artist, hair stylist, fashion stylist, manicurist and a model, who all come together to shoot stories that produce beautiful digital images that each of you can showcase in your online portfolio with the express purpose of:

1. Securing more and better testing opportunities with better photographers.

2. Securing paid work assignments from decision-makers.

3. Producing images that can you can use to market and promote yourself in print and online through social media.

4. Attracting and engaging new and existing followers.

Simply put, you gotta' get pictures to show folks so they can hire you for work. Kapish?!

Not every test will include every one of the artists mentioned above. A testing collaboration might be a makeup artist and a photographer and the model for a beauty test where only the face and slicked back hair is being shot. Or, the collaboration could be a photographer and a manicurist for a still shot of a model's hands holding a glass or a purse in several different angles and a couple of polish changes. Or it could be the full-blown execution of a fashion story in the desert that your team has been meeting about on FaceTime and over coffee and arranging for weeks.

From the simplest idea of two artists working together to photograph a gorgeous red lip for a holiday story, to a fashion stylist using their relationships to pull a couture gown from the hottest designer showroom so it can be photographed at night on the steps of the New York Public Library—testing is where artists can let their imaginations run wild.

The images from your best test shoots become the foundation of showcasing your work in your online portfolio. The people you work with are your collaborators, and the photographer's names become entries in your growing list of credits that can be transferred onto your résumé.

Images are everything.

Any job (or test) that you do that results in work being published in a magazine, on an outdoor billboard, as a mobile [that hangs from the ceiling in a gas station], on packaging or a book cover, is called a tearsheet.

While a TV commercial, music video or feature film is not called a tearsheet, it serves the same purpose. It gives you credibility, tells someone else who is considering hiring you that another decision-maker trusted you with something important and adds credits to your growing résumé.

Examples of print-related tearsheets include magazine editorials (stories), ads in magazines (L'Oréal), CD covers, book covers, packaging, overhead hanging mobiles, point of sale merchandise, direct mail inserts, catalogs, newspaper, billboards, bus sides, etc. If it's a piece of flat art and you worked on it, it's your tearsheet, and you should collect it for your portfolio, photograph or scan it and upload it to your site, and if it's cool enough—share it with your followers on Instagram and Facebook.

indispensable and relevant. Study all of it. Get to know that the cat eye was created 2000 years ago, not in the 90s.

Why do you think so many new makeup artists aren't looking for inspiration in the fine arts?

Sir John: So many just want to be famous without actually putting the time and work into it. You really have to think about what you want to contribute via your work to this moment in time. The projects we work on as makeup artists are like a time capsule. For example, I want to do work that I can look at 50 years from now and find relevance in it. If you study art, you'll realize that every era in time had its relevance. That's what we want to continue doing with our artistry.

How do you feel about social media?

Sir John: Social media is like our own personal channel. It's your personal version of HBO or NBC. We need to look at it like an editorial space and treat it that way.

> Curate what you post because people are watching. I think social media is our vehicle to show the world our ideas and our judgment call.

It shows how much judgment you have, how much creativity you possess, and what your voice is. I'm aware of so many social issues and haven't always felt like I could have a voice about them. But now, I know that I can talk about beauty, and I can discuss what society has done to beauty. I can speak about the intersection between politics and beauty and how they also run parallel.

Which Way Go I?

In the early stages of your career (first 1-2 years), choice should be used as a starting point. Why? Because often, when embarking on a new path, we only think we know what we want because 1) we haven't done it yet and 2) we don't know what the job actually entails. Everything looks sexy when you're sitting on the sidelines trying to get on.

My sister went to law school. She had an idea in her head about what it would be like to work as an attorney. The reality was far from what she imagined, and she spent the next 20 years happily working for a judge instead.

New York Makeup artist, Monifa Mortis, received her Bachelor's degree in Fashion Merchandising from the Laboratory Institute of Merchandising and thought that high fashion would be her schtick when she became a makeup artist. Not so. It was only after working backstage at a fashion show during New York Fashion Week (NYFW) that she learned that she hated the fast pace and non-meticulous nature of makeup artistry on fashion shows. That genre just wasn't for her. But she soon found out that celebrities were. The pace, privacy, and extended time allotted for perfecting the makeup application suited her personality, and she developed a successful business by finding and owning her niche: working with celebrities who favored clean, modern, sexy makeup.

LA-based makeup artist, Uzmee Krakovszki, has worked in television with her beloved client, Jeannie Mai of *The Real* for several years now, and while she loves her client, she isn't so stoked about the singular nature of working in a studio all day for days on end and she's even less thrilled about the drop in her income. She liked it much better when she had more flexibility, worked on TV just a few days a week and could augment that work with other 1-2 day advertising and editorial print jobs with photographers and television commercials. Her life in a studio five days a week is not what she had in mind.

The moral of these three stories are, you won't know what's real for YOU until you get a little muddy. Get out there in the trenches and see what you like and what you're drawn to.

Along the way, you may fall in love with other things. Leave room to be surprised. When Uzmee's mom passed a year or so ago, what's important started to change for her. Life seemed shorter and as if it could end at any time. She wanted to make more of a difference in people's lives, and discovering the transformative powers of microblading has made this possible for her. "Makeup is wiped off at the end of the day, but eyebrows frame a person's face, and you haven't seen joy until you give someone brows who has been living for years with the loss of hair on their face from alopecia," she says.

If you're just getting your feet wet in this industry, now is a great time to experiment with different genres.

At this juncture, choice serves an important purpose: to help you find a starting point. You can mix it up—a film here, a print ad there, a play, a TV commercial, an editorial, etc. It's all fine, and I encourage it because I want you to find your niche. Also, and this is crucial—while you may do lots of different jobs, you will always have the option to choose what does and does not go in your online portfolio, on your résumé or out there for the world to see and hear about in social media. In other words, CURATE! Put the work into context, categorize

and organize it. Some jobs are just money jobs and should never see the light of day. The work itself or the working conditions of a particular job or project may have prevented you from producing great imagery. That's okay. Just don't show it to anyone. Don't talk about it. Just take the money you made and reinvest it in yourself.

If, on the other hand, the work wasn't good but the credit is everything, add it to your résumé and get that little professional bump that may get you hired on the next project that will net you some beautiful images.

Curate is the hot new word that started gaining popularity in 2012 when [in an article] Fast Company magazine called Pinterest a content-curating site. To curate means to contextualize, and organize information. That is what you will be doing for the rest of your career online and in social media. You will be making decisions about what will be seen when it will be displayed , how it will be arranged, and how long it will be seen. In essence, you will be creating an experience for the people who visit your site and social media platforms. These people have the power to hire you, or move on. With that in mind, give them something beautiful to look at, and arrange your images in the order that you want them to be seen. That is how you create an experience.

Did you ever work as an assistant?

Sir John: I got to where I am because I worked really hard. New artists shouldn't turn down the opportunity to assist a key. I gave up makeup for a while and started working as a visual artist for a store in New York. I would stay up all night doing their window displays. But then one day, one of my old artist friends ran into me on my lunch break and told me he was working with Pat McGrath. At the time, I didn't know who Pat was, but he said she needed an assistant for Fashion Week. I hesitated but then decided to do it. After my first show with her, she asked me to go to Milan two weeks later. So, this was a turning point in my life, and all because I didn't turn down the opportunity to be an assistant. Everything sort of aligned after that.

What did you learn?

Sir John: Going to Milan was my first trip out of the country. My first show there was for Dolce & Gabbana, and after that, I was booked to work for Prada. It was all kind of a whirlwind. Pat just took me under her wing and the next thing I knew, I was in Paris. I started meeting all the top girls in the fashion industry, making connections, alliances, and relationships. I was learning every day without the pressure that the key artists had. Assistants weren't under that type of pressure or scrutiny from the fashion directors. I just worked and took it all in. I allowed myself to be an assistant and decided to become the best assistant possible. I learned what Pat would need before she even asked for it. I was always one step ahead. And that's the problem now, nobody wants to

What's important right now is that you:

1	Position yourself to be ready for opportunity.
2	Say YES more often than you say no.
3	Find out which opportunities and situations make you light up like a Christmas tree.
4	Learn to stay away from opportunities that don't bring you joy.
5	Build relationships.
6	Practice your craft.
7	Invest in more education.
8	Be someone who can be depended upon.
9	Ask more questions than you answer, and listen more than you talk.

Along the way from one yes to another, from one relationship to another, from one class to another, and from one experience to another, you will find your niche. And as you do, your objective will be to curate your work in such a way that creative decision-makers will come to know and believe that you have an area of expertise, vision and an approach to creativity that they desire and need. In that space, you will be well paid!

WHAT'S IT LIKE TO WORK ON. . .

...Print & Electronic Media

Print and electronic media is a whole different ballgame. The picture, the entire picture and EVERYTHING including the picture matters! That's why the glam squad is so important. The collaboration of people (makeup, hair, stylist, photographer, manicurist, and model) who produce the image are all part of the magic. Earlier in this chapter, I talked about testing. The objective of testing is the production of WOW that makes a creative decision-maker want to book you for their next project.

As a print artist, you are always updating your book, and in pursuit of creating or collecting (from a photographer or a client) images and tearsheets (published work) that will get you to your next great job, collaboration, meeting, opportunity or level.

To secure work in print and electronic media, your primary goals are to build an online portfolio and social media presence, and cultivate followers that will:

1 Position you to be considered and booked by decision-makers who are hiring for beauty, fashion, lifestyle advertising, celebrity press junkets, CD covers, magazines, catalog, runway and e-commerce assignments, etc.

2 Attract the attention of top agencies who will consider you for representation or their assistants list.

3 Elevate your profile along with your day rate and get you well compensated by advertisers.

4 Get you noticed by brands who can supply you with FREE product because you have a dedicated and growing group of followers who can put new eyeballs on their products.

The better your portfolio is, the higher the day rate and the better the perks (business and first class flights, 4-5 star hotels, car service, etc.) you can command for your expertise (creative interpretation).

Better, in this case, means published work (tearsheets) with major lifestyle, beauty and high fashion advertisers; magazines, celebrities, recording artists; and even cutting-edge highly stylized tests.

Catalog is the television work of the print industry. It's steady work, and shoots often go on for several days. It pays well, averaging $500-$850 per day, and is usually very consistent once you get on board with a photographer or the company that is producing the catalogs. The stores—think Bloomingdales and Banana Republic—that produce catalogs often hire the same teams over and over again for years on end. Utilizing the same people ensures the consistency they require to meet the discerning needs of their customers. It's great work when you can get it.

E-commerce is like a catalog on steroids. The studios that produce the multitude of images we see online operate at least 5 days a week, hire both freelance artists and, in some cases, maintain full and part-time glam squads and typically pay be of service anymore. But then, you lose out. When you become the best assistant possible, who do you think your key is going to call if they can't make it to a job? That's what happened to me. Pat wasn't able to go to a booking with Naomi Campbell, so she sent me. I couldn't believe it, but I did it! Naomi was my first celebrity client.

I believe in assisting. I'm glad that you do, too.

Sir John: Yes. Being an assistant is really impactful. The fact that you can learn from all these different teachers gives you such a multifaceted education and one that your counterparts won't have. You make relationships and connections that are invaluable. All of these important people in the business get to know you by name, know you by face, and know that you helped the key and what you brought to the table.

I'm also really huge on energy and feel that it's crucial and impactful. I know that when you are on a set as an assistant, and you make everyone feel good and ensure the room feels more comfortable, you will keep getting called back.

How you make people feel is important isn't it?

Sir John: A lot of people can do beautiful hair and makeup, but clients will always remember how you made them feel. And I'm talking about not just being nice to the celebrity or the key artist, or the director, but also the person sweeping the floor. If you have good energy with everyone, people will start whispering your name, pointing at you, and making sure that you come back.

$500 - $650 a day for freelancers and $50,000 - $100,000 per year for full-time, on-staff makeup, hair and stylists.

Advertising, which includes print ads and TV commercials, is the cream of the crop. It pays very well, usually $700-$4,000 a day, is high profile and exposes you to some of the best photographers and commercial directors in the world. Let me distinguish advertising from editorial for you because people do get confused, since both end up in magazines.

Every magazine has four covers:

Back cover	Front cover
Inside front cover	Inside back cover

The front cover is the only one that is considered editorial because it is the only one that the magazine's editorial staff decides what content appears on it, and then hires artists (photographers, makeup and hair stylists, manicurists, fashion stylists, models, writers, etc.) to execute the editorial vision. The other three covers are sold to advertisers who want to promote their products to YOU! The average cost of a full page ad in Vogue is $203,412.00. That's one page for one month.

If you work on an ad for Prada Eyewear and it ends up inside Vanity Fair magazine, you do not get to add Vanity Fair to your résumé because Prada Eyewear purchased that page in Vanity Fair and many other magazines. You may very proudly add Prada to your résumé and the tearsheet [from that ad] to your online portfolio and your social media account. However, do not get it twisted. In this instance, you did not work for Vanity Fair.

...Runway

Runway shows are great fun, intense, high-pressure and a super way to build and nurture relationships and get on the fast track to doing more fashion and to being invited into the fashion circle. But it is NOT where you make your money. In fact, sometimes, you don't get paid at all, and when you do, it's somewhere between $150 and $350 per show regardless of whether you're in New York, Paris, Milan or London.

...Television & Film

Television is attractive to many because it offers a sense of security and camaraderie. Many artists get jobs on television shows and work there for many years, collecting a steady paycheck as if they worked a 9-5. Because you often develop close friendships with the other crew members, going to work feels like hanging out with your family.

Working on a film, while not quite as steady as television, can go from a few weeks to several months, providing a paycheck that you can plan on. Every day you work with the same people, make friends and develop relationships that can turn into referrals and bookings on upcoming projects.

In film & TV, you build a résumé; it's your calling card. It is bolstered by the positions/titles (1st, 2nd, key, department head, etc.) and thus, the amount of responsibility you hold on the projects you work on. There are two primary goals:

1 To gain enough experience working on projects that you can apply for better positions and pay on subsequent films until you are qualified to be head of the department.

2 To get into the union so that along with your position and a certain amount of security, workplace protections, medical insurance and a pension, you get added to a roster of eligibility that provides opportunities to work on better projects.

Except for the few right-to-work states (see www.thebalance.com/right-to-work-2071691), most big-budget films—think Wonder Woman, Spider-Man: Homecoming, and Transformers: The Last Knight—are union productions, and if you're not in the union, you cannot work on them, with the exception of occasional day-playing (getting called in sporadically when no union members are available).

I notice that this younger generation, when on set, are only nice to the celebrities and then go on texting, checking Instagram and ignoring everyone else. No, sweetie. Start up a conversation with the people around you. You aren't better than anyone else there, and you don't know who is responsible for bringing you back on set or who will be promoted and in charge of booking. The stylist's assistant might end up being a fashion editor in a few years , so should you be ignoring him or her?

Any other advice for artists trying to rise to the top?

Sir John: Be respectful. Work hard, and don't talk behind people's backs. Everything comes back around in this industry. Just do you and be the best at that. Be willing to walk away from situations that don't feel right because you need to protect your career and at the end of the day, you are the only person that can do that.

IN HIS KIT: 4 THINGS SIR JOHN CAN'T LIVE WITHOUT

- Tom Ford Bronzer
- MAC Blacktrack Fluidline Liner
- Urban Decay Naked Concealer
- Embryolisse Moisturizer

 sirjohnofficial

 www.sirjohnofficial.com

In film & TV, the objective is to create believable characters. On the television show SCANDAL, the CHARACTER, Olivia Pope, played by Kerry Washington, does not change from day-to-day. Each week, when the television audience returns, they find the same Olivia they left the week before—looking pretty much, exactly the same—FABULOUS. That was the case until Season 4 Episode 10 when the plot took a [ridiculous] turn and Olivia got kidnapped and thrown into a Washington, DC basement made to look like a Middle Eastern prison for several episodes. In those weeks, there was no designer clothing and flat-ironed hair. She looked a hot mess, and I'm sure the glam squad had a blast dirtying Olivia up every week until she got rescued and went back to looking FAB!

Helen Mirren won an Academy Award for The Queen in 2006. As a makeup, hair or costume designer on a film, you don't get to come in on Tuesday morning half way through the movie and decide it's time for The Queen to chuck the bifocals and go with a more interesting pair of frames. That kind of creativity is reserved for working on magazines, music videos, and runway.

The film & TV makeup artist must be proficient with techniques that include cuts, bruises, bald caps, etc. The hair stylist must show proficiency with wigs, period styles, and contemporary looks.

It's perfectly normal to see before, during, and after digital images and movie stills in a film and television portfolio. Unlike a print portfolio, the quality of the photographs is not (nor does it have to be) high end. In film and TV, technique and continuity are everything.

Over time, the résumé replaces the portfolio and a successful makeup, hair or costumer is often heard saying, "Gee, no one has asked to see my portfolio in years." Not so with print, TV commercials or runway.

...Video & TV Commercials

I often compare the work pace of music videos and TV commercials to a basketball game. Everything is fast and compressed. As a freelancer, you may spend two days on a television commercial, and then move on to an editorial shoot for a fashion magazine, and then on to a music video. Unlike the camaraderie of working in film and television, you probably will not see the same people at the editorial shoot that you just spent those two days with on the TV commercial.

Music videos pay really well when you're working with big-name talent like Beyoncé and Taylor Swift. However, there are a lot of 12-14 hour low-budget music videos made every day. Don't get burned out. Get what you need for your résumé, establish some great connections, give 100% while you're there and move on.

Directors on music videos are usually working from a 1-2 page treatment that was created and submitted by them to the artist or record label based on a 2-5 minute song. While not always this loose, instructions to makeup, hair and styling talent can sound like "We're going for a kind of edgy urban feeling"—whatever that means.

Regardless of the genre, artists typically start out testing to build their books, assisting key artists to gain real-world experience or both.

Melissa Mangrum

Makeup Artist & Founder

Melissa Mangrum & Co.

BIG
IDEA
AHEAD

GETTING FAMILIAR WITH THE GENRES

The following are brief descriptions of each genre category. They will familiarize you with the subtle differences between print, videos, television commercials, film, TV shows, e-commerce and live performance. By supplying you with some basic information on the type of work assignments you can expect in each genre, I hope to help you zero in on where you would like to focus your energy as you build your freelance career. You'll see spaces for check marks, but don't mark anything just yet. You'll come back to these spaces later.

Print

Makeup, hair, fashion stylists and manicurists who work within the print arena will find themselves working closely with photographers, art directors, graphic designers, artist managers, fashion, beauty and photo editors, sittings editors, model bookers, and photo producers. And those of you who want to work with celebrities will eventually meet the all-powerful celebrity publicist, also known as the handler. Print assignments include but are not limited to working on the following:

PRINT	EXAMPLES
_____ Magazines	Fashion: Vogue, Elle, W, Bazaar,
	Beauty: Allure, Glamour, New Beauty
	Lifestyle: Essence, O, InStyle
	Entertainment: Rolling Stone, Entertainment Weekly, US Weekly
_____ Advertisements	Lifestyle: Nike, Coca-Cola, Mercedes-Benz
	Fashion: Prada, Burberry, Zara
	Beauty: Maybelline, CoverGirl, Bobbi Brown
	Fragrance: J'Adore, Paco Rabanne, Jo Malone London
	Hospitality: Hilton Hotels, Starwood, Four Seasons
_____ CD Covers	Recording Artists: Beyoncé, Rihanna, Justin Timberlake
_____ Catalogs	Brands: Victoria's Secret, J. Crew, Banana Republic
_____ Book Covers	Authors: Lean in (Cheryl Sandberg), Chasing Light (Michelle Obama)
_____ Stock Photography	Getty Images, Wire Images, iStock
_____ Movie Posters	Logan, Kong, Aftermath
_____ Corporate	Annual Reports (multi-page booklets of corporate earnings)

Celebrity

The ideal artist that works with TV & Film celebrities and recording artists has the patience of Job, brings calm to the set, is always ready to serve, doesn't mind stopping to pick up a cup of coffee, is ready to travel at a moment's notice, doesn't mind interruptions while practicing their craft, has a passport and is hella' cool to have around all day.

Melissa Mangrum, *Makeup Artist*

Melissa "Missy" Mangrum is Founder of Melissa Mangrum & Co. She is well known for being a beauty expert in bridal and pageant artistry. Her flawless work and eye for natural beauty has afforded Melissa the opportunity to work with such clients as Glamour Magazine, Nickelodeon, the NFL Network, and Vanity Fair, to name but a few. Melissa shares what motivated her to pursue makeup.

Was becoming a makeup artist something you fell into or was it something you always wanted to do?

Melissa: I wasn't into makeup at all when I was growing up, but in 2004, I was looking for a part-time job and applied to work at Ulta as a cashier. At my interview, I was asked if I could do makeup because they needed someone for their Prestige counter. I said that I did and they hired me. I was clueless! I knew nothing about makeup, but I needed this job, so I decided to fake it until I made it. I would practice and make it a point to learn everything. I wanted to know how to work with all skin tones and be ready for whoever walked in that door. People would come in and request me, and I still couldn't believe it! I took this part-time job and five years later, in 2009, made it my career.

Do you have to do hair in the pageant world as well as makeup, or is it usually a separate thing?

Melissa: You don't have to do both in the pageant world, but I fell into doing hair because there was a need for it. I saw some things happening with the hair that I knew wouldn't look good on stage, so I wanted to help with that. I didn't really know anything about hair, but I knew what looked good and what didn't. But you really don't need to do both.

Celebrity assignments include but are not limited to the following:

CELEBRITY	EXAMPLES
_____ Press Appearances	Junket: Promotion of a product (Film, TV/Radio, Web, Book)
	Red Carpet: Oscars, Emmys, Grammys
_____ Magazines	Covers & Inside Spreads
_____ Television	Talk Shows: James Cordon, The Real, The View

E-Commerce

The artist that works in e-commerce, a.k.a. e-comm, often hails from a print background and may already be working on catalogs and print advertising. Think of e-commerce as print photography and video content created for online. An entire industry has sprung up in the last three years to meet the growing demands of online content. Mega studios produce photo and video content at a dizzying pace that keeps makeup, hair and stylists busy five days a week.

E-COMMERCE	EXAMPLES
_____ E-commerce	Online Content: Catalogs, Looklets, Lookbooks, BTS Video, Social Media Advertising

Runway

The artist that works on runway shows loves fashion and beauty, thrives in a fast-paced, frenzied environment, strives to make their mark in the fashion world and doesn't get stressed out when they get yelled at by the temperamental lead on a show. This artist is focused on building a portfolio that will eventually get them booked on major high fashion ad campaigns such as Gucci, Donna Karan, Prada, Guess, Tom Ford, etc. Your print portfolio is everything when it comes to securing a spot on a top fashion week team.

Artists often pay for their own flight and hotel to work the circuit from NY to London to Paris and Milan. They maintain a tight network of colleagues who keep them informed of who needs artists on shows and pick up shows via text message once they land in each new city. Following is a typical annual fashion week schedule:

2018 FASHION WEEK	SCHEDULE
_____ Paris FW Men's	January 2018
_____ Paris: Haute Couture	January 2018
_____ NYFW Fall/Win	February 2018
_____ London FW Fall/Win	February 2018
_____ Milan FW Fall/Win	February 2018
_____ Paris FW Fall/Winter 2018	February-March 2018
_____ Paris FW Men's	June 2018
_____ Paris: Haute Couture	July 2018
_____ NYFW Spr/Sum 2019	September 2018
_____ London FW Spr/Sum 2019	September 2018
_____ Milan FW Spr/Sum 2019	September 2018
_____ Paris FW Spr/Sum 2019	September/October 2018

Music Videos

The artist that works on music videos quite often has been working with one or more recording artists on their CD covers, publicity and perhaps even their editorial magazine shoots. A good way to break into this area is to develop a print portfolio that showcases beauty and fashion work on tests, editorial assignments, CD covers and publicity shoots. Video assignments include:

VIDEO	EXAMPLES
_____ Music Videos	Beyoncé, Wiz Khalifa, Justin Timberlake, Taylor Swift

Industrial, Educational & Corporate Videos

The educational/training video area is exploding! In addition to the typical videos that have been around for years of men in hard hats walking around a construction site or on an oil platform, the plethora of online courses is generating a ton of new opportunities for glam squad artists. The artist who gets chosen for these kinds of projects might showcase a range of lifestyle, corporate, grooming and clean beauty work in their portfolio, and have some experience working on television and on TV commercials. Video assignments include:

How did you choose pageantry as your niche?

Melissa: It kind of happened organically. I didn't set out to do it, but it found me in a sense. Initially, I was all about doing bridal makeup, but the pageant world isn't all that different. It's still helping a woman look beautiful on her "big day." Really, one job led to another, and that turned into becoming national director for one system and then another. I kept connecting to women in the pageant circuit and the different systems, and everything expanded from that.

Do you remember your first pageant job?

Melissa: My first job was assisting another artist. I'm originally from Richmond, VA and there was an artist there that was working for the Miss United States system. I had met him while freelancing. One day, I saw on Facebook that he was looking to hire people for his team, so I reached out to him. At first, I didn't hear back, but I kept following up. I kept reaching out again and again until finally, he asked me to join the team. I worked for him for two or three seasons after which he felt like he needed to move on, so I weaved my way into his position.

What professional traits or skills helped you gain entry into the pageant niche?

Melissa: I would say it's mainly two things. I was a bill collector for many years, so that helped me learn how to deal with every kind of personality imaginable. In the bridal world, there are bridezillas, and in the pageant world, you can say there are pageantzillas. Being a bill collector prepared me to deal with all of those attitudes. I know that the attitude doesn't represent them, but it's their big day, and they are nervous, also stressed out. I have to

Industrial | Educational

CORPORATE	EXAMPLES
_____ Industrial Videos	Boeing, Microsoft, Shell Oil
_____ Informational Videos	Cancer Research Foundation, AIDS Hospice
_____ Instructional and Training Videos	Online Courses: Virtual Business Academy, Win Now Mentorship Program

TV Commercials

Artists that work primarily on television commercials often have a good deal of experience working on print, advertising, and music videos and know their way around a set. In LA or New York, it's fairly easy to get a job on a low-budget music video to gain experience and learn what goes on on the set of a television commercial.

Artists who work frequently on TV commercials, probably started working on print advertising assignments and then moved into commercials.

In Los Angeles, music video directors soon make their way into directing television commercials and bring their music video glam squads with them. TV commercial projects include the following:

COMMERCIAL	EXAMPLES
_____ Commercials	Burger King, Coca-Cola, Volvo, Nespresso
_____ Infomercials	Proactiv, P90X, Total Gym, George Foreman Grill
_____ Public Service Announcements	SAFE, All American Girl (Heroin), It Can Wait

Live Performance

The daily challenge of working on live shows prepares an artist for addressing issues of timing, the illusion of spontaneity, and the necessity for continuity. These skills are an asset for the rigors of the hectic, demanding and constant pace that is associated with working on episodic television and feature films, which are usually shot out of sequence (last scene first, and so on) and require an artist to keep track of what was done last week, or last month. Live performance includes:

LIVE PERFORMANCE	EXAMPLES
_____ Concerts & Tours	Beyoncé, Taylor Swift, Janet Jackson
_____ Fashion Shows	NYFW: Zac Posen, Marc Jacobs, BCBG
_____ Theatre	Phantom of The Opera, A Raisin In The Sun
_____ Dance	Goffrey Ballet, Dance Theatre of Harlem
_____ Musicals	Hamilton, Book of Mormon, The Color Purple

Television

Artists who work in television often started building their portfolio by working on unpaid student film projects, low-budget independent films, and assisting veteran artists on set. Every [good] job, paid or not, goes onto a résumé that showcases their growing experience on set. The artist who wants to work in television can expect to work on the following projects:

TELEVISION	EXAMPLES
_____ Sitcoms	The Big Bang Theory, Brooklyn Nine-Nine, Blackish
_____ Episodics	The Handmaids Tale, Scandal, Riverdale
_____ Movies	Second Chance Christmas, The Punisher
_____ Miniseries	The Defenders, Big Little Lies
_____ Drama	Orange Is the New Black, The Americans
_____ Action-Adventure	Game of Thrones, Iron Fist, Black Sails
_____ Soap Operas	The Bold and the Beautiful, Days of Our Lives
_____ Science Fiction	Doctor Who, The Expanse, Falling Skies, Defiance
_____ Awards Shows	Grammys, Emmys, Oscars, VMA's, BET Awards
_____ Reality	Project Runway, The Profit, The Bachelor, Survivor
_____ Comedy	Blackish, Parks and Recreation, Saturday Night Live

make them comfortable and realize that it's not about me. Another thing is that I learned that my artistry is not for everybody. I'm okay with that, and I don't let it defeat me. I move on because I know some people love me and want me to work with them.

When you hire assistants and other artists to work with you, what do you look for in their portfolios?

Melissa: I look at online portfolios and social media. I talk to everyone beforehand because I want to know if they are right for the job. I look for someone who can adapt to change, who can take direction, and be selfless. They have to be a team player. I need someone that is a people person and will be professional all the time. Being able to deliver the product that you are selling is very important too.

You mentioned the ability to adapt to change. What types of things can go wrong?

Melissa: It's really not so much about what can go wrong, but with pageants, it's such a big production, and there are so many people involved that things can change at the drop of a hat. Like, call times, for example. Those can change leaving you with a lot less time to get your work done, but you can't sit around with a bad attitude about it. You have to accept it and put in the extra work to get things done on time. Whether that means we are pinning dresses, helping with shoes or adding body glue. Being able to do whatever it takes to make sure the show starts on time is what I mean by being adaptable to change.

Is your team part of the hair, makeup and wardrobe department?

Melissa: We are whatever they need, yes. If one of them

Feature Film

Like television, the artist who works in film often worked their way up by seeking out student and independent film projects and assisting veteran artists on set. In film and TV, the makeup artist and hair stylist retain their titles. However, the word fashion stylist, that is associated with working in print, advertising, editorial and on music videos, changes to wardrobe stylist, or costumer.

The artist who wants to work in film can expect to work on the these kinds of projects:

FILM	EXAMPLES
____ Features	Baby Driver, Wonder Woman, Logan, Get Out
____ Short Films	Fish Story, I Know You From Somewhere, The Rabbit Hunt
____ Student Films	Blood and Water, Luna, Female, Smell The Roses
____ Documentaries	City of Ghosts, Casting JonBenet, Icarus, Whose Streets?

You may be surprised at the vast array of opportunities and exciting career choices. It is here that you begin the process of drilling down your interests.

Let's get focused. Using the list that follows, number each area of interest from 1-8 in order of its importance to you. One being the MOST important, and eight the LEAST.

AREAS OF INTEREST	TYPE OF WORK
____ PRINT	Magazines, CD Covers, Ad Campaigns, Movie Posters Catalogs, Book Covers, Outdoor (Billboards)
____ CELEBRITY	Press Junkets, Red Carpet, Talk Shows
____ E-COMMERCE	Online Lookbooks, Catalogues,
____ VIDEO	Music, Industrial, Educational
____ COMMERCIALS	Commercials, Infomercials, PSA's
____ FILM	Features, Shorts, Documentaries, Student Films
____ TELEVISION	Sitcoms, Soaps, Dramas, Movies of the Week, Specials, Mini-Series
____ LIVE PERFORMANCE	Concerts, Road Tours, Fashion Shows, Theatre Runway

Now, I want you to GO BACK through pages 33-38 and place check marks on the underlines next to the kinds of projects that correspond to your #1 and #2 choices in the AREAS OF INTEREST above.

By choosing two areas to focus on, you can now begin to approach photographers who have the same interests, to collaborate with and start building your portfolio.

Why not 3 or 4 choices? Because I don't want you to become overwhelmed. Let's start by getting focused on something manageable and build from there. You can always add more!

For instance, if you choose PRINT as one of your GENRES, then ask yourself, "What kind of print work would I enjoy doing most?"

I did my best to expand on each genre by giving you plenty of examples to ponder. You might even think of some new ones.

From time to time, we will call upon our fictitious Makeup Artist, Mary Coletti, to help us understand a concept or solve a problem. Check out her choices in the shaded area that follows.

PRINT	Magazines, CD Covers, Ad Campaigns, Movie Posters, Catalogs, Book Covers, Outdoor (Billboards)
CELEBRITY	Press Junkets, Red Carpet, Talk Shows

What do we now know about Mary? From reviewing the highlighted selections, we know that her #1 choice is PRINT, and she wants to work on magazines, advertising campaigns, catalogs and billboards. Her #2 choice is to work with CELEBRITIES.

This information tells us that Mary should begin her freelance journey by focusing her efforts on building a beauty portfolio with photographers who have similar interests and passions.

Now that you've identified your areas of interest and studied and checked off the corresponding vehicles, you can see has a meltdown, then we also have to be a counselor and let them know everything is going to be fine. We have to be motivators and coaches—whatever it takes to keep them coming back.

What could an artist do that would make you never hire them again?

Melissa: Showing up late. That is one of the biggest things because, like I said, we are on a time constraint. We have to be on, available, and ready on time. You also have to watch how you behave at work. Artists need to understand that they are always being watched. The girls are watching, the team is watching, the pageant staff is watching. You have to be professional and have a good attitude. I have hired a lot of your PYP graduates because I believe they work to a certain standard. I was a PYP grad too, so I know what we are taught.

What are some of the more exciting pageants you've worked on?

Melissa: All of them are exciting because they are all different. I've had the pleasure now of being with the Miss Earth United States Organization for the past two years. What I love about this system is that the women are all professionals. You have lawyers, doctors, engineers, etc. It's all types of girls, and they care about the environment and social issues. Talking to them, I've learned so much that I didn't know about our earth and other things. It's fascinating to me.

What are the first steps an artist should take to be a part of the pageant niche?

Melissa: The first thing I would do is reach out to the

more clearly the different kinds of work available to you in the marketplace. The Guide is designed to help you set and achieve your goals as a freelance artist. Hopefully, you'll find yourself flipping back to these pages often as you begin to understand exactly how the business works.

DO YOU

I can think of only a few professions where personal imaging is as important as it is in our business. Whether you're a hair stylist, makeup artist, fashion stylist, or manicurist, you must be current, creative, and coifed. Individual style is applauded, and people who have it also appear confident and self-assured. Creative decision-makers look for those two qualities when they are considering hiring you. Develop your personal style and roll with it.

Keep up with fashion trends. You don't have to adopt every one. However, you should be aware of them, as you may be called upon at any time for your opinion about them.

Right after I started my business, I had the good fortune to meet an extraordinary woman, Elka Kovac, who was also a photographer's rep. She became my mentor and friend. In a brutally honest moment, she told me that my personal style needed some work. I had quit my sales job, but I was still wearing the uniform: a navy blue suit, white blouse, bow tie, pantyhose and low-heeled pumps. 'There are no navy blue blazers and white shirts in this business,' she informed me. I had left corporate America, but my presentation was still very Fortune 500 and inappropriate in my new creative work environment, where all the art directors, producers, and photographers wore jeans and T-shirts.

My response was what yours should be, to look at what others in the business were wearing, pay attention to the trends and adopt [only] those that suited me personally and professionally.

Some of you will work and prosper in the small to medium towns you live in. Others will do the same in the big cities. Let me tell you that big city style and small town dress are two different things. So, if you're coming to the big city (Los Angeles, New York, Chicago, Miami or Dallas), heed my words.

If you're over 25 and still wearing the same haircut that you had when you were 18, you probably need to get a new one. Be contemporary. An up-to-date look helps in this business regardless of what city you're working in. It says: I know what's going on; I keep up! I'm on top of my game.

Presence

One other thing that usually goes hand-in-hand with personal style is presence. People often tell me that I have presence. I finally figured out what they were talking about. I stand up very straight, hold my head up when I walk, project my voice into the next state, speak the Queen's English, have a firm [not crushing] handshake, I'm very approachable and always assume that I'm going to get what I came for. I believe that is what people see when they say that I have presence.

In the house that I grew up in, if I were slouching in a chair, my grandmother would walk up behind me, grab my shoulders and force them back. "Sit up straight," she would say. She never slouched.

An agent, who sat on the panel at one of my PYP Workshops, spoke candidly to the artists about presenting themselves to agencies and clients. "There's nothing more offensive than an artist who comes in for a meeting, sits slump-shouldered in a chair and mumbles about why they came to see me. I will not sign an artist like that. I can't imagine that they would go to an interview and present themselves to a client any differently than they are presenting themselves to me."

Your style, posture, and presentation say a lot about you and is vital to the people who hire you. Every agency owner I've ever spoken to has had something to say about the importance of signing artists who had an understanding of fashion, and personal style.

pageant director of the State they are in. The director is who puts the whole production on. I would ask if they already have a hair and makeup team, who they are, and if you could get an introduction. If they don't already have a team in place, I do offer my services anyways. State directors often work with regional pageants. I would send a comp card, links to my work online and a nice signature with contact information. Let them know you are interested in offering your services to the girls that are competing and they can pass that info along or put it in their directory.

They also need to be aware that the makeup for pageants is very different than bridal or advertising. Pageant hair and makeup are not like what most artists in the freelance world are used to. It's beauty, but an entirely different type of beauty. It's hairspray and eyeliner for days. So, you actually have to study pageant makeup because it's different than other forms of makeup. But that also varies from pageant to pageant. I would say it's important to look up all of the systems and their websites and look around and see what each one wants, get a feel for it.

IN HER KIT: 3 THINGS MELISSA CAN'T LIVE WITHOUT

- Mario Badescu Rose Water Spray
- Southern Flair Lashes
- My brush belt

 melissamangrumco

 www.melissamangrum.com

I'll end with this little story. A makeup artist came to the agency to show me her book. It was very, very good. But her look was totally outdated, and she couldn't understand why photographers in the LA (Los Angeles) market weren't responding to her. While she was an attractive woman, her hair was much too long for her age. Her jacket sleeves were pushed up above her elbows exposing the lining, and she was wearing flesh colored pantyhose and black pumps. I took a deep breath and said, "Well, since I assume you aren't paying me a coaching fee to look at your book, and blow smoke in your eyes, I'm going to tell you what I think. Let those darn sleeves down on your jacket. Dump the pantyhose or wear pants if you're not comfortable with showing your legs, trade in the pumps for some clunky sandals, and chop off some of that hair, or pull it up and let some of it fall around your face in a messy cool way." After implementing these small changes, she found it much easier to connect and book appointments.

THE FIRST YEAR

What To Expect

Getting started means preparing yourself, becoming aware, identifying your passions, and fine-tuning your peripheral vision so you don't miss anything valuable that might help you now and in the future. It also means knowing what to look for, and how to use the information once you find it.

The first six to nine months of your new career can be the toughest. Many artists have full-time jobs they work diligently to juggle while testing to build their portfolio and work on student and independent films on their off days and hours. Some try to do it with part-time jobs, often taking on roommates or moving back home with parents to make up for the loss in income. Still, others quit their day gigs all together and get jobs assisting or apprenticing with more experienced artists while they test with photographers to build their portfolios.

All three choices involve sacrifice. I offer this advice: get your business in order. Make some early sacrifices, cut spending on luxuries like clothes, restaurant outings, entertainment, cocktails, Starbucks coffee and valet parking. Put some money in the bank and save up for a rainy season, not just a rainy day. You'll need enough to pay your rent, bills, food, and entertainment expenses for at least six to nine months and you can do it if you're taking YOURSELF and this business seriously.

Becoming a freelance artist is not an inexpensive venture. The least costly area of expertise is hair, nails are second, makeup is third, and fashion styling can send you to the poorhouse. A hair stylist, makeup artist, and manicurist can often strap kit supplies around their waist and get away with leaving most of their tools in the parked truck a block away from the photo shoot. The fashion stylist, on the other hand, is in constant fear that the $500 Louis Vuitton handbag and the $2,500 Narcisco Rodriguez dress that is charged to her mom's American Express card are going to be the only items the neighborhood thief wants out of the truck.

In addition to the basic materials and requirements artists have in common, each discipline (makeup, hair, fashion, and nails) requires its own specific set of accoutrements (tools) that must be purchased.

Unlike a tube of lipstick or nail polish whose shelf life can be extended because it can be used over and over again and mixed with something else to make an entirely different color, clothing can be trendy, seasonal or so specific that it cannot be worn over again until deemed retro or vintage in the next decade. This means that the financial commitment can be staggering. Plan ahead now; you'll be in a better position to celebrate year two as a freelance artist.

What To Do First

The most important activities you will participate in during your first year as a freelancer will be things like testing with photographers to build a strong portfolio, getting on as part of the crew on someone's first student film, putting yourself out there to work on an independent film, working your way up from gopher to makeup artist on a low budget music video, or convincing your boss at the corporate office to let you help out with the grooming for the company's annual report. It doesn't really matter where you start, just as long as you do… start, that is.

As your creative passions grow and develop, you will find that the work of some photographers or directors excite your senses while others don't do it for you at all. This narrowing down process is quite natural and will help you to focus on the people you would like to work with and the kinds of projects you see in your future.

The most important advice we got from the artists we interviewed was that you shouldn't waste your time testing with photographers whose work you don't like. The expense of testing (time + money) is too great to fool around with photographers whose work is not going to help you get to the next level. The same goes for directors. There are as many of them as there are photographers, and you will have to search until you find the ones who fit your sensibilities. In closing this chapter, I encourage you to venture forward and just go for it. Don't overthink your next move. Get in. Get muddy and get acquainted with your marketplace.

"Curate your portfolio with regularity. Edit, get outside perspective and put your best foot forward.

—Craig Brooks

Director, Renn Films

2

Tools Of The Trade

Every industry has its own TOOLS OF THE TRADE: the skills, equipment, products and services that [as a group] makeup, hair, fashion stylists and manicurists need in order to do their job properly. I've laid out a set of business tools that I believe are necessary for you to manage the day-to-day business of freelancing effectively.

The following are the list of tools I'll cover in the upcoming pages:

ONLINE PORTFOLIO DOS & DON'TS

DO

- ☑ Put your name, phone number and email address at the bottom of every page.

- ☑ Create an electronic comp card that can be downloaded from the contact section of your website.

- ☑ Keep a copy of everything on your website in your Dropbox.

- ☑ Make your résumé available on your website.

- ☑ Create an electronic résumé that can be downloaded from the CONTACT section of your website.

- ☑ Update all the content on your website at least once a month.

DON'T

- ☒ Do not allow anyone to purchase your .com for you, it's too easy for them to name themselves as the owner, and you may NEVER get it back!

- ☒ Don't use too many tabs on your site.

- ☒ Don't use flash. People hate downloading plugins.

- ☒ Put an actor's headshot in your portfolio

- ☒ Copy anyone's bio word for word and use it as your own on your website.

TOOL 01	ONLINE PORTFOLIO
TOOL 02	SOCIAL MEDIA
TOOL 03	EMAIL
TOOL 04	RELATIONSHIPS
TOOL 05	SELF-PROMOTION
TOOL 06	DEAL MEMO
TOOL 07	CREATIVE DIRECTORIES & PRODUCTION GUIDES
TOOL 08	INSPIRATION
TOOL 09	CONSUMER & TRADE MAGAZINES
TOOL 10	EDUCATION
TOOL 11	PRINT PORTFOLIO (BOOK)

TOOL 01

THE ONLINE PORTFOLIO (WEBSITE)

Tool #1 is your website—your online portfolio. It's everywhere you want it to be, and it's open 24/7. Step one is to decide what you want to call it. Step two is to purchase it, and Step 3 is to make sure that people can find it.

What's In A Name?

How you brand your business is pretty important. Quite often, freelance beauty and fashion pros choose what they consider are cutesy memorable names like:

- Makeup Your Face
- Glamour Puss Makeup
- Kiss and Makeup
- Natural Beauty Makeup
- Rosy Cheeks Makeup
- All Made Up
- The Tangle Warrior
- Hair State of Mind
- Hair, Here, and Everywhere
- Nearer My Shears to Thee
- Love My 'Do
- Hair City

These may work in the brick and mortar salon/beauty bar business, but as a freelancer, you get known by your name. When you arrive on set, no one is going to ask, "Rosy Cheeks Makeup" or "Tangle Warrior" to touch up the model on set. They are going to call you by name. If your website, social media and Facebook page don't match, it's easy for decision-makers to get confused. Use your name if you can. If it's already taken, consider adding a word like beauty, makeup artist, hair, nails, manicurist, or fashion stylist to the end of it.

Here I Am: Being Found On The Web

Your site can, if you include the right SEO (search engine optimization) tools (keywords, tags, and description), appear magically when creative decision-makers search the internet for a freelance artist with your professional profile and discipline (makeup, hair, fashion or nails) in your city with your focus (beauty, lifestyle, fashion, celebrity, etc.).

When a decision-maker logs onto Google and types in the words: *lifestyle makeup artist in Washington DC,* it's your M.O. that you want them to find if you are a makeup artist in the DMV (DC, Maryland, Virginia) area.

I typed in the words: *lifestyle makeup artist in Washington DC,* and what follows is what comes up. If you fit this profile but don't see your name listed in the top 15-20 results, this strategy can help.

GETTING AROUND YOUR WEBSITE

8 THINGS YOU NEED TO KNOW TO MAINTAIN YOUR SITE

Knowing nothing about how to purchase and maintain your own dot com is courting disaster. Here are eight basics you'll need to know to maintain control and update your website.

1 How to access your site using your own password.

2 How to change the password.

3 How to upload, resize and replace images.

4 How to change the names of your images

5 How to upload and embed videos.

6 How to make minor changes such as:

    a. Fix typos

    b. Update, upload and delete your bio, résumé and electronic comp cards

7 How to add keywords, a description and name on your backend to improve SEO.

8 How to submit your site for indexing on Google.

Learning these basics will empower you and give you confidence. Everything you need to know is available on YouTube.

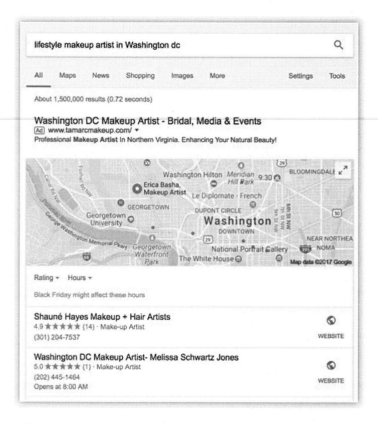

There are five things that you can do [besides pay for ads] to increase the odds that your website will pop up prominently in the Google search engine results. They include:

1 **Make sure that the backend of your website includes a**

    a. Name   c. Keywords

    b. Title   d. Description

2 **Go to your clients and ask them to review your business on Google.**

3 **Make sure that your Facebook business page has been completely filled out to include your:**

a. Phone number   c. City & State

b. Email address   d. Website

4 **Name your images something besides DCV1074225.jpg before uploading them onto your website.**

Utilize your brand name, professional title and category in the title of your images.

EXAMPLES:

Caroline Jones Makeup Artist Beauty 001.jpg

Caroline Jones Makeup Artist Lifestyle 001.jpg

5 **Ask Google to re-index your site.**

Visit www.google.com/webmasters/tools/submit-url

If you've recently added or made changes to a page on your site, you can ask Google to (re)index it using the **Fetch as Google tool.**

What follows is the **backend** information for three Washington DC, Maryland, Virginia (DMV) makeup artists. When you add this (title, keywords, description) information to your website, you become much easier to find.

The backend of your website is easily accessible through your web host provider (the company that is hosting/displaying your online portfolio). The thing is, if you don't ask them where you should input this information, or request them to do it for you, you may not be able to find it on your own.

TAMAR C

```
<meta charset="utf-8"/>
<title>www.TamarCMakeup.com - Makeup Artist in Northern Virginia</title>
<meta name="fb_admins_meta_tag" content=""/>
<meta name="keywords" content="Bridal Makeup, Event Makeup, Hair and Makeup, blog, weddings"/>
<meta name="description" content="Makeup Artist in Northern Virginia serving the DMV for the past 8 years, specializing in bridal and beauty makeup. "/>
<link rel="shortcut icon" href="https://static.parastorage.com/client/pfavico.ico"
        </script>
```

AUDREY BETHARDS

```
<title>Audrey Bethards, Best Makeup Artists &amp; Hair Stylists Services in Washington, DC - MD - VA</title>
<meta name="description" content="Voted Best Hair Stylists and Makeup Artists Services for Fashion, Bridal, Photography and Special Events in Washington, DC Baltimore, MD N Virginia Maryland"/>
<meta name="keywords" content="best hair stylists services, best makeup artists services, makeup artists for weddings, hair stylist for weddings, hair and makeup artists, bridal hair and makeup in washington dc"/>
<link rel="canonical" href="https://www.mymakeupbook.com/" />
```

RENATA LYNETTE

```
<title>Renata Lynette Makeup | Wedding Makeup and Hair Artist </title>
<meta name="fb_admins_meta_tag" content="renatalynettemua"/>
<meta name="keywords" content="dc wedding makeup artist, maryland makeup artist, richmond makeup artist, virginia makeup artist"/>
<meta name="description" content="Renata Lynette Makeup, offering on-location makeup and hairstyling services to brides in Washington, D.C., Virginia, Maryland and beyond. If you want a timeles"/>
<link rel="shortcut icon" href="https://static.parastorage.com/client/pfavico.ico" type="image/x-icon"/>
```

49

Daniel Chinchilla

Celebrity Makeup Artist

Choosing A Platform

Now that you know what to do, I am going to share some really great resources for getting your website up and going as quickly as possible, for as little as possible.

An excellent online portfolio will only cost you about $72 - $300 a year to acquire and maintain. So, if you already have a site and you're spending more than $300 a year—you're paying too much. You can get a ton of bells and whistles for $300 a year or less.

One of the things that plague freelance artists is whether to purchase a pre-made [turnkey] solution—which IS what I'm suggesting—or to go the route of hiring a web designer to create your website. You may have a cousin, friend or relative who is a web designer or wants to be one. "I'll build your website for you," they say, and you're off to the races. Except that, from experience, I can tell you that what should take a week to get up and going often takes six months.

What's the problem with web designers? Everybody thinks they are one. Anyone with a copy of Adobe InDesign thinks they are a webmaster. They're not. As someone who has been through her share of good and bad professionals, and flakes—I've seen and wasted thousands of dollars on website design, hosting, and maintenance. Please read carefully, and you won't have to. But, you need a web presence, so what do you do? What follows are some options:

1	Hire a webmaster to build a site from scratch—but please, don't go this route with your first website—it's painful because it's hard to know what you like or don't like in a site until you've had one for at least a year.
2	Do it yourself—Please, don't, unless you were a web builder in your other life. Most home-made websites look just that—home-made.
3	Sign up for an AWESOME subscription-based online portfolio that offers several pre-set templates for you to choose from—YES! Now we're cooking with gas.

The best answer—at least in the beginning for your first website—is "Number 3." There are many great sites with lots of awesome features that were created just for the freelance community of photographers, makeup artists, hair stylists, fashion stylists, and manicurists.

NOTES

....

....

....

....

....

....

....

....

Daniel Chinchilla loves all things beauty. Originally from San Francisco, he moved to Los Angeles in 2001 to pursue a career in the fashion and entertainment industries. It soon became clear that he had a unique talent for makeup artistry and he felt compelled to delve into that world. His natural abilities soon became apparent to people in the industry, and it wasn't long before he was able to make a name for himself.

Daniel's ability to create flawless looks have led him to work with some of the top names in the industry. His work has been featured on the pages of Allure, Women's Health, Cosmopolitan, and InStyle amongst many others. Daniel is also responsible for Ariana Grande's enviable makeup looks, and he is a favorite of many of Hollywood's hottest young stars.

Daniel recently took the time to share a glimpse of how he pursued his passion and turned it into a successful and fulfilling career.

Daniel, was becoming a makeup artist something that you always wanted to do?

Daniel: Actually, I was 19 years old, and I was enrolled in community college studying psychology. I was there for a semester and was great at it. I loved being in school. It was easy for me. But I was bored, and I knew that sitting in a classroom was not what I wanted to be doing.

The problem was that I didn't really know what else to do. Then one day, I walked by the MAC counter at Nordstrom. At that point, I didn't even know what makeup was. I had never touched it, knew nothing about

All of the sites listed below are subscription-based programs that allow you to upload a specific number of images, a résumé, video, a bio, social media and contact information onto your little piece of website heaven for a monthly, quarterly or annual fee. Additionally, most of them have a 7-30 day free trial period so you can try before you buy.

PLATFORM	MONTHLY COST
Format.com	$ 6 - 12
Livebooks.com	$ 20 - 60
Krop.com	$ 10
Dripbook.com	$ 10 - 39
Viewbook.com	$ 16
Foliolink.com	$ 19 - 29
BigBlackBag.com	$ 9 - 30
PortfolioBox.net	$ 7
Squarespace.com	$ 12 - 26

Another benefit of these turnkey solutions is that these sites cater to a specific industry and have a vested interest in submitting the community [of sites] to search engines like Google, Yahoo, and Bing. Ongoing and scheduled submissions to search engines are one of the ways these companies help drive traffic to their community and your site.

Every picture should not make it into your online or print portfolio just because you worked on it. Artists sometimes make the mistake of putting every test or paid assignment that produces a tearsheet into their portfolios in an effort to fill it up. I've got news for you folks, great hair on a photograph with bad makeup is a bad picture. Bad photography and great fashion styling is simply—a bad picture. An art director isn't going to separate your fabulous hair from bad makeup, photography, or fashion styling, so be discriminating! Pick only your best shots to display in your portfolio! It's crucial that you understand what makes a book stand out, and increases your chances of being singled out and booked for jobs. In order of importance, the two factors are content & presentation.

A. Content

By content, creative decision-makers consider these four things. Read the definition below and ask yourself the questions as they relate to the images and tearsheets that you will add to your own growing portfolio.

	CONTENT	QUESTIONS
1	The quality of the prints, tear sheets, and images that are displayed in your portfolio.	Are they sharp and in focus, not over or underexposed, not overly retouched and free of distractions—a string hanging, a tag exposed, an eyelash coming loose, chapped lips?
2	The choice of images (photographs or tear sheets) and stories that make it into your portfolio.	Do the images feature a combination of good makeup, hair, styling, nails and photography? Do some of the stories (2+ pages) show what you can accomplish in the course of a single 8-hour day?
3	The creativity, inventiveness, interest, and enthusiasm with which you completed each assignment.	Are the subjects and environments interesting and well thought out, or is everything just thrown together with little or no thought to the stories that you are telling?
4	The arrangement/layout/flow of the images.	Is there a flow in your book that keeps the viewer interested and engaged till the end?

Over the years, I have learned that what most creative decision-makers mean by range is variety within the context of what you do consistently as an artist. For example, if you are a hairstylist, and what you do best is hair that is simple, neat and clean—then show plenty of it. Include different models, variations of styles, with lots of changes and creativity. That means short hair, medium length hair, and long hair. Show it swept up off the back of the neck, cascading down over a single eye. Show it on White girls, Black girls, Asian girls and Hispanic girls. Be sure that it works with the wardrobe, and the environment the photographer is shooting in.

it. I hadn't even considered being a makeup artist. I ended up stopping, picking up some glitter, and thinking that it looked fun and cool. Everyone seemed excited to be working there, so I decided to apply. They told me they couldn't put me at the MAC counter but that I could work for Clinique and I went for it. I was just so excited to be there!

I fell instantly in love with making women feel good. It's funny because psychology is what I started off studying in school and is something that has always interested me. I feel like I am a psychologist every day at work because women talk to me, they open up about their lives, and I listen, and give advice. People love being heard. I feel like I've been able to merge the two…makeup and psychology.

Where were you living at the time?

Daniel: I was still in San Francisco. I just kept falling more in love with making women feel good and look good, and I knew that the next step would be to move to LA. I was about to turn 21, and I told my mom that I was moving. She thought I was crazy! I ended up applying to Makeup Designory in Burbank. I packed my car, and headed to LA.

So, what would you consider your first big break in Los Angeles?

Daniel: Well, after makeup school, I got a job at MAC. I worked for them for about five years as an artist, then as a freelancer. While there, I met a woman who told me she did these glamour parties and needed a makeup artist on the weekends. I ended up working for her on

If I open up your portfolio and see 17 images of girls with shoulder length hair, all I know about you is that you're good with shoulder length hair. If you assume that the art director "should know" that you can do what he/she is asking, you'll assume yourself right out of a lot of jobs.

Makeup artistry is the same. If I open up your portfolio and see 15 images of girls with the same smoky eye, you can't convince me that that you can do clean beauty unless you have it in your portfolio.

Often, an artist will say, "Well I can do that" or "that's nothing, I do that kind of work with my eyes closed." My response is, "well then close your eyes and put it in your book because clients are only interested in what they can see with their eyes."

If you do a fashion spread with four changes of clothes, then show me what you did with the hair to ensure that it works with the clothing changes. But don't ever overdo it just because you can when the shot doesn't call for it.

Confidence is born out of experience and comes with time; however, do your best to trust your gut on shoots and know when you DON'T need to make any changes at all. Know when the answer to a question like, "What do you think we should do with the hair for this shot?," is "Nothing. I think it's perfect just the way it is."

That is real confidence.

Remember that makeup, hair, and nails are NOT done in a vacuum where you singularly decide to apply makeup, start the hair or paint the nails without knowing:

1	What the photographer wants (the vision).
2	What the client wants (has in mind—intends).
3	Where the story is being shot (the location/ environment).
4	What the model will be wearing (the wardrobe).

This process is a collaborative one that works when everyone is on the same page. Always ask questions to gain understanding. It will make everyone's job easier and more enjoyable.

The LA Times Magazine fashion spread featuring Tyra Banks is an example of a beautifully executed fashion editorial where everyone was on the same page. The makeup artist, hairstylist, and fashion stylist are in sync with the simplicity of the photographic and editorial vision shot on a simple gray backdrop. Celebrity hairstylist, Neeko Abriol, worked on this shoot when I represented him. This was a one day shoot with several clothing, hair and makeup changes, as you can see. It's worth mentioning that this shoot took place in 1995. However, the classic nature of the looks makes the layout a timeless one that can remain in your portfolio for many years without looking dated.

What you see in these classic images is Neeko's ability to execute subtle changes in the hair, while considering the environment that the photographer has created and clothing that the fashion stylist has selected.

Look at these photos. A one day shoot. Four different looks. A story perfectly told.

Imagine for a second that you have conceived and executed a similar story with a photographer as a test. The only thing missing would be the type and page numbers. When your tests are consistently this good, you will—as the Brits say—have cracked it!

the weekends, and even though I would do makeup on 20 women in one day and was exhausted, it was how I started freelancing.

I liked the idea of being my own boss and making my own hours. From there, I started e-mailing a bunch of headshot photographers, letting them know that I was available to work. This was at the time when there was social media, but it wasn't as big as it is now. It was just MySpace, so there weren't a lot of resources. I literally e-mailed headshot photographers and landed a job with one of them as a makeup artist. It was just the beginning, but it felt so liberating.

I feel like my first job that made me feel truly legit was when I did a hair campaign for FHI Heat. I actually booked that job on Facebook because, by that time, I was posting pictures of my work online. I didn't even realize I was "friends" with the company on there. But one day, they contacted me and told me that they loved my work. From that point on, I knew that I had to keep updating my presence online because that was how I was going to get recognized.

Did you find it easy to manage your money and business when you started freelancing?

Daniel: Well, I've always been good with my money, but back then, I started gaining more clients and got a little ahead of myself. At one point, I was making a lot of money for me, so I was also spending a lot. I was like, "Let me go buy these pants. Let me go do this and do that." Good and bad. I'm a lot better now. But back then, I was still able to handle my money to where I was not

B. Presentation

The online presentation begins with the visual impact of seeing your home page, name and title font, includes the online experience of reviewing the images in your portfolio, accessing and reaching out to you through your contact page, extends to the ease or difficulty of being able to download collateral materials such as your comp card and résumé, and ends with being able to access your social media through links on your website. Every element comes together to create an impressive package.

Building A Strong Portfolio

The process of building a portfolio is ongoing. As long as you are a working artist, it will be a work in progress and you will always be adding something to it. This in turn means that you will always be adding something new to social media and your résumé and thus your list of credits will continue to grow. It's the perfect circle.

Our goal here in building Tool #1—your online portfolio—is so that you can easily use it to market yourself right into paid work and even better tests with exceptionally talented photographers.

So lets begin by getting some questions answered.

 1 HOW MANY IMAGES DO I NEED?

Most decision-makers we interviewed thought that an artist should have at least 10-15 great test shots in their book before they start showing it around to get work, and 6-10 tearsheets before looking for an agency for representation. There are of course exceptions to every rule. We suggest you use these as targets to aim for.

The biggest turn off is work that was dated. Everything in

the book should be current (12-24 months) or timeless and classic. Audrey Hepburn in Breakfast at Tiffany's is timeless. The images never get old. If you've never seen the movie, do yourself a favor and cuddle up to a bowl of popcorn for this one.

2 | WHAT'S WRONG WITH THE IMAGES IN MY BOOK?

We found that the two universal wrongs were bad photography and bad models. While mediocre work in any of the disciplines, (makeup, hair, props, styling or costume) can present a problem, photography and wanna-be models were the most common errors noticed by book reviewers such as art directors, photographers, and magazine editors.

3 | CAN I USE MY SALON CLIENTS AS MODELS?

Sure, if their names are Gisele Bündchen, Adriana Lima or Joan Smalls. Ladies and gentlemen, your clients, unless they are real models, are really not capable of projecting on camera what you will need to impress decision-makers and paying clients. While they are pretty to you and the average person walking on the street, most women and men who are considered beautiful by the general public would not pass muster at even the smallest [reputable] modeling agency.

4 | HOW LONG WILL IT TAKE BEFORE I HAVE A BOOK TO SHOW?

That depends on whom you want to show it to. The process of building a portfolio is ongoing, everlasting and ever-changing. While there are always exceptions (I signed Neeko to my agency with one image), typically it will take no less than six months to a year before you are ready to show your book to most paying clients for work. The same goes for getting on the assistants lists at most agencies and more like 2-3 years before you get signed. However—and I can't stress this enough—you must show your portfolio to decision-makers. You need feedback.

All too often, artists are afraid to show their work to anyone because they are perfectionists, or they fear rejection. Not everyone is going to like your work. Do you like everyone's potato salad? NO! Only by showing your work will you know where you need to focus your energies to improve. Show it to photographers. Show it to art directors. Show it to producers. Show it to magazine editors. Show it to other key artists that you respect and want to assist. Ask for constructive criticism, and then don't be upset because you didn't get the answer that you wanted.

You must show your book to photographers at every stage of the game and often. If you have one or two images then show them. It's the only way to get more and better photographers to want to work with you.

5 | WHERE DO I FIND GOOD PHOTOGRAPHERS TO TEST WITH?

Go to Chapter 4 where we discuss this subject in depth. Good photographers are found in art schools, magazines, in photo programs at universities, community colleges, vocational schools, through word of mouth and so forth.

struggling. I was always able to pay my bills and handle business.

Was your focus the same back then? Where did you see yourself sort of ending up?

Daniel: I've always been in love with beauty and seeing a face that is beautifully made up. I've always been pulled to the beauty and hair ads. That's what calls to me. Beauty. And despite everything I've done, I still have a long way to go. I feel like I haven't done everything I desire to do yet. I want to end up creating those types of ads.

Do you think you will have to venture outside of LA to get those kinds of campaigns?

Daniel: I feel like a lot of those campaigns are shot in New York, but I also perceive a lot are shot here in LA. Social media is really changing everything too. It's a little bit easier to get these jobs because you just connect with the companies via social media, and I feel like I don't need to move. If a client is in need of my services, I would just fly to New York or anywhere else.

Are you signed with an agency right now? Have you ever been with one?

Daniel: I have never been with an agency. I actually just recently started to talk to agencies but what I've learned is that you can't rely on an agent alone. I feel like people are so stuck with the idea that if they sign up with an agency, they will automatically get all these jobs. In my opinion, that's just not how it works. They can connect you with

 ## 6   HOW DO I KEEP MY IMAGES SAFE?

Take advantage of the hottest technological development of the last decade—Dropbox. By storing all of your images and scanned tearsheets in Dropbox you will always have a way of reproducing your entire portfolio at a moment's notice should something go wrong with the technology. The artist full of regret is the one that lost a portfolio full of images on a site that went belly up and didn't have a backup plan.

Dropbox provides you with a FREE online receptacle in which to store images indefinitely and you can get to your photos regardless of what computer, phone, or tablet you're using.

 ## 7   CAN I RETOUCH MY IMAGES?

Yes, but don't overdo it. A good retoucher can remove imperfections from an image for $5 - $20. You can spend a lot more—but why? Visit www.fiverr.com for inexpensive retouching.

 ## 8   CAN I USE BLACK & WHITE IMAGES IN MY PORTFOLIO?

Yes. Every artist wants to know whether or not they can have black and white photos in their portfolios and on their comp cards. The person who can have the most black and white images is the hair stylist. Photo shoot hair is about styling not color, and the art director doesn't assume that you colored the hair. However, with makeup, fashion styling and nails, the color choices are an integral part of the shot. It's impossible for an art director to know whether you put purple, green or silver eye shadow on a model if everything is in black and white. Yes, you can use black and white, just don't create a portfolio with MORE black and white images than color. I would err on the side of 75% / 25%.

Objectivity

One of the toughest things for an up-and-coming artist to learn is how to accept constructive criticism regarding the contents and quality of the work in his or her portfolio. Inevitable and sometimes painful decisions must be made regarding what to keep in, or remove, from a book. Artists must be careful not to perceive the advice of professionals as a personal attack on their creativity or talent. The suggestion to remove one or more images from your book due to obvious flaws may have nothing to do with the quality of your work. Making people look good requires the involvement of several people to pull off the miracles we love to behold in print, video, film and television. The obvious players on any variety of shoots (still and moving) include the following:

hair stylist	makeup artist	fashion stylist
manicurist	prop stylist	special FX makeup artist
photographer	actor	director
director of photography	digital tech	wig maker
model	costume designer	costumer

This is a list of key people who you can least afford to have show up on set and have a bad hair day—so to speak. However, it can and does happen. The results vary from mediocre still photography that doesn't quite cut it to moving film that has to be tossed and re-shot.

The emotional toll of having put so much work into a day or days that produce nothing can be frustrating to the young artist building their book. The longing to include something new in a portfolio often causes artists to compromise their portfolio with photographs that are less than perfect. While you are vacillating on whether or not to include a so-so photo in your portfolio, remember this: a busy art director will not separate your great hair styling from bad makeup, photography or fashion styling to conclude that you should be hired to work on an upcoming project. On the contrary, the art director or producer will look at your portfolio and decide against hiring you, convinced that the one unflattering photograph in your book [that you couldn't part with] is the very same one you will produce at his/her photo session or commercial.

In most instances, you will not be present during the portfolio review because the decision-maker will be reviewing your portfolio online. Who then is going to say to the art director, "Don't pay any attention to the bad makeup, just look at my wonderful hair?" One bad photograph can mean a lost job assignment. Most decision-makers prefer to see five great photographs in your book rather than five great shots and three okay ones just to fill up space. Be selective.

their clients, but most of it is going to be what you put into it and your legwork.

What are some of your most exciting jobs?

Daniel: I love anything fast paced. I love performances. I love the VMAs (Video Music Awards) and that's kind of my thing. I love anything exciting because I live for the challenge. For the past three and a half years, I've been working with Ariana Grande pretty much full-time. It's great. I have realized that TV and film are not for me, though. There's too much waiting, and I get bored. I'll take the photo shoots and music performances, press days and anything that is fast-paced. I just like to be busy.

Do you ever hire assistants? And if so, how would you want them to contact you?

Daniel: Not too often, but I do once in a while. I have had more bad experiences than good ones with assistants, though. This is why I tend not to hire them. It's just so important to take your job as an assistant seriously and show up on time, be professional, and work hard. That doesn't always happen.

If I were to be contacted by a would-be assistant, I'd prefer email, but I would want to see a professional page. For example, if someone messages me on Instagram and gives me their link and their Instagram is full of pictures of them partying or pictures of their kids, that's fine, but that doesn't show me you as an artist. It doesn't show me you and your career.

TOOL 02

SOCIAL MEDIA

I know, I know, for those of you who have figured it out, social media is the dream medium that powers your marketing engine. Your followers are growing, and the perks are rolling in. If you're not getting paid for all of the followers, your shelves are stocked to the brim with so many makeup, hair, fashion and nail products that you can't remember the last time you actually had to purchase something for your kit.

For the rest of us, it's the elephant in the room, a chore that makes us feel inadequate, behind the 8-ball and wondering if we'll ever catch up. You're either sitting atop the beast with a clear vision and voice that resonates with your ever-growing audience, or you're looking up at the beast, trying to figure out how to mount that son-of-a-gun without falling off.

There are millions of marketing people claiming to have all the answers that you need to grow your base, engage your audience and increase your followers. But there's also this disconnect because as a visual learner, some artists find it difficult to see how amassing followers for widgets and washing machines is the same as collecting followers: art directors, celebrities, photographers and producers who can hire them for upcoming gigs.

Experts have convinced us that followers are the answer to all of our...well...we're not sure what they're the answer to, but we know we need to have more of them.

Listen, I'm not in disagreement that you want to create and grow your social media presence. Doing so can only be good for your business. But what I don't want is for you to obsess about it to the point that it controls your life.

If you hear me say it once, you'll hear it from me a thousand times: PLAN TO WORK AND WORK THE PLAN. Without a plan, a vision and goals you can measure, you will remain a slave to the notifications on your mobile phone, chiding you to take yet another look at your social media account which only serves to depress you if your numbers have gone down, instead of up.

The thing is, without a plan, checking your social media account each time it buzzes you is like weighing yourself on a scale every day when you're on a diet. Sometimes, you're up, and another time, you're down. You may be making progress, but if you're not losing half a pound every single day, you can often feel defeated. Whereas with social media, if you're not gaining 100 followers every day, you can feel that way. Worse still, you'll start comparing yourself to others, always feeling like you have to catch up, and the self-comparison goes on and on and on. STOP THE MADNESS! Help is on the way!

When I interviewed celebrity hairstylist, Oscar James, for the *Guide*, he revealed some guiding principles for what he shares on social media that totally line up with his goals, values and his truth.

Oscar says,

Truth	*I'm silly*
Truth	*I'm a giver*
Goal	*I like to make people laugh*
Goal	*I always want to come from a place of giving*
Value	*I like to lift people up*
Value	*I like to share my heart*

Could it be any simpler? He seeks to share his authentic, silly, empathetic, flawed self with the rest of us and that is how he chooses what to share. His approach resonates with his audience, and so, they stick around.

I know that for me, I sometimes struggled with being "too much!" For a while, I was traumatized by a makeup artist whose work I loved, and I wanted to sign her to Crystal Agency, but she didn't love me. She was making the rounds of showing her portfolio and decided to sign with another agency instead of mine. What got back to me was that she had said, "That Crystal Wright is just too much."

The thing that I have learned and now embrace [and you will too] is that you are never going to be everything to everyone. I am a lot. I have a big personality, and not everyone is going to like me. Even so, there are lots of people who do and will, as long as I consistently share my authentic voice with them, and that voice is [quite often] loud and boisterous and challenging. It is also honest, loving and protective.

NOTES

....

....

....

....

....

....

What's one quick piece of advice you have for someone who wants to break into makeup artistry?

Daniel: Educate yourself. I wanted to know everything when I was starting out. I knew that research was the way to go. I was always reading, surfing online, looking at stuff and checking what other artists had to say. Just reading and gaining knowledge of the industry was so important to me because I knew nothing before that. I had no mentors, and I had nobody to look up to. Again, Sam Fine and Kevyn Aucoin but they were huge. You have to take the initiative to educate yourself about everything regarding the career you want.

   beautybydchinchilla

   www.danielchinchilla.com

Crystal says,

Truth	*I'm serious*
Truth	*I'm a giver*
Goal	*I like to challenge people to think*
Goal	*I always want to come from a place of honesty*
Value	*I like to give people confidence*
Value	*I like to share my hopefulness*

Take a moment and ask yourself: what is your truth? What is your goal, and what value can you bring to the lives of others? I think that this is a great place to start a social media posting strategy.

Now, it's your turn.

....

Truth   *I'm*

....

Truth   *I'm*

....

Goal   *I like to make people*

....

Goal   *I always want to come from a place of*

....

Value   *I like to*

....

Value   *I like to*

....

Once you have filled in these blanks, you have essentially created a litmus test for your posts. You need only to ask yourself:

Is this post achieving either of my truths?

Is this post achieving either of my goals?

Is this post adding value to anyone's life?

It's simple, isn't it? Do your social media posts serve any of your truths, goals or values?

Curating Your Instagram Account

Collecting, selecting and presenting your images is known as curating and should be done with an eye toward the experience you are creating for the end user—the decision-maker. It's no different than laying out your online portfolio.

Here are some simple steps:

1 Choose a vibe (aesthetic) for your Instagram Feed. For example, is your vibe going to be bright, edgy, golden, moody, dark, or colorful? Switching back and forth from day-to-day can look tacky and cause you to lose followers.

2 When editing and using filters, limit yourself to 2-3 filters. You don't want to make people dizzy.

3 Give your feed some order. Look at your feed as a whole and make sure everything fits together. Images should look good beside each other.

4 Post mostly images.

5 Make your life easy by planning ahead. Set aside a 2-hour block once each week to prep your images before posting. It's less stressful than trying to figure out what to post the night before.

Your Audience. Your Community.

Know the difference between your audience and your [freelance] community. Yes, they can be one and the same if you are teaching classes. However, in many cases, artists create content for their community of other artists instead of creating content that will attract potential clients. Are you creating a makeup line or hair product that you hope to sell to makeup artists and hairstylists? Or are you showcasing your art because you want to be hired by decision-makers who need someone for their upcoming project? Hmm? It's worth considering, isn't it?

While I never say never, I'll say this: it may be difficult to become a 6-figure freelance artist by creating content for your artist community unless you have a product to sell them, and I don't mean another class.

If your goal is to become a celebrated freelance artist, your audience is photographers, art directors, fashion and beauty editors, celebrities, publicists, line producers, art producers, and photo editors who hire people like YOU for jobs.

Cleaning Up Your Act

The way your business uses social media says a lot about your brand, and if you're making rookie mistakes, you risk losing credibility in the eyes of your audience.

If your business is actively using social media, you're on the right track, but being active doesn't mean you are effectively using social media to market and grow your business. You have to ensure that your content is shareable, interesting, and valuable to your audience, and also includes your personality and a bit of your personal life. All work and no play makes our fictitious makeup artist, Mary Coletti, a dull girl. Your audience wants to feel like they know you.

Social media experts will tell you that you should be posting every day. What I want you to know is that it's okay to ramp up to that schedule over a 12 to 18 month period.

Start to think of your business in quarters the way companies market to you. Spring, summer, fall, and winter.

Ask yourself: What can I do realistically and consistently on social media from now through the end of this quarter? If that is posting once a week, do it. To be effective in social media, you have to find your voice and gain perspective while experiencing growth and through an increase in numbers and engagement.

The beauty of ramping up, is that it gives you time to get to know your audience and tweak your strategy.

You may decide to share inspirational quotes with your audience every once in a while. If you don't have a list of inspirational quotes sitting around on your desk, ramping up will give you time to find and stockpile those quotes.

STRATEGY

In quarter 1 post once a week. In quarter 2 ramp up to twice weekly posts. By summer you're posting three times a week and then in the fall you're up to four. Slow down and get consistent. You're not losing weight for a family reunion.

Read on to learn about the most common rookie social media mistakes and how you can steer clear of them.

1 Clean up your act

a. Delete or edit posts with profanity in them.

b. Prune (remove), edit or rearrange images that pigeonhole you and make your artistry appear one-dimensional.

c. Stop commenting on hugely controversial posts that might cost you a job or your reputation.

d. Spell check existing posts.

e. Separate your personal and professional brands.

f. Make your personal brand private if your followers could stall your upward mobility.

g. Check your posts against your quality litmus test by asking yourself if what you are about to post:

1. Is a downer
2. Is angry, mean-spirited or hateful toward another person
3. Is troll-like in nature
4. Is too political

2 Be discerning about whom you follow.

Unfollow people whose work, philosophy, or posts don't inspire you, or whose social media antics could cause decision-makers to be concerned about your character.

3 Untag yourself.
Check your social media to see if you're being tagged by unscrupulous folks who can ruin your reputation.

The power of social media is evident. Use it wisely. We'll talk more about social media in the Marketing Yourself Chapter.

TOOL #3

EMAIL

In a perfect world (and it can be a perfect world), as far as your email is concerned, your email address should be the same as your web address, which in turn matches your brand (Chapter 1). Check out the examples that follow:

WEB ADDRESS	EMAIL ADDRESS
MaryColetti.com	Mary@MaryColetti.com
MaryColettiBeauty.com	Mary@MaryColettiBeauty.com
HairbyJonathanAzod.com	Jonathan@HairbyJonathanAzod.com

Many use Gmail addresses for their business websites. It's not ideal, and you should seek to change it as soon as you can afford the $36 per year at GoDaddy.com. Using an email address that matches your brand when communicating with decision-makers puts your professionalism and seriousness just ahead of other candidates who are applying for the same position.

When your email address matches your brand and website, it is easy for potential clients to associate and remember. Email addresses with strings of numbers are difficult to memorize. Why don't you try remembering something like MaryColetti41773@gmail.com? When you use it, you are branding the wrong thing.

If you have to stick with Gmail, Yahoo or any other carriers for the time being, what is best and most professional is simply your first and last name.

Here's the good news, once you have secured your newly branded email account from Godaddy.com, you can send and receive mail from your Gmail account.

Simply log into your Gmail account, click on the settings gear icon and then click on the words: Forwarding and POP/IMAP. The instructions are simple, and you should be able to set up your branded email account in about 5 minutes or less. Instructions for Yahoo and others will be similar, but if hazy, look it up on YouTube!

If you have a common name like Jim Jones, it is quite possible that it's already taken. If that is the case, try variations that incorporate your professional job title. Here are some good alternatives:

JimJonesMakeupArtist@gmail.com

JimJonesMakeupandHair@gmail.com

JimJonesBeauty@gmail.com

KellyClawsonHair@gmail.com

LisaMichelleFashionStylist@gmail.com

HairbyKellyClawson@gmail.com

FashionStylingbyLisaMichelle@gmail.com

CrystalWrightLive@gmail.com

Remember, professionalism is the name of the game. If you want to be remembered as a PRO, your email address is a good place to start!

If you start posting 7X a week and can't keep up the pace you can lose your audience because they can't depend on you. Don't create an expectation for yourself that you can't maintain. Instead, create a pace that you can live and grow into. The world will still be here in the spring.

QUARTER	MONTHS	POSTING STRATEGY
SPRING	MAR, APR, MAY	1-2X PER WK
SUMMER	JUN, JUL, AUG	2-3X PER WK
FALL	SEP, OCT, NOV	3-4X PER WK
WINTER	DEC, JAN, FEB	4-5X PER WK

Check out these awesome visual planning tools for curating and planning your social media feed:

$0 - $7/month   Planoly.com
Create a cohesive Instagram feed by visually planning, managing and scheduling your posts

$0 - $9/month   Hashtagify.com
Maximize your social media strategy by searching and using the top hashtags on your feed

$0 - $19/month   Hootsuite.com
Social media marketing and management dashboard for scheduling, managing and measuring results.

TOOL #4

RELATIONSHIPS

Celebrity makeup artist Renny Vasquez says, "Relationships are NOT microwavable," meaning that they take time to develop and grow. They are one of the most powerful tools that an artist has and often overlooks.

Contrary to what you might think, your relationships are ultimately more powerful and valuable than Instagram. You see, your website and social media can't give you a job, only people can. What your online presence does is expose you to people and magnify everything that is good, or bad.

Anyone can be discovered online and get booked once. But longevity and growth creatively and financially are based on your ability to get re-booked and referred, even loved by those who work with, and around, you.

Because things move so very fast these days, artists often think that they can "microwave" their way into being booked on magazine covers, red carpet events, TV commercials and music videos. Well, if you're just starting out, and you think that you are just one Instagram post away from the celebrity selfie that will launch your freelance career—read on.

Every moment on the set provides you with an opportunity to impress someone. My friend Oscar says, "First impressions are non-refundable." Are you building up your relationship stock or is it losing value day by day?

Adhere to these four business-building principles, and you are sure to get a return (re-booked and referred) on your relationship investment.

1 Make a Great First Impression

- Dress like a professional: Wear clothing appropriate for the shooting environment.
- Be on time: Arrive 15-30 minutes early.
- Be courteous: Say Yes, thank you, and excuse me.
- Don't gossip: Don't gossip!
- Listen more than you talk: Shhhhh.

2 Be Trustworthy

- Be reliable: Do what you say you're going to do.
- Be dependable: Stay ready.
- Be honorable: Have high standards.

3 Be a Team Player

- Work with others to bring about great outcomes.

4 Expend Energy on the Relationship

- Be a giver.
- Show interest in people when you don't want anything from them.
- Remember important dates (birthdays, anniversaries, etc.)
- Follow up by sending hand-written thank-you cards in the mail.
- Support the charitable endeavors of bosses and peers.
- Volunteer to help out on a project or a task when you have nothing to gain.

Relationships grow when you put time into them. Don't we all have a relative or acquaintance who only calls when they want something? You can see them coming from a mile away, and you're looking for a place to hide. Is that the way you want people to think of you? No, of course not. In the same vein, it won't take the decision-maker long to notice if you ONLY ever call them for work and never send a thank-you card, or tender a small gift during the holidays to show your appreciation for the work they have already awarded you during the year.

How much would ten $750 full-day bookings be worth to you in a single year? This is not just a mathematical calculation. We all know it's seven thousand, five hundred dollars. The question is, "What is it worth?" What kind of impact does the money that sprang out of this relationship have on your professional goals and aspirations? Don't value the money. Value the relationship. A $50 Starbucks gift card goes a long way toward building a relationship with a coffee lover who happens to be the producer who donated $7,500 toward your rent this year.

The money is a by-product of the excellence you bring to each working relationship and the maintenance of the four principles above. If you care for your relationships, they may double in value next year. Get it?

When I represented artists, I had a very close relationship with one of my photographers. Together, we decided to save $150 from every photo shoot all year long and put it into a separate checking account that I could use whenever I felt the client relationship warranted a special gesture. When the Christmas Holidays rolled around, we had over $5000 in that account. I spent every dime of it on our clients. Each one of those clients had contributed to the growth and development of our business, and we knew it was good business to let them know how much we appreciated them.

Jennifer Macdougall

Hair Stylist
New York
Jennifermacdougall.com
Focus: Beauty, Fashion
and Celebrity
IG: jennifermacdougall

ADVICE

Being successful in the beauty and fashion industry is simple—be amazing at your craft and build strong working relationships with those you work with.

You will learn over time that the circle of pros is not that big and that people move up the ladder fairly quickly. The assistant photographer may soon be the next photographer shooting for Vogue; so, leaving a great impression on everyone matters.

Be flexible with how you work but not to the point that you lose your sense of self. People feel more confident with your work if you believe in yourself instead of trying to please everyone.

TOOL #5

SELF-PROMOTION ARSENAL

The 5th most important tool is your Self-Promotion Arsenal of printed and electronic materials that you can hand out, email and make available for download on your website. These materials along with your website and social media platforms make it possible for you to implement a marketing plan to promote yourself. Your plan should include print and web-based comp cards, a website, social media, and involvement in the creative community in which you choose to work and play.

1 PRINT COMP CARD

Quite simply, a comp card is a postcard with your beautiful images and contact information on it. Its purpose is to get the viewers' attention and make them want to see more. The more I am referring to is your website and Instagram account.

Every artist should have a comp card. I hear artists debate this point from time to time. "Why do I need a comp card," they ask, "when everything is done electronically?" To that, I say, "Then why do Nieman Marcus, Nordstrom, L'Occitane, Banana Republic and Crate & Barrel still send me brochures and other promotional postcards in the mail?" Quite simply, because print is not dead.

Comp cards are your very own mini-brochures. They show potential clients what you do, your style, and the way you approach your art. It acts as your calling card and "conversation

The Hair Makeup & Fashion Styling Career Guide

piece" all rolled into one. It will remind others of what your work is like long after they have moved on from your website, or you and your iPad have left the studio.

Success can be an elusive promise without marketing (self-promotion) materials. You may never know how many jobs you didn't get because after reviewing your portfolio and liking it, the photographer or art director didn't have a comp card to hang on to when it was time to hire someone for an assignment.

When it's time to review online portfolios for a project, most decision-makers open up their files or glance up at their walls lined with their favorite comp cards. They call the individual artists or their agencies and inquire about availability for upcoming projects.

It's not unusual to walk into the office of an art director,

producer or beauty editor for an appointment and find the walls and tabletops covered with comp cards of stylists, photographers and makeup artists whose work they find particularly interesting or stimulating. It would be a shame for your card to be missing from that pile.

Basically, what we're talking about here are postcards. We call them comp cards, but a piece of light-weight cardboard with pictures on it is after all—a postcard. As the demand for postcards grows as a means of marketing everything from movies and parties to lingerie, the price of printing postcards has become very reasonable.

One hundred 4x6 or 5.5X8.5 full-color postcards typically cost around $47. Commonly used comp card sizes are 4X6, 5.5X8.5 and 6X8.

Michele Gay

CEO & Co-Founder
Limelight by Alcone

How Many Pictures Should I Put On My Card?

Now there's the million-dollar question. You could put 10 on a card but I don't advise it. Why? Because less is more and the purpose of a comp card is to give the decision-maker a taste of what they'll find in your portfolio, not the whole shebang! Personally, I don't want to see more than four pictures on a small card and one-three is better.

Black & White Only?

Artists often ask whether they can have an all-black & white card. Fashion stylists and hair stylists can sometimes get away with using only black and white images on their cards. However, this technique rarely works for (unknown) makeup artists because black and white photography can easily hide the details. A photographer looking for a great makeup artist won't be able to tell whether the makeup artist inappropriately applied blue eye shadow on a model wearing a brown tweed suit if he can't see the color. Very few photographers would take a chance on hiring someone they've never worked or never heard about if all they've ever seen of the artist's work is in black and white.

Do I Need Permission To Use A Photographer's Pictures On My Card?

The photographs are owned by the photographer who took them. They call it copyright. There are times when the photographer sells his copyright or grants certain rights (usages) to clients such as magazines or record companies. Because of this, it's very important that you ask the photographer for permission to use his/her photographs before having them printed on your comp card. In most cases, the photographer will not withhold permission unreasonably; however, as a professional courtesy, you should ask. And whenever possible, get written permission. Always get the correct spelling of the photographer's name and provide them with written credit on your card. Yes, I know, they rarely reciprocate the credit for makeup, hair, styling or nails on their own card, but that's the world we live in.

For more information on copyright and how to get what you need from photographers, read Copyright Law and You in Chapter 4.

Listen up! Getting anything from a photographer after a shoot is almost impossible. Make it a habit to ask up front for permission to use the photographs from the shoot on your card and in your book (See Chapter 5 for more information on working with photographers).

Many a makeup, hair, and fashion stylist and manicurist complains of being too broke to invest in a comp card that will showcase their skills and creativity and bring them more and better quality work on a regular basis. That same stylist, however, is rarely too broke to buy the latest Dolce & Gabbana dress or Manolo Blahnik shoes. The operative words here are INVEST & BUY. INVEST in a card that will bring you higher fees and steady work, or BUY a new dress to wear to the unemployment office. Don't allow your misinformed peers to convince you that printed self-promotion pieces are a waste of money in the internet era.

When Banana Republic, Nordstrom's and Zara stop printing look books, and stuffing their promotional pieces into your shopping bags and online purchases, you can archive [forever] your comp cards. Until that time, print on boys and girls, print on!

 TIPS:

| 1 | When looking for a place to print your comp card, look up post card printing instead. Why? Because a comp card is a post card with a different name. |

| 2 | Go to www.uprinting.com, www.gotprint.com and www.moo.com and sign up for their mailing lists. You'll soon start receiving advance notices of sales and special offers and discounts afforded only to their subscribers. |

Here are three GREAT resources for printing comp cards:

* UPRINTING.COM
* GOTPRINT.COM
* MOO.COM

You should keep your comp cards with you at all times. Drop a few into a ziplock bag, or keep a few in your kit and off you go. Your comp card is a much more impressive presentation than your business card, and most women's handbags are big enough to drop one in. While your business card may get lost in the bottom of someone's bag, your comp card will not.

I recommend that in addition to handing out your card, you should display it prominently in the makeup and hair or dressing room where you are working. I've known many artists who turned one job into another booking because they taped their comp card to the mirror in the room where they were prepping their clients.

Michele Gay, *CEO & Co-Founder, Limelight by Alcone*

Michele Gay is the CEO and co-founder of Limelight by Alcone. Launched in 2015, Limelight harnesses the knowledge and expertise of professional makeup artists to bring the best professional cosmetics to everyday women. Her passion for empowering women has turned this 2-year old brand into a powerhouse. Empowering makeup artists and consumers via high quality products and education is what sets her and the company apart from the competition. Michele gives us an insight into what makes Limelight the empowering career opportunity that it is and shares what it can do for makeup artists at all junctures of their careers.

How did Limelight come to be?

Michele: Well, when you are involved in a family business, like Alcone, you get tapped whether you want to or not. My sister was leaving the company at the time to pursue other endeavors, and my dad called me to come in and work. I said I'd come in and work for 6 months, but it's been 7 years now!

Two years into working at Alcone, I came up with the idea for Alcone Pro which was a great platform for pairing up makeup artists with people who needed their services. That's when I started thinking about what we could do to give the makeup artists compensation for sending clients to Alcone. I wanted to do something that would allow them to make a real income, not just a few pennies here and there. I wanted to create a program that could become a safety net for pros.

3 ELECTRONIC COMP CARD

An electronic comp card is simply a card that has been turned into a .jpg, .jpeg, .png (each is a type of image) or .pdf (portable document format). Your electronic comp card can easily be stored in your Dropbox. If you create a download link and attach it to your website, a decision-maker who finds you online can download your comp card right onto their own desktop, laptop or mobile device. A decision-maker who likes your comp card will be able to print it out in color and get EXACTLY what you intended.

2 BUSINESS CARD

A business card is smaller than your comp card and fits in your wallet. In order for it to work for you, it must be printed with your name, professional title, cell phone, web and email address and your Instagram account on it. It is shared with potential clients or colleagues during introductions, and at events where you are networking and connecting with people with whom you would like to work and collaborate. Some business cards have images on them. That's cool as long as it's only ONE image and it is not on the same side as your contact information. Additionally, the image should be of your work and not you.

Some freelancers have gotten entirely too creative with their business cards by making them extra small or extra large. Let me ask you something. What have you done with all of the itty-bitty business cards that have ever been given to you? Were they harder or easier to find in that oversized bag you carry around all day? They were harder to keep track of, weren't they? And they got beaten-up in the bottom of your bag, didn't they? If you're anything like me, eventually, you tossed those cards in the trash. Don't let that happen to you. Order a normal-sized business card and purchase a business card holder to keep your cards in. They should look brand new when you hand them out.

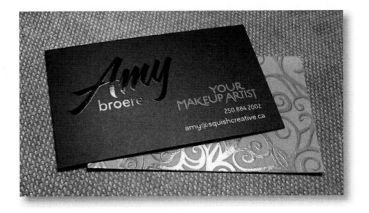

4 RÉSUMÉ

It's often said that a résumé won't get you the job, but it can cost you the job if not put together thoughtfully and formatted correctly. It may not guarantee you the job assignment, but it can and will help you get your foot in the door of many television and film company decision-makers who won't entertain meeting with you until they review it.

The résumé for an artist who works on feature films, television and commercials, is quite different from the résumé of an artist whose work focuses on print, commercials and music videos.

When asked if they looked at résumés, and whether or not they were important as a means of hiring artists for jobs or signing an artist to an agency, decision-makers who worked mostly on print weren't really interested and were happy to focus on the portfolio. For producers who worked on television commercials, TV and film, the résumé was a must.

My advice to ALL artists is that you should start building your résumé right along with your website and social media presence. There is nothing sadder than getting an unexpected opportunity to work on a film or television project and not getting hired because you don't have a list of your credits—which is exactly what a résumé is.

As you can see from our samples, they look very different, but they serve the same purpose—to acquaint the decision-maker with the important projects that you have worked on. And by the way, it doesn't matter whether you got paid or not because work is experience and experience matters.

NOTES

....

....

....

....

Michele Gay, *CEO & Co-Founder, Limelight by Alcone*

What kind of safety net?

Michele: My sister was a makeup artist. I could see how hard she and her colleagues worked, the time they invested in their craft, developing skills, and constantly learning new aspects of the industry. But, what if they became ill? What if they couldn't work as a makeup artist, or be on their feet for hours anymore? My sister developed MS. She knew that her time of doing makeup was limited, so what could she or would she be able to do then? Really, she was my inspiration for this.

When did you launch Limelight?

Michele: On February 1st, 2015. We launched it and it just grew exponentially. We took our professional products and repackaged them to appeal to the consumer. Originally everything was very pro-centric, but we wanted to expand our client base and deliver pro quality products to women for everyday use. We wanted them to see and experience how much better pro quality products are. The higher pigmentation, the blendability, and quality ingredients were things that most women weren't getting from their regular makeup. Our pros would also be able to sell [the same] products to their clients that they were already using as a way to make money to support their dreams. As soon as we started interfacing with customers and makeup artists, we knew that what we had was lightning in a bottle because it's always a good idea to invest in women.

NOTES

SAMPLE RÉSUMÉ FOR FILM AND TELEVISION MAKEUP ARTIST

MARY COLLETTI
MAKEUP & HAIR

LOCAL 555, mary@firstnamelastname.com
www.firstnamelastname.com, (555) 555-1212

FILM

CATCH ME IF YOU CAN Amblin Entertainment Dir: Steven Spielberg	MAKEUP THIRD
DID YOU HEAR ABOUT THE MORGANS United Artists Productions Dir: Marc Lawrence	MAKEUP THIRD
ANIMALS Magnolia Mae Films Dir: Michael Di Jiacomo	MAKEUP
DECEIVER MGM / MDP Worldwide Dirs: The Pate Brothers (Joshua & Jonas)	MAKEUP
GREAT EXPECTATIONS 20th Century Fox Dir: Alfonso Cuaron	MAKEUP
MY FELLOW AMERICAN Warner Bros. Dir: Peter Segal	MAKEUP
SICKO Sony/Albemarle Prods. Dir: Michael Moore	1st.ASST.MAKEUP
MY TEACHER'S WIFE Savoy Pictures Dir: Bruce Leddy	MAKEUP

MARY COLLETTI
MAKEUP & HAIR

LOCAL 555, mary@firstnamelastname.com
www.firstnamelastname.com, (555) 555-1212

TELEVISION

LAW & ORDER SVU WB/Columbia-Tristar Prod: Greg Prangemonster	ASST. MAKEUP
LEGACY(Pilot) UPN/Atlantis Productions Dir: Stuart Gillard	ASST. MAKEUP
THE DAY LINCOLN WAS SHOT TNT Dir: John Gray	MAKEUP
WHAT THE DEAF MAN HEARD Hallmark Hall of Fame/CBS Dir: John Kent Harrison	ASST. MAKEUP
UNSOLVED MYSTERIES (episode: Picture Taking Fugitive) Cosgrove/Meurer Productions Dir: Jim Lindsay	KEY MAKEUP
THE STEPFORD HUSBANDS CBS/Edgar J.Scherick Assoc. Dir: Fred Walton,	ASST. MAKEUP
I AM BRUCE LEE CBS/Warner Bros. Dir: Pete McCormack	KEY HAIR
BLUE RIVER (MOW) Signboard Hill Prod/Fox Dir: Larry Elikann	ASST. MAKEUP

The Hair Makeup & Fashion Styling Career Guide

Michele Gay, *CEO & Co-Founder, Limelight by Alcone*

Your consultants are called Beauty Guides. How many did you start with and how many are there now?

Michele: We started with one and just built from there. Now we have 20,000 Beauty Guides across the United States!

Do the Beauty Guides teach their customers how to use the makeup?

Michele: Each Beauty Guide has their own way of presenting the product to their clients. For example, we have one who creates videos showing how to use the products, the different brushes, sponges, etc. Whenever someone places an order from her she sends them a link to her video highlighting that product and the other products that work well with it. Her clients watch the video, learn how to use their product, and end up ordering the other products she's highlighted!

We're also finding that our Beauty Guides are growing their client base as makeup artists because a lot of the women who are ordering products from them will also tap into them to do their makeup for weddings, and other special events. They'll have all the products, but they still want a pro to apply it on them.

Who are some of your top Beauty Guides?

Michele: We have several, but one of them goes by the name "Angie" on YouTube and she has cultivated a huge following. Her videos are hilarious and she's created this character that talks like an Italian grandmother and it is so fun to watch. Her videos go viral, and she makes upwards of $20,000 in sales per month.

MARY COLLETTI
MAKEUP & HAIR

LOCAL 555, mary@firstnamelastname.com
www.firstnamelastname.com, (555) 555-1212

COMMERCIALS & MUSIC VIDEOS

PEP BOYS (4 spots, English and Hispanic) Manhattan Film & Tape/Maximum Marketing Dir: Mark Sitley	KEY MAKEUP/HAIR
FEDEX Colelli Productions/Sheehy & Assoc. Dir: Ralph Colelli	KEY MAKEUP/HAIR
BANK OF AMERICA Jack O'Brien Agency Dir: Jack O'Brien	KEY MAKEUP/HAIR
OSCAR MAYER BOLOGNA Michael Daniels Assoc. Dir: Mark Piznarski	KEY MAKEUP/HAIR
KENTUCKY FRIED CHICKEN Brad Christian Films Dir: Roger Tonry	KEY MAKEUP/HAIR
McCOY'S CRISPS K.P.Foods U.K. Dir: Syd Macartney	KEY MAKEUP/HAIR
SUSIE BOGGUSS "Drive South" (Music Video) Deaton Flanigen Prods. Dirs: Deaton & Flanigen	ASST.MAKEUP/HAIR

MARY COLLETTI

MAKEUP & HAIR

LOCAL 555, mary@firstnamelastname.com
www.firstnamelastname.com, (555) 555-1212

SPECIAL EFFECTS

BRAVEHEART, (U.K.)
ANIMATRONIC HORSE f/x crew
Paramount/Icon Productions.
Dir: Mel Gibson

IMPERIAL WAR MUSEUM EXHIBIT, (U.K.)

FINAL TOUCH-UP & LASHES
Lifelike Replicas Cazaly-Schoonrad

TEENAGE MUTANT NINJA TURTLES

CREATURE DRESSER
Golden Harvest Productions
Dir: Steve Baron

References Available Upon Request

MARY COLETTI
MAKEUP & HAIR
LOCAL 555
mary@firstnamelastname.com
www.firstnamelastname.com
(555) 555-1212

or not the artist should be considered for the same position on an upcoming film, or if the artist might be ready to be elevated to a status of more responsibility and thus, a new title.

For example, an artist who has keyed many projects may consider him/herself ready to interview for the department head position.

NOTES

....

....

....

....

....

....

....

....

A film and television résumé like Mary Coletti lists an enormous amount of information that includes the production company, director, producer, artists' title and the project name. A film makeup artists' résumé will give the producer or director an opportunity to see the kind of responsibility an artist has had (by looking at his/her title) to determine whether

77

Michele Gay, *CEO & Co-Founder, Limelight by Alcone*

Another is Christina Hernandez. She had to borrow money to start her business, but worked hard and was dedicated and is on track to make a million dollars this year. We actually have five Beauty Guides on their way to making a million dollars!

Who is the ideal beauty guide?

Michele: People with a sincere desire to do something incredible and who want to have an extra revenue source. We have so many makeup artists who are successful with us who are also doing other things, following their passions, helping sick children, working in outreach for the poor, teaching, etc. We want people on board who see the possibilities that we have to offer and that their careers have to offer. We want to bring in people with the mindset that they can own what they want to do with their careers and just do it.

Michele: In what ways do you use pro makeup artists in the development of Limelight?

Michele: We love bringing in celebrity makeup artists to pick colors and customize palettes. It's a true collaboration as opposed to other brands because we don't just put their names on the brand. We let them test everything and really get to know the products, make suggestions, and be an actual part of the process. We are never in a hurry to launch new products. We launch once everything is perfect.

We've just started working with Danessa Myricks and she's amazing. She's helping us create incredible products

SAMPLE RÉSUMÉ FOR A PRINT, & CELEBRITY FOCUSED HAIR STYLIST

NEEKO
HAIR STYLIST

PHOTOGRAPHERS

Jon Ragel
Kate Garner
Albert Sanchez
Bob Sebree
Alberto Tolor
Dan Winters
Firooz Zahedi
Patrick Demarchelier
Robert Erdman
Larry Bartholomew
Isabel Snyder
Troy House
Ken Bank
Dewey Nicks
George Lang
Greg Hinsdale
Dorothy Low
Bonnie Shiffman
Wayne Stambler
Richard Hume

EDITORIAL

Esquire
Vibe
Movieline
Entertainment Weekly
GQ
fitness
Essence
YM
Heart & Soul

NEEKO

HAIR STYLIST

EDITORIAL

Elle
Allure
InStyle
US
Stuff
Maxim
LA Times Magazine
Italian Max
Vanity Fair

RECORDING ARTISTS & CELEBRITIES

Halle Berry
Nikki Taylor
Lil Kim
Elizabeth McGovern
Tyra Banks
Veronica Webb
Debra Cox
Mary J. Blige
India Davenport
Shara Nelson
Amanda Colville

ADVERTISING & COMMERCIALS

Cover Girl
Bill Blass
Schlitz
Dark & Lovely
McDonalds
Revlon
M&M's
Macy's

NEEKO

HAIR STYLIST

FEATURE FILM

Executive Decision starring Halle Berry

TELEVISION

Keenan Wayans Show
Vibe Television
Nickelodeon

CRYSTAL AGENCY
www.CRYSTALAGENCY.com

(323) 555-1212

The Hair Makeup & Fashion Styling Career Guide

Neeko's résumé, on the other hand, is indicative of a print artist's résumé. As you can see, it makes no mention of a particular position on a shoot. He is the hair stylist. This résumé is designed to communicate a sense of the artistic/creative company he keeps, i.e., the level of talent he has worked with on most projects. Creative decision-makers who work mostly in print want to know what well-known photographers, top-notch magazines, high-profile directors, cutting-edge projects, campaigns, and notable people you have worked with. Most print résumés are like this, listing only categories, key individuals, projects, and clients.

5 THE ELECTRONIC REEL

The electronic reel is a collection of your television commercials, music videos, TV show episodes and feature film segments that have been edited together into a single 3-4 minute compilation which can be shared via email link or uploaded onto a platform like Vimeo or as part of your online portfolio.

for different skin tones and complexions. Her ultimate goal is to make women feel more beautiful and she knows Alcone will do that. It's the perfect collaboration.

Do you have any advice for new makeup artists trying to break into the business?

Michele: So many young makeup artists now are constantly being told not to do this or that. They are being told what to do to launch their careers instead of being given the freedom to grow their own businesses. They are immediately getting put into a box and their dreams and hopes are being stifled. They need to listen to their own intuition about what they want to do and shut out the other voices. They need to go for what they want in a way that feels right to them.

What about seasoned pros?

Michele: I find that a lot of the ones that have worked with big beauty brands need to be deprogrammed. They are used to old management styles which feed fear and penalize the artists. We want them to know that it's ok to fail and learn from it. We don't want them to fear that if they don't meet quota that they'll be fired. We don't operate that way. We want them to have the freedom to recommend other lines and products that may work better for their client. But pros who have been in the business for a long time are afraid to do that. So, we need to deprogram that fear.

A reel is a production. It is created by editing ALL of the media down to a few fabulous minutes of an artist's best work which then has some mood music laid over the top of it.

In my experience, artists who work in TV and film do not usually have reels. One reason might be because the cost to edit five feature films down to a few minutes can be quite prohibitive. The real reason is probably because most well-known artists who work in film and TV are hired by their résumés and word-of-mouth.

For example, let's say that you are a hair stylist who has worked on five music videos totaling 20 minutes of tape. First, you collect each of your videos. You can do this any way you like, but I can guarantee that you will spend a few hours of emailing and phone calling to get what you need emailed back to you or burned to a DVD. The task can test your patience because production companies are in the business of making movies, videos and TV shows, not copies of those shows for everyone who worked on them.

Collecting Your Stuff

Make sure to email a request for the video and include the information that follows in a single email to the production company. Providing these details will make it easy for them to find the video and drop the requested media into your Dropbox.

- Video & Commercial Title
- Director
- Producer
- Job Name
- Artist/Subject
- Job No.

Sound like a lot of work? Maybe. But it worked, and it was the only sure-fire way I found to get what we needed 80% of the time for the artists I represented at Crystal Agency. I said, "sure-fire," not "foolproof." Repeat this process until you have collected each one of your videos, commercials, webisodes, TV episodes, etc.

Music Selection

Remember that you are going to be editing these videos down into a single electronic reel of 3-4 minutes. You will remove the sound from these videos and overlay them with a selected piece of music that represents you while at the same time choosing something that a majority of decision-makers will respond to favorably. TuPac's "How Do You Want It" probably would not be a good choice.

In choosing your music, take into consideration the feeling and flow of the video and commercial clips that will appear on your new electronic reel.

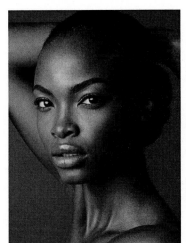

DELINA MEDHIN

MAKEUP ARTIST

DELINAMEDHIN.COM
DELINA@DELINAMEDHIN.COM
929. 251. 4404

Your name, phone number, profession and any snazzy graphics make up what's known in the business as a Title. Hence, a title card. Most editors will have the ability to create something pretty sophisticated on a computer or use something you share from your Dropbox to serve as your opening and closing titles. Your comp card can be great for this. It pops up at the beginning and the end of your electronic reel to inform people where to contact you. Be sure to ask the editor what format and resolution they would like the artwork in to work on their editing system.

Planning

Your next step is to view all the videos, commercials, TV and film clips and compile a list of the shots you desire in the finished product. It's also a good idea to think about your beginning (opening shot), ending (closing shot) and your middle. Planning your shot list in advance will save you time and money at the editing bay, since the editor usually charges by the hour or has a set number of editing hours for a specific rate. Before scheduling your editing session, give yourself enough time to view your videos and create or decide on your title card.

The Delina Medhin comp card sample on the left would make a great title card for an electronic reel. Just add Instagram.

6 LISTINGS

Listings are one way to get found on the web. A free one means that you don't have to pay to tell everyone who you are, what you do, and where you can be found. Free and paid listings are marketing tools that you don't want to pass up. Check out the list that follows and simply call, and ask for the deadlines and requirements for submission.

Michele Gay, *CEO & Co-Founder, Limelight by Alcone*

What would you like makeup artists to know about Limelight?

Michele: I want them to know that they can help build our company. We are a group of entrepreneurs building something different and successful. We are open to ideas. We want to hear what they have to say, what their suggestions are.

We have an incredible sense of community here at Limelight. That is what I am most proud about. We have a built-in sense of family, full of support and mentors ready to help. We want people to feel like they can find their focus and their home with us.

How does a makeup artist get involved with Limelight?

Michele: If they already know a Beauty Guide, reach out to them and ask how to get started. Don't worry about being pressured or hounded. That's not what we do. Talking to another Beauty Guide just allows you to figure out if this is the right opportunity for you.

If you don't know a Beauty Guide, visit our website at www.limelightbyalcone.com and go to "Become a Guide". Then just follow the steps to join.

limelightalcone

www.limelightbyalcone

1 **ProductionHub.com** is just one of the online communities that makes it possible for you to list your freelance business online in a forum that is designed to attract decision-makers who are looking for artists just like you. www.productionhub.com/get-listed

2 **Mandy.com** touts itself as the world's largest creative community of actors, film and TV crew. They help professionals to find work in TV studios, on movie sets, in training institutions, events, concert halls, theatre companies and art collectives. www.mandy.com/#signup

3 **Variety411.com** provides listings of film, video and TV commercial producers. They provide the best, most trustworthy production resources for commercials and music video production. variety411.com/apply-to-be-listed

4 **Shootsonline.com** is a one-stop shop for all production crew needs in the USA and around the world. For $149, you can add your profile, images, videos and more. my.shootonline.com

5 **KFTV.com** is an essential international resource for producers who are hiring crew members for films, TV shows, and commercials. www.kftv.com/register

On the print side of things, we find LeBook, Workbook, Models. com and the APA.

6 **LeBook.com** is pricy and prestigious. A page can cost you $2,500 or more. While you may not be ready to pay for an ad, it's a great resource when you're searching for new clients, photographers to work with, and to learn who's out there doing what. Additionally, if you have any national tearsheets from advertisements or magazines, you can submit them to LeBook with your credits to be considered for inclusion and that is FREE! www.lebook.com/contribute

7 **Workbook.com** is one of the most important print production guides in the country. It has been around for over 25 years and is dedicated to providing the creative community with a website that offers comprehensive resources for finding top photographic and glam squad talent. You can get a free listing right here: www.workbook.com/directory/free_listing

8 **Models.com** offers a collection of professional fashion images, modeling agencies, hair makeup & styling agencies, a directory and news. Sign up for FREE and get a listing along with an online portfolio to display your work. www.models.com/register

9 **APAnational.org** is a national organization that is dedicated to elevating the art and works of photographers while protecting their content. What's in it for you? For $125 a year, you will get listed in the directory, become privy to everything that goes on in the photography community and get invited to events where both the newest and most experienced photographers will assemble to discuss art and commerce. If I were a freelance artist, I would be hanging out at APA events with a stack of business cards, comp cards, and an iPad to show off my work. It's just .34 cents a day. It will cost you more than that to valet park your car at the W Hotel, have an appetizer and buy two martinis. www.apanational.org/join

Production guides (moving media) and creative directories (print) each have their requirements for getting listed. However, most listings are free or have a nominal charge between $10 and $500 each year. This is a small price to pay for getting a job that might pay you hundreds of dollars and open the door to a business relationship that could last a lifetime.

Remember, you are in BUSINESS and running a business is not free. You have to spend some money to make some money and now is as good a time as any to get started.

The following is an example of the typical information you might find listed in a directory. This one is for an agency:

Celestine Agency (Makeup, Hair, Styling & Nails)
1666 20th St. Ste 200B,
Santa Monica, CA 90404
(Reps: makeup, hair & stylists)
PH: (310) 998-1977
Email: info@celestineagency.com
FAX: (310) 998-1978
Web: celestineagency.com

Lisa Smedley

Fashion Stylist/Costumer
Los Angeles and Atlanta
fashionstylingbylisa.com
Focus: Commercials, Movies, TV
IG: lisa_loves_fashion_

ADVICE

I moved to Los Angeles right after graduating from high school to pursue a career in fashion. I started working at Saks 5th Ave in Beverly Hills, believing that it would be a great way to open doors. It was. I wanted to freelance and be more creative, so I started putting the word out to my Saks clients that I would personally pick out wardrobe and create a look for them when they had upcoming events.

I used my retail job to create opportunities for me to learn and grow. While at Saks, I met a lady who introduced me to Crystal. Fashion was my passion, but I had no idea that fashion stylist was a job title and that people with that title shopped for celebrities.

Crystal believed in me and took me on. She was tough, but it never made me weak, only stronger and more determined. I wanted to learn all I could. I worked hard, listened and watched the fashion stylists I assisted, and took every constructive criticism to heart.

I worked in Hollywood for ten years before I took a 10-year break in 2005. After caring for my mom, who passed on, my kids were now teens: 17 and 14 years old. I resolved to get back in the business despite being discouraged by others.

Crystal once again stepped in as my coach with the right advice at the right time. On December 15, 2017, my latest project, Gotti, starring John Travolta, will hit movie

The agency information above is considered a business listing. With only slight variation, they all give the same basic information to the reader and potential client.

An individual listing, like the one that follows for Mary Coletti, applies to directors, producers, and yes, makeup, hair, and fashion stylists, and manicurists. In most cases, you merely request one, fill out a standard listing form and beat the deadline for the following year's directory.

Mary Coletti

323.555.1212

mary@marycoletti.com

www.marycoletti.com

CATEGORY: Hair & Makeup Artists

SPECIALTIES: airbrush makeup, celebrities, events, fashion/beauty, film/commercials, grooming, hair, makeup, manicures, print, special effects

REPRESENTED BY

Zenarbia Agency, Inc.

323.555.1212

keith@zenarbia.com

www.zenarbia.com

Listings can be of even greater benefit to you if you provide them with a phone number that remains stable even when you're not. A Google Voice number is best. Since these numbers are not attached to a residence or business, you can move around as much as you like and people will still be able to get in touch with you.

This is especially important if you change agencies. Take it from an agency owner. As great and wonderful as we are, we're in business to make money. When someone leaves the agency and a client calls and asks for that person, most agency owners are not going to give out your forwarding phone number when a booking is at stake.

A stable phone number is very important. So many people are unlisted that most creative decision-makers don't think to call information looking for you, especially with so many area codes to choose from. Do yourself a favor. Get those free listings, make sure you're in 411 and stay in touch.

7 Pre-Production Services

Pre-production service companies gather the crew and shoot details on upcoming movies or television projects, and sell the information to anyone at a monthly or quarterly rate. They are best suited to artists who are interested in or are working in film and television. While they do list production companies who produce television commercials and music videos, these are not their focus, and you will be disappointed if you intend to find a list of 100 television commercials that are crewing up locally.

When searching through the Internet, use terms like Production Report and then add your city or state for more local information. The most well-known are The Mercury Report, Production Weekly and Production Leads. They're not cheap, but one job could more than pay for a year's subscription.

The Mercury Report	$52/month
	www.thempr.net
Production Weekly	$50 - $75/month
	www.productionweekly.com
Production Leads	$299/3 months
	www.productionleads.com

NOTES

theatres. Some said it couldn't be done, but I'm doing it! To everyone, I say, "Be humble enough to know that you can always learn and improve your skills." Then remember these few tips:

1 **Stay motivated.** Even when work is slow or non-existent, read fashion books, go to fashion shows or look online (it's free), initiate and accept invitations to test, and find ways to increase your business knowledge in areas like invoicing, production deals and negotiation, etc.

2 **Be persistent!** One, two, or even three setbacks is not a reason to give up! This business is tough. You have to be a strong person who can handle setbacks, and constructive criticism without giving up or becoming resentful.

3 **Use your time wisely!** Do everything you can to improve your skills. I read fashion magazines, attend fashion shows and visit designer showrooms to build relationships. Become more business-savvy by looking at the new ways that things are being done.

4 **Set goals.** Make an action plan. Write it down. Give your goals a date and then follow through! Writing down what I want to accomplish by a specific date keeps me focused and on task.

In 2016, I wrote down that I wanted to transition from commercials to doing more movies and TV. I wrote it down and began calling production offices, sending my résumés and following up with phone calls. Since setting that goal, I have worked on several movies and TV shows and just recently got called to work on three shows at the same time! I could only choose one but what a great problem to have!

DEAL MEMO

The deal memo is one of the most essential tools because you will use it every time you book a job. The deal memo confirms the terms and conditions, days, dates, and rates under which you will work and get compensated for a particular job.

It specifies how and when you will be paid your fee and overtime, reimbursed for out-of-pocket expenses, receive written credit, be compensated in the event of cancellation or postponement, how long you will [typically] wait to receive your pay, and whether you are to be paid by check, electronic transfer or credit card. Without this single sheet of paper, you may never get paid, or you may wait forever to collect your money.

When I started Crystal Agency, I soon figured out that without something in writing, it was very easy for a decision-maker or a company to walk away from our verbal agreement. That's when I created my own deal memo. I needed something that would confirm the days, the dates, the rates plus the terms and conditions under which my artists were going to work.

We'll talk more about the deal memo later in the Freelancing chapter. For now, just know that there are five crucial pieces of information that you need to collect each time you are being booked for a job:

1 PO Number

2 Job Name

3 Job Number

4 Name of the Key Decision Maker

5 Signature of Someone in Authority

In the case of the PO number (Purchase Order Number), one may not always be issued by the company that is hiring you; however if they are issuing (supplying) them and you don't get one, you WILL NOT get paid.

DEAL MEMO

This deal memo confirms that _____ will work on _____.

CLIENT: _____ CLIENT JOB NO.: _____
CLIENT JOB NAME: _____ CLIENT PO NO.: _____
ARTIST JOB NO.: _____ PHOTOGRAPHER/DIRECTOR: _____
CONTACT PERSON: _____ JOB TITLE: _____
PREP DAYS: 0 DATES: _____
TRAVEL DAYS: 0 DATES: _____
SHOOT DAYS: 0 DATES: _____
WRAP DAYS: 0 DATES: _____
WEATHER DAYS: 0 DATES: _____
ASSISTANT DAYS: 0 DATES: _____
TOTAL DAYS: 0 NOTES: _____

RATES • TERMS • CONDITIONS

DAY RATE/FEE: 0.00 PER ___ FULL OR ___ HALF DAY UP TO ___ HRS
STRAIGHT TIME FEE @ 1.0 X THE RATE/FEE: 0.00 PER HOUR FOR EACH HOUR IN EXCESS OF ___ HRS
OVERTIME FEE @ 1.5 X THE RATE/FEE: 0.00 PER HOUR FOR EACH HOUR IN EXCESS OF ___ HRS
OVERTIME FEE @ 2.0 X THE RATE/FEE: 0.00 PER HOUR FOR EACH HOUR IN EXCESS OF ___ HRS
PREP RATE/FEE: 0.00 PER ___ FULL OR ___ HALF DAY UP TO ___ HRS
TRAVEL RATE/FEE: 0.00 PER ___ FULL OR ___ HALF DAY UP TO ___ HRS
WRAP (RETURN) RATE/FEE: 0.00 PER ___ FULL OR ___ HALF DAY UP TO ___ HRS
ASSISTANT RATE/FEE: 0.00 PER ___ FULL OR ___ HALF DAY UP TO ___ HRS
OVERTIME FEE @ 1.5 X THE RATE: 0.00 PER HOUR FOR EACH HOUR IN EXCESS OF ___ HRS
EXPENSES: 0.00 FOR _____
0 % AGENCY COMMISSION: 0.00 _____
MINIMUM BOOKING: 0.00 _____

CANCELLATIONS & POSTPONEMENTS
IF NOTICE OF CANCELLATION OR POSTPONEMENT IS GIVEN LESS THAN THREE (3) BUSINESS DAYS BEFORE THE SCHEDULED SHOOT DATE, THE CLIENT WILL BE CHARGED 100% OF THE FEE.

INVOICE PAYMENT
The invoice associated with this job assignment is due and payable no later than _____. If payment has not been received by that date, a new invoice will be generated with a 2% late fee per month due on the unpaid balance. To avoid this charge, please pay your invoice promptly. If you will be paying by credit card, please initial here: _____, and complete the additional paperwork titled Credit Card Authorization.

AUTHORIZATION
Your signature, working title and today's date is required below, and will serve as confirmation and agreement of the number of days and dates booked, and agreed upon fee/rate. Once signed, you have agreed to the terms and conditions as they are stated above. Please email a signed copy to me at _____ by ___ :00 on _____.

NAME: _____ TITLE: _____ DATE: _____
SIGNATURE

CREATIVE DIRECTORIES & PRODUCTION GUIDES

Creative directories are resource guides for the print industry. Production Guides are resource guides for moving media such as music videos, television, film, and commercials.

In addition to being the vehicles you can use to place your own free and paid listings, they provide you with names, addresses, phone numbers, email and web addresses as well as other important information that will help you reach out to decision-makers such as photographers, other artists you may want to assist or collaborate with, producers, art directors, production coordinators, directors, fashion editors, beauty editors, etc.

Kristine Murrillo Hair Stylist
631.374.9583
kristine@kristinemurillo.com
www.kristinemurillo.com

bookmark

CATEGORY
Hair & Make-up Artists

SPECIALTY
hair

Carol Oliveto

Photo and Art Director

INSPIRATION: FIND YOURS

The dictionary says of inspiration that it is:

- a divine influence
- a sacred revelation
- the action or power of moving the intellect or emotions
- the act of drawing air into the lungs
- the quality or state of being inspired

My favorite is "the act of drawing air into the lungs." I am inspired by many things: books, fashion magazines, people who succeed against the odds, a walk through an art gallery, photography, old ruins, travel, being around my friends, and anything about history.

Owning your own business—which is what freelancing is—won't always be easy. Rewarding YES, but easy, not always, and certainly not in the beginning. I encourage you to go inside. Not your house, but inside yourself. Find what inspires and breathes life into you. Like love, it will carry you through the tough times.

Inspiration comes from within, and it is very different from motivation. Motivation is about psyching yourself out/up to do something that you may not want to do, like going to the gym and working out. It often has more to do with what you feel you should be doing.

Inspiration, on the other hand, makes work feel like play because you love it so much. Staying up all night to do research on the internet or pouring through magazines feels effortless. Working on the TV commercial set for 15 hours fills you with the exhilaration of WINNING a marathon. When you're inspired, you can barely hold yourself back from practicing your craft right now. The flame inside you never seems to go out, and the projects you dream of completing leave no space in your head for anything else but the fruition of your dream.

Dr. Wayne Dyer said, "Motivation is when you get hold of an idea and carry it through to its conclusion, and inspiration is when an idea gets hold of you and carries you where you are intended to go."

Find yours, and protect it with all your might. It will carry you through.

NOTES

Carol Oliveto is the Photo and Art Director at Belk. She is a highly regarded creative professional with over 20 years of experience working in-house and with top agencies as a visual artist and creative director. Some of her clients include Rodale, QVC, Pure Red, A.C. Moore, Coldwater Creek, Mervyns, and World Market, to name a few.

Her passion for her work is evident every step of the way through to the final product. From lighting to casting, design concepts, and photoshoots, Carol brings professionalism, and attention to detail. She has worked with some of the top clients, models and photographic teams in the industry.

Originally hailing from Philadelphia, Carol's career intention was to become an illustrator. However, once she set foot on her first photoshoot, she knew that, that was where she wanted to be. The rest is history.

In this interview, Carol shares her thoughts about where the industry is headed. She touches on the importance of retaining authenticity and professionalism in a world and industry that has become far too fast-paced for its own good.

Carol, where do you see the industry going?

Carol: Honestly, it's crazy. I mean you still have to have all the photography no matter what, but what I'm seeing is the lack of personality in the photography. It's becoming more and more assembly line. There are all these companies that just want everything on white. They just want the model to stand there so people see clothes.

Things have changed so much. Like when I first started at Strawbridge's, there was a Strawbridge's and Wanamaker's

CONSUMER & TRADE MAGAZINES

While you may want to subscribe to every fashion or trade magazine known to man, you probably won't have time to read them all. My advice: subscribe to the print or online publications that will serve as your resource materials and inspiration for growing your creative side. Make a list, price the magazines, and purchase your subscriptions all at once at the same time each year.

If you've ever subscribed to magazines, then you know what a drag it can be to remember the exact month you paid for your subscription to a specific publication. It seems as though publishing houses begin sending renewal notices as soon as they process your credit card. This can become pretty unnerving if you have more than two or three magazines arriving each month. I've paid for Vogue more times than I care to remember.

One great way to get your consumer magazines is through www.texture.com, a monthly subscription service. The monthly fee is $14.99 and they offer a free 14-day trial. Visit www.retailmenot.com to see if you can snag a discount coupon for the service.

Makeup

Two publications fulfill the needs of the freelance styling community of makeup artists: On Makeup and Makeup Artist magazines.

Makeup Artist magazine focuses on the needs of makeup artists who work on film and TV projects throughout the US. They cover current events, feature makeup artists who work behind-the-scenes and produce the annual International Makeup Artist Trade Show (IMATS) in Los Angeles, New York, Toronto, Vancouver, London and Sydney, Australia. Makeup Artist magazine is published bi-monthly, and is available at www.makeupmag.com.

On Makeup magazine is published in NY and endeavors to service freelance makeup artists who work on print, video, runway and television commercials. Turn to On Makeup for news, information and trends in the industry. www.onmakeupmagazine.com

Hair

American Salon and Modern Salon magazines, while directed at the salon industry, do offer the opportunity to work on their covers and will keep you abreast of product announcements, events, opportunities and changes in the cosmetology landscape. Check out www.americansalon.com and www.modernsalon.com.

Behind the Chair touts itself as the largest community in the world for salon professionals. They provide articles, galleries, how-to and formulas and step-by-step instructions for their subscribers. Visit behindthechair.com.

EDUCATION

It goes without saying that there is always more to learn. Be one of those artists who takes advantage of new classes and seminars that can make you an even better, more well-rounded, and employable artist than you are today.

Look For Opportunities Tthat Add Value

If you are a makeup artist or hair stylist in a small or lifestyle market (Chicago, Seattle, New Mexico, Cleveland, etc.), you should be well-versed in both makeup and hair. It will help you to get and stay booked. The jobs in these markets typically call for one person who can do both makeup and hair. In fact, it might be worth your while to add basic nail skills to your repertoire. Imagine how grateful the producer will be—even though you don't publicize yourself as a manicurist—when you whip out an emery board and a bottle of nude polish to touch up the hands of the model who came in without a perfect set of nails. Your action could save them hundreds, even thousands of dollars on retouching. These are skills that you can actually charge more for.

In markets like Los Angeles and New York where focusing on just one discipline—Makeup, Hair or Nails—is often the norm, choose classes that will help you to sharpen and master specific skills that will help you get to the next level—better, more challenging jobs with more interesting people and better day rates.

The Hair Makeup & Fashion Styling Career Guide

and the Lit Brothers and there were different personalities to each store. You would shop at a certain store because of some kind of feeling it would give you, but nobody does that anymore. They click on Amazon where they can find it cheap, and if it doesn't fit then they just return it. There are still some lifestyle clients producing shoots that tell a story. They try to connect their brand with the consumer. I love seeing that because it's refreshing and adds such a human touch.

The personal stuff is still out there but is getting harder to find. Fewer people take the time to shoot according to the store or client's personality. They think that if it doesn't work or look right, they can just Photoshop it. Remove a head here, add one there, do this, do that. It's almost becoming like a robotic thing. So that's why I'd be thrilled doing more TV and video work. You get the same players but the end result is different.

Are clients still investing in producing television commercials, or do you see that going away?

Carol: I don't see it going away unless they can figure out how to take that human part of it out and illustrate everything. I mean that's why people still go to movies and watch TV. There still is that human element to it. It makes you feel something. So, you're still going to need all the stylists and hair and makeup people for that because, let's face it, nobody looks good on camera without all those people prepping them. I don't care who you are. The lighting isn't conducive to just natural unless you're naturally talking to someone in person.

Take advantage of one-on-one, extension and online classes that are being taught by professionals in the industry who can teach you something new. However, be discerning about the classes you take. Don't sign up for expensive classes without thoroughly examining the offering and the offeror. Not everyone who posts a new class has the qualifications to teach it.

Don't be seduced by slick ads with lots of promises. Ask for referrals, send out direct messages to individuals who have taken the class, and check out the educator's credentials. Have they had success in the area that you are about to invest in? Is the instructor happy to give you the names of some of their former students? Can you see the fruit (results) being manifested in the lives of other artists who swear by their methods? One testimonial by a single person does not prove anything when it comes to investing hundreds, even thousands of dollars in a course.

Before signing up, exercise the muscle of asking questions, read the fine print, and be brave enough to confirm that you are going to get what you're paying for. Anyone who has something of value to offer isn't afraid of a few questions from a potential student. In fact, they embrace the opportunity to share.

This is what we call due diligence: a comprehensive appraisal and evaluation of the offer to establish its value and commercial potential in your professional life!

NOTES

THE [PRINT] PORTFOLIO BOOK

The portfolio book is the physical manifestation of your hard work from testing and jobs placed into a coffee table-sized book. While it won't be getting the workout it once did (before online took over), it's still a very valuable tool, especially at photo shoots where decision-makers you haven't met yet will be milling about, chit-chatting, drinking coffee, returning phone calls, browsing through magazines and YES—discovering your portfolio if you brought it with you, and laid it out on that coffee table in the lounge area.

I know what you're thinking—why can't I just take my iPad? You can take your iPad, but are you really going to let it out of your sight and leave it sitting 200 feet away while you are slaving away in the makeup, hair or wardrobe room prepping the talent? I think not! Besides, that iPad has a code on it, shuts down every fifteen minutes and could be filled with images that you don't want other people to see. Furthermore, they disappear. Heck, even Winona Ryder steals.

By contrast, no one is going to run off with your 8lb portfolio if you leave it sitting on the coffee table in the studio, but they just may leave that shoot with one of your comp cards and a business card if you make it available to them.

The portfolio book provides another benefit to you, the artist. There's nothing quite like gazing at all of those big beautiful 11X14 prints. It presents the real you to you. Not the 3X5 inch version of you that you see on the face of your mobile phone. Seeing your work in this large format gives you an opportunity to evaluate, scrutinize and appreciate the breadth of the art that you are producing. Artists have told me that seeing their work in this format inspires them to work harder and correct mistakes they hadn't noticed in the smaller format, and gives them the confidence to go after opportunities they didn't know they were ready for until their work was staring back at them.

Print Presentation

So, how do we prepare the work to show? The print presentation encompasses the inside, outside, and collateral (business card, comp card, résumé, etc.) elements of your book. The size, cover font, accessories and YOU all come together to create an impressive package. In the presentation of your work, four elements must be considered:

- Size
- Style & Type
- Appearance
- Accessories

Tearsheets ripped sloppily from magazines and photographic prints that bare the uneven scissor cuts of a six-year-old will not cut it when $500/day or more is at stake. Make it nice! Don't let your book be one of those inadequately produced and prepared portfolios that doesn't make the cut.

Size

Professional glam squad artists show their portfolios in one

So makeup, hair and fashion stylists will be able to keep their jobs a little longer?

Carol: That's right. As for print, it's just going in a strange direction. I was talking to some people who works for a clothing company and they have just one person on set. No photographer or art director. The whole crew is gone. The camera is focused on the mannequin and there's one person dressing it and hitting the button on the camera. So, how crazy is that? Everybody wants everything faster, and leaner, and meaner. I understand wanting to save money, but I would love to see a return to that connection between the images and the people looking at them.

How do you feel about models being hired through Instagram rather than agencies?

Carol: There are clients that don't want to pay the 20% agency fee. They want to cut rates on the models and these girls are too young to remember that, that is why Eileen Ford started her agency. So that models wouldn't get caught in bad situations. With Instagram, no one is looking out for these models. The agencies' purpose is to filter all of the bad stuff out.

What about makeup artists and hair stylists? Are you seeing that most clients prefer to hire them separately, or someone that can do both?

Carol: It depends on the project, but I can actually get more done with a separate hair and makeup person. I think a lot of clients feel this way. You can have one person on set and the other in the makeup room. That way there's no lull in productivity. There's always movement which is essential during a photoshoot. You don't want to lose momentum.

of two sizes, 9.5x12.5 and 11x14. DO NOT choose an 8X10 book; it's unacceptable in this business—it reminds everyone of headshots, and makes you look like an amateur.

Style & Type

There are custom (made-to-order, handcrafted) and off-the-shelf portfolios. Custom portfolio makers offer books that can be built according to your taste and wallet. The combination of preferences (color, materials, page type, and embossing) that you choose are personal. Customization options include:

- Color, which ranges from black to the brightest shade of yellow and just about anything in-between.

- Materials, which include a faux leather-like fabric, aluminum, plastic, real leather and more. If you can imagine it, a custom portfolio maker can produce it for you.

- Embossing, which comes in a variety of colors from blind to black, red, gold, white, silver and yup, just about anything.

- Page type, which can be plastic or acetate. The plastic is matte. The acetate has more of a glassy appearance.

Appearance

Prints and tearsheets should be trimmed neatly and mounted so that they don't move around in your book. To keep your book looking neat and polished, invest in a precise paper cutter from an art supply store.

Accessories

PORTFOLIO FRONT

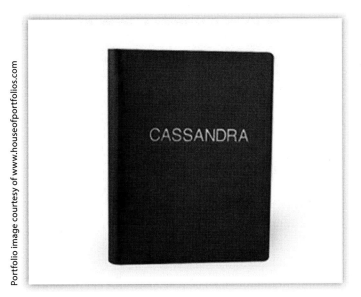

Portfolio image courtesy of www.houseofportfolios.com

PORTFOLIO INSIDE

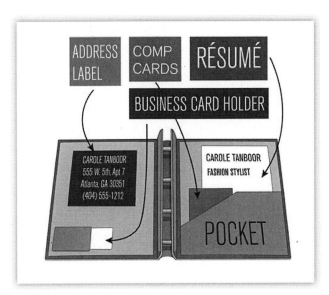

Portfolios can be ordered with pockets for the inside back, inside front covers or both. I'm in favor of one inside back pocket to hold your comp card, business cards and résumé. You can make business cards available to clients without worrying about whether they were going to slide unnoticed into the big pockets of the portfolio by purchasing a pressure-sensitive business card pocket from Cardinal or Smead. They are available in most office supply stores.

You apply them to the pocket by simply peeling off the self-adhesive backing and pressing them into place on your portfolio. You can then slide two or three business cards into it, and clients can remove them at will.

WHERE TO PURCHASE

Custom USA

www.houseofportfolios.com

www.brewercantelmo.com

www.kloportfolios.com

Custom UK

www.hartnackandco.com

Off The Shelf

www.adorama.com

Carol Oliveto, *Photo and Art Director*

What advice do you have for someone who wants to work in the industry?

Carol: I would say to be relentless and focus on somebody you want to work with and go for it. For example, I sent QVC 13 résumés. They actually called me and told me to cease and desist. I told them I would as soon as they hired me. And they did! I mean, it's better to hire somebody who wants to be there than somebody with an attitude.

If you want to work in hair or makeup or as a fashion stylist, I would say to go pound on every door of every photographer you've ever heard of and tell them you're serious about working. The thing about starting out is that everyone needs to trust you because the jobs are fewer and fewer and it's their reputation on the line. So if they hire you, they have to trust that you're not going to screw up the account. You've got to make sure that everything you do is professional. Be relentless about really wanting to do this. When you are on set, don't talk on your phone all day. I see that on sets, where the makeup or hair artist will be on their phone instead of watching the shoot, which makes me worry about how they are going to do their job. You need to be present and be part of the team. This is one profession where everyone depends on each other.

 carololiveto

 www.carololiveto.com

NOTES

NOTES

_____

_____

_____

_____

_____

_____

_____

_____

_____

_____

_____

The Hair Makeup & Fashion Styling Career Guide

You have to love to work. You have to love yourself, and you have to love promoting yourself. And then you have to love your clients. You gotta do a lot of loving.

—Rose Cefalu

Photo Director - Emmy Magazine

3

Marketing Yourself

KEEP ME UPDATED
FOLLOW UP   CALL ME
SHOW ME
LEAVE ME
FOLLOW THROUGH

Frank Garguilo

Art Director

What do you do as an art director?

Frank: In most places the term art director means coordinating the project, going to the photo session, articulating the overall look of the project and handing it over to a designer. That's very different from what we do here at the record label. Here we art-direct and design the project. Very rarely do we hand anything over to a designer, unless we are extremely busy and records get bumped into other releases and things begin to overlap due to scheduling issues.

Art direction changes from project to project. The process begins with being assigned an artist or band. You have a meeting with them where you listen to

Show Me Whatcha Got	a portfolio, résumé and your Instagram account.
Leave Me a Reminder	a print or an electronic comp card.
Call Me	follow-up with a phone call.
Follow Up	send a thank-you card.
Follow Through	do what you say you are going to do.
Keep Me Updated	show me your new stuff every month.

6 RULES OF MARKETING ENGAGEMENT

Above and below are my six rules of marketing engagement. These are the essential steps/actions that are required to launch and SUSTAIN a successful marketing plan. It doesn't have to be complicated. It just has to work, and in order for it to work, it has to be executed consistently, tweaked and repeated.

The freelance artists who have graduated from my portfolio-building and marketing course, known as PYP Grads, created a T-Shirt with three words on it. DREAM. DO. REPEAT. Believe it or not, to be successful in this business you have to have a dream. You have to take action, and you have to repeat your steps in order to manifest the fruits of your labor.

If you are good at what you do, commit yourself to following these six simple rules. Things will happen. Work will come.

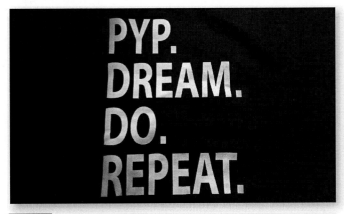

RULE 01 — SHOW ME

It is not enough just to tell people what you've done. You have to show them. That means sharing your online portfolio, social media and résumé.

RULE 02 — LEAVE ME

Once they've seen your work, you must give them something to remember you by. That is where your comp card and résumé come in. It's the physical piece of evidence that reminds the decision-maker of the kind of work you do.

RULE 03 — CALL ME

You've sent everything. Now it's time to follow up with a phone call. A good rule of thumb is to call back within two-three days of online sharing, mailing or emailing. Remind them who you are, and ask if there is any work coming up that you might be well suited for. At worst, they can tell you no, not right now. At best, you may just be in the right place at the right time, with the right skills and creativity, and get booked for an awesome job.

RULE 04 — FOLLOW UP

It means engaging and staying in touch by phone, email, social media and snail mail. Oh yes, buy some stamps. Sending a thank-you card when you need to say, "I really appreciate that you took the time to look at my work, meet with me, give me advice, or give me a job" is like stacking money in your savings account. If you're good at what you do, and you take time to appreciate people, you will ALWAYS be in demand.

RULE 05 — FOLLOW THROUGH

Do what you say you are going to. PERIOD. Don't beg out of commitments because you got a better offer. Don't call in sick as if you are on your death bed when all you have is the sniffles. Be someone who can be counted on, and if you really do have to cancel on a client or colleague, be proactive and try to find another artist to cover you.

RULE 06 — KEEP ME UPDATED

Keep potential and existing clients in the loop on all of your new work. It's your responsibility to keep expanding and informing their idea about what you are capable of creatively. You don't have to get stuck doing work that you accept just to pay your bills. As long as you are sending out an email every 30 days to share your new work, activities and updated résumé with decision-makers whom you want to do work with for the first time, and clients that you want to continue working with, something will break. The universe wants you to succeed!

what they have to say, hear their music, and try to get an understanding of what they're thinking about and their feelings about their own music. At that point I start reviewing photographers' portfolios online, and sometimes stylists and hair and makeup people at the same time, depending on the schedule. I like to try and pinpoint a photographer first, and move on to styling, hair and makeup.

The entire process is very collaborative. I want everyone to have an opportunity to create. It starts with the selection of a photographer, the stylist next and the rest of the crew, and that's how you begin preparing for a shoot. Hair and makeup is much more technique so I'm just looking for someone good. Unless it's something outrageous, then you are looking for something really special. Styling is really important, people notice clothing more than makeup, and that's the way it should be. You shouldn't notice someone's makeup unless makeup is the focus.

With styling I look for creativity, even in the simplest things. The music starts the direction of what you are looking for and then the artist. I look for artists I feel are in the same sort of mode. I present the artist with three to five portfolios, sometimes less.

What's the best advice you can give to artists who are just starting to build their portfolios?

Frank: It's really important for hair and makeup to work with good photographers. When the photography isn't

Listen! You can't win, I mean really win, without making these six rules an integral part of your plan. You've got to show 'em, leave 'em, call 'em, follow up, follow through and update decision-makers with what's new and exciting in your work life. It may sound clichéd, but the squeaky wheel gets the grease.

You Are Your Brand: Curating Your Work & Your Message

Now that you understand the 6 Rules of Marketing Engagement, let's talk about how we share information about ourselves and engage with others in the business. We CURATE. It means to organize, collect and share. As a freelance artist whose career is on the rise, you will want to curate what decision-makers see of you, hear from you and learn about you. You do that by stepping into your I AM MY BRAND shoes when deciding what you'll share on social media and in your online portfolio. In other words, not every aspect of your work, home life, politics or religion needs to become public knowledge in your workplace.

Before you release every job detail into a world where you cannot take it back, consider the upside of first collecting, organizing and sharing details with the public during moments when you believe you will garner the most attention and traction for your brand.

You manage your brand by managing perception. And you manage perception by making good CHOICES about what to share and when to share it, and what to keep to yourself. This is the first lesson in marketing yourself and managing your brand.

The goal should be to curate your persona in such a way that the rest of the world sees a put-together, savvy artist with clear focus and a creative agenda, even though, early on, you—like the rest of us—may still be trying to figure it out. No one needs to know what's going on behind the veil except you and your closest friend.

How you curate your online persona will impact who wants to work with you. It's not really nice to judge people, but we do it all the time, don't we? You may be the best person for the job, but if a decision-maker visits your social media pages and finds that you or your closest friends are the next coming of 'the mean girls', they can simply close that tab on their Google browser and move on to artist number two. Manage perception.

Ask more questions than you answer, and listen more than you talk. Before you tell everyone at the party that you voted for Clinton or Trump—listen. Work and politics do not make good bedfellows in this polarized world we live in at the moment. Mentioning that you are a Democrat at a networking function full of Republicans or vice-versa could cost you jobs that you didn't even know you were about to be awarded. Shhhhhhh. Listen first. Sometimes when you're in a room full of people who think differently than you do, the best response is a non-committal hmmmm, wow or really.

NOTES

Just the other day, I called a warehouse to inquire about fulfillment services for my books. When the woman who answered the phone heard my name, Crystal Wright, she proudly blurted out, "I just want you to know that we espouse the same values as you do." I was surprised, stunned and taken aback. But I wasn't as surprised as she must have been when I calmly responded, "Oh, I'm not that Crystal Wright." TMI. You can see how important it is to curate what you put out there? That was $3,000 worth of business lost, just because she didn't think to learn more about me before she jumped to a wrong conclusion aloud that then cost her a new client.

FREELANCERS TOOLKIT

In Chapter 2 you learned about the tools of the trade. These skills, equipment, products and services will help you do your job. Now I'm going to show you how to maximize some of those tools along with the 6 Rules of Marketing Engagement and your new-found ability to curate your message, so that you can supercharge your freelance career in print, video, film, television and e-commerce.

good, or the lighting is all wrong, it's hard to focus on the hair and makeup. Sometimes it's hard to get beyond the photography, even though I've trained myself to be able to look beyond it at just the hair or makeup. When a recording artist looks at the book and the photography is bad, it ALL looks bad to them. Musicians are not trained to look at books the way we are.

What is your aesthetic?

Frank: I like really clean, non-existent makeup. But I like to see both extremes in a book. During a photo session I may want to go to both extremes depending on the artist. I think makeup and hair artists should show a range in their book. A fashion stylist should show what they really like to do.

If a portfolio doesn't work for you, how do you handle it?

Frank: When I had more time, I used to write notes. I would say what I did like about the book and what I didn't. If an artist calls, I will try to give them some feedback.

What do you need from an artist on the set?

Frank: Aside from their technique, I look for someone with a good attitude and spirit. I like a collaborative team of artists. If an artist has a suggestion, I want them to let me know. I like my shoots to feel like a real team effort. I want it to be an experience for everyone. Those are the people I feel compelled to work with again. And no attitude.

Best practice

There are 11 items in the freelancer's toolkit. You will probably use one or more of them every single day. Now I'm going to show you how to use them to get work. They are:

1	Online Portfolio
2	Social Media Presence
3	Professional Email Signature
4	Bio
5	Comp Card
6	Business Card
7	Résumé
8	Thank-You Card
9	Savvy Networking Skills
10	Phone & Email Etiquette
11	Elevator Pitch

1 USING YOUR ONLINE PORTFOLIO TO GET WORK

Whether it has five images or 25, your portfolio is you. The moment you start sharing it with people, it becomes part of your brand. It should not contain work that you have to make excuses for. A decision-maker is immediately turned off by the artist who shows his or her work and adds the proverbial disclaimer with every photo or tearsheet.

If you say things like, "This photo would have been better if…", or "I keep intending to take this out of my book" or "This really isn't my best work", the typical decision-maker's response will be to thank you kindly and hire the next artist who shows up with a positive self-image and belief in their own work. If the work is in your book, you should have only good things to say about it. If not, take it out!

Be proud of your portfolio. I once got a job for a fashion stylist who did not have a portfolio of her own work. And I don't mean a rinky-dink job. I mean a full-on four-day styling assignment to create a look for a new recording artist's CD cover. Her fee was $750 per day. How did I do it? I didn't. She did. She sashayed into my office with an old-fashioned zippered portfolio full of magazine pages that she had cut out of the top fashion magazines and mounted them neatly into this portfolio. She looked me right in the eye as if she were herself the fashion editor of Vogue, and said [as she flipped through the portfolio], "If I had styled this picture, I wouldn't have put that skirt on her!"

The next 5 minutes were a blur. She couldn't be bothered with what I might have thought. She was there to get me to represent her, and represent her I did. The very next day Tom Bricker, an art director at Atlantic Records, called me about needing a stylist for an upcoming job, and I convinced him that this little fabulous girl—who had never styled anything besides herself—was the right person for the job. She inspired me with her nerve, determination and preparation. Lisa Michelle Boyd walked into my office without a single picture of her own and boldly took me where no one had before. Long after I had closed my agency, she went on to become Charlize Theron's fashion stylist.

The point: Don't apologize. Don't make excuses. Don't try to hide the fact that you only have a few images. Be as proud of one photo as you are of 100. Take the meeting! And, if someone says, "You only have three photos", agree with them and tell them what a great job you're going to do for them and why you're the right person for the job.

NOTES

....

....

....

....

....

....

I worked with a really great stylist that I may not ever hire again. We were doing CD on an artist who wasn't a thin person. We communicated this to the stylist, but when she showed up at the meeting and saw the artist, her mouth dropped open and she made the artist feel terrible. And that just cannot happen. After spending more than eight hours together at a photo session, I bumped into the stylist and she didn't even remember who I was. And we've been re-introduced a couple of times since then.

It's really important for makeup, hair and fashion stylists to know that we are not working with models, these are real people with real feelings. They are musicians, not models.

How do you like to be contacted?

Frank: If someone has been recommended, I check out their online portfolio and Instagram and then I try to meet with them. Comp cards are good, too. If I get something really amazing, then I'll visit their site and Instagram, and call the person or their agency and ask to meet them. An artist should have some sort of card. I keep the ones I like and write a note on them. When I'm looking for someone for a job, the first thing I do is go through my files.

What do you want to see?

Frank: Personal work. When someone brings me a lot of commercial stuff, I will ask to see their personal stuff.

Portfolio Formatting

If you want decision-makers to spend some time on your website looking at your portfolio, these attributes are a must:

1	Simple to navigate (easy to use)
2	Have 5 essential tabs • PORTFOLIO • ABOUT/BIO • CONTACT • BACK STAGE | RED CARPET • RÉSUMÉ
3	Load quickly.
4	Have no music or flash.
5	Include all of your contact information.
6	Be mobile-friendly.
7	Have an email link that activates and opens up a browser when you click on it.
8	Have a phone number that launches a dialer when clicked on.

Showcasing Your Videos, TV Commercials & Television Credits?

The electronic reel is an extension of your online portfolio. It becomes a pull-down selection when someone hovers over portfolio. If you have music videos, television commercials or snippets from TV shows or feature films that you would like to share on your website, the electronic reel with a two-four minute compilation of moving media is the way to do it. An electronic reel doesn't replace your portfolio; it gives you another way to approach marketing yourself to producers who hire for commercials, music videos, television and film.

Additionally, your reel can be burned to DVD if necessary, duplicated relatively inexpensively ($1-$3 each) and sent, with a résumé and comp card, to a variety of people at various production companies. You can also upload your finished reel free on websites like YouTube and Vimeo, and add your résumé and contact information.

2 USING SOCIAL MEDIA TO GET WORK

There's a difference between being focused on growing a consumer or professional audience for influence and being focused on using the platform to get freelance work. I'm here to help you get work from creative decision-makers.

I was fortunate to interview celebrity hair stylist Oscar James for this book. What a joy. In Chapter 2, I do my very best to break down the beautiful and simplistic approach that Oscar uses when he posts to his social media account. If you're searching for a simple approach to help you get started posting to your social media account on the regular, revisit the social media tools in Chapter 2 and be inspired to find your own truth and authenticity as an artist. It will make social media much more fun and less stressful. From there, you can consider my tips that follow to get you on a path to building an audience that will get and keep you working as a freelance artist.

Consider that you want to:

1 Curate and upload:

- good work that you do
- something personal
- something inspirational
- behind-the-scenes

Consider that you want to follow:

Glam squad artists whose work you admire who are in and outside of your specific discipline (makeup, hair, fashion styling, nails).

1 Glam squad artists whom you would like to assist.

2 New and established photographers whose work you admire.

3 Beauty and fashion brands whose products you use and love.

4 Magazines whose content interests and inspires you.

5 Celebrities whom you hope to work for (if that's your thing).

6 Decision-makers and colleagues who hire and refer you on paid and unpaid jobs.

What advice would you give an artist who's in the process of building his /her book?

Frank: Like the work you are putting online. Gear your book towards something you like and feel strongly about. Find a few good photographers that you can collaborate with. I think it's also really good for a fashion stylist to be able to create things themselves, or find people who can help them. Using young designers is a good idea. A really good fashion stylist who can't find something will make it, or have it made.

I think it's even great when a stylist can take a household item and make something out of it, or just find that extra something. I think good styling is all about putting things together in interesting, flattering ways. What I look for most in a stylist's book is how they put things together, mix and match things, their sensibilities. It's really important for a stylist to make connections.

Do you look at résumés ?

Frank: Not really. What's in someone's book is more important to me.

Remember to:

1 Engage with followers and people you follow by liking and commenting on their posts and asking questions.

2 Look for ways to engage with followers and people you follow on subjects other than work.

3 Acknowledge people who make positive comments on your posts.

4 Mention brands that you use by @ and # tagging them.

5 Credit the artists whom you collaborate with on tests as well as paid and unpaid jobs.

3 CREATING AN IMPRESSIVE EMAIL SIGNATURE

It never fails that, several times a month, I get incomplete emails from freelance artists and random folks who want advice or help from me. I am astounded by the lack of professionalism in these correspondences, and I rarely respond.

Following is the kind of email message that doesn't get a response from me:

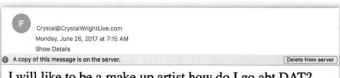

Crystal@CrystalWrightLive.com
Monday, June 26, 2017 at 7:15 AM
Show Details
A copy of this message is on the server.   Delete from server

I will like to be a make up artist how do I go abt DAT?

A professional signature should ALWAYS contain the following six elements, and it should be included on all of your devices—if you expect to get a call back. Use the space provided to create your own professional email signature.

First & Last Name

Job Title

Phone Number

Email Address

Web Address

Social Media

Titilayo Bankole

Manicurist | Nail Stylist

301.555.4525

titilayo@titilayobankole.com

www.titilayobankole.com

@titilayomanicurist

Linda Zirkus

Hairstylist | Make-Up Artist

323.555.1212

linda@lindazirkus.com

www.lindazirkus.com

Delina Medhin

Makeup Artist

323-555-1212

delina@delinamedhin.com

www.delinamedhin.com

@delinamedhin

As an option, you may also want to add other social media accounts to your signature, such as Facebook, Twitter, Snapchat, YouTube, etc. I would, however, limit it to a maximum of 3.

NOTES

....

....

....

....

Jeanne San Diego
Makeup & Hair Stylist
JeanneSanDiego.net
IG: jeannesandiego

A career in makeup and hair seemed far-fetched while I was in school pursuing a "stable" vocation in healthcare. Everyone doubted me when I decided to pursue my passion in the beauty industry. But a year after getting my cosmetology license, and training in makeup artistry, I was on my way up. Ten years later, I reached what I thought was a significant accomplishment in my career—I won the 2012 North American Hair Award for Makeup Artist of the year. But somehow, I felt STUCK and asked myself, "Now what?" I knew of Crystal for years and decided to take her workshop in December 2012.

What came after proved to be the most productive (not busy) 30—60—90 days of my career. The goals I set for myself partnered with activities and a plan that Crystal masterminded with me, which helped me to gain unprecedented momentum in my business.

You can have amazing products in your kit but not knowing how to properly use them is a waste of your time and money. Similarly, you can be the most talented artist in town, but not knowing how to land a gig makes you a starving artist. Create a clear vision of where you want to go in the industry and be accountable to your dreams and goals. Someone once told me, "The day you stop learning is the day you stop growing!"

4 GETTING TO KNOW YOU THROUGH YOUR BIO

Since so much business is done over email and on the web, your bio is another way to give decision-makers a window into your personality and an opportunity to get to know you. When I interviewed Frank Moore, the agent at Celestine Agency in Los Angeles, he said, "The majority of clients we deal with just want people to hang with all day who have the right personality, do their job really well and quickly, and don't demand attention."

The question to ask yourself is, "How do I share a piece of my passion, my expertise, my personality and my professionalism with the world in two-three paragraphs?"

This is a good time to go back to that list of artists that you are following on social media. From Instagram or Facebook, you should be able to find a link to their website. Once there, look for a link or a tab that says BIO or ABOUT or MEET. Sample two-three and get a feel for the way that they talk about themselves, their work and their passions. One of my favorite yet simple bios is that of a fashion stylist that I represented some years ago. You can find her website and bio at www.melindatarbell.com. I'm sure you'll agree as I do that the image and the description in her bio are a perfect match.

5 COMP CARD MAGIC

As I mentioned in Chapter 2, your comp card has one purpose: To grab someone's attention and make them want to see more, and more is on your website.

A comp card is to a freelance artist what a magazine cover is to Condé Nast. Would you buy Vogue magazine if it didn't have an interesting or captivating image on the cover? Publishing companies put beautiful people on the covers of their magazines because we the public buy pretty pictures of recognizable people or striking images that we cannot turn away from. The same is true of how you market yourself.

Your comp card should be with you at all times. Drop a few into a Ziploc bag, keep a few in your kit and off you go. Your comp card is a much more impressive presentation than your business card, and most women's handbags are big enough to drop one in. While your business card may get lost in the bottom of someone's bag, your comp card will not.

I recommend that, in addition to handing out your card, you should display it prominently in the makeup, hair or wardrobe room where you are working. I've known many artists who turned one job into another simply because they taped their comp card to the mirror in the room where they were prepping clients.

It's always a great idea to take comp cards with you to events. Wherever there are women who are dressed in their finest, there are opportunities to pick up clients. I am the first person to leave a few post cards for one of my events on the counter in the bathroom at a nice venue.

In fact, I used to get in trouble at the Makeup Show every year because I printed 11X17-inch posters with our booth number on them and instructed my volunteers to tape them to the insides of the women's bathroom stalls. Our booth was always packed!

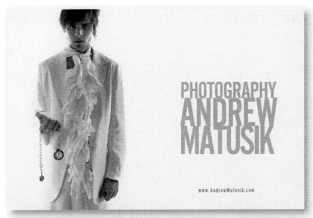

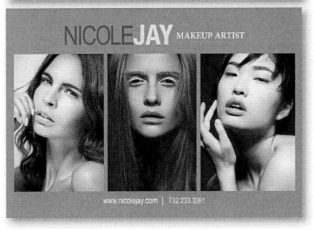

Rose Cefalu

Photography Director

Emmy Magazine

Do not allow the creation and printing of your comp card to become a last-minute thing. If your intention is to produce one twice a year, pick the months and set an alarm on your calendar to remind you 30 days in advance that it is time to select an image for your comp card.

When it comes to creating an effective comp card, less is more. I encourage you to stick to one, two or three images at most. Be aware that while your comp card may be five to seven times the size of your business card, it's still a pretty small piece of real estate. The more images you add, the smaller they have to be to fit on the card. As they become smaller, you begin to lose the detail of the images, and the impact is diminished for the end user.

NOTES

6 THE MOST IMPORTANT BUSINESS CARD

Every artist should have a business card. It should be clean and simple, and the person you hand it to should be able to write on it with a regular ink pen. Shiny cards are for kids. Always remember that the most important business card is not the one you give, it's the one you get, because the one you get is the only one you can follow up on.

The same basic information that goes in your email signature should be printed on your business card. If you can fit your social media on the card without making it look cluttered—go for it. If not, leave it off. You can include it on your comp card.

I have always been a fan of putting one single image on the back side of a business card.

7 RÉSUMÉ

A résumé gives you credibility. It says, "Someone else trusted me with a project, and you can, too." What I want you to know about compiling your résumé is that the most important, prestigious and recognizable entries should come first. There is no need to put your résumé in chronological order. Most people scan a résumé looking for things that they recognize. You may have just done a movie last month, but, if it's not as well-known as something you did last year, put last year's movie at the top. (see Chapter 2 Pages 75-77)

This is also true for the print-focused résumé that is full of the names of photographers, directors, celebrities, publications, etc. Stack the good stuff at the top of each category. (see Chapter 2 Pages 78-79)

Don't date yourself by adding the year that you worked on a project. Leave the dates off of your résumé wherever possible, and it should never be more than two pages long.

NOTES

....

....

....

The Hair Makeup & Fashion Styling Career Guide

| **Rose Cefalu,** *Photography Director* |

Rose Cefalu is the Photography Director at Emmy Magazine and an adjunct photography instructor at the Art Institute of California. She has racked up an impressive list of publications since her early days as an intern at Detour magazine, including Movieline, Flaunt, Variety's VLife, Treats Magazine and internationally on the UK-based Loaded, and New Zealand's Pavement.

In her job as photography director, she hires the crew and manages all aspects of photography including cover shoots, research, and budgets. Recently, Rose discussed how she broke into the industry and how you can rise to the top.

Can you tell me what steps you took to become a photo editor, and what you love about your job?

Rose: In my last quarter of photography school, I had a project in which I worked with a team to put together a magazine. I worked with a graphic designer, a fashion designer, a painter, and a few others. I thought it was the coolest thing and decided to try and intern at a magazine.

I interviewed with Detour and interned with them for a year. I made myself as valuable as I possibly could as an intern. I did everything. I picked up dry cleaning. I worked with photographers. I copy edited. I created a valuable position for myself when there wasn't one, so they offered me a paid position and hired me as the Photography Director.

I'm currently at Emmy Magazine which is part of the Television Academy. I love it. It's so much fun. We just

8 THANK-YOU CARDS GIFTS & MORE

The thank-you card is everything. Cultivate an attitude of gratitude, and you will last a very long time in this business.

If there was ever an area that I fell short in, it was that I didn't show my clients that I appreciated them enough. There were times when I got it right, but I wasn't consistent with it. As an artist, it's important for you to remember that when you're working on set doing what you love and making $500, $800 or more than $1,000 a day, the person who hired you and gave you that great gig is probably making a fraction of what you are earning on any given day. A thank-you card with a Starbucks gift card in it, remembering their birthday or sending over a nice bottle of wine goes a long way toward showing appreciation and getting booked again sooner rather than later.

Get over to Ross or TJ Maxx and spend $4.99 on a box of thank-you cards. It will be the best $4.99 you have ever spent. I can almost guarantee that the return on that investment is about 500%.

THE GIFT THAT KEEPS ON GIVING by Celebrity Makeup Artist Sam Fine

In a business where many articles stress "How to Keep Up With The Latest Trends" or "How to Make It Big in Business" you'll rarely find any "real" information on how to maintain the business you have.

The fact is, that in a sea of talent, part of your job is working at being remembered long after the booking is over. I know what you're thinking—after becoming an established artist your work is remembered simply because you're at the top of your game—not true! In an industry that feeds on its young, with clients always searching for the next new artist to reinvent their image, you learn not to rely on your craft alone.

Ask makeup pros how many of them believe they've retained a client simply because of their skills and I'm sure they'll tell you that it's not enough to be artful, you have to go a step further and master how to become irreplaceable! It begins with what I like to refer to as "care taking." After you've performed your duties, what makes them remember you? When you're finished for the day and a week passes, what makes them say, "That artist was great?" We'd like to think that working our hardest to make them beautiful is enough. NOT! What helps people remember you comes in many different forms.

Imagine that you've just finished an assignment and the client loved that new lipstick you used or has inquired as to where you found that perfect foundation. How thoughtful would it be to purchase the lipstick she loved, and send it to her with a note card describing what a pleasure it was working with her? Not only have you just made her day by giving an unexpected surprise, you've also provided her with bragging rights to say that her favorite artist has given her something no one else has.

Remember that giving isn't always about a gift; it also speaks to giving of yourself. Gifts come in many wrappers and care is one of the best gifts to give. I have been referred to as "a full-service salon. On many occasions, I've found myself calling upon hairdressers and manicurists, selecting the right

Dorothy Dandridge

shoe for an outfit and making appointments at jewelers. Oh, and yes, painting her face! Someone would call it going above and beyond the call of duty; I call it "The Gift That Keeps on Giving".

I didn't always think this way, but one day to my surprise I received a thank you note from actor and songstress Vanessa Williams (The Emily Post of the entertainment industry). As if working with one of the most beautiful women in the world wasn't thanks enough, she sent a gracious card relaying that she enjoyed my artistry and looked forward to seeing me again soon. I realized how special it felt to be remembered, so I made it my job to remember others.

The time it takes to write a note or call a florist is nothing compared to the lasting relationship you begin to forge! This new relationship can also become helpful in future endeavors. If the client at Revlon relocates to L'Oréal, don't you want to be the first person they remember? So, keep in mind, our jobs put Elisabeth Moss on the cover. She just won an Emmy. And we put Seth MacFarlane on the cover with the kids from Stranger Things this year as well.

What has changed over the last 5 to 7 years about the way you do your job?

Rose: My official title started out as photo editor and then went to photography director. I'm also producing video because there has to be a video component to every photo shoot. I'm dealing with social media. I'm dealing with the website. Things have changed so much. Things move so fast. With magazines, we used to have a 3-month lead time. And it's hard to keep a secret now for three months.

We shoot something for the magazine and people want to share it right away, but they cannot. We really have to limit what gets seen to when the magazine is actually released.

Do you require the glam squad to sign an NDA, so they don't start posting selfies online?

Rose: Most of the people that I'm working with on Emmy Magazine are experienced. They are veterans so we don't have that issue. My call sheet always says, "No posting until the magazine has posted first." So, there's nothing signed, but it's on the call sheet.

I often get celebrities who want to share pictures before the magazine comes out, and I'm happy for them to do that because that brings a bigger audience to the magazine. But I don't want the crew to post anything before the magazine does.

as artists don't end after the final stroke of the brush or once everyone packs their kits.

It becomes everyone's job, both beginners and pros alike, to give a bit of yourself and provide the client with a lasting impression. At the end of the day everyone wants to be appreciated. And in the beauty business—which is all about feeling good—make sure to find ways to keep your clients happy. There are no guarantees to keeping a client, but good manners and kindness endure.

9 SAVVY NETWORKING SKILLS

If I could only give you one piece of advice about networking, I would say be genuine. Networking is easiest for people who are inquisitive by nature, and like other people. People who are inquisitive ask questions, and then they listen intently for the answer, which leads to more questions, which makes the other person feel important.

I'm like that now, but I wasn't when I was younger, because I always thought that I was the most important person in the room. I didn't listen to what other people had to say, I just waited for them to finish talking so I could regale them with my fabulousness. Back then, I always got invited to a party once, but I rarely got invited back. It took me more than a decade to figure it out. Someone gave me a book entitled *It's Not All About You.* I was insulted, but soon realized that it was a book I needed to read. Since then, I have made great progress.

Doing your research before heading out to an event will make your networking more effective, satisfying and interesting. Prepare for the event like you would a cocktail party where you have to impress your significant other's boss. In prepping for an event, find out in advance who's going to be there. Look up two-three people, and write down a couple of questions that you will ask them. This is especially important with famous people, because most people who meet them just walk up and say the same thing, "I like your movie", or "I read your book", or "I like your work." Not one of those comments will get you to first base. However, when you can ask a question that peaks their interest, makes them think and inspires them to engage, you've really done it right.

Set a networking goal for yourself before you leave your house. Decide how many new people you are going to meet, and don't leave the event until you have met your goal and collected business cards that you can follow up on the day after.

Connections happen in both planned and unexpected ways, so always be prepared with your elevator pitch when you get an opportunity to:

- Connect via email.
- Chat on the phone.
- Follow up after sending out a comp card.
- Request a meeting.
- Meet someone on set.
- Be introduced at a social gathering.
- Get a reply back on social media.

Take the initiative to make each engagement purposeful. Before picking up the phone or leaving the house, it helps to know the who, what, where, when, why and how objectives of your encounter.

WHO:	You're Calling, Meeting or Emailing	The Decision-Maker
WHAT:	You Expect to Accomplish	The Goal
WHERE:	You Expect This Encounter to Lead	The Result
WHEN:	You Would Like to Connect	The Date & Time
WHY:	You're Calling, Meeting or Emailing	The Reason
HOW:	You Expect to Accomplish It	The Plan

Armed with these facts and a purpose before you pick up the phone or head out the door, you will be better prepared for success in any situation.

NOTES

....

....

....

....

Rose Cefalu, *Photography Director*

We recently did a shoot with the Rock, who has 98 million followers. He has a whole social media team, and he did some videos and posted the cover before we did, which is fine because he has a much bigger audience on that platform and he's a huge star.

So, what hasn't changed over the last 5 to 7 years?

Rose: The process is still the same. Celebrities come in. They discuss what they want to do with the creative team regarding the creative process and the direction they're going in.

In fact, I think if anything, the communication from the celebrities has gotten stronger, and there's more involvement with hair and makeup and styling. So, in that aspect, it hasn't changed, but maybe the mentality has changed.

How do you like being contacted by artists?

Rose: I know a lot of new artists don't have agents. So, I'm open to forums like yours, and obviously, your PYP graduates. If I'm introduced to an artist by someone, then I'm more likely to use that person.

When I do bring someone new into the mix, and they have a good portfolio, it's usually on a small job. That small job can lead to a lot more. It just depends on the chemistry. They have to remember that it's their opportunity to sort of climb the ladder when it comes to having that particular celebrity or executive request them on another job.

10 | PHONE & EMAIL ETIQUETTE

Giving Good Phone

The most effective outgoing phone calls are planned in advance and scripted when necessary. Early on in my sales career, one of my primary activities as an account representative was "cold calling". Cold calling is a term used in sales to describe the act of contacting someone on the telephone, in person or on email who doesn't know you and isn't expecting you.

For me, the experience was almost paralyzing. I would find a thousand things that needed to be done just to keep from calling a perfect stranger on the phone, having a door closed in my face or having an unhappy customer screaming at me because the last rep sold them the worst product ever made. Fortunately, I could only clean out my briefcase, straighten my desk or refill my stock of brochures so many times before I uncovered the telephone on my desk staring back at me.

So, what do you think happened? You guessed it. With practice, I got very good on the phone, stopped taking the NO personally, learned to close the deal and remained in the top ten percent of my region during my five-years at the company. You see, we all have to overcome something. For me it was fear of the phone.

Answering Your Business Phone

How you answer the telephone may determine whether you are presented with a job opportunity or not. I have returned calls to artists only to be caught in the loop of a three-year-old answering Mommies incoming calls and playing on the phone? Nah, it couldn't be, because freelancing is your business, not your hobby. If you owned a clothing store in Manhattan, would you let your child answer the phone? If not, then don't do it from your home office, which is probably your cell phone. Clients don't think it's cute or funny. If they're chuckling, it's nervous laughter. Once they hang up the phone, they will move on to book the next artist on their list.

Voice Mail

When your voice mail picks up, the message potential clients hear should be professional, succinct and informative. I want to know where you are (unavailable or on a job), how I can reach you (cell phone), when you're going to call me back (within what time frame), what to do if it's an emergency (cell phone) and where (email or text) I can send instructions or information. What decision-makers don't want is children gurgling in the background for 15+ seconds while your favorite musical selection plays in the background. REALLY?

Let's call Mary Coletti and listen to her outgoing message:

Hello,

And thank you for calling. You're reached LA based makeup artist Mary Coletti. I am not available to take your call at this moment, however if you will leave me a message at the sound of the tone, I will get back with you within the hour. If your need is urgent, please send me a text message to this same number. You can email me at mary@marycoletti.com and please visit my website at www.marycoletti.com.

Simple.

Giving Good Email

Now that you have that great email signature we created in this chapter back on page 109, how about a few email etiquette Do's and Don't's.

- Include a clear subject line. Email messages without a subject line appear to be spam. When I get emails from artists, I perk up when I see subjects like: New Work or Portfolio Update or Makeup Assignment with Rhianna.

- Include your new signature on every email. Visit your email providers **SETTINGS** tab and automate your new signature so it appears on every email you send or respond to.

- Say hello professionally. Yo and Whasup are not professional. Hello Denise or Hi Denise is quite acceptable.

- Don't try to be funny with people you haven't developed a relationship with.

- Proofread your message three times before sending.

- Don't be cryptic or clever thinking that the recipient will know what you're talking about. Just tell them.

The talent has to be there. But it's 90% marketing and putting yourself out there. If you're not marketing yourself, no one is ever going to know you even exist. Also, perception is so much of it. If you're creating new content for your social media and website, then people are going to see that you're working and people want to work with people that are working.

When somebody is contacting you, how much is too much?

Rose: Once a month is good. I love it when I'm out and I'm meeting people, at a show and someone gives me a card. But I'm not a fan of the cold-call from hair and makeup and styling. I'd rather just have an email maybe once a month

What should an artist put in the subject line of their email to get your attention?

Rose: I think the ones that stand out the most are the personal ones. Make it personalized so it doesn't feel like it came from an email bot that just put my name in there.

Do you use social media when sourcing artists for a project?

Rose: No, I don't. But I do know that a lot of people are getting hired through social media, especially from Instagram. Instagram is really the biggest platform I think for people in entertainment-based media or fashion media.

I think an artist's Instagram account is just as important

11 | ELEVATOR PITCH

Everyone needs an elevator pitch. It's a brief persuasive declaration that you use to spark interest in what you do, and inspire the person you're speaking with to take action on your behalf. It should last about 20-30 seconds and be interesting, memorable and succinct.

My elevator pitch is just under 24 seconds.

> *I get people unstuck. I am a freelance business development coach with 30 years experience representing artists. In my practice, I focus on helping beauty, fashion and photography professionals find their own version of creative success in print, video, film and TV. I want to help more people, so I'm looking for opportunities to share my expertise and my methods with a much bigger audience.*

Let me break it down for you:

When people ask me what I do, I say, "I get people unstuck." The next questions is usually, "Well how do you do that? Or "Who do you do that for?" At that point I say, "I am a freelance business development coach with 30-years experience representing artists. In my practice, I focus on helping beauty, fashion and photography professionals find their own version of creative success in print, video film and TV. If I were in the elevator or on the escalator with the education director for the IBS show, I might say something like, "I want to help more people, so I'm looking for opportunities to share my expertise and my methods with a much bigger audience."

Your elevator pitch is all about you: who you are, what you do, and what you want to do. It's a great way to share your expertise and credentials quickly and effectively with people who don't know you.

Sample Elevator Pitches

Following are some sample pitches that you can use to craft your own elevator pitch. Make sure your declaration includes at least three of the five credentials that follow:

What you do.

Your background.

Your special skill.

Your strength. (Experience)

What would you like to do? (Goal/Aspiration)

- I recently graduated from Makeup Designory where I specialized in beauty makeup. I work part time at Sephora to continue to build my product knowledge, and I assist artists at Celestine and the Wall Group to hone my skills and learn set etiquette. I'm looking for freelance jobs that will put my skills as a beauty makeup artist to work.

- I have several years worth of retail fashion experience styling regular people. If your production company is ever in need of an extra set of hands, I'd be thrilled to support one of your more seasoned stylists.

- My name is Jeanine, and after years of working in a hair salon, I've taken the plunge and started freelancing. If you know anyone who's looking for an on-set hair stylist, I hope you'll send them my way!

- I create fantasy nail art for beauty and fashion brands. My passion is coming up with creative ways to help them express their message on fashion runways and in advertising campaigns.

Use the spaces that follow to craft at least two elevator pitches that you can use the next time you meet someone of influence.

Pitch #1

....

....

....

....

....

....

....

....

as their website in how professional they are. You want to see an Instagram grid that's curated to the work if you're a hairdresser, a makeup artist or stylist. I don't want to really see personal pictures. I want to see the work.

Do you still want to see a website with a full body of work?

Rose: Yes, because it shows me that this person understands a little marketing, and putting together a body of work. I want to work with people that actually know how to do grooming and can shave, cut, style, do light, natural makeup, glamour makeup, and just healthy, glowy skin. I want to see the range that a person can do in each particular category. I don't want to see the *contour* artist.

Do you have any preferences or pet peeves for the way a portfolio is arranged online?

Rose: No music. I don't like music because you might be pulling something up somewhere and all of a sudden, this music starts playing and it's just kind of annoying. I also like to see an online portfolio clearly separated by categories.

What advice would you give an artist who is in the process of building his or her portfolio?

Rose: Reach out to the modeling agencies because they have a bunch of test photographers that they're working with, and you're going to get great subjects. If you're just starting out, you should do at least two shoots a week and post new content on your website and Instagram, because

Pitch #2

Pitch #3

GETTING WORK IN ADVERTISING

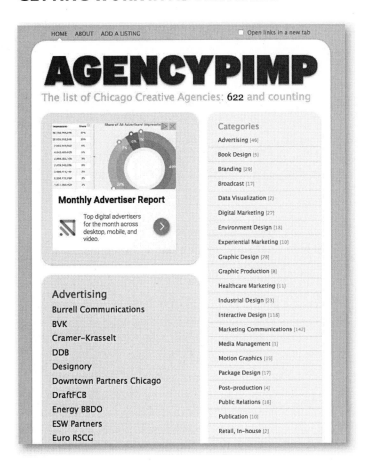

Advertising's finished product refers to both print and television commercials. They include everything from print ads in magazines and on billboards, to point of sale and point of purchase pieces such as hanging mobiles and life-size cardboard cut-outs often found in the aisles of neighborhood grocery and drug stores, to the packaging of everything from Aunt Jemima Pancake Mix to L'Oreal Hair Color to television commercials that feature a kid on a skateboard carrying a can of 7-Up to an infomercial on the latest weight loss product. All are methods used to promote and sell products, services and events commonly called advertising.

NOTES

Advertising is by far the most lucrative area of freelance work. Typically paying $750 per day in smaller markets, and up to $2,500 or more in cities like New York and Los Angeles—or whenever a major celebrity is involved. The ad shoot is a coveted assignment. The prize—those all-important "tearsheets."

The Hair Makeup & Fashion Styling Career Guide

out of sight, is out of mind. I think as a makeup artist; you want to level up. You want those brands to see you, all the makeup brands. You want celebrities and editors to see you, so follow those people.

What are your expectations on set for an artist?

Rose: Be on time. Understand when to open your mouth and when not to. I want someone who is going to jump in if they see a hair sticking out. Have clean, sanitary makeup and hair products. I don't want to work with anyone that's messy or dirty. Cleanliness is super important.

What are your top three turnoffs from freelance artists?

Rose: Emailing and calling too much, a dirty kit and being late.

Is there anything else that you would like to share that you believe can empower freelance artists to land more jobs?

Rose: Be ambitious, on time, friendly and be for the client.

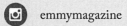 emmymagazine

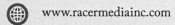 www.racermediainc.com

---

Getting advertising work can be a time and resource consuming endeavor—but the dollars and steady work are well worth it.

Let's start with a few facts:

1 What does an advertising agency do?

It uses marketing strategies to create ad campaigns tailored to sell and create awareness for their clients' products. The employees of the ad agency (art directors, creative directors, account executives) work closely with the client (Nike, Coca-Cola, L'Oreal, US Army, etc.) to gather information and pitch their campaign ideas, which, if chosen by the client, begins the creative process of actually making and distributing the ads in magazines, on billboards, on television in the form of commercials, etc.

2 There are [stand-alone/outside] advertising agencies that work like the one I just described, and there are in-house creative departments that take the place of advertising agencies and exist in the companies themselves.

3 Sometimes, companies with outside advertising agencies get fed up with the creative ideas that the agency is coming up with to promote their brand, and they bring their advertising in-house.

4 How can you find out which advertising agencies are based in the city or state where you live? Go to Google and search for: ADVERTISING AGENCIES + CITY/STATE. When I went online and searched for ADVERTISING

> AGENCIES CHICAGO I found a phenomenal site entitled AgencyPimp.com. It has a list and link to over 600 agencies. Click on the link and then look for the WORK or CLIENT link, which will typically show you the kind of campaigns the agency works on.

These are the basic facts you need to know to understand what an agency does and how you can find them. Now let's get down to the nitty gritty. What follows is a six-step program for getting work in advertising that should make the going a little easier:

1	Research! Research! Research!
2	Keep Track of the Information.
3	Tailor your Presentation.
4	Submit your Work for Review.
5	Follow Up.
6	Follow Up Again.

NOTES

....

....

....

The Hair Makeup & Fashion Styling Career Guide

STEP 01 — DO YOUR RESEARCH

Think locally, nationally, then globally. Begin by assessing the type of work that is available in your city. You may want to work with Michael Jordan on a NIKE commercial, but unless Weiden and Kennedy, Nike's Portland, Oregon-based advertising agency, decides to shoot in Widefield, Colorado, where you live, you may be waiting a while.

Comb the local newspapers and magazines. Are there department, clothing, or grocery stores in the vicinity? Is a local doctor or gym doing ads or commercials? Are people in the shots? If so, someone prepped them for the camera and it might as well be you. Create a hit list of local, national and international clients you would like to work for. A sample list for a Seattle-based makeup artist might include:

- **LOCAL**
  Mario's
  Butch Blum

- **NATIONAL**
  Nordstrom
  Starbucks

- **INTERNATIONAL**
  Microsoft
  Boeing Aircraft

With this list you can begin getting some questions answered. Do the local businesses have in-house marketing departments? Do they use ad agencies? It's easy enough to find out. Get the phone numbers of the local businesses. Call them up and

Jennifer Jackson

Hair & Makeup Artist
Chicago
JennJackson.com
Focus: Film and TV
IG: JennJacksonhmua

I was first introduced to the 'Guide' by a friend and fellow hair stylist. We both worked in the same salon and wanted to get into doing freelance work. She gave me her copy of the Guide and I read it from cover to cover. She booked our first test shoot from Craigslist. She did hair and I did the makeup. It was so amateur, yet it was the beginning.

Eventually I met Crystal at a makeup trade show and the next month I took her PYP workshop in New York. I began to assist other artists and eventually ventured out into my own projects. But I wasn't all the way in. I was all over the place.

By now, I had my own copy of the Guide, but YOU CAN'T JUST READ THE GUIDE, you have to PUT IN THE WORK! Sure, I read it, but I hadn't begun the work. I didn't have a résumé, comp card, or portfolio... just some funky business cards that I hated. Yet I still managed to get plenty of great work (feature films, TV, editorial, commercial, music videos, etc.) because I networked and talked a good game...but I really wasn't in the game.

I spent a couple of years just floating through. Then opportunities started to pass me by. Why? Because

politely ask the receptionist to transfer you to the marketing department. With your foot placed firmly in that door, request the name of the person who hires photographers or reviews portfolios for freelance hair, makeup and fashion stylists. It is often one and the same. Once you get connected to someone who knows, ask if you can get an email address to send your online portfolio to. You may learn that their advertising is handled by an outside firm. If so, ask for all the pertinent information: company name, phone number, art director on the account, and the email address.

To find out the names, addresses and phone numbers of local advertising agencies, use the search technique I just shared with you; #4 on page 124.

"The Red Books Standard Directory of Advertising Agencies", can be found in the library's reference section. Yes, I said the library. Remember those? The Red Books provide everything from basic company information and e-mail addresses to complete listings of all creative and administrative employees, plus a list of the clients each agency handled at the time of printing.

For more current information, consider an annual subscription to Adweek or AdAge. It's cheap and will not only keep you abreast of all the contact information you need, it will avail you of the trends in beauty and fashion.

Either of these two publications will give you up-to-the-minute data on the accounts that are being maintained by a specific agency, which ones are up for grabs (review) and who's in contention (i.e., other agencies) to get them—usually within the next six months. You can learn the names of creative and art directors for specific campaigns and how to reach them.

STEP 02 — KEEP TRACK OF THE INFO

Make a list of 10 clients that you want to work with. Look only for the advertising agencies and decision-makers for those 10 clients. Why? Because those 10 clients may produce up to 30 people to contact. That's a lot of folks to contact and follow up with. Anything else becomes overwhelming, and I don't want to see you go down that rabbit hole of collecting more information than you can handle.

Look at my Seattle example on page 125. As you can see, there are six companies. Those six companies may produce one-three contact people at each company.

A few hours of emails, phone calls, taking notes, forwarding your portfolio, mailing comp cards, and scheduling follow-up emails and appointments can leave you exhausted if you try to do too much, or don't lay out your plan of attack and execute it properly.

Decide now where you are going to keep your appointments, tasks and follow-ups: on paper or in your mobile device. I'm still a paper girl. However, I set an alarm on my phone to remind me of anything I am supposed to do that I write down on paper, or I will forget it for sure.

The notes you take are an important part of prospecting—that's what the rest of the business world calls "soliciting work". Write everything down, from the name of the receptionist who may become your best ally to any mention of upcoming projects or referrals.

Be sure to collect:

- Name, title, email address, phone and social media of art directors and/or creative directors

- Agency submission policies and guidelines

- Current clients

Be patient! It may take a few calls to reach your desired party but politeness, persistence, follow-up and follow-through are your keys to success. Be aware that the stress levels at ad agencies can border on suicidal. Staff are often stretched to their limits in an effort to meet impossible deadlines.

However, if you are patient and reach out with consistency (three+ times), your persistence will usually be rewarded with an appointment or even a job. Just don't become a stalker.

STEP 03 — THE PRESENTATION

With account and staff information in hand, you can begin to lay out your portfolio, decide which shots should be included and in what order, and whether or not you need to test with a photographer to add new images to round out your book. These decisions will be based on the general nature of the accounts you intend to go after.

If, after doing your homework on the advertising agencies in your area, you find that 75% of the clients they work with fit into the Lifestyle category, I wouldn't suggest sending a link to a portfolio full of tearsheets from the last ten rap and hard rock CD cover shoots you worked on. They aren't going to get it. They can't use it and they won't be impressed. Besides, you are wasting their time.

Jennifer Jackson

I wasn't prepared, or as Crystal says, "I wasn't READY!" I didn't have the tools in place to move me forward. You can only do enough to get by for so long.

I had just completed the cover and two fashion spreads in a national publication, yet I was still STUCK! I had come to rely on someone else to funnel work to me. I wasn't working MY plan. I was working everyone else's plan.

Then the light bulb came on. I wasn't in charge of my own destiny. I had no presentation. Nada! Nothing tangible that was reflective of me or what I did. Outside of people that I knew, there was no way to expose myself to new potential clients.

So, I pulled out my Guide, and stopped making excuses. I just had to figure it out. I had to redefine my target audience, and learn how to differentiate myself from other artists and how to engage and attract new clients.

I decided to brand myself. I wanted to brand my name, and use that for my domain, but it had been taken. I sought out the owner of my name and purchased it. It wasn't cheap either (I paid about $300 for it, but it was now mine.)

I got a new logo designed and new business cards. I got a new website. However, I had more behind-the-scenes pictures, tearsheets and videos than

An LA based photo rep says, "Not all images are created equal, and one or two bad photos can bring the image of the book way down. Every artist should live with their own pictures. It may sound old fashioned, but print your images. It's cheap at Costco. Then put them all over the house. In the bedroom, bathroom, kitchen, everywhere. Live with your own images for a month and the ones that really start to bother you should be taken down. The photographs that are left hanging on the walls at the end of the month should go online and in your print portfolio."

Connecting with an art or creative director should be a rigorously pleasant experience, provided that you have done your research, are prepared to show them examples of your work that relate to their clients and you have a comp card to share that is representative of the work they are going to review in your book.

Says one makeup artist, "Tailor your presentation to fit the market you work in. I moved from San Francisco, where I was booked solid working on cutting-edge editorials and advertising, to Charlotte, NC, a very lifestyle-oriented market. I had to start all over building a new portfolio and putting together a comp card. I explain to the photographers I meet that I can do the scaled-down clean work that they want, but they want to see it. I'm even having a hard time getting an agency to represent me. They say my work just isn't right for this market."

Her experience isn't uncommon. The tendency of many established artists who are successful in one market is to assume that what they have in their portfolio will work in any market. Unfortunately, that is not the case. Do your research. Plan strategically. Knowledge of the area will help you rearrange your book to make the biggest impact on your new target audience. You wouldn't go into battle without knowing as much about your opponent as possible, so don't do it with your livelihood.

STEP 04 — SUBMITTING YOUR WORK

Submitting work is pretty standard throughout the industry:

1   Send a link to your website.

2   Send a comp card.

3   Follow up with a phone call within two-three days, and leave a message if no one answers.

4   Repeat once a month until you get a YES, some advice or a flat-out leave me alone.

In a crowded market where everyone is sending something to decision-makers, here's what I did:

I designed a small invitation-style card that looked just like a party invitation. I hand addressed each envelope and sent them out to 10 decision-makers who worked in advertising agencies. I then followed up each month with updated materials. Two of those 10 decision-makers became our client within a six month period. Plan to work and work the plan.

NOTES

....

....

....

The outside of the card read:

YOU ARE CORDIALLY INVITED

Once the card was opened, the purpose was revealed. **The inside of the invitation read:**

To review the portfolio of

DAVID ROTH

please pick it up from your creative coordinator
Carolyn Jones.

It will be at her desk on
Monday, January, 9th, 2018

The portfolio will remain at your agency
until the 13th of January.

Should you wish to reserve
David Roth

for an upcoming assignment,
please contact me at

323.299.0500

Sincerely,
Crystal Wright

129

actual useable portfolio images, so I began to test with quality photographers. It was starting to come together. I became a brand. I am not just Jennifer who does hair...I am Jenn Jackson, Hair and Makeup Artist. This was a good start, but I was still struggling to find the time to actually execute a successful marketing plan in order to remain competitive.

My foundation was finally in place—now I needed a marketing plan. The purpose of marketing is to create interest in your brand. But between being a hockey mom, taking care of home, doing my regular hair clients, traveling out of state for my private hair clients, and doing weddings, I still found it a challenge to keep up and stay on top of my game. Remember, there are so many layers when it comes to marketing and effectively getting your name out there.

So, I decided to hire a publicist (someone who generates media coverage for individuals and companies). She is majoring in public relations at DePaul University. She is building her book, so her fees are not as expensive as an established publicist. She is also being mentored by a well-established publicist who works with some of the best in the industry.

She is responsible for getting my name out to media outlets with press kits, news releases, meet and greets, etc. She manages my schedule and keeps me abreast

Art directors loved it because they appreciate creativity, and, unlike the fashion and entertainment businesses where an artist's fate can be tied to the whims of a famous face, advertising has a much more loyal and stable side to it. If you get in and do your job well, you are almost guaranteed to be booked over and over again for jobs, and to be referred as well.

A New York art director said, "People think we only hire superstar talent like Charlotte Tilbury, Dick Page, Pat McGrath, Sir John and Pati Dubroff. Not so. We are always on the lookout for new fresh talent."

"Superstar rates are going through the roof. And, let's face it, when the same artist works on several campaigns, they can tend to look similar. In the world of advertising, with 25 beer cans or cosmetic products lined up next to each other in the local Rite Aid or Walmart, we want our product to stand out from the crowd, not blend into it."

STEP 05 FOLLOW UP & FOLLOW THROUGH

This is the most important step of all, FOLLOW UP, by any means necessary. It gives you the feedback you need to further sculpt a winning portfolio, track responses, make changes and assess creative needs.

If you had an appointment in person, on the phone or on Facetime—send a thank-you card (see page 114 The Gift That Keeps on Giving by Sam Fine). An art director's time is valuable. Thank him/her for their time and recommendations, and enclose another comp card as a reminder. It jogs the memory and demonstrates that you are a professional and detail-oriented business person who respects others' time and talents.

FOLLOW UP AGAIN

Every 30 days without fail you should be following up with an email that includes a link to your website, mention of any new work and even an embedded image in the body of the email that will get them excited to click on your website link to see what's new. After sending that update email, wait two-three days and follow up with a phone call.

I am consistently amazed at how many artists tell me, "I'm too busy to do 'all that'", or assume their efforts will be ignored or pointless.

Everyone appreciates being acknowledged. When you solicit feedback you are, in effect, asking for advice. And, to echo what I said before, ALWAYS send a thank-you card when someone, anyone, offers you professional advice (whether you think it's useful or not). It will go a long way toward establishing yourself as a professional.

You now have some basic tools to help you approach the advertising industry. Consider assisting artists who are already working in advertising. Working artists often recommend assistants to their clients for key spots on jobs they are unable to accept a gig due to scheduling conflicts or vacation.

Finally, I offer this bit of advice: "As BIG as the advertising industry seems, it's a small community. Art directors network with one another often. So, put your best foot forward and really give them something to talk about!"

Resources

Adweek: www.adweek.com

AdAge: www.adage.com

NOTES

The Hair Makeup & Fashion Styling Career Guide

of industry-related events I need to attend as well as arranges guest and speaking appearances. Her results are measurable, as she provides weekly and monthly status reports. Our business relationship is solidified by a contract, not a handshake, so everyone knows what to expect. It is fair and above-board.

I say all of this to say, there is no way of getting around doing the work. Lay the foundation, and if you need additional help—get it! It's about working smarter, not harder. Figure out the method that works best for you, and WORK YOUR PLAN!

PLAN TO WORK AND WORK THE PLAN

At Xerox, we learned to "**Plan to Work and Work the Plan**." We were required to write our goals down on paper, and then present them to our sales manager who wanted to know how we intended to close deals on the prospects we believed would purchase equipment from us by the end of that month. It was a plan, and, once it was written down, we became accountable to it. Katherine Paterson, author of *The Invisible Child*, said, "A dream is just a wish without a plan."

That's the stage that we're at here in the Guide. It's time to start formulating a plan.

Your first job may not be as the key makeup artist on the next Katy Perry music video or a film with Martin Scorsese but, if that's what you want, I'm here to tell you that you can get to that level. Committing your goals to paper makes them real. It's easy to say you want to be a high-fashion makeup artist like Sir John or Lottie Tomlinson, and work with famous photographers like Rod Spicer and Patrick Demarchelier on the covers of America's top fashion, beauty and entertainment magazines like Vogue, Elle, W, Allure, Glamour, Entertainment Weekly and Rolling Stone, but what it takes is a plan.

How are you going to get there? Do you have a plan? Do you have an online portfolio? Do you know what these photographers are looking for in a glam artist? Do you know what glam squad artists they are currently working with? Do you know what city they live in? How will you email your portfolio to them? Do you have their email addresses? Do these magazines only hire glam talent from agencies? Lots of questions, huh? Well, I'm going to give you some of the answers and teach you how to find the rest.

It feels like a lot. I know. But let me tell you what Neil Fiore, author of *The Now Habit*, says about working on big projects: You don't have to worry about the whole thing. Just find a way to START for 15 minutes. All I'm asking you for is 15 minutes. Neil says, "If you start for 15 minutes, the finishing will take care of itself." Just think of it. Your life-long goals and pursuits can be accomplished 15 minutes at a time. Now, breathe!

Come with me into the thought realm. Get somewhere by yourself. Turn off the notifications on your phone for just 15 minutes, and let's start with choices.

Choices

Choices are important. Why? Because you don't want to be all over the place trying to test and collaborate with everyone as it relates to building your book. Remember, I already said that you could experiment with different genres and accept different kinds of jobs; however, when it comes to building and curating your portfolio as well as your social media, it's important that they have a focus.

You may not know right now whether you want to focus on beauty, fashion, lifestyle, celebrities, feature films, television, etc. That's okay. However, if you do makeup, hair or nails, the first five-seven images in your portfolio need to be full-on in-your-face beauty! START WITH BEAUTY and END WITH BEAUTY. The last three-five images in your portfolio need to be full-on in-your-face beauty. This is how you set the tone of your portfolio. This is where your creative signature begins to emerge. The choices you make and put out in the world inherently affect the way others view your brand. Start with beauty.

You might think it's cool to open with a wide shot of a model walking through a field, and then use up the next six pages (print) or spaces (online) revealing the rest of a fashion story where the model's face is so small it can be covered up with a quarter, but the decision-maker won't. They might need to book a makeup and hair artist for a celebrity, a beauty ad, a book cover, a beverage ad or a CD cover. All of those require the decision-maker to be able to SEE the makeup, hair and the nails.

Fashion stylists are different. Their portfolio may open and close with that wide shot. Their close-ups can be elements. A shoe, a bracelet, the fold of a lapel, the contrast between two fabrics laying on top of each other, the overlapping of patterns.

As an artist, your decision to focus on a specific genre—for example, lifestyle advertising or music—will determine which photographers you should collaborate with to build 'the rest' of your book. But, ultimately, even the photographers want to see beauty first, so mesmerize them by focusing on that first.

A photographer will be making these same choices when deciding whom to work with, and will seek out glam artists who he or she believes can most accurately produce looks which will help his or her book to stand out amongst competitors in front of decision-makers.

You are building a portfolio to market yourself. You must choose your collaborators wisely, or it will take you twice as long to get where you want to go. Twice as long to get good paying jobs. Twice as long to make a name for yourself, simply because you didn't choose the right people to collaborate with.

Katherine Rothman

CEO and President

KMR Communications

Remember what I said earlier, choosing well is easy when you know the difference between good and bad photography, and you have a standard by which to measure the artists you are choosing to collaborate with. Train your eye to recognize good photography, and you will make better choices about whom to work with. This will ultimately produce better images.

Aspiration:
a hope or ambition
of achieving something.

If your focus is high fashion and beauty, working with a photographer who wants to focus on lifestyle for companies like Crest toothpaste and the U.S. Army is going to be a complete disconnect in the growth of a portfolio that can help you secure work for Maybelline and Calvin Klein. It will take twice as long to build a body of work that can get you high fashion and beauty assignments because you and your collaborator are not on the same page, nor do you have the same goals.

Knowledge

Knowledge levels the playing field. For instance, if you want to kick it with the kids in the beauty and fashion playground at the highest levels, it's vital that you know who is already showing up at that playground. The kids are the photographers and glam squad artists who are already working on the biggest accounts and editorials. Haven't we all experienced that awkward moment when someone asks you a question that you are sure you should know the answer to? "Do you know so-and-so?", they say, or

"What did you think of so-and-so's work?", and you don't have a clue about whom or what they're talking about? That's because you are on the outside looking in. You haven't done your homework. You showed up to the playground without any gear—the knowledge you gain from doing your research. Saying you want to work in fashion but not being able to name three fashion magazines shows everyone that you don't know who's in your playground, and consequently no one wants to play with you in your sandbox. You can fake it until you make it—for a while, as long as you go home and do your research so that you show up better equipped next time. Look at every question you can't answer as an opportunity to gain more knowledge, be better informed and get to know the masters of the game in your fashion, advertising, music video, feature film, television, editorial, e-commerce or bridal playground.

5 Reasons You Need Knowledge

One online description of knowledge says, "Knowledge is a familiarity, awareness, or understanding of someone or something, such as facts, information, descriptions, or skills, which is acquired through experience or education by perceiving, discovering, or learning."

1	Levels the playing field.	Do your research about noteworthy and historical industry icons, art, trends, and popular culture. It gives you power, and makes you look smart, interested in the work, and interesting to chat with.
2	Allows you to participate in the creative process.	Knowledge gives you confidence to speak up and contribute ideas, opinions and suggestions that can enhance a project.
3	Helps you to get in the game.	People can't talk around you, or exclude you, because you understand concepts, and you have valid perspectives and historical references.
4	Brings you an understanding of the market.	Knowing what kinds of opportunities your market (state) has to offer will make you more efficient at prospecting for and securing work and collaborators.
5	Keeps you from being fooled.	Knowing the difference between good and bad work, ballpark pay rates and what you like and are drawn to artistically will keep you from being hoodwinked, bamboozled and led astray by photographers, directors and producers who will waste your time and resources, and pay you less than the industry norm.

Katherine Rothman, *CEO & President*

PUBLIC RELATIONS: THE NEXT LEVEL

At some point in your career you may decide that if only the world knew how fabulous you were, it would crave your very presence. Becoming well known is often the job of a publicist. In the interview that follows, New York-based makeup artist and men's groomer David Maderich, talks with Katherine Rothman, CEO and president of KMR Communications, Inc. about the importance of publicity in the life of a freelance stylist.

Ever wondered why certain artists get quoted in all the right magazines? Is it their artistic endeavors that garner them press, or is it something else? On a cold Manhattan day, David sat down with Katherine Rothman, CEO and president of KMR Communications Inc. for a chat about the importance of PR in the quest to become a beauty star.

David: Does KMR specialize in the beauty industry?

Katherine: Yes, we do. Beauty, health and fitness public relations.

David: Why should an artist want a publicist?

Katherine: Anyone who wishes to remain competitive in the beauty or fashion industry today needs to hire a publicist. Now more than ever, consumers rely on what the media dictates as quality. There are many makeup artists whose entire reputations were made as a result of media exposure. There are many talented people in the beauty industry today. But what sets the superstars apart from those without a "name" is the use of savvy

I always like to start doing research from a point of aspiration. The point of aspiration is the place you want to end up—for instance, working on a Maybelline advertising campaign. From there, you can work backwards.

Gaining Knowledge & Focus Through Research

Let's assume for a second that your goal is to focus on beauty, and that you see yourself working with beauty photographers on major ad campaigns that will ultimately end up in magazines and on billboards, buses and subway trains. Where do you start? Simply by identifying ten beauty accounts that you would like to work on.

 STEP 01 Go through several of your favorite magazines and put Post-it Notes on ten beauty advertisements. Examples of beauty accounts (a.k.a. clients) include: Maybelline, CoverGirl, L'Oréal, Pantene, Iman, etc.

 STEP 02 Visit www.lebook.com and www.models.com. One by one type in the names of each of the ten beauty accounts you identified [on your Post-it Notes] into the search bar. From this vantage point, you can start to collect the names of the kids (photographers, makeup artists, hair stylists, manicurists, producers, etc.) who play at the high-end beauty playground.

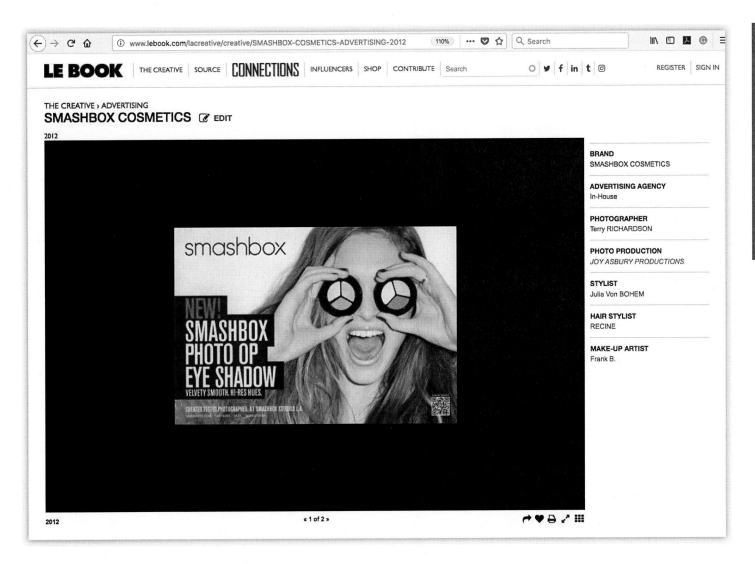

promotion in the form of media exposure in magazines like Vogue, Allure, and InStyle.

David: What should you expect a publicist to do?

Katherine: A publicist's main function is to secure media coverage, be it on television, in newspapers, magazines, or websites that offer beauty information. Publicists should write innovative original press releases for their clients. It is also extremely helpful for a publicist to arrange "meet and greets" with key beauty editors. This affords an artist a chance to demonstrate their techniques in person as well as elaborate on any products he/she may be selling. This facilitates a much more personal interaction between an artist and a press person. In this manner, they are not just another name on a press release. We have found these meetings to be invaluable to the long-term success of our clients. Publicists should also be in contact weekly with their client, updating them on progress either by phone or e-mail, whatever the client wishes. A client should never be left in the dark regarding progress on their account.

David: Do you think a publicist can turn an artist into a star?

Katherine: Absolutely. Those who hire publicists must be mindful that a public relations campaign is a cumulative process. Long-term success is not achieved by sporadic media coverage. It must be the right media coverage and it must be achieved with consistency and mindfulness of an artist's target market.

Are you starting to get the picture? Not only will you begin to see who's doing what, you can also start to identify artists that you may want to assist. What a great way to kill two birds with one stone.

Another benefit of doing this research is that you can also click on the links of these artists to see other work they have done, and which agencies they are represented by (see LeBook graphic featuring Bryce Scarlett). Go a step further and follow the artists on your top-10 list on Instagram. Take a look at what the top 10% are doing, how they curate their Instagram accounts, what they post alongside their images and the hashtags they use. If you notice any patterns that you find helpful, write them down.

Study them later on and you just might be able to use what you have learned to fine tune your own posting strategy.

NOTES

LE BOOK

THE CREATIVE | SOURCE | **CONNECTIONS** | INFLUENCERS | SHOP | CONTRIBUTE | Search

REGISTER | SIGN IN

Bryce SCARLETT

CLIENT LIST

NAME	TYPE	YEAR	SEASON
VOGUE KOREA | GIGI HADID	EDITORIAL	2017	September
MAYBELLINE	ADVERTISING	2017	Spring / Summer
MAYBELLINE | GIGIxMAYBELLINE EAST COAST GLAM COLLECTION	ADVERTISING	2017	

BRYCE SCARLETT
HAIR STYLIST

USA

Agent
THE WALL GROUP LA
LOS ANGELES USA
(310) 276-0777
(310) 276-0107

Agent
THE WALL GROUP NY
NEW YORK USA
(212) 352-0777
(212) 462-2778

Creating a grid like the one that follows is a great way to collect information for your playground and ultimately your own sandbox. To help, I created a blank one for you, just visit **www.crystalwrightliveacademies.com/p/careerguideexclusives** to download.

ACCOUNT	PHOTOGRAPHER	GLAM	
Maybelline	Andrew Day	MUA:	Carole COLOMBANI
		Hair:	Bryce SCARLETT
		Stylist:	Marie-Amélie SAUVÉ
		Model:	Adriana LIMA
Wet & Wild	Dorit Thies	MUA:	Sally WANG
		Hair:	Benjamin MOHAPI
		Stylist:	David ZAMBRANA

David: What about established makeup or hair artists?

Katherine: Even stars such as Bobbi Brown and Francois Nars still need media coverage. There is always going to be a "new kid on the block" and no one can afford to be complacent in a country so overrun with beauty experts.

David: At what point should an artist seek a publicist?

Katherine: A publicist should be hired when an artist feels that all components are in place. This means that the artist has a good online portfolio, satisfied clients who might be willing to talk with media people or allow their photos to be printed, a competent assistant who can field inquiries that come in as a result of media exposure, and finally they should feel as if they have truly honed their talent. Also, public relations must be something they are able to comfortably afford without having to sacrifice other necessities such as supplies or office space.

David: How does an artist find a publicist?

Katherine: First, look for another artist whose name appears frequently in the media and then find out who has been responsible for their public relations campaign. Call a beauty editor at a large women's publication and ask them what public relations firms handle beauty accounts or makeup artists. PRSA which stands for the Public Relations Society of America is an excellent resource.

David: What does a publicist charge?

Katherine: There is that old saying, "you get what you pay for." An artist could find someone for as little as $500 a month. But be wary if the fees are so small. That person

SANDBOX

Once you start to know more about your playground, it's time to populate your sandbox.

Your sandbox is three things. It's aspirational, inspirational and a work-in-progress. It has four sides.

Outside the Sandbox

We start with the outside of the box, which is aspirational and inspirational. These are the glam artists and photographers or directors at the top of their game whose work you are inspired by. You may have discovered some of them while researching artists on LeBook.com and Models.com, or you may have found them on Instagram. Perhaps some of them are the reason you decided to become an artist yourself.

These are the artists you study and use to train your eye. They set the bar. You follow them on social media. These are also the artists that you reach out to, to assist. Yes, I said it. If you're a makeup artist, why shouldn't you assist Sir John, Charlotte Tilbury, Pat McGrath or Mario Dedivanovic? Hair stylists such as Frederick Fekkai, Sam McKnight and Adir Abergel are but a social media page away, and, if you're paying attention, you might catch a post where any of these artists is looking for an assistant for an upcoming gig. Manicurists like Tom Bachik, Julie Kandalec and Eichi Matsunaga need assistants, too, and if your shtick is fashion styling I would aim for the clouds and reach out to people at the Marni Senofonte, Maeve Reilly and Melinda Tarbell levels.

If you don't recognize these names, along with the names of top

FASHION STYLISTS

HAIR STYLISTS

PHOTOGRAPHERS

MAKEUP ARTISTS

does not likely have the media connections or expertise to do the job. Typically, firms in New York charge more than the rest of the country. By virtue of this location, they can make valuable inroads and connections with key media people that would not be possible elsewhere. A quality PR firm would typically charge an individual makeup artist anywhere from $2,500 to $3,500 per month. It is important that artists choose firms who make their niche in beauty public relations as opposed to fashion or entertainment.

David: That's a lot of money. What can an artist do on their own if they can't afford a publicist?

Katherine: They should compile a list of all of the women's publications such as Vogue, Allure, Elle, New Beauty, Glamour, etc., and find out the names, email addresses and social media handles of the beauty editors. They can also do the same with their local publications. They should email and call and introduce themselves as a resource for stories pertaining to makeup artistry. Emailing over a bio and accompanying cover letter is also helpful. If they have their own product line, they can also speak with editors and ask if they wish to try complimentary samples and invite editors for "open house" makeovers. This last tip can be extremely helpful if an artist has celebrity clients who will allow their name(s) to be revealed. An artist should not be afraid to name-drop with permission from the celebrity. Magazines love to able to say, "Jane Doe, whose list of celebrity clients includes…"

Finally, do not make the mistake of being too aggressive, or demanding of an editor's time. They receive dozens of emails and calls each day and they will call you back if they

photographers or directors, you should. Populating the outside of your sandbox will open your eyes to the names of artists whose work you may have admired for years, and help you to discover new ones. Regardless of your specific discipline, you have room on the outside of your sandbox to add 12 artists in four disciplines.

You might be asking yourself, "Why should I care about hair and fashion styling, or fashion styling and nails when I'm a makeup artist?" It's simple, what you do, all by itself, does not a picture make. These images, whether still or moving, are made with teams of people who all come together with a common goal for a day, days, weeks or months. Remove a single element and the result is something that is NOT portfolio-worthy. As individual as freelancing can be for a graphic designer, for makeup, hair, fashion stylists, nail artists and any photographer who shoots people, it is a team sport and the team is only as strong as its weakest link.

Standing behind you on the side of the sandbox closest to you are the artists who match your specific discipline. These are also the artists you will want to assist if you're starting out, or trying to get a leg up in an area of the industry that you haven't worked in before.

The right side of the sandbox is always photographers or directors. If your focus is print, it's photographers. If your focus is television and film, it's directors.

The left side of the sandbox and the side opposite you can be populated with makeup artists, hair stylists, fashion/wardrobe stylists or manicurists.

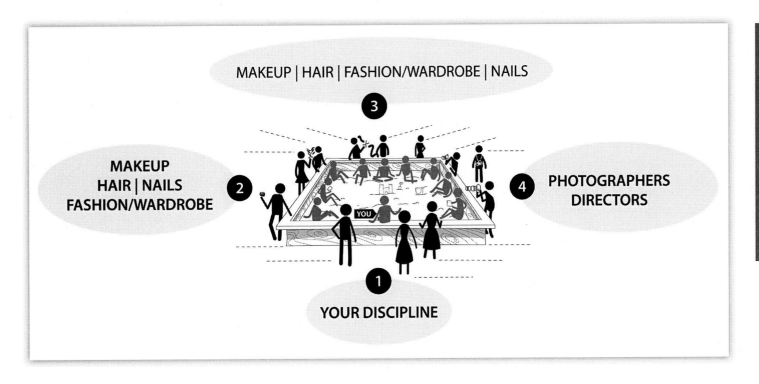

MAKEUP | HAIR | FASHION/WARDROBE | NAILS

3

MAKEUP
HAIR | NAILS
FASHION/WARDROBE

2

YOU

4

PHOTOGRAPHERS
DIRECTORS

1

YOUR DISCIPLINE

Inside the Sandbox

Now let's talk about the inside of your sandbox. Earlier I called it a work-in-progress. That is because it is filled with the artists that you connect and network with, get introduced to, get referred to, meet on other shoots and reach out for. They are part of your journey from testing to building your portfolio, to referrals for jobs, to lifelong friendships. Some will come. Some will go. There's an old saying: People come into your life for a reason, a season or a lifetime.

One of the reasons we get stuck is that we don't know how to let go of the people who are only there for a reason, or a season. Testing to build your book can be like this. It's hard to tell a teammate who introduced you to the best photographer you've ever met that while you intend to continue developing your relationship with that photographer, you don't want to work alongside them anymore because they never show up on time, or they're not prepared or they've bailed on you at the last minute one time too many. But this is the reality of being successful. Some people have to be removed from your sandbox if you want to move forward.

You'll notice that the inside of your sandbox has room for you to add nine artists. Why nine? Because it's enough people to have in

Katherine Rothman, *CEO & President*

have an interest in what you are pitching. Prove yourself useful and you will be rewarded; prove to be a pest, and media coverage will vanish.

David: What do you think when artists complain about not getting enough for their money?

Katherine: The client and publicist need to be clear from the outset about what is expected, and what can realistically be delivered within a specific time frame. An artist should not just say to a publicist, "I want media coverage." They should be clear about the kinds of publications they want to see themselves in, and the nature of the coverage. The publicist should be honest about the frequency of coverage that the artist can expect.

An honest publicist should be truthful about what they can and cannot achieve. It is really important that an artist realizes that publicists are responsible for securing media placements. Beyond that, a publicist cannot guarantee new business as a result. If a client is unhappy, a publicist needs to understand why.

If the publicist is securing consistent media coverage in line with the types of publications a client had indicated, then the publicist is doing his/her job. It's helpful if a client gives a publicist a wish list of publications, as well as outlines long- and short-term goals. Any skilled publicist will ask these questions.

 davidmaderich

 www.davidmaderich.com

rotation without spreading yourself to thin. Don't forget, even an NBA basketball team only has 12 active members.

The sandbox is built so that you can remove and replace people as you need to. And it's quite possible that it will never have nine people in it at once—that's okay. You may have one, two or three different teams of people that you are working with. You will build and dismantle teams until you find just the right mixes and magic. You may even be in someone else's sandbox—although they may not call it that.

Your sandbox is a visual representation of your professional playground.

Use it to stay focused on the big picture, build your portfolio, build your relationships and grow your business.

Start using the sandbox on the following page to create your own professional playground. You can download additional SANDBOX worksheets from my website.

NOTES

....

....

....

....

Suzie Moldavon

Makeup Artist
SuzieMoldavon.com
Focus: Brows, Bridal
& Celebrities
IG: suziemoldavon
flybrow

I never planned on being a freelance makeup artist and running my own businesses, but it suits me as a person, and I feel very blessed and proud of the success I've had thus far. I'm so grateful to be doing something I love, that fits my talents and personality, and something that allows me to create balance between my work and my personal life. My job is not just to make someone look beautiful, but to really feel beautiful. I am fulfilled and grateful to have a hand in someone else's journey to discovering and sharing that inner beauty.

I love freelancing. There are rewards and challenges to being a freelance artist. I love that each day brings something new. I am usually outdoors or in my car instead of being stuck in an office, and sometimes I'm in amazing locations from commercial sets, to elephant farms, and because I live in California, there is the occasional photo shoot on the beach. Many of my clients have become friends. I appreciate what the travel and backstage access some of these work relationships have brought to my life. I love that my

Focus

Let's move ahead with our fictitious makeup artist Mary Coletti. By looking back and reviewing some of her choices in Chapter 1 on page 39, we know that Mary is print-focused and wants to work on magazines, CD covers and advertising campaigns, to name a few. She is also interested in working with celebrities on their red-carpet events, press junkets and talk-show appearances. Since photographers are key decision-makers for print assignments, Mary takes the time to research the names of a few photographers, and some of the projects they have worked on recently. Her aspirational list—and the outside of her sandbox—are starting to take shape.

PHOTOGRAPHERS	RECENT EDITORIAL & COMMERCIAL CITINGS
Isabelle Snyder	US Weekly, Italian Elle, Emmy, Oprah
Danielle Federici	American Vogue, German Vogue, Photo District News
Nigel Perry	Vanity Fair, InStyle, Men's Health, Esquire

This list tells us that Mary has given thought to the photographers she aspires to work with long term. She has taken the time to research the kind of work they've done recently by skimming through fashion, entertainment and photographic [trade] magazines as well as Instagram, LeBook.com and Models.com. This kind of research will also help Mary to make better choices about which photographers to test with. She's training her eye to recognize good photography when she sees it. We'll discuss this more in Chapter 4: Photographers.

Magazines contain a wealth of information, that can be gleaned from the on-page or back of the book credits. You can find out:

- Who photographed the cover and feature stories.

- Who the makeup, hair, fashion stylist and manicurists were on a job.

- Which agencies the glam squad artists are signed to—or not.

- [sometimes] Who the assistants were on the job.

- Which store(s) or designer(s) loaned out the clothing and accessories.

- Which makeup, hair and nail products were used.

- The location where the shoot took place.

- The name of the model(s) and their agency.

- The name of the company or the person who produced the shoot.

While all of this information is not included on every single editorial page, variations of it are included in most magazines.

There was a time when it was nearly impossible to find out who worked on an advertisement or a television commercial. Online databases like LeBook.com and Models.com have made it much easier to learn who did what on a shoot. Visit one or both of these online resources and you can find out:

- Who photographed the advertisement.

- Who directed the commercial.

- Who "art directed" the photo shoot.

- Who did makeup, hair and fashion styling as well as nails.

- Who produced the shoot or the commercial.

- Who retouched the images.

- The name of the model.

Additionally, clicking on the links makes it easy to obtain the addresses, phone numbers, email and social media accounts of the decision-makers who should receive your comp card or receive a link to review your portfolio when it is ready to share.

CAREER MISSION STATEMENT

At this juncture, like Mary you have plenty of tools and resources. You know where to go to get the information you need to contact the people who can help you. So, what's missing? What she does, whom she serves and how she's going to serve them—a career mission statement.

This is where you take over. It's time for you to create your own personal career mission statement, the purpose of which is to help you focus and give you a clear direction for your freelance business. Its purpose is to inspire and motivate YOU, and it should be revisited often.

I suggest writing it out on several pieces of paper and placing them all over your house. Writing your ideas and goals gives you clarity and focus in a busy and hectic world. Rewriting them reaffirms your seriousness in accomplishing them. C'mon now, pull out that black Sharpie!

schedule is my own and that I can be a present mom available for after school pick up and field trips while juggling work around my priorities. I thrive on the hustle.

As much as running my own business is a 24-hour a day job, I am proud when I have a full calendar with work that fuels me and allows me to keep putting food on the table. My guilty pleasure is being able to go to the gym in the middle of the day! There are no paid vacations, no sick days and no benefits, and I often work weekends. But for me the pros of working for myself outweigh the cons of having to budget for vacations, pay for my own health care and business insurance while staying healthy at all costs! As Crystal would say, "It's just the cost of doing business."

A great freelance artist is someone with an amazing work ethic; it takes a certain kind of person to succeed on their own. As a makeup artist in the freelance world, there is no reward for laziness. In the infamous words of musician Rick Ro$$, and probably the theme song of my work life, "Everyday I'm hustlin'". You just have to get busy living and get after 'it'. Do your thing, network, and be open to opportunity. Continue learning and growing, as artists and as people. As the jobs come, the goals should grow. Be aware of your energy and attitude,

Those of you who are just starting out may find it necessary to amend your career mission statement in six months, because without experiences in the business you can only dream and guess that doing celebrities, or working in film, is EXACTLY what you want to do. Don't beat yourself up about it, just go back in with the new information you will gain from taking advantage of opportunities, tweak your statement and keep it moving! Life is fluid.

Those of you who have been in the business for a while or are in transition may have the benefit of insight gained from on-set work experience when you write your statement.

Your career statement may consist of two parts:

1	Goals and objectives.
2	Past achievements.

Why do I say may consist of two parts? Because not everyone has won a marathon, been promoted to vice president on their job, written a best-seller or gotten a plaque for employee of the month. That's okay. Being enthusiastic about where you want to go and your willingness to write it down is good enough for me.

In fact, some of us with big résumés, work experience and past achievements can lean on those past laurels to the point that our egos get the best of us, causing us to miss opportunities that we believe are beneath us. An example of that would be a hair stylist who doesn't want to accept an assisting gig for $150 or no pay because he/she has owned their own salon for 15 years, or a makeup artist who became the manager at the MAC counter and now thinks testing with photographers for free is a waste of time—even though the artist doesn't have a single image for their portfolio. Can you say self-sabotage?

Past achievements can be a blessing or a curse. Sharing them when they are kept in perspective makes them a blessing. If you're not sure what I mean, I've included excerpts from the elevator pitches on page 121 of this chapter.

An achievement is:	I recently **graduated** from Makeup Designory.
	I have **several years'** worth of **retail fashion experience.**
	I am a freelance business-development **coach** with **30 years' experience representing artists.**

Before you write your statement—which by the way is short, sweet and to the point—I want to address the two questions below that sometimes trip people up.

1	What do you value?
2	Describe past achievements, experience and qualifications for this career.

Value can be more freedom to spend time with your friends, family, significant other or kids. It can be self-determination, traveling or the desire for a more artistic life. Value is simply what's important to you.

Secondly, focus on how what you HAVE done can positively impact the dream you have for the rest of your professional life. Don't let the fact that you have worked in IT for the last ten years cause you to feel like you're not qualified to transition into makeup artistry, hair styling, fashion styling or nails. Being able to manage your crazy boss on the job day-to-day may qualify you to work with temperamental celebrities. Working in a warehouse managing inventory may make you a great department head. Handling chemicals in a lab may have prepared you for a career in special FX. Add any of these skills to your creative side and you have a winning combination!

Now you are ready to consider the clarifying questions that follow before you write your statement. Do not run from writing things down, or hide from the 15 minutes of quiet time that you deserve to complete this exercise. Just do it! The reward is coming.

NOTES

....

....

....

....

....

clients hire artists that want to be there; repeat jobs are quantifiable proof of a job well done. Know that you are the engine of the machine; you are the artist, the publicist, the agent, the bookkeeper, and the social media maven that is responsible for making your business run.

You might have an agent that helps facilitate negotiations and acquire jobs, or an assistant that clean your brushes, but at the end of the day, you are the one that is responsible for getting jobs and doing them well.

And most of all, have passion, for both the art and the success, because with genuine passion, you can be successful at anything.

Clarifying Questions

What do you want to achieve in life?

....

....

....

....

Why are you interested in this career?

....

....

....

What do you value?

....

....

....

Why does this career fit you?

....

....

....

....

....

What do you expect to achieve from this career in the next five years?

....

....

....

....

Describe past achievements, experience and qualifications for this career.

....

....

....

NOTES

....

....

....

....

....

....

....

....

....

....

....

....

....

NOTES

I read a lot. And it was my journey through Simon Sinek's book and online program *Start With Why* that helped me to write my own mission statement in 2017. Here it is, the Crystal Wright Mission:

To provide every freelance beauty, fashion and photography professional with a clear, concise path to his or her own version of creative success, financial independence and freedom of choice.

Following are two other examples to get you thinking:

To touch the lives of as many women as possible during special events and on their wedding day, by creating a beauty experience that they will cherish and remember for the rest of their lives.

To deliver cutting-edge editorial hair styling to the world of commercial photography and advertising throughout the midwestern United States.

Now it's your turn:

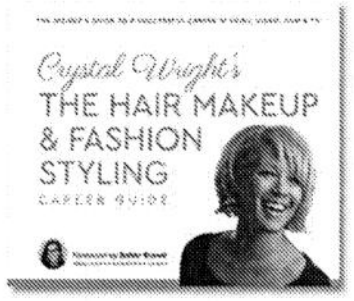

NAME: ______
TITLE: ______
CITY & STATE: ______
EMAIL: ______
PHONE: ______

INTENTIONS WORKSHEET | DATE RANGE: ______

STATE YOUR INTENTIONS

1. ______
ACTION 1.1: ___ ______
ACTION 1.2: ___ ______
ACTION 1.3: ___ ______
2. ______
ACTION 2.1: ___ ______
ACTION 2.2: ___ ______
ACTION 2.3: ___ ______
3. ______
ACTION 3.1: ___ ______
ACTION 3.2: ___ ______
ACTION 3.3: ___ ______
4. ______
ACTION 4.1: ___ ______
ACTION 4.2: ___ ______
ACTION 4.3: ___ ______
5. ______
ACTION 5.1: ___ ______
ACTION 5.2: ___ ______
ACTION 5.3: ___ ______

CRYSTAL WRIGHT LIVE | www.CRYSTALWRIGHTLIVE.com | 323.299.0500 | @crystalwrightlive

You can download this Intention Worksheet and more, from my website.

Beyond your career mission statement are the intentions and your how's. What do you intend to do to make your mission a reality, and what steps or actions (how's) will you take to achieve these new intentions?

For example, if you INTEND to build a portfolio, in order to fulfill your mission to deliver cutting-edge editorial hair styling to the midwestern advertising community from where you are right now, what are some of the actions that you will need to initiate in order to fulfill your intention? Here's an example:

1 Add 2 new 4-page lifestyle editorial stories 2 my portfolio.

ACTION 1.1: ___ Contact modeling agencies new faces division.

ACTION 1.2: ___ Call 2 photogs I met @ NYC photo expo abt testing.

ACTION 1.3: ___ Check with Ericka abt doing makeup for test.

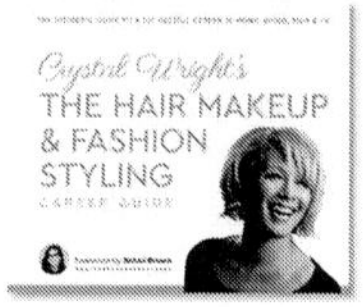

NAME: Brittney Evans
TITLE: Makeup ARtist
CITY & STATE: Baltimore, MD
EMAIL: prettydivamakeupartist@gmail.com
PHONE: 323.555.1212

INTENTIONS WORKSHEET | DATE RANGE: Feb 4 - 10

STATE YOUR INTENTIONS

1. Add 2 new 4-page lifestyle editorial stories 2 my portfolio
ACTION 1.1: ___ Contact modeling agencies new faces division.
ACTION 1.2: ___ Call 2 photogs I met @ NYC photo expo abt testing.
ACTION 1.3: ___ Check with Ericka abt doing makeup for test.
2. Rebrand my makeup business as Brittney Evans Makeup Artistry
ACTION 2.1: ___ Purchase www.brittneyevansmakeup.com from
ACTION 2.2: ___ Replace www.prettydivamakeu
ACTION 2.3: ___ Create new

If you INTEND to establish or revamp your social media presence in preparation for decision-makers who hire freelance beauty professionals to work on print advertising campaigns in the Midwest, what are some of the actions that you should take in order to fulfill your intention?

2 Rebrand my makeup business as Brittney Evans Makeup Artistry

ACTION 2.1: ___ Purchase www. brittneyevansmakeup.com from GoDaddy

ACTION 2.2: ___ Replace www. prettydivamakeupartist.com w/new brand

ACTION 2.3: ___ Create new email & signature w/ brittneyevansmakeupartistry

NOTES

In this order, you will:

1 Write your career mission statement.

2 Write down the things you intend to do to fulfill you mission.

3 Write down the steps/actions you will take to complete each intention.

4 Check off the actions as you go.

5 Store your used intentions worksheet in a binder for reference, inspiration and motivation.

6 Celebrate.

7 Repeat #2 through #6 for the rest of your life in all things that matter to you both personally and professionally.

Craig Brooks

Commercial & Film Director

Renn Films

You Are Here

Before we move on to creating a hit list, I want to remind you that **YOU ARE HERE**! Everyone who is reading this book is HERE, but in a different place. You may be sitting next to your new bestie makeup artist that you met a month ago and the two of you are now kindred spirits. You are still in different places with different skills, experiences, relationships, resources and personalities.

Some of you have portfolios and others don't. Some of you are starting from scratch, and others are starting over after taking time off from having a baby, raising a family, the break-up of a marriage, experiencing a death, illness or moving to a new state or perhaps a new country. Some of you have just quit or are preparing to leave a corporate job after pleasing your parents by getting a degree that you didn't really want.

It's very important that you DO NOT start comparing yourself to others. Each of you is in a different lane, with different goals and a different time frame for arriving at your destination. Celebrity makeup artist Renny Vasquez says, "Comparison is the thief of joy." If you spend too much time looking around, you will start to feel like you are not keeping up. That feeling produces fear and FEAR is **F**alse **E**vidence **A**ppearing **R**eal . You don't have to keep up with anyone but yourself. That's why it's so important to set goals, create intentions and then map out the steps that you will take to achieve those goals.

The truth is, life is a freeway and someone is always going to be in front of you, behind you, and on either side of you—but it's not a race.

I don't want you looking over your shoulder every day to see who is gaining on you or who has passed you. Artists experience this every day on Instagram. Following people and checking your account starts out as a way to keep you inspired and motivated and quickly descends into a 100-yard dash with Usain Bolt.

Celebrity makeup artist Monifa Mortis says, "You can't cheat the journey." Enjoy it. All of it. The ups and downs, the ins and outs are all here to teach you something about yourself, the work, where you fit best, what you like and the genres you will ultimately make your home in.

A HIT LIST: PROSPECTING FOR WORK

The pages that follow provide an excellent opportunity for you to zero in on the who's and what's you will incorporate into your marketing plan and your future. Filling in the blanks will crystallize what you know, challenge you to find out what you don't and give you the energy and insight to keep your eyes on the prize.

At every level, there is a hit list. In corporate America, we called it a prospecting list. If getting more on-set experience is a priority for you, then you should be creating an ASSISTING HIT LIST. Identify ten people whose work you admire, and who are working in an area of the industry that you have an interest in learning more about or whose focus is identical to the kind of work you see yourself keying in the future.

If building your portfolio is a priority and you don't have any images, or just a few, you should be creating a hit list of photographers who are also building their books in your area of interest.

LIST 5 ARTISTS THAT YOU WANT TO ASSIST

KEY ARTISTS   NOTES

NAME:
EMAIL:
PHONE:
IG:
WEB:

NAME:
EMAIL:
PHONE:
IG:
WEB:

NAME:
EMAIL:
PHONE:
IG:
WEB:

NAME:
EMAIL:
PHONE:
IG:
WEB:

NAME:
EMAIL:
PHONE:
IG:
WEB:

LIST 5 LOCAL MAGAZINES THAT YOU WANT TO WORK FOR

LOCAL MAGAZINES   NOTES

CO:
WEB:
PHONE:
DM:
EMAIL:

CO:
WEB:
PHONE:
DM:
EMAIL:

CO:
WEB:
PHONE:
DM:
EMAIL:

CO:
WEB:
PHONE:
DM:
EMAIL:

CO:
WEB:
PHONE:
DM:
EMAIL:

Craig Brooks is a commercial and film director at Renn Films in Seattle, Washington. But that's not where the story begins. In his 20's, Craig moved to Los Angeles to persue a career as an actor when he fell in love with production and everything that went on behind the camera. After years of hard work that included driving RV's and trucks for production he got to see firsthand what makes a good producer and he knew he wanted that job.

From that road to this one, his commercial reel of clients includes BMW, Microsoft, Alaska Airlines, Jet Blue, Thom Jones, Shwood Sunglasses and many more.

I met Craig years ago when one of my fashion stylists was hired to work with one of his clients, Mervyn's. We connected immediately and continued to work together for several years until I closed Crystal Agency. Here Craig talks about his journey to success, what he learned in the process, and how hard work and perseverance will help you master the career of your dreams.

Can you tell us a little about your journey from producer to director?

Craig: Sure. Along with working on commercials and some independent films, I started driving RV's and trucks for production. So, I really got to see all sides of the business. I got to see firsthand what makes a good producer. At that point, I didn't really want to be in front of the camera. I wanted to be behind the camera.

So honestly, I like to say, I BS'd my way into production,

If you already have a portfolio that gets you work in one area, but you see opportunity by adding images in another genre, you too should be creating a list of photographers at a more advanced level who can help you build stories that will attract new clients.

If you have a great portfolio, and you're ready to start booking jobs in a specific area, it's time to write down a list of 10 clients that you want to work for. They could be beauty brands, lifestyle brands, recording artists, celebrities, magazines, TV shows, e-commerce brands, etc. And the hit list goes on.

On my website, I have created full-sized hit lists for you like the thumbnails on page 157. You can download them and start gathering contact information. They will help you to start thinking about the people you want to work with and the brands that you want to work on.

The Battlefield Is In The Mind

Now here's where the rubber meets the road (the point at which a theory or idea is put to a practical test). It's the point where you actually have to write those 10 names down on a sheet of paper. For many, this is where your mind starts to play tricks on you.

You might be a makeup artist. You're sitting there staring at that piece of paper. For a moment, you get bold and write down names like Sir John, Billy B, Pat McGrath, Rick Baker and Renny Vasquez. But the longer you look at that piece of paper, the more doubt starts to creep into your mind and you start to scratch out those names and replace them with less established artists. STOP the madness! 5, 4, 3, 2, 1. Just DO IT! In her book, *The 5 Second Rule: Transform Your Life, Work, and Confidence with Everyday Courage*, author Mel Robbins pushes you to be better than your excuses and bigger than your fears.

Your mind tells you:

- It's not what you know, it's who you know.
- They're never going to return your call anyway, so don't bother.
- Why would they respond to your CM, you're a nobody?
- Just wait and do it tomorrow.
- Do it after you have lunch

And the list goes on. Your mind wants to protect you. But protect you from what? Writing down the names of artists who truly inspire you, whom you would like to support on upcoming projects by assisting them? Reaching out to photographers who could use your help on their upcoming test shoots? You have five seconds before your mind plies you with excuses. It's just names on a piece of paper. Write them down.

Do The Work

I am summoning you to action now. This book is good, but it is not a silver bullet unless you DO THE WORK! Do the written exercises in the book. They offer you an opportunity to:

- Get familiar with the names of the real players in the game and the language of the business.
- Focus in on, and be specific about, your goals and aspirations.
- Begin a process of thinking about the "how's" of your career.
- Learn the basics of research, gathering and cross-referencing information that will benefit and assist you in meeting your goals.
- Focus and keep your eyes on the prize.

Don't rush. Linger over print and online magazines, get to know their editorial style and focus. Check out the fashion and beauty layouts, feature spreads and ad campaigns. Compare these aspirational tearsheets to the photography that you are or should be producing with the artists in your sandbox.

Browse through the calendar sections, and highlight upcoming events that you should attend and possibly participate in on some level (i.e., fashion shows, trade shows, photo exhibits, photo expos, etc.). Become part of the beauty, fashion, e-commerce and entertainment scene. Get involved, be visible and, by all means, look the part!

Completing the job of filling in the worksheets will take some time, but it will take less time than you think if you get quiet and focused for 15 minutes at a time.

These exercises may require print focused artists to purchase the latest fashion, beauty, entertainment and industry trade publications, visit your local library or subscribe to magazines online at texture.com. Film and TV focused artists will invest in trade publications like Variety.com, HollywoodReporter.com Reporter, ShootOnline.com, and BackStage.com.

It's a great way to learn who is doing what, who is using whom, who is getting the good jobs, what agencies are involved, etc.

Who's In Your Sandbox?

Not knowing who's in your sandbox translates to a lack of knowledge and seriousness about the business. It is like being in a crowd of people at a party who are talking about a subject you know nothing about or a book you didn't read. It's the sense of being on the outside looking in. I know, I've been but I spent a lot of years watching producers to see how they operate and what they did. There's nothing better than backing yourself into a corner where you have to do what you must do. That was kind of a little lesson. One of my very earliest instructors for acting in Los Angeles said, "Your intention is to do what you must do."

What was the first thing that you produced and was it print or moving media?

Craig: It was a short film. A 17-minute short film called Mart. I went headfirst into it not knowing fully what I was doing. You get caught up in the romanticized version of filmmaking.

But you have to remember that it's still work. It's not just fun and games. At the end of the day, there is a budget you have to be accountable for and it's a job.

You can't get wrapped up too much in just the romance and the fun. I was able to get out of that unscathed and learned the lessons. But that's the important thing. You kind of fall into it, and there's a tremendous amount of work that's involved.

How did your earlier gigs, like driving trucks and RV's, help you with your career in production and directing?

Craig: Well, it taught me a valuable lesson about hard work. When you're a truck driver or an RV driver, you get to know the bottom of the totem pole. You're the first on set. You're the last one to leave. You're the one that cleans up the toilets and you're one that picks up all the trash.

there. It's an uncomfortable feeling. And the only way to get rid of that feeling is to become knowledgeable and informed to the point of contribution.

Some years ago, I had a conversation with one of my makeup artists. We'll call her Nancy. She was quite successful. In addition to doing some print work, she was the department head of makeup on a popular Fox Television show as well as a day player on two soap operas. She had several feature films to her credit, and was frequently assigned male grooming for CD covers and music video work as well.

Nancy and I would have conversations periodically about her desire to land more editorial assignments. She wanted a cover of Elle magazine. We often discussed her need to test with beauty and fashion photographers. Her book lacked high fashion.

Months went by, the work came in; however, it was not editorial. The more CD covers she booked, the more CD covers she booked. After landing her an assignment to do a cover of Essence magazine with a well-known male celebrity, the coordinator, who was very pleased with her work, called to book her on another assignment featuring the female stars of a top-rated TV show. After the two-day shoot, the coordinator called me and said, "Very nice with men ; however, her work with women left a little to be desired. It was nice, but it wasn't high fashion." She went on to give me specifics about lipstick color choices, the lack of definition in the models' eyebrows, and a word of caution that anyone who had been paying attention to Essence should have been more familiar with the style of the publication.

When I passed this information on to my artist, she became very defensive. She had lots of rationalizations about why the lips were this and the eyebrows were that. The bottom line was, she *wasn't* paying attention. And if she wasn't paying attention to Essence, she certainly wasn't ready for Elle.

If you want to work for a publication, you should know something about its look, feel, style, audience and the photographers who are hired to shoot for it regularly.

Learn The Lingo

The beauty, fashion and entertainment business loves to talk about itself. Day in and day out at parties, photo shoots, coffee shops and anywhere else that the hippest of the hip gather to discuss the newest of the new, you hear the words, "Did you know...?" The topics of conversation move from who photographed the cover of X, to what celebrity was on Y, to who the glam squad was for that highly coveted beauty brand, to why so and so didn't get the cover of Z, to who almost got the job but didn't because...well, you know.

In this business, nobody talks about "the" shoes, they talk about the "Blahniks". Your job is to know who Manolo Blahnik is and what he produces. The same goes for Narciso Rodriguez, who makes dresses and perfume. Can you tell me how many U.S. magazines focus on beauty? What's the difference between DKNY and Donna Karan? And who is Billy B anyway? And who is doing Beyoncé's makeup? Well, that's what this homework is all about, being in the know about the industry you hope to call home.

Over a decade ago, Entertainment Weekly magazine featured

Younger (TV Land Network) star Debi Mazar on its cover with a headline that read, *"How Style Became the Star: Models, designers, and photographers are the latest breed of media darlings—the new Hollywood, if you will. Even hairdressers and makeup artists are celebrity timber now."* This was the precursor to the age of the glam squad.

WORKING & THRIVING IN YOUR OWN BACKYARD
By Cristy Guy
Founder, On the Set Styling

Cristy Guy is a makeup, hair and wardrobe stylist based in Kansas City, Kansas. She is also the owner of On the Set Styling, a group of exceptionally talented artists who specialize in print, television, video and live events. Cristy works all over the world from her home base in Kansas City. She wants to tell you how she did it so you can too!

I work with professional athletes, musicians, politicians, executives, personal clients and brands, including 7UP, Under Armour, Nike Golf, ESPN, the U.S. Army, BOSE, LG, Jim Belushi, J.J. Watt, Deion Sanders, Curtis Stone and professional golfers Paul Casey and Kevin Chappell, to name

So I've learned and I've seen every side of the production business. Most of the productions that I was driving on were still photo shoots. There were campaigns. There were catalogue shoots. There were ad shoots. Some huge budgets. Some really small budgets. A lot of the people that I had connected with from the production side were on those catalogue and print shoots. So I started to make good inroads with some of those people. I was a PA with them. And again, starting from the very bottom and being willing to put in the work.

When I got to the point that I had to really strike out on my own, I identified a list of 25 companies that I wanted to produce for and I created a list. I called every single one of them every three weeks. I think it took three and a half to four months to actually get someone to hire me. At that point, I was two weeks away from having to declare a bankruptcy. I had exhausted all of my financess, was going through a divorce and trying to figure all this out, but I kept at it and I kept calling and I kept calling. I had my eyes on the target. I broke into the business because of the connections I made and my persistence. I told myself there's one path out of this and I just have to go after all the people that I had met on the shoots and take names, do the best job that I possibly could, and listen to outside influences for direction.

When you find your path, you need to put everything into it. And you have to be willing to fail in order to actually get something. It's a super crazy business and it makes little to no sense. But you have to find your way, be persistent and you have to do the work.

a few. I started over 18 years ago right in my own backyard of Kansas City with an early edition of Crystal's book and a list of contact names. My career now takes me around the world.

I'm excited that you're reading the 'Guide'. It puts you one step closer to kick-starting your career and being successful. My reason for contributing to the Guide is to help other artists, who, like me 18 years ago, are struggling with how to be a part of this industry without moving to a major city like L.A., New York or Chicago. If your own life circumstances will not allow you to move, and you love living in your current cozy city, keep reading!

I lived in Tempe, Arizona, graduated from The Fashion Institute of Design and Merchandising in L.A., and spent a few years in Denver, Colorado before settling in Kansas City.

I knew that I could face challenges in developing a credible, consistent and lucrative career here, but, for me, family came first. My dad was fighting cancer and I could not imagine not being near him during that time. So, I called Crystal to see if she thought I needed to move to L.A. to be successful in the industry, and she said, "Cristy, look in your own backyard." I did just that, and 18 years later I'm based out of Kansas City and still going strong.

The benefits of working in a smaller market are obvious. Your money goes further and lasts longer, and housing is typically reasonable. The day rates you earn are comparable to middle markets like Chicago and Atlanta, and, without the big city traffic, getting around is much easier and more efficient. You are a bigger fish in a small pond, and if you are comfortable doing makeup, hair and wardrobe you can work all the time.

Allow me to share my personal insights and information on what it takes to flourish in your own "backyard".

Define Your Starting Point

It's been said that starting is the hardest part. Let's start with these four key steps:

1 **Get Your Mind Right.** Create a vision for your business that not only includes working locally, but throughout the U.S. and internationally as well. I never pictured myself working only in a small market. My vision was to live in Kansas City and work all over the U.S. That then grew into working around the world.

2 **Identify your niche by thinking about your core passions.** Do you enjoy working with real people? Are you excited about supporting brides on their big day? Are you a news junkie? Do you love sports? Are you a fashionista? Do you love learning from people in the business world? Every one of these passions has a place for makeup, hair and wardrobe stylists in small-town America.

3 **Create a Written Plan.** It will be your working business plan. It will keep you on track, guide you and be your accountability partner. Or, as Crystal says, "Plan to Work and Work the Plan." You can mold it, edit it and shape it along the way as your business grows and changes.

4 **Start thinking of yourself as a business and a brand.** Recognize that everything you do and say, how you carry yourself from hello to your handshake, your web and social media presence and the materials you present to creative decision-makers and consumers regarding what your business does and how you run it, contributes to the reputation of your brand.

Achieving Vertical Focus

The sooner you know your core passions and where you would like to go—your BIG picture—the quicker you can apply what I call, "Vertical Focus". With vertical focus, you imagine each effort, task, test, job, workshop, and marketing promo stacking on top of each other towards your major goal. Horizontal focus on the other hand is when you chase many different ideas and go in all different directions.

So the relationships you make along the way are very important.

Craig: The biggest thing is relationships. Whether it's with the photographer or with an art director or it's with your actual client that hires you. Whether it's a catalogue company or an advertising agency, you have to be mindful of your reputation. And you learn by making mistakes. You learn by being arrogant. You learn by having an ego and thinking that you're fancier than you are.

What advice would you give to someone that aspires to work in production or other aspects of the industry?

Craig: I think it's important for people to know that there is a need for everyone to be mindful that this is a real job. It requires work and practice, testing, and studying. The same as if you are going to be a cabinet builder, a woodworker, a boat builder, a scientist. You have to put in the work and you have to put in the time.

From the hair, makeup and styling perspective you need to have a conversation with yourself and ask why you want to be in the business. Do you just like clothes or do you have a point of view? Or do you have a really great element of, "I can do something to support someone else's vision?" It needs to be about supporting the vision of the client. And if you're able to understand what your aesthetic is, you'll be able to identify the clients that you should be working for and then you'll work.

If you are going to work for J. Crew but you keep styling in a completely different manner, you'll never work for J.

Big-City Opportunities Available in Small Markets

Following are 8 big-city opportunities that you can find in smaller markets:

1	Commercial Advertising
2	News and Sports
3	Local & National Magazines
4	Corporate Communications
5	Weddings
6	Conventions
7	Fashion Shows
8	Personal Clients

Sports

If your city is home to successful sports teams, there is a good chance you can work on national advertising campaigns with national TV networks. There have been many times when brands such as Nike, Under Armour, 7UP and Bud Light have hired me to work with the athletes they sponsor for major advertising campaigns and for television appearances.

Since securing work with my first professional athlete (who happened to be endorsed by Bud Light), the calls have just kept coming in. The more athletes I work with, the more sports opportunities I receive.

Makeup & Hair Priorities in Small Markets

One of the keys to your success in a smaller market is understanding makeup, hair and grooming priorities. Surprising, perhaps, but I've used my character and special effects skills to make female models look like "old school" gold diggers, face-paint a crowd of fans for a football scene, and create UV black light makeup designs for a major electronics brand. My top 10 list of skills you should master if you want to keep work coming your way are:

1 Make talent and actors look natural.

2 Perfect the "no-makeup makeup look" in 15 minutes.

3 Master the skin tones and types of all ethnicities.

4 Identify makeup priorities quickly.

5 Manage shine and tame fly-a-ways.

6 Become an expert at men's grooming.

7 Master the 'man' application technique:

- Make men comfortable by working quickly and keeping the process feeling as masculine as possible.
- Apply fewer products to target priority areas.
- Answer questions about what you are doing.
- Keep all lipsticks and eye shadows out of sight.
- Verbalize that 'we are just about finished' when you notice a man getting fidgety, or they stop talking.

8 Be fast (able to complete a full makeup and hair in 30–60 minutes) and thorough.

9 Wedding Makeup

10 Master these 5 Character & Special Effects techniques.

- Body Painting
- Injury Simulation: Cuts and Bruises
- Dirty, Grimey and Sweaty
- Sunburns and Frost (Frozen Looks)
- Zombies and Gore

NOTES

....

....

....

The Hair Makeup & Fashion Styling Career Guide

Crew. You have to be targeted. The same way that you would approach any other business.

You have to do the research, the same way that I research cameras, lighting, story, and how to develop everything. I ask myself if I'm telling the right stories, am I seeking out the projects that really speak to me. If I am continually trying to go a different route then I'll never be successful.

> *From the hair, makeup and styling perspective you need to have a conversation with yourself and ask why you want to be in the business. Do you just like clothes or do you have a point of view?*

What about resumes? Do you look at them, and what do you look for in them?

Craig: I want to know who you've worked with and if we like your work and it's interesting, I want to know who to contact to vouch for you. If you're really the real deal. I want to know that you are ready to put in the work.

Do you use social media when sourcing talent?

Craig: Absolutely! All producers look you up. They'll

Wardrobe Priorities in Small Markets

As a wardrobe stylist or combination artist who supplies all three services to your clients, your priorities are different. My top 5 list of skills you should master if you want to keep wardrobe work coming your way are:

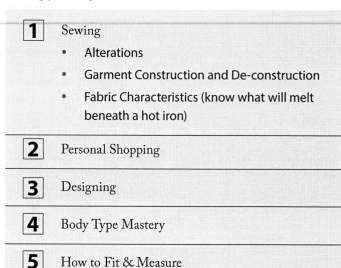

1. Sewing
   - Alterations
   - Garment Construction and De-construction
   - Fabric Characteristics (know what will melt beneath a hot iron)

2. Personal Shopping

3. Designing

4. Body Type Mastery

5. How to Fit & Measure

Commercial advertising can range from shopping and pulling "real-world" authentic looks to sourcing a marching band or football and cheerleading uniforms for a TV commercial. I've added felt teeth to a mascot's head and designed and produced a costume based on what Mother Earth would wear to the Kid's Choice Awards. You just never know what the day will bring!

As a triple threat makeup, hair and wardrobe stylist, my design and sewing skills have helped me to land jobs to key makeup, hair and wardrobe departments where I hired a team to assist me.

Small Market Challenges:

Smaller markets do have some challenges, but, with good planning and a little creativity, you can eliminate these bumps in your road in no time at all.

Challenges

How to Master

Challenges	How to Master
Industry-Focused Makeup Supply Stores	Check out local area costume shops.
Skills Development	Plan ahead. Search for classes and workshops in New York, Los Angeles, Miami, Atlanta and Chicago. Budget and set aside for skills and knowledge-based course opportunities that can open up new doors and bring better, higher paying jobs to you. Traveling away from home will keep you inspired and enable you to connect with other artists all over the world.

A smaller market will dictate the type of work you do. The jobs may not be cutting-edge, but, if you continue to test, develop your portfolio, and set new personal standards you'll keep getting new work and growing your market.

When marketing yourself in a smaller market, it can help to break the market up into two categories: business to business and business to consumer. The former is YOU, a business selling your services to other businesses. The latter is YOU, a business selling your services to other people. With business to business, you identify the entity and then locate the decision-maker who should receive your materials. With consumers, you go directly to the individual who needs your service.

Small Market Opportunities

BUSINESS TO BUSINESS (B2B)	BUSINESS TO CONSUMER (B2C)
Photographers	Brides
Production Companies: Producers, Production Managers, Production Coordinators	Special Events: Galas, Charity Fundraisers
Corporations	Imaging: Personal Wardrobe, Makeup & Hair
TV Studios	Holidays: Christmas, New Year's, Halloween
Public Relations Firms	Festivals
Advertising Agencies: Art & Creative Directors	On Camera Appearances
Magazines	
Festivals	

check your LinkedIn page, your Facebook page. We want to know what you look like and that you're not an idiot. You have to have a social media presence. You have to curate your social media. If I pull up your Instagram page and it's all party pictures and beer and weird stuff you're probably not going to get called unless you're willing to shoot for TMZ. If your facebook page is totally innapropriate you're not going to get called for the higher end jobs. Without question. And if they're not current... better to not even have them.

Is there anything else you would like to share with freelance artists that will help them land more jobs with people like you?

Craig: Take your job seriously. You aren't owed anything. You aren't fancier than anyone else. You're not better than anybody else. You have to work to get it. Take your job seriously. If you want to be in this business for 10, 15, 20 years, approach it as a business and a job!

 craigbbrooks

 rennfilms.com

Commercial Marketing – B2B

Attracting sophisticated advertising agency creatives demands that your website and promotional materials include relatable language and imagery. The art director from Under Armour who is traveling to your small town to produce a shoot is looking for makeup, hair and wardrobe talent that can deliver the same quality they have come to expect in larger markets like Los Angeles and New York. To be considered for high profile jobs, the imagery on your site must contain an advertising look and feel, not "before and afters" of your friend or cousin's makeup and hair. Maintaining a universal aesthetic in your branding, marketing materials and personal presentation will open doors to working with bigger brands and names.

Consumer Marketing - B2C

Consumers, while they enjoy seeing all of the big projects and people you have worked with, also want to see images that they can relate to. A woman who is about to get married will want to see beauty and bridal shots in your portfolio, because they often struggle with visualizing themselves in the pages of your commercial work unless they see exactly what they want.

It's tricky to present commercial and consumer imagery on the same website. You will rarely see them together on the websites of artists who work commercially in large or mid-sized markets. Crystal recommends separating them, which also streamlines the process of establishing different rate structures for each opportunity. Ninety percent of commercial (B2B) artistry will be based on full and half day rates plus overtime and expenses for travel, etc., while consumer (B2C) artistry will often be billed as per face, per hour or a flat rate.

Keeping Track of a Growing Business
Cristy's Big Black Book (BBB)

Early on in my business, I purchased a huge black binder notebook and designed my own contact template in Word. Crystal has one that is available as a free download for those of you who, like me, still like to put pencil to paper. Over the years I have made hundreds of copies of it. I have a thriving business and still use it to this day.

My process was to search and brainstorm every imaginable client who could use my services. Once I located their contact information, I entered it into my BBB and tracked every move I made. By logging every movement, including the time and day I called, whom I talked to, what was said, when I followed up, the date I sent them a promotional piece through the post or email, and when to follow up again, I was able generate business for myself in a very short period of time. I used this same information to follow up and share new work with my clients. Yes, you can do this digitally now; however, for me and maybe you, the power is still in the pen. When I connect my thoughts and ideas to paper with a pen—as Crystal suggests throughout the book—the opportunities come to fruition much faster. This method immerses me in the actual process, and in my business.

Diversify

Unlike large metropolitan markets where you can choose to do either makeup or hair, small markets operate much differently. Diversifying your skill set to include makeup and hair and even wardrobe will enable you to accept more jobs, and clients will benefit greatly from your new knowledge.

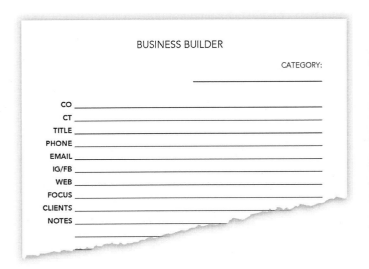

To work steadily in markets such as Kansas City, Denver and Indianapolis you will need to do both makeup and hair. Clients rarely hire separately for those roles.

WORKING AS A LOCAL: GROWING YOUR PHYSICAL REACH

Working as a local means that the client does not pay the travel expense of transporting you from where you live—your home base, to where you will be working—anywhere in the U.S. or beyond. You will be responsible for your own airfare, car rental, hotel and meals outside of the shoot.

You can often raise your rate to be in line with the higher "local" day rates, which will help to offset out of pocket expenses, and many times you'll still make *your* day rate. If the opportunity to work as a local will only cover your expenses, but the client, tearsheets or credits will be a great addition to your portfolio, résumé or future marketing efforts—go for it!

Jennifer Cunningham
MAKEUP & HAIR
jennifercunningham.com
Focus: Commercial
IG: jennifercunninghambeauty

I went to beauty school during high school because I knew that I wanted to work in fashion. I didn't know how to get involved, so I started talking to people who owned modeling agencies in the area, and they referred me to photographers to do tests with and build my book. I started getting pictures for my book with good makeup, hair, and styling and just O.K. models.

I learned that I could get better girls (models) by showing the work I had accumulated to agencies, photographers, and decision-makers. Crystal taught me that the tests in my book should look like they could fit into the top beauty and fashion magazines. They had to look like real jobs that I wanted to work on in fashion, music or advertising.

You should practice on everybody that you can get your hands on. Get good girls in your book by connecting with the bookers at the modeling agencies. Show them what you want to do, and be prepared to work for free for a while.

You can't expect to make a lot of money off the bat, but you've just got to stick with it. It's frustrating at the beginning, because nobody knows who you are when you're just starting out. Get experience, get your name out there, and work on your book so you'll have something to show. Just stick with it!

It's as good as being paid to gain experience working in a new "local" environment. You don't have to accept these assignments indefinitely, however, a few of these jobs on your resume can produce a future of high paying gigs with new clients.

The artist who is good at working as a local has a YES mindset. The glass is always half-full, and they are always thinking first of the how they can make something happen instead of why it can't be done. This artist is resourceful, makes friends quickly and doesn't freak out when they arrive in a new city and all of the regular stores they shop at in their local market have new names.

A good way to challenge yourself and your abilities as a local is to start out seeking work that is not too far away from your home base. Answer these questions when considering opportunities:

- What cities are within a three to four hour driving distance from my home?

- In what states do I have a support system of friends, family or colleagues?

- Do I have friends or family in other cities that I could stay with for a few days up to a week?

- To which cities/states could I purchase affordable airfare?

- In what cities/states can I find affordable lodging and inexpensive ground transportation?

Keeping An Open Mind

The 90's musical group En Vogue recorded a rock song entitled, "Free Your Mind." The first chorus went on to say, "And the rest will follow." This is what taking advantage of opportunity requires. Be open to possibilities like moving to get more work. Is there a state you've been interested in moving to? Consider booking a few jobs there and checking out the city at the same time. You can write off most of the expenses for work and get a feel for the local culture.

Do you like the beach but live in Oklahoma? Choose a city like Houston where there is plenty of work. On your off days visit Galveston and sink your toes in the sand.

As an aside, never broadcast that you are not local when working in other markets. You never want a client to feel uneasy, or concerned that you might not have a grasp of local market culture, customs, or resources. You don't want to give them a reason NOT to hire you again.

I'm also a firm believer in listening and observing new situations. This practice will allow you to learn a lot about the market, crew members, and who's who.

Smooth Operator

Following are four tips for making a smooth transition when working as a local:

- Get a deal memo signed as early as possible. Once the job is confirmed on paper, you can book a flight, reserve a hotel and secure ground transportation. If anything goes wrong, some airlines offer a 24–72-hour hold as well as a cancellation reimbursement policy.

- When your job is wardrobe styling, choose a hotel in a safe area with good retail shopping nearby, even if it's farther from the actual shoot location. It will make life easier when completing returns before heading to the airport to catch your flight home.

- Be sure to pick up a steamer, wardrobe rack, storage tubs and hangers. You will want to have all the tools you would have at home. If you start working often in that area, consider renting a small storage space to house all of your equipment, and have an extra kit there as well.

- Be sure your makeup and hair kit is travel-friendly.

- If you don't have a passport, get one ASAP.

Follow my advice and, before you know it, you'll be working on national projects with top athletes on major ad campaigns. This kind of exposure can do wonders for your career!

I don't have a recipe for going international. A series of positive outcomes which included doing a great job for all my clients, being genuine, hard work, preparation, connecting with crews doing big things, and applying for my passport years before I used it made me ready when the opportunity presented itself. Believe me, it happened to me and it will happen to you.

NOTES

_____

_____

_____

_____

_____

_____

_____

_____

_____

_____

_____

_____

_____

Success In A Small Market

In a small market you will be expected to wear different hats. If you want to stand out and work steadily, adding wardrobe styling services is beneficial. Seek out an agent in a city near you. Be willing to work as a local in other states, and offer your services to both businesses and consumers. Keep your marketing material updated. Always carry business cards in your kit, purse, set bag and vehicle, and post regularly on social media. Develop a 110% work ethic. Do a great job no matter who the client is and treat everyone like a VIP. Don't gossip. Respect the crews you work with and help them out from time to time. The effort goes a long way toward being seen as a team player. Know that your role, whether makeup and hair, wardrobe or all three is to bring your client's vision—not solely your own—to life. Show up on set ready to work. Leave your personal life at home. Be personable, prepared, flexible, and friendly. You will be amazed where your career can take you. Every single day do something to market and care for your business. I mean every single day.

Contributing to this edition of The Hair, Makeup & Fashion Styling Career Guide is a full-circle moment for me. This book truly kick-started my career 18 years ago. I've kept in touch with Crystal the entire time. Now, I'm sharing some of my knowledge with those of you who are ready to kick-start your career. So awesome! Wishing you all the best!

Cristy Guy
Makeup, Hair & Wardrobe Stylist
www.cristyguy.com | www.onthesetstyling.com

Think Big, you can settle later.

NOTES

If it comes down to two people, I'm going to hire the person who is easy and nice.

—Mike Ruiz
Photographer

4

Photographers

B efore we talk about photographers, let's talk about
photography. Throughout my journey as an artist's rep and
teaching artists how to develop successful freelance businesses,
I have come to understand that a hair, makeup, fashion stylist
and manicurists understanding of and appreciation for good
photography makes you a better artist. Additionally, having a
historical perspective and appreciation for what came before
you, will make you a better collaborator because it empowers
you to come to the creative table with ideas of your own.

For years glam squad artists have entered into testing
relationships with photographers feeling like they were at the
beck and call of those photographers and often erred on the side

Mike Ruiz

Beauty & Fashion Photographer

of, "Let me just do what I'm told so I can get my pictures." Sadly, many of them were still trying to 'get their pictures' months after the shoot was over, and some never have.

While some photographers treat their glam squads as disposable and downplay the artistic contribution as a minor part of the overall creation, there are others who are wonderful collaborators that will value your role and treat you with respect.

Throughout this book I stress the importance of testing to build a strong portfolio. In this chapter, I will go a step further and share:

- Guidelines on how to distinguish good photography from bad photography.

- Tips for becoming a true collaborator.

- A process and procedure for getting your photos.

- A strategy for getting your work published.

- Where you should go to find photographers.

- Before, during and after actions that you should take if you want to get rebooked.

- How to work with your photographer as an equal and become a successful collaborator.

DEVELOPING COLLABORATIVE RESPECTFUL RELATIONSHIPS

Would you like to be invited to the collaborative party, have a say in what's going on and even be asked about your opinion on shoots? Well, in the December 2017 issue of PDN (Photo District News magazine - pdnonline.com), Victoria Granof, one of the most influential stylists in the business said she has noticed an industry-wide change in the nature of collaborations between photographers and their stylists because stylists are being asked to contribute and come up with ideas right alongside the photographers. "Changing the dynamic of serving at the pleasure of the photographer must be undertaken carefully and thoughtfully," she says.

I believe the place for glam squad artists to begin is by taking the initiative to understand a little more about photography, lighting, art and history. One of the ways to start this process of learning is by taking classes. In fact, two types of classes that will change your perspective on photography and art, and open up your mind to allow new ideas to flow in are lighting and art history.

Angelika Shubert the founder of the Celestine Agency for makeup, hair and styling in Los Angeles suggested that adding knowledge in these two areas could significantly elevate an artist's value on set.

An art history course typically covers several eras—often from ancient to medieval, or renaissance to modern—and gives you a more expansive view of the world and its different cultures. All of which has impacted the world of beauty and fashion for thousands of years. Wouldn't you like to be part of that?

Classes

Classes can be very enlightening and also build confidence. Knowing the origin of things is very empowering. You can educate yourself by reading and studying on your own the same way you research what's coming up in fashion and beauty. Local community colleges offer great content and the internet has exploded with online courses.

www.CreativeLive.com has some amazing photography lighting classes. One taught by celebrity and lifestyle photographer Matthew Jordan Smith has been watched by over 31,000 people. Portrait photographer Annie Leibovitz's MasterClass teaches artists how to tell stories through imagery.

www.coursera.org has a wonderful selection of art history classes that you can enjoy online.

Start here.

Research

I would like you to add Photo District News to the list of trade and consumer magazines you'll start reading. Found online at pdnonline.com it not only showcases the work of some of the greats—whom you must familiarize yourself with if you intend to be part of the creative conversation—it highlights the work of exceptional newcomers, which PDN refers to as 'emerging photographers.' For beginners, these are the men and women that you will want to align yourself with. Why? Because these are the new stars who are just beginning to form their glam squads. These emerging photographers will be more receptive to setting up appointments and collaborating with you.

Each calendar year, PDN publishes several special issues. You should pay special attention to PDN's 30 which highlights up-and-comers and the Wedding and Events Issue which features top wedding shooters and the hot new trends in wedding photography.

Take The Meeting

I've often said, 'never underestimate the power of a cup of

Highly acclaimed beauty and fashion photographer, Mike Ruiz, is based in New York City. At the age of 28, he began working as a photographer and has since then built an impressive client list including Vanity Fair, Flaunt, Conde Nast Traveler, Interview, Paper, Citizen K, Vogue, Ellen and more. His ability to create art with his camera has led him to work with fashion giant Dolce & Gabbana, as well as celebrities like Iman, Traci Lords, Kelly Rowland, and Kelly Clarkson to name a few. Mike took time sit and talk about how he got started in the industry and what it takes for glam squad artists to work successfully at his level.

Was photography something you always wanted to do?

Mike: Well, I got a camera for Christmas at the age of 28. Prior to that, I didn't really have an inclination to become a photographer, but once I opened that camera and started using it, I became obsessed. I started shooting models, and then their agencies would see the images and send me more models to shoot. It kind of snowballed from there. It took me about a year and a half to really get started in it as a profession. But during that time, I did everything I could to learn about all of the intricacies of photography and the industry. What started off as a fun passion turned into the career I have now.

What qualities do you look for in the glam artists that you hire?

Mike: What it really comes down to is how nice and easy to work with the person is. There are a lot of talented people, so it can't come down to just talent. I'm at a point

coffee." Because you and the photographer are both freelancers, quite often you both have the same routine and schedule when it comes to building your portfolios. You're sitting at home doing research on your computer, flipping through magazines, rearranging your vision board, making phone calls and sending emails. Mostly sending emails. This routine plays out day-in and day-out while everyone else you know goes off to their 8-5 job. They have contact with their colleagues and bosses, go in and out of meetings and often have lunch and breaks together while you sit isolated at your kitchen table researching 1960's hair styles on Pinterest.

Inviting a photographer that you are trying to connect with, out for a cup of coffee to share and discuss ideas can be just what the doctor ordered. Trust me, they want a break too. And what better break than to sit down with another creative person, and potential collaborator to share a cup of java and discuss cool ideas for an upcoming shoot. Never, underestimate the POWER of a cup of coffee!

Recognizing Good Photography

"What's the big deal about photography," you ask? It's simple. If you don't know the difference between good photography and bad photography you can't possibly make good choices about who to collaborate with. Without a discerning eye the process of testing can be long, hard and discouraging.

Here's what you need to know, you train your eye to recognize good photography, by looking at good photography. There is no bad photography in Vogue, or Elle or Glamour or W or RollingStone or Essence or GQ or Oprah or ESPN or Sports Illustrated. These publications hire the best photographers in the world.

Training Your Eye

Pour over the pages of these magazines for three months. Put yellow Post-It Notes on the work that speaks to you. Look in the seams of each magazine for the names of the glam squad members who collaborated on the stories that you cannot take your eyes off of. This is the beginning of your re-education. It is the beginning of your transformation into someone who recognizes the best work in the world. Love it. Devour the pages. Burn them into your memory and in time, you will emerge with a more discerning eye toward the kind of world class work that you will someday create for the pages of those same magazines! I said it. Believe it.

Remember Tool #8 in Chapter 2? It is INSPIRATION. Create your own photography look book or idea diary of images that inspire you. Review them often. Pay attention to the composition, the lighting, the placement of shadows or the lack thereof. There are no accidental shadows in good photography. Inspired work should take your breath away, the same way a painting does in an art gallery or a dancer in the ballet.

I interviewed Reesa Mallen for the 'Guide.' She was my first agent at Crystal Agency and went on to become the photo editor for Teen Magazine, the creative director for Lands' End, and hold creative decision-maker positions at many other great companies. Reesa's way of keeping up with the work of the photographers she admired and hoped to convince to work with our artists at Crystal Agency was to create a hybrid scrapbook/notebook. She cut the photographers picture out of the contributors section of a magazine and glued them into her notebook. It looked like a messy three ring binder [to me] but from her vision sprung many wonderful relationships, great bookings and a ton of tearsheets that our artists parlayed into long successful careers.

Each time Reesa saw a favorite photographer's work in a magazine, she ripped out a page from the story or their portrait from the contributor's section, added it to her binder and wrote copious notes next to each image. When she made her phone calls she knew a heck-of-a-lot more about them than they knew about her. They felt that she really had taken the time to get to know their work, and she found it much easier to get appointments with them.

Pictured here is a scan of a page from that old notebook which included everything she could find on the photographer; where they hailed from, whom they had assisted, when they got their first break, etc.

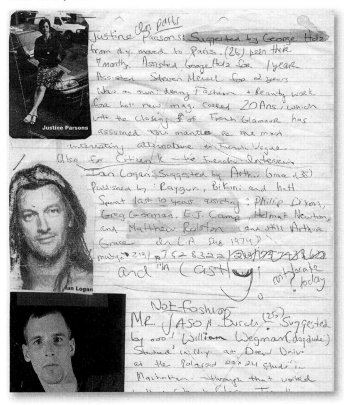

in my life where it's the path of least resistance. I don't care who someone has worked with, or who they think they are. If they aren't easy to work with, then I can't hire them. That really is the most significant criteria for me.

When you look at an artist's work, what do you look for?

Mike: I pretty much work with the same people most of the time. I have five makeup artists, five hair stylists, and two or three fashion stylists that I always go back to because they're easy to work with and they're all great. I don't have to worry about them showing up or being on time. People who are habitually late are just disrespectful. But you are asking what I am looking for creatively, right? Ultimately, I look for someone who can elevate the project. If I'm working on something gritty, then I will look for someone that can do that type of work, same goes for more polished, or natural looks. I look for people who will be appropriate for the project I am working on.

You said you have a pool of artists that you generally hire from, but if you needed someone new, where would you look?

Mike: Instagram is pretty much the go-to these days. I haven't even checked out a website in a long time. I've been asked to send websites to clients, but personally, I can assess their work ethic from the way they present themselves and the work they have online.

You can pick up on work ethic on Instagram?

Mike: I can. Being in this business for so long and

Let's say you meet a photographer who says he is testing for his book (a.k.a. TFP) and he would like to work with you. You ask to see his book. He shows you several pages of photos. Are they good? Are they bad? Are the subjects lit properly? Do random shadows appear all over the subject? Is the lighting flat? Is he using different colored gels to mask his lack of skill? Are the pictures washed out? Are the photographs overexposed or overly retouched? Are they all black & white actor or model head shots? If you don't have answers to most of these questions then you don't know enough about photography to make an informed choice about who to work with.

Artists looking to get signed by an agency have brought their portfolios to me for review and I have cringed. The conversation goes something like this:

Crystal:	"How long have you been testing?"
Artist:	Oh about a year or so.
Crystal:	Hmmm. Where did you find this photographer?
Artist:	Glamour Shots.
Crystal:	Oh Darlin' [shakes head] that's all wrong.

That is Scary! Stereotypical maybe, but good photographers with vision and the desire to do BIG things creatively, don't usually set up shop in the mall. The artist I met with didn't know any better. Without creating your own standard by researching, studying what you see, pouring over magazines, identifying the imagery that takes your breath away, you won't have anything in your mind to compare to what you're looking at. This is why the outcomes of your hard work and testing is often imagery that doesn't make the grade.

As you begin to study, you will be drawn to the work of certain photographers. Your reality will change, and so will the photographers you choose to work with. I used to play a little game with myself. When there were tons of magazine stands, I would go, stand back and see if I could identify the photographers whose work was on the covers. I was right a 85% of the time. That level of knowing comes with study.

As time passes, you will no longer be impressed just because a photographer has a book full of pictures. You will be more impressed with the photographer who shows you five fabulous images on an iPhone. When the work stirs you from the inside out and reminds you of some of the photographers whose work you have been collecting, you will be on your way to making great choices about who to spend your valuable time with.

Imagine the surprise of a young photographer when you complement him/her by saying that their work reminds you of Mario Testino, Steven Meisel, Mike Ruiz or Terry Richardson. Photographers like these have launched the careers of many makeup, hair, fashion stylists and manicurists. And they were, at one time, that young photographer whose iPhone you may have been looking at just the other day. Everyone is impressed by people who do their homework and show genuine interest in what they do. Be that person.

TESTING WITH PHOTOGRAPHERS

You'll remember what I said in chapter 1 about testing, it's a collaboration between a makeup artist, a hair stylist, a fashion stylist, a manicurist, a photographer and a girl (model) who all come together for a common purpose—to create something wonderful that each can showcase on their websites, in their print portfolio and on social media that will be so compelling

to a decision-maker that they will want to hire the artist for a paid assignment (job/gig) on a magazine, CD cover, ad campaign, book cover, TV show, etc. Or, and this is often the case in the beginning of building your portfolio—the work will be good enough to get you an even more fabulous test with an even better photographer!

I once represented a celebrity photographer in LA who said, "If I could do the hair and makeup myself, I wouldn't even have these people around." I was getting him $5,000 a day to shoot a recording artist for Atlantic Records and he was bummed because the makeup artist was making $850. This statement pretty much sums up the attitudes of those photographers who treat their glam squads like second class citizens. These same photographers made it impossible for artists to get their images. They were never available after the shoot to provide the artists who needed their images the most with the photos that would help them get to the next level in their careers. The scenario usually goes something like this:

It's Wednesday afternoon, your telephone rings, and the voice on the other end of the phone is that of a photographer you've been dying to work with. He wants to do a test and claims to have a great girl from one of the local modeling agencies lined up. He wants to know if you are available for a test with him on Friday.

"Yes, of course," you reply. You speak with him several times during the week. The two of you brainstorm and come up with some great ideas for the shoot. You discuss, at length, the location, the time of day that is best, the lighting, and everything concerning the logistics of the shoot.

working with such a wide variety of people, you become something of an expert on human nature and human behavior. I feel like you can peg someone in two seconds. For example, I can make a pretty accurate assessment of someone's work ethic based on the kind of work they are doing. If they're doing Vogue or Elle covers, I can assess that they have good work ethic, are talented, and well liked.

When you're hiring artists, do you care if they're agency represented?

Mike: I don't really care. Some are, some aren't. I, very rarely, go through an agent to book people. I normally text them to find out if they are available and it doesn't matter to me if they are agency repped or not. Actually, Instagram has become the new mother agent for everyone anyways.

Do you like to meet a person before you work with them?

Mike: I always like to meet people first. If it's a smaller, personal project, I might hire someone just off their work online, but when I'm working on a bigger project, with a client, I'm not just going to hire someone off Instagram. But, like I said, I have a group of people that I use that I've been working with for years that I don't have to worry about. This new generation, millennials, I am wary about. They tend to have quintessential millennial behavior because they have no idea what the protocol is on a photo shoot and there actually is a protocol.

Back when we started in the industry, we entered into that protocol, we learned it, and we understood it. We

The photographer pulls together a great team and you are looking forward to the opportunity to get new images for your portfolio. The day of the shoot arrives.

The model is two hours late. She overslept. She has bags under her eyes and her stomach is swollen from all the pizza and beer she consumed the night before. But what does it matter, this is your chance. The hair stylist has some fabulous new looks he has been dying to try out and the makeup artist can't wait to do her signature 3-D lips on this girl.

Six, eight, twelve hours of shooting. Mickey Dees for lunch, and a coke every hour. What the heck. The photographs will be worth it.

Back at the photographers' studio, hugs and kisses all around. Everyone agrees, "it was great." Goodbyes are exchanged and the photographer agrees that he will Dropbox an electronic contact sheet to you on Tuesday. You can view the images and choose which are best for your portfolio. What a great feeling. You can't wait for the weekend to end so you can get a look at the great photos everyone worked so hard on. Guess again.

Tuesday rolls around and you text the photographer in the morning. The end of the day draws near and no return message. Wednesday comes and still no word. You check with the rest of glam. No one is having any luck. The hair stylist even claims to have overheard a conversation at Starbucks about the photographer leaving town to show his book around—with your pictures, no doubt!

And so, the story goes. If you have been testing with photographers to build your portfolio this story may be all too familiar. Some of you may even meet the kind of photographer who uses you to build his portfolio but doesn't hire you when the real paying jobs start to roll in. It's sad, but it does happen.

I remember a photographer who tested with one of my fashion stylists when they were both just starting out. I helped him secure a celebrity for a photo shoot with a magazine that he had a relationship with and I also got him a fashion spread in one of the few hair magazines that produced pages good enough to use in a fashion and beauty focused portfolio.

The editor of that magazine couldn't see his brilliance, but I could and convinced her to use him for the shoot. The pictures were really special.

Neeko, my top hair stylist from that shoot went on to become Halle Berry's hair stylist. Lisa went on to have an amazing career, styling Charlize Theron and others. But at no time since those pictures were taken did he ever hire either of them to work on his paying jobs.

He preferred the bigger agencies with bigger artists names and thought nothing of it. That's life. It didn't stop me from working my butt off to get them great jobs, but it made me very sad and still does.

These stories are not intended to paint so dismal a picture that you decide against a career in this business. On the contrary, I endeavor to educate you about the realities of working in the business, steer you clear of the potholes, and lead you to success without all the battle scars that those before you have already endured. You can't avoid all of the pitfalls, but you can learn where to look for them and how to succeed in spite of them.

Collecting Your Images

Getting pictures from photographers after photo shoots necessitates that arrangements for acquiring the photos be made and understood prior to the day of the session. The onus is on you to confirm with the photographer or booking party (sometimes a studio manager) when the images will be ready for you to view online, and how soon after making your choices you can expect to receive them. Here's what you will need to do before you show up for the test:

- Negotiate up front. Newsflash! You can't negotiate anything with a photographer at the end of the shoot. He holds all the cards. It's too late. Set boundaries up front. Make your expectations clear and follow everything up with a really nice email that begins with a compliment about how fabulous the photographer is, and how excited you are about the project and then wind them into who, what, where and when will you get your images. Answers to these three key questions will go a long way toward giving the photographer a sense of your seriousness toward your work.

1	When can I expect to receive a link to the electronic contact sheet?
2	How many images will you be retouching for me? (Ask for at least one image from every look.)
3	How long (a specific date) after selecting MY images can I expect to have the 11X14 (300dpi) retouched images delivered into my Dropbox?

practiced it. But, it's gone out the window with this young generation. I can't tell you how many interns I've had on set that I've had to ask to leave. I'm happy to step aside with them and answer questions and help them learn, but what I see is that the minute I turn my head, they are approaching the celebrities I'm shooting and handing out business cards and taking selfies with them. I appreciate someone who is ambitious, but you have to be respectful. I was ambitious, but I never stepped on anyone's toes. I made the calls, I pounded the pavement, I did the work, but I never showed up with the expectation that I was owed any work.

Tell me more about this on-set etiquette you've mentioned.

Mike: For me, it's all just common sense. It is respect. If somebody gives me an opportunity, I won't bulldoze my way past them to make it all about me. If I am brought into a situation, I would be grateful and appreciate it and learn from it. That applies to everyone across the board; makeup artists, hair stylists, fashion stylists. There are people out there that will step on toes and take credit for things they don't deserve credit for.

What has changed over the last five to seven years about the way you book artists, and what hasn't changed?

Mike: Everything has changed, yet nothing has changed. I still book people based on the same criteria based on personal and creative aspects. That's been the way I've done things my entire career. I would have to say that is the one thing that has stayed consistent. The way I

- Don't ask IF you are going to get your pictures, discuss when you will receive them. Don't ask how something is going to happen as if you have no control over it. Instead, offer a solution: I'll send you a link to my Dropbox.

- Ask around. Talk to other artists. There are dozens of Facebook and LinkedIn groups where creative people huddle and share. Find out what other glam squad artists have experienced with a photographer. Photographers who exhibit selfish behavior have skeletons in the closet, and you only have to rattle the door a bit before all of the bruised glam artists who STILL haven't received their photos start falling out around your feet.

- Tactfully let the photographer know that you consider testing for your book to be a serious investment, and that the skills you bring to the session are valuable.

- Confirm that YOU will be able to select the images that are right for your book, and while you appreciate that the photographer may want to choose the images for you, that won't be necessary. If he/she insists, explain that what you need for your book can be completely different than what he/she needs. Additionally, you feel it's very important that you learn how to choose the images that best represent your work. **Drops the mic!**

- Some images from tests are good enough to be published. Many magazines accept submissions and everyone benefits when your images are among the lucky ones to get selected and published. If getting published becomes a possibility, discuss how long you will have to wait [during the submission process] before you can add the images to your online portfolio. Without discussing a time table up front you can end up waiting several months for the photographer to shop the images around and they never get picked up by a publication while you sit idly by waiting for images that can potentially generate paying jobs for you.

What To Expect From Testing

Understanding testing is knowing that twenty-five test shoots will probably yield 30 to 40 pictures for your book not 60 or more. Of course the intention is always to net four to five amazing new images per shoot. However, that ambitious goal doesn't always mean you will end up with 4-5 portfolio worthy images each time. Why not? Variables. There are always some unpredictable variables. Every photo shoot can potentially be affected by MURPHY'S LAW, "What can go wrong, will go wrong." Photo shoots are like that. Here's what can happen:

The Model	Doesn't arrive.
The Model	Arrives late and everyone is packing up to go home.
The Model	Is 10lbs heavier than her agency profile states and none of the clothes fit.
The Photographer	Gets a paying job at the last minute and bails on the test.
The Photographer	Trips over the c-stand and sends the camera crashing to the floor.
The Hair Stylist	Forgets the curling wand.
The Makeup Artist	Couldn't get to the mall to grab the right foundation before the store closed last night.

The Fashion Stylist	Ran out of room on his Visa card.
The Budget	There isn't one.
The Transportation	Breaks down on the freeway in rush hour traffic.
The Designer Gown	Was sent FedEx 2-Day Delivery instead of overnight and it never arrives.
The Location	Wasn't scouted beforehand and is now a McDonalds.
The Electricity	Fails.
The Weather	Pours down rain.
The Weather	Turns out to be the hottest day on record and everything melts.
The Manicurist	Has a reaction to the sun and is rushed to the hospital for heat stroke.
The Props	Don't arrive.
The Food	Gets delivered to the McDonald's location.

You name it, it can happen. Be prepared to improvise, and keep a good attitude regardless of the circumstances. The magic of the day may be the bond that you all share by making it work in spite of the obstacles.

What Should Make It Into My Book

I have a simple test for determining whether an artist has met their objectives when it comes to adding a new piece in their portfolio. Ask yourself this question. If I laid some type on conduct myself, and interpersonal relationships with the artists…that has remained the same. I have always had respect for the work people do, and I expect the same respect for what I do.

I think the biggest thing that has changed the most is social media. For 20 years, I put in the time and work, and slowly climbed the ladder to get to the point where I felt like things were good and I was on a roll. Then social media just pulled the carpet from under all of that because then, like 20 years ago prior to Instagram, your value was based on something completely different than what it is now. So, now I feel like I have to hustle in a very different way than I used to. People's attention spans are so short nowadays. I have to hustle continuously and curate my Instagram page very specifically because it's the only viable way to market yourself now. I suspect it's the same for stylists, hair and makeup artists. Posting daily and how many followers you have is something people put a lot of stock into.

Do you think that they put a lot of stock in it from a commercial standpoint as well as an editorial one?

Mike: No. I think that social media clout doesn't influence the bigger more established clients like the Vogues and the L'Oreals. I don't think they see the same value in it as the younger companies do. The bigger clients are more likely to hire someone based on relationships and accolades which is the classic, old-school way.

this photograph, would it look like it could be a beauty feature or fashion editorial in my favorite magazine? If the image is a portrait, could it be a cover?

As an agent to photographers as well as glam squad artists, I worked with magazines such as InStyle, Rolling Stone, ESPN, Essence and many others. Mikki Taylor, the beauty and cover editor at Essence, would always bring a small transparency that was made to look like an Essence cover with her to the shoot to lay over the image. Each time the photographer took a picture, Mikki would fold it neatly, and place the transparency over the image. She could then see how the setup, lighting, look, clothes, hair and makeup were going to read on the cover.

You won't have a transparency to lay on top of the iMac or iPad screen but you should create one in your mind (or find an app) and use it every chance you get. That, and a dry erase marker could work wonders for helping you to see how an art director, fashion editor or photographer might view your work. That's a little old school magic.

Paid Tests

Portfolio building tests are done most often without compensation. However paid testing happens in two situations:

1	Models, actors, actresses, and dancers pay photographers and glam squad artists to do their makeup, hair, and styling for headshots and comp cards.
2	Makeup, hair, stylists and manicurists hire a photographer to produce images that they can use in their books.

In situation number 1, the test is usually orchestrated by a modeling agency for a new face, or a public relations firm for an actor who needs pictures. These sessions have not been commissioned by a commercial entity (magazine or advertising agency), and are being paid for by the actor or model. A day's compensation typically ranges from $50 to $150 for a session with a model, and from $50 to $500 for a session with a celebrity.

In situation number 2, the glam squad artists are usually fed up with trying to find good photographers to collaborate with and decide to pay the photographer to do EXACTLY what they want.

There are different schools of thought about situation number 2. Some artists regularly pay photographers to produce the images they need. Some artists do it rarely, but I don't like it, because that is not a collaboration and it makes artists lazy. Connecting and communicating with a photographer creatively is magical. Reaching out enough times so that you fine tune your coffee pitch is exhilarating. Paying a photographer is just hiring someone to do a job and other than the money, they have is no vested interest in your success. I certainly can't blame you for doing it the other way, but I hope you'll try relationship building first.

NOTES

Working With Modeling Agencies
By Reesa Mallen

Modeling agencies are a good way to get fabulous photos for your book. Every agency has what's called a New Faces division. The purpose of which is to, find "New Faces." The chance that you will discover a super model sucking on a Smoothie in front of the local Jamba Juice who happens to have a hot portfolio of herself is about one in a million.

A "new model" who wants to get bookings needs a good portfolio. What makes a good model portfolio? Pretty much the same elements that you need; good photography, fabulous hair, a well beat face (makeup), a pretty set of nails and great threads. It's a team effort. Each of you need each other because you all need images for your books and social media.

You, and the photographer who just graduated from photography school, all need good models, makeup, hair and clothing. This is especially important if the photographer intends to focus on fashion. Modeling agencies set up tests for their new faces (models) all week long.

Mike Ruiz, *Bicoastal Makeup Artist*

How do you prefer to be contacted by artists? What works for you?

Mike: Obviously, I can't respond to all of my DMs and work with everyone that contacts me. I don't want to give false hopes. I can say that a lot depends on the tone of the message and if they sound aggressive or not. It's also a two-way street. If I see new, young talent that I want to work with, I'll message them as well. If they are inspiring to me, then I'll want to reach out to them and work with them.

What advice would you give an artist who is in the process of building his or her portfolio?

Mike: Be honest with yourself. You have to learn how to assess the quality of your work quickly and put what you're most proud of forward. A lot of people put a bunch of junk in their portfolios just to fill it up, but I'd rather see six amazing images than 40 mediocre ones. If you are on the fence about something, take it out. Also, if you have a vision for your work, don't change it because someone else tells you to.

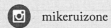 mikeruizone

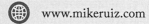 www.mikeruiz.com

Follow these 6 easy steps for building your portfolio with real agency girls!

1 Call modeling agencies in your city and ask for the New Faces department. If you're just starting out, the agencies will not give you their "Super Models" to test with until they see that you are a "Super Artist".

2 Ask the "New Faces" booker if you can come by and meet them. Explain that you want to test with their "girls" (the word that refers to a model). The more you use their lingo the quicker you'll get in.

3 Request that they call you for tests. However, when the agencies start to call you BEWARE! You will not want to test with every one of their girls, so ask the booker to email the models comp card (zed card)? Beauty to one eye may be bland to another. If after reviewing the cards you decide to go ahead and test with the model, make sure you can speak with the photographer beforehand to get an understanding of the "Look" he is aiming for.

4 Keep the direction of your book in mind. You don't want to have to many pictures with the same exact "look" in your book, or a decision-maker will assume that you have limited talent—or worse, that you are unimaginative!!

5 Always pick out your own images. What a photographer thinks is right for his or her book, may not work in yours at all. The gig is not over until you get images for your portfolio. Remember, you are going for an editorial look in your book. Have you ever flipped through Vogue and seen a one-page editorial? Never!!

6 Recognize when you have leverage. When a photographer calls you on his own to test (instead of the modeling agency) he likes your work. Now is the time to put forth some ideas of your own.

Have fun and remember you do not accept every test that the modeling agency or photographer calls you for! You may not like the model, the photographer, or the rest of the makeup, hair and styling team. It takes a bit of luck to make a fabulous test fabulous. Good Luck and Happy Testing!!

Getting Published

Getting published is a wonderful thing. Who doesn't want to see their work and name in print? While not all magazines accept submissions (Vogue, Elle, Glamour, W, Essence, etc.), plenty do—both print and online.

New York-based photographer, Lindsay Adler, publishes a magazine submission resource guide known as Get Published. The most up-to-date edition is Get Published 2. Lindsay suggests this publication is for photographers, however, I think it is a great resource for the glam squad as well.

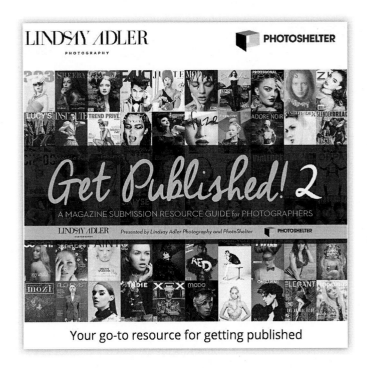

Your go-to resource for getting published

Here are just a few things it will help you to accomplish:

1 Getting your work published.

2 Finding new photographers to test with.

3 Getting connected to all the right people at magazines.

4 Learning how things work.

5 Being a better collaborator.

I encourage you to be proactive regarding submissions. There is no law that says you can't reach out to the magazines yourself,

Jaleesa Jaikaran

Beauty & Fashion Makeup Artist

however, I suggest that you offer to assist the photographer before going solo. This is the time for you and the photographer to pool your resources and connections.

Getting published provides an opportunity for everyone to get credited. Turn on your savvy business hat, and you might be able to get studios, equipment rental companies, locations, and cosmetics companies to loan or gift you the products or services you need to produce a shoot for FREE—as long as they receive a visible credit with a link that others can use to find them. Businesses want awareness and sales. Just put on your thinking cap. You can do this!

Check out the link that follows, read the magazine profiles, develop your pitch, make a few calls to see who might be interested and go for it. http://promo.lindsayadlerphotography. com/getpublished

On Page Credits

The time to discuss your on-page credit is the moment submitting the images to magazines becomes a serious consideration. If the photographer is going to submit the images to magazines, you want to make sure that your on-page credit reads exactly as you would like it to appear. Due diligence. There's that word again. Go through magazines and see how the glam squad artists are credited. Not every magazine credits the same way. Some credit on the first page of the editorial (story), others further in, and still others, like InStyle, credit at the back of the book—that's magazine lingo for the back of the magazine. Either way, there will be a formula for the way each publication approaches crediting. Create your credit line according to the magazine's formula and be prepared to email or text it to the appropriate person (photographer or magazine editor) on demand. However, if no one asks you—inquire, and send it in.

Following are examples of how your editorial credit could read under certain circumstances:

> Makeup by Mary Coletti/marycoletti.com (just you)
>
> Makeup by Mary Coletti/BailyGroup.com (when agency represented)
>
> Makeup by Mary Coletti at Beauty Bar/BailyGroup.com (salon/studio + agency)
>
> Makeup by Mary Coletti at Beauty Bar/marycoletti.com (salon/studio + just you)
>
> Makeup by Mary Coletti for MAC Cosmetics/marycoletti.com (brand + just you)

Be aware that some magazines will restrict credit lines to a certain number of characters, in which case…adapt! Get ready for the opportunity by using the spaces provided to formulate your own myriad of possible editorial credits:

....

....

....

....

WHERE TO FIND AWESOME PHOTOGRAPHERS

There are hundreds of places to find and meet photographers, but only a few of them are the right places. Commercial and editorial photography requires a team of people to accomplish an assignment. As someone who wants to be on that team, ask yourself, "Where could I connect with photographers who need glam squad artists for an upcoming photo shoot? If you're thinking about places like Facebook, Instagram, and photo and high end bridal expos then you are right. But I want you to do more. Using the space that follows, take five minutes to do a brain dump. Stop and think of other places where you could meet photographers.

....

....

....

....

Following is an exhaustive list of physical and online places where you can find, meet and connect with photographers. Add them to the list you just created and you'll be busy networking for awhile.

> Photography Schools
>
> Social Media: Instagram, Facebook & LinkedIn
>
> Events
>
> Online Creative Directories
>
> Photo Organizations
>
> Magazines
>
> Coffee Shops
>
> Word of Mouth
>
> Model Mayhem

Jaleesa Jaikaran, *Beauty & Fashion Makeup Artist*

Jaleesa Jaikaran is a bicoastal makeup artist who grew up in Trinidad. Having worked with her home country's top photographers, designers, and artists, she made the move to New York to further follow her passion. Her ability to naturally enhance her clients' natural beauty has landed her work with companies such as Nylon, Elle, V Magazine, Paper, Seventeen, W, and Vogue. Jaleesa gives an inside look on how she established herself as a makeup artist and gives advice to novices in the industry.

What was your path to becoming a makeup artist?

Jaleesa: I took makeup classes in Trinidad just as something fun to do on weekends. I didn't plan for it to become a career. Soon I began assisting my teacher on jobs and things took off from there. I started working on my own photoshoots and earning clients. Soon after, I left my office job and went to work at a MAC store as a product specialist. Moving to New York was something I wanted to do, but I knew that I needed a plan before just relocating. I let MAC know that I wanted to move and they helped me relocate. That's when my career really started to grow. Assisting Sir John Barnett and several other well respected and well known artists paved the way to my career growth.

What is your focus as an artist?

Jaleesa: My focus is beauty, fashion, and commercial. Although I have found myself working across all arenas.

Photography Schools

Many different types of schools have photography departments. Art schools, universities, community colleges and vocational-technical schools provide opportunities for you to meet photographers.

Some schools still have student information boards where you can post a three by five (3X5) card with your contact information, an image of your work if you have one, your professional title, a business card and your intention—what you want from them.

Others will have online forums or marketplaces where you can connect. Call the school and say something like:

> *"Hi, My name is Mary Coletti. I'm a makeup artist here in Phoenix, and I am looking for a way to connect with the photographers in your program who are building their portfolios. Do you have a place online where I can share my information with your students?"*

Be prepared to reach some receptionist who doesn't know what the heck you're talking about. Just don't let that stop you. Keep digging. Ask to be transferred to the photo department, the career center or one of the professors.

LISTEN TO ME! Everything you need to know about that school, its program, the schedule of classes, and upcoming events, is on the school's website. Gather the info you need and hightail it over to the campus. Be standing outside the door when class ends.

Introduce yourself to the professor and every photographer coming out of that classroom, and hand them your business card. Give them your elevator pitch, but this time, make sure to add your focus which may be beauty, fashion, lifestyle, celebrity, etc.

You can adapt this elevator pitch for the photographer or the professor:

"Hi Professor Johnson. My name is Mary Coletti; I'm a beauty and fashion makeup artist here in Phoenix, and I would like to connect with some of the more promising beauty and fashion photographers here in your program so we can collaborate on building our portfolios. I brought a few of my images to share with you. If you like them, I hope you'll introduce me to some of your favorite photographers?"

In Los Angeles, there is Art Center College of Design. In New York, there's SVA—the School of Visual Arts. In Massachusetts, there is the Massachusetts College of Art and Design. Somewhere in or near your city, there's a school of photography. Finding it is as easy as typing in the words: PHOTOGRAPHY SCHOOLS + CITY OR STATE in the Google search engine. You will be rewarded with a list of schools that offer photography as a field of study.

Now, go forth and slay!

The trick, as always, is getting their attention. The 3X5 card is one way, posting something in their online forum is another, and stopping by the campus—which I totally support—is better. Most schools will even help you to schedule a tour. No need to divulge your real intention. Just go for the visit.

Just be PERSISTENT. Don't take NO for an answer; someone needs what you have to offer. When it becomes important enough, you'll do what it takes. Don't be afraid of the word no. No backward is ON. So, get ON with it!

Social Media: Instagram, Facebook & Linkedin

It really is everything, isn't it? Instagram I mean. Post your work. Identify and follow good people. Engage by commenting on their images. Hashtag your work appropriately. Look for common ground to start a conversation with people whose work you admire and be aware that the common ground could be a hobby, children, having the same dog, loving dogs, working out, cooking, family, etc.

Often times, artists overlook the obvious opportunities to engage because they think it must come from them waving their hands in the air and saying, "Hey, here I am, can you see me? Can I work with you? Can I be your assistant? Can we do a shoot together?" The common thread could just be that both of you are raising miniature schnauzers. It doesn't matter. Just engage, be consistent with your posting, try not to microwave the relationship and look for the open door.

Are you signed with an agency?

Jaleesa: No, not yet. I believe that because the trajectory of the industry is changing so much, it's important to focus on getting your own clients and building your brand first.

Can you share some of your most exciting jobs or clients with us?

Jaleesa: I love getting to work with brands that I grew up with or grew up seeing on TV. Clear Eyes and Shea Moisture are at the top of the list.

How would you describe your job as a makeup artist?

Jaleesa: My job as a makeup artist is really to assist with bringing the creative vision to life. Whatever the job may be, whether it is natural or creative, the end goal is to match your work to the overall goal the client wants to accomplish.

What did you learn as an assistant?

Jaleesa: I learned to be intuitive and quick on my toes. I learned to keep the mindset that every assisting job is an opportunity and to absorb as much as possible. Also, working with so many personalities helped me become a better team player.

Why do you think the key artists you assisted kept hiring you?

Jaleesa: I always gave 110%. I was proactive and respectful.

A great way to find photographers on Facebook is by logging into your account and typing the words PHOTOGRAPHERS + STATE/CITY into the search bar at the top of the page. You will get a new page with an additional selection of links, and one of those is GROUPS.

Click on GROUPS, and a list of photographer's groups in the city or state you selected appears. From here, you can click on the links, learn what the group is about and join them.

LinkedIn works very much like Facebook when it comes to groups. Go to your profile page, and type the word GROUPS into the search bar at the top of the page. You will get a new page with additional links, and one of them is GROUPS. Click on it and then type the word PHOTOGRAPHERS into the search bar above and voila, a plethora of photographers to choose from.

Events

Looking for a way to meet 2000 photographers in one day? Photo conferences are the way to do it. This is where photographers congregate to network, be inspired and learn. From the activity in the conference venue lobby to the live courses to the expert panels, and evening soiree's, this is the place to hang out, network, see and be seen. Show up with your iPad, business cards and comp cards in hand, and you are sure to leave with more than a few new connections.

A favorite event is the PDN Photo Plus Expo. Each year 20,000 professional photographers, videographers, students and educators attend. Visit photoplusexpo.com to learn more.

To search for others in your neck of the woods visit Google and type in the words: PHOTOGRAPHY + CONFERENCE + CITY/STATE.

To help you get started filling up your calendar, here are a few:

Photo Plus Expo	New York, NY
Imaging USA	Nashville, TN
WPP	Las Vegas, NV
Shutterfest	St. Louis, MO
Photography Show	Birmingham, UK

MEETUP provides organized event opportunities for people with common connections to meet, connect, brainstorm and work together. Join and search for photography pros at www. meetup.com.

LEBOOK produces workshops and conferences that focus on photography, commercial production and industry trends. CONNECTIONS is one of those events and brings together an international network of creative talent and decision-makers to discuss and share what's going on in the world of trendsetting image-making. It happens five times a year in New York, London, Paris, Berlin and Los Angeles. For more information visit: lebook.com/connections.

Online Creative Directories

Creative Directories are essentially databases full of information and inspiration that serves a specific industry—in this case photography. These print and online directories are full of resources that include: photographers, photo and glam squad agents, artists and more. Creative decision-makers use these directories to source talent for upcoming projects.

Recognize that creative directories have levels. Lets call them A and B list. An A-List directory will showcase the biggest and highest paid photographers in the world. They are almost always agency represented and work on the national and

international advertising campaigns that you see on billboards, in magazines, and on bus sides all over the world. In these directories you may not find the photographers that you will be testing with to build your book, however, they are the photographers you should aspire to work with. Three that come to mind are:

1 LeBook.com

2 Workbook.com

3 ProductionParadise.com

These directories are great for populating your sandbox, becoming knowledgeable about the best and highest paid photographers both stateside and internationally, and for training your eye to recognize good photography.

The B-List creative directories are local in nature. They showcase the work of photographers in a specific region. Creative directories that fit that bill include:

Chicago Creative Directory	creativedir.com
The San Diego Creative Directory	sdcreativedirectory.com
Philly Creative Guide	phillycreativeguide.com
Minnesota Creative Source	mncreative.com

You can find directories in your area by going to Google and searching for

Creative Directory, Photography, City, State

| Jaleesa Jaikaran, *Beauty & Fashion Makeup Artist* |

Did you find that you had to stop assisting in order to key your own jobs?

Jaleesa: No, it happened simultaneously. I continued assisting while keying my own jobs. I just became more selective about what jobs I would take.

Do you ever hire assistants? If so, what qualities do you look for?

Jaleesa: I do hire assistants, and I look for people who are proactive and have great set etiquette.

What tools do you expect an assistant to have that wants to work with you?

Jaleesa: I want them to be eager to learn and work hard.

Do you ever use social media as a tool for finding assistants? If you do, what do you look for?

Jaleesa: I do sometimes, via private Facebook groups. Great assets to have would be being proactive, helpful, and engaged. Turn-offs would include talking too much on set, using their phones, and asking too many questions while we're working.

Have you ever hired someone directly from Instagram without looking at their portfolio?

Jaleesa: I haven't. Even if a recommendation comes from Instagram, for me, it's probably through a trusted colleague.

Do you use social media to market yourself?

Jaleesa: Yes. I mainly use Instagram for my professional work. I also create content on YouTube to highlight the

Photo Organizations

Photography organizations are an underutilized resource for finding photographers. Many are nationally and internationally recognized around the world and always have some kind of event, symposium or seminar going on in a city near you. The APA (American Photographic Artists) is national in scope, has local chapters in most large cities, and maintains a state by state membership directory that includes photographers and glam squad artists.

Once a member, you become part of the directory and gain access to all of the workshops, symposiums, talks and online events that they host at a discount. The membership directory is updated annually and circulated to all members. The APA has monthly meetings that are attended by...guess who? Photographers. As a bonus, the workshops and gatherings often include art directors, photo and glam squad reps, art buyers and more as part of panel discussions they host. It's worth the price of admission. They also publish a monthly newsletter.

Magazines

Magazines are a great place to discover new photographers to work with and be inspired by. The photo credit in most magazines can be found in one of five places:• On the contents pages (cover credits are usually printed here).

- On the first page of a feature, beauty or fashion story.
- In the front of the book on the contributors page.
- Next to the makeup, hair and styling credit in the seam of the magazine.
- At the back of the magazine, in the resources section (Ex: InStyle magazine).

When a photographer's name is run in the credits of a magazine that is published locally, there is a good chance the photographer has a website and an Instagram page where you can find all of his/her contact information.

Coffee Shops

What better place to meet someone than the watering hole of the 21st century—the coffee shop. Unlike the seedy donut shops of yesteryear, today's coffee shop offers gourmet coffee, Italian sorbets to cleanse the pallet, fancy European pastry (the names of which everyone except the Europeans mispronounce), comfy chairs, three-prong outlets for your laptop, and quite often, creative people sitting around sharing lots of great ideas. Photographers, video producers, beauty and fashion editors (if you live in New York), stylists, designers, and celebrities are all part of coffee shop scene. In Europe they call it cafe society.

Model Mayhem

I feel compelled to talk about Model Mayhem because it has been around so long, has gone through many transformations and it's still here. Go-Figure! It's been bad—really bad. But then, when I stopped by to investigate it for this latest edition of the Guide, I noticed that six years ago, Roshar did an interview with Model Mayhem. Model Mayhem is like a soap opera that goes up and down in popularity but never goes away.

So, here's my one and a half cents about Model Mayhem. It can work for some people who are starting out, but only if you:

| **1** | Know what you are looking for. |
| **2** | Have done your homework and created a standard by which to measure the photographers that you connect with. |

Without having a lock on #2 (knowing the difference between good and bad photography), you are doomed to spin your wheels and work with losers.

If on the other hand, you have really developed a discerning eye for photographers and models, you could spot a diamond in the rough and build a relationship that just might take you places. Check it out!

TWO KINDS OF PHOTOGRAPHERS

There are two kinds of photographers. The ones who are going somewhere, and the ones who are not. Along the way, you will surely meet both. Use this checklist to determine whether you can go the distance with your photographic muse. Five or more check marks in the 'Going Somewhere' category is a keeper. Three or more in the 'Going Nowhere' category means you should turn and run in the opposite direction.

NOTES

....

....

....

....

....

behind-the-scenes of being a makeup artist.

Was it easy for you to find your voice on social media?

Jaleesa: Over time, I discovered that your voice is really just being yourself and having confidence in that.

Can you describe a week in your life?

Jaleesa: When I'm not busy freelancing, I like to spend time prioritizing my calendar around the projects I'm working on, events to attend, and of course a little fun. I try to keep myself busy even on my "off" days.

Who is on your bucket list to work with?

Jaleesa: Big beauty brands like Maybelline and Cover Girl.

How do you prefer to be contacted by assistants?

Jaleesa: I will always prefer to receive a personal email versus a direct message on social media. Texts may be used for last minute communication, but always confirmed via email.

What advice do you have for newcomers?

Jaleesa: Focus on creating a body of work that you're proud of. Have a book that is a representation of the type of work you want to book. And remember that your only competition is and always will be you.

Characteristics Of A Photographer Who's Going Somewhere:

____ Has established working relationships with modeling agencies.

____ Has an online portfolio and Instagram Account.

____ Shows respect for his/her team of assistants and glam squad artists.

____ Values what you have to say.

____ Trusts you enough to let you do your job on set.

____ Is knowledgeable about the great photographers who came before him.

____ Is willing to collaborate with the glam squad on tests.

____ Returns emails, texts and phone calls within 24 hours.

____ Knows how to tell a story through his pictures.

____ Doesn't give you watermarked photos.

____ Has a pleasant professional demeanor and attitude.

____ Provides you with an electronic contact sheet within 3-5 days after the test shoot.

____ Doesn't insist on choosing your images for you.

____ Provides a clean, organized studio environment to work in.

___ Is open to reviewing and sharing inspirational photos/storyboards/vision boards.

___ Has a collection of inspirational books and magazines in the studio.

___ Will listen to you even when they don't agree.

___ Is Creative.

___ Understands the natural lighting cycle and positioning of the sun when shooting on location.

___ Is respectful of other people's time.

___ Provides the crew with pertinent information regarding the location name and address, parking instructions in advance.

___ Knows how to get "the shot" without taking 500 photos of the same pose/look.

___ Sends a thorough and timely call sheet, introduces everyone on set, takes a collaborative minute to confirm what everyone is there to do.

___ Gives you images in 300 dpi or better for printing and your digital portfolio.

___ Doesn't become offended when you share your feelings about retouching and is willing to tone it down so you can use the image(s) in your portfolio.

NOTES

The Hair Makeup & Fashion Styling Career Guide

Is there anything else you want to share that you believe will empower freelance artists?

Jaleesa: Understand that someone else's way does not have to be your way. The beauty about being a freelance creative is the ability to design an environment that's conducive to your life and growth. Stay true to your path and know that it happens differently for everyone.

IN HER KIT: 3 THINGS JALEESA CAN'T LIVE WITHOUT

- A great moisturizer
- MAC Face & Body Foundation
- A brow gel.

 jaleesajaikaran

 www.jaleesajaikaran.com

Characteristics Of A Photographer Who's Going Nowhere:

____ Insists on giving you images with watermarks or their logo splashed all over the photographs.

____ Insists on choosing your images for you.

____ Insists that you credit them on every image you load up on your site and social media even when they won't do the same for you.

____ Never gets good girls from modeling agencies.

____ Always testing with someone they met on the street or a neighbor.

____ Has been testing with modeling agencies for five years or more and still doesn't have a magazine editorial in their portfolio.

____ Doesn't have an online portfolio.

____ Thinks Facebook is their website.

____ Constantly talks in technical terms you don't understand.

____ Often criticizes the work of their peers.

____ Takes days to return emails, phone calls and texts or doesn't return them at all.

____ Thinks they're a better makeup, hair, fashion stylist or manicurist than you are.

____ Brings you on the job but doesn't trust you to do your job.

____ Doesn't get booked on paid jobs but is always afraid that someone is going to steal their images.

___ Often cancels at the last minute.

___ There is never any food or drink on the set.

___ Is not Photoshop proficient but insists on touching up their photos which results in over-retouching or mediocre work.

___ Unwilling to use a professional retoucher, even when retouching is not their strong suit.

___ Not proficient in lighting.

___ Thinks that beauty shots are simply wide shots cropped tight.

___ Edits the images down to a small selection of their choices for you to choose from.

___ Makes you wait for months to get your retouched images.

___ Has the images from the test up on their website and Instagram months before they give them to you.

___ Doesn't understand that your portfolio image needs are different from theirs.

___ Uses excessive "locker room" talk that makes the set environment uncomfortable.

___ Is not growing creatively from the standpoint of their lighting, editing or photo quality.

___ Only shoots one type of model.

Glamour Shots, Boudoir And Pin-Up Portraits

No offense to the glamour shots, boudoir and pin-up photographers of the world, but getting work in that genre of the industry is not serviced by this book. That said, I am all for you working on jobs that are going to help you become a better artist, provide you with more experience and compensate you while you're doing it. In fact, Ariana Grande's makeup artist, Daniel Chinchilla whom I interviewed for this book, got his start doing what he calls weekend glamour parties where he did makeup on 20 women in a day. Be encouraged. Everyone starts somewhere.

The Photographer Psyche

Photographers with names like Steven Meisel, Mario Testino, Annie Leibovitz, Patrick Demarchelier, and Mike Ruiz have glam squads that they have been working with for years. They demand that specific people work with them at all times, and have been known to reschedule shoots when their favorite artists are unavailable.

Seem unfair? Only when you're not on that list, huh? In the first five years of building your book, it's likely that you may not work with a photographer at this level. If you do, it's often because you have been brought in by a celebrity and their glam squad request trumps what the photographer wants.. This would happen with an artist who works with a celebrity at the level of Beyonce, Ariana Grande, Charlize Theron, Mariah Carrey, etc.

For the artist, this is a golden opportunity. We all have to get in where we fit in. What matters most is that you are up to bat.

Titilayo Bankole
Manicurist
TitilayoBankole.com
Focus: Fashion, Beauty
& Commercial
IG: @titilayomanicurist

ADVICE

I began this freelance manicurist journey in 2010. In the beginning, I tested with photographers every chance I got. It took almost three years before I was signed by my agent. During that time, I experienced an up-hill battle with fear and confidence. Once I decided to work through my fears, one of my PYP sisters helped me design my comp cards and I started sending them out to agencies, magazines, and photographers.

After three years of ups and downs, I was still working on my book when I received a phone call from an agency that was interested in representing me. A few weeks after that, a second and much bigger agency called me, scheduled a meeting and actually signed me on the spot. Today, I can say that when you package yourself the way Crystal shows you, you will be armed with everything you need and more to succeed as a freelance artist.

Start prepping yourself to hear the word NO because you are going to hear it from time to time. But use it like a light switch and flip it to "ON"! The key to making it in this business is persistence. Remember, NO spelled backward iss ON. Just keep ON keeping ON.

I have personally witnessed photographers being standoffish, even downright nasty to artists that were not part of their regular glam squad on a photo shoot. It's not fair, but it does happen. Remember that this is your chance to excel, shine, and dispel any notion that you are any less of an artist than their regular stylist just because you don't have a Vogue or Elle cover in your portfolio.

The trick, in such situation, is to make it clear that you are coming to the party and you are on the photographer's team.

One of the things photographers dislike about working on photo shoots with artists who have been chosen by the celebrity, is that [typically] when differences of opinion arise about the makeup, hair or styling direction of the photo shoot, the artist takes the side of the celebrity. This can handicap the photographer from creating that 'slice of wonderful' that they are known for and deliver with regularity when they are working with 'their own team.'

A hypothetical scenario with our hair stylist, Denise, could go something like this:

Photographer: Denise, we're going for a 60s retro look, and I would like to do something with a part down the middle of Beyonces hair. Something like what Cher or Ali McGraw would have done in 1963.

Denise: [smugly] She doesn't like to wear her hair like that.

STOP! WRONG ANSWER. *You'll never get back into the studio with that attitude. Let's try again.*

Photographer: Denise, we're going for a 60s retro look, and I would like to do something with a part down the middle of Beyonces hair. Something like what Cher or Ali McGraw would have done in 1963.

Denise: Oh, (Mr. Photographer) that sounds great. I've been dying to try some new things with her hair. She doesn't like a lot of change, but I think I can get her to do it for you. Do you think I could meet the fashion stylist and take a look at the clothes first? Then I can see where you really want to go with the hair and create something wonderful for you.

At that moment, the photographer has an inkling that you may be on his side, and whether the celebrity allows you to part her hair down the middle or not doesn't matter because the photographer believes that you are working with him to make it happen.

This may just be the first test of the day. All of your actions will answer these questions in the photographer's mind:

- Do you get along with the rest of his regular crew?
- Did you understand the direction, after listening to the photographer and speaking with the fashion stylist?
- Are you personable?
- Are you offering up creative suggestions and solutions?
- Are you assisting the photographer in his or her efforts to get the subject to buy into his vision for the day's shoot?
- Are you a team player?
- Are you attentive?
- Are you cool?
- Do you know fashion or beauty?

Take it all in, stride and think of it as a rite of passage. You're not being singled out. It happens to everyone. I'll share a story with you.

Many years ago, while representing photographers, the photo director for a popular entertainment magazine gave my photographer, David Roth, an assignment to shoot a little-known actor for a small feature in the magazine—another rite of passage.

Even though we were already shooting celebrities for other magazines, those weren't her magazine. The photo director's message was clear; you perform well on this little assignment, and I'll give you something a little bigger next time, and so on.

Many photographers choke upon getting their big break to shoot for a major magazine. Photo directors can ill afford the expense of a photographer screwing up a cover, any more than a photographer can afford to have a fashion stylist pull the wrong clothes, or the makeup artist put clumpy mascara on an actress like Jennifer Garner.

Don't be surprised if a photographer gives you the same test that the photo director gave us. Take that small job. Be excellent and the next day, send a hand-written thank-you card, add a little follow-up, and you will more than likely get another chance to work with that photographer or that client on another project. If you are not sure what I mean, fast forward to Page 237 in Chapter 6 and read Career Building Blocks by Celebrity Makeup Artist Monifa Mortis.

Following are some things you can do before, during and after the photo session to ensure yourself a second opportunity.

Terria Fontaine

Hair & Makeup Artist

Chicago

TerriaFontaine.com

IG: terriafontaine

ADVICE

As an advertising executive in charge of beauty accounts, I was surrounded by hair and makeup artists, manicurists, and wardrobe stylists.

Looking back, I realize that I chose a career in advertising because it allowed me to live vicariously through my true love—hair and makeup artists.

As time moved on, I began to feel like there was some part of me that had never been fully realized, at least not in the way I wanted deep down. The artist in me was screaming to be set free! In my corporate role, I built a reputation on being the one who kept an eye on the budget, required strict adherence to strategy, and who, at times, repressed the creative process in order to please my client! I followed artists careers, and read the 2nd and 3rd editions of the book you are now reading. Things began to change, when I allowed myself to think, "I am an artist." A passage from the Bible became my mantra; "As a man thinketh, so is he!"

I changed my thoughts. It was not too late! By executing the steps in the 'Guide,' following the lead of other successful artists and building on what I'd learned as an advertising executive and yes, as a fly on the wall in the glam rooms, I began to grow my freelance career as a hair and makeup artist. Today, I am well on my way to achieving my goals. Be encouraged. Change your thinking. It is NEVER too late!

SUCCESS = OPPORTUNITY + PREPARATION

Before The Session

Get the photographers name and do your homework. Familiarize yourself with the photographer's work—easy enough to do on Google and LeBook.com. Jot down 2-3 projects the photographer has worked on in the last few months, make a note of his favorite makeup, hair, fashion stylists and manicurists and be prepared to use the information to engage when you speak with him.

If you were booked by the celebrities' manager or publicist, request the name of the creative person in charge of producing the photo shoot. This might turn out to be the art director, photo editor/director, fashion or beauty editor. Call and introduce yourself. Let them know that you've never worked with the photographer before and you were wondering if you could get a little background so you can familiarize yourself with his work. This knowledge will give you a leg up and something to talk about before or during the photo shoot.

I call this leveling the playing field. Almost everyone is flattered when you know something about them and their work. At this point, you know more about the photographer than he knows about you.

The Day Of The Session

Arrive at the shoot at least 30 minutes early to set up. Introduce yourself to the photographer and anyone else on the crew that you don't know. Be friendly and pleasant regardless of the reception you receive. Remember, it's all a test.

Use the information you gathered about those 2-3 projects to strike up a conversation with the photographer if he isn't too busy. Mention the recent work that you discovered, and be prepared to share what you loved about it. Arm yourself with a couple of questions to engage the photographer. People love to talk about themselves.

Now is also a good time to discuss the direction of the shoot if you haven't done so in advance, or to clarify that nothing has changed since your conversation. Don't be afraid to ask the photographer to show you what he wants.

During The Session

During a photo session that lasts all day, there will be opportunities for you to assess how your work is being perceived by the photographer and his crew. Be confident, and don't be afraid to offer up suggestions when you think they are appropriate and will benefit the common goal.

After The Session

1 Be sure to make the rounds, shake hands or hug everyone and let them know how great it was to work with them.

2 Mail the photographer a hand-written thank-you card and don't ask for anything.

3 A week or so later, send the photographer an email, restating how much you enjoyed the shoot and requesting the photographer to take a look at your online portfolio and mention that his feedback would be much appreciated.

4 A couple of weeks after that, send one of your comp cards, wait 2-3 days and follow up with a phone call.

5 Once a month and for the next 12 months, shoot over a short email that says something like, "Hope to work with you again one day. Here's some of my recent work."

Remember, that no today is ON tomorrow. Don't give up. Persistence is KING!

NOTES

....

....

....

....

....

....

....

10 Tips For Getting To 1st Base With Photographers

1 Do your homework! Spend time researching the photographers you want to work with. Query them on Google, visit their website, and come up with two questions to ask that will engage them on the phone. Write down something that inspires you on their website, and be prepared to share how it touched you.

2 Recognize that photographers who shoot fashion have a point of view, and are influenced by magazines like French and Italian Vogue, Elle, Bazaar and W.

3 Curate your portfolio and Instagram for the kinds of photographers that you're showing your work to. Don't turn a fashion photographer off by showing catalog shots and posed test photos, or a lifestyle photographer off by showing them a portfolio full of CD covers of rappers.

4 Be prepared to talk about what you did to enhance and contribute to the shoots in your portfolio!

5 Have answers to these 5 questions from a photographer:

1. How did you contribute to the vision for this shoot?"

2. If you could change one thing about this shoot, what would it be?

3. What are your three favorite fashion magazines?

4. Where do you go for inspiration?

5. What do you enjoy working on most?

6 Remain positive in the face of on-set mishaps. The best photo shoots are 80% good planning and 20% magic. No one wants to miss the wonderful accidents which can turn a good photo into a great one.

7 If you're an artist—CREATE! The most creative photographers look for artists who can come up with wonderful, off-the-wall combinations, interesting twists and new ways to do, show and present things.

8 Collaborate. When you meet or talk with the photographer, be prepared to come up with ideas—it will make you part of the creative process.

9 Create your own notebook or vision board of ideas you're dying to try out. Sharing it with photographers can inspire them to want work with you. If your focus is fashion, stay current on what's going on in the U.S. and European worlds of fashion and beauty by studying major and underground fashion magazines.

10 READ magazines that are pertinent and crucial to the success of your business. Read and study Photo District News (pdnonline.com). It's an invaluable resource that will give you a bird's-eye view of what's going on in photography, how photographers approach their business and how they think.

NOTES

....

....

....

....

....

....

The majority of clients we deal with just want people to hang with all day who have the right personality, do their job really well and quick, and don't demand attention.

—Frank Moore

Agent Celestine

5

Agency Representation

Finding the agency that is best suited to your needs, temperament, and personality requires some research, leg work, and a bit of detective work. There are hundreds of agencies throughout the U.S. and abroad. Each has its own market focus. Because of that, the agents recruit to serve the client base within that market focus. By focus we mean beauty, fashion, lifestyle, catalog, corporate, entertainment, ecommerce, etc.

An agency's physical size is determined by the number of artists it represents. Large agencies often keep a roster of forty or more artists. A small boutique agency may represent only five or ten artists.

Frank Moore

Agent

Celestine Agency, Los Angeles

Size is one thing, prestige is another. Cloutier Remix, Celestine and Opus Beauty are among the largest and most prestigious agencies for makeup, hair, styling and nails in Los Angeles. In New York, Bryan Bantry, The Magnet Agency, and The Wall Group are among the heavy hitters. Between them, they garner the greatest number of high-profile editorial, fashion, celebrity and beauty campaign bookings on the west and east coasts. It is rare that you open a magazine like Vogue, Elle, W, InStyle, Esquire, Essence or Rolling Stone and don't see at least one of these agencies beside the name of a glam squad artist. Their client lists read like a Who's Who Behind the Scenes in Beauty, Fashion and Entertainment.

HOW AGENCIES WORK

An agency is a firm whose job it is to secure work for the talent it represents. That is if you have a client list and a portfolio that demonstrates experience, good taste, versatility, imagination, personal style and range. Oh, and as of late—more than a few social media followers.

A good agency should:

- Provide sound & honest advice regarding your career.

- Procure and securely book jobs on your behalf.

- Create new opportunities for you.

- Confirm your booked jobs with a deal memo.

- Verify and submit your on-page credits to magazines.

- Promote your talent to new and existing clients.

- Circulate your online portfolio to new and existing clients.

- Update your résumé.

- Negotiate fees, expenses, and travel arrangements on your behalf.

- Collect your fees and expenses.

- Issue and follow up on all outstanding invoices.

- Pay out fees and expenses within 14 working days of receipt and clearing the bank.

- Discuss goals, direction and new opportunities with you at least twice a year.

Sounds great, doesn't it? It is, when it works. For many a talented and lucky artist, this is exactly the way it happens. Be forewarned, however, that agencies are in the business of getting work for people who already have work.

For many artists, the agency search becomes a frustrating Catch 22. You can't get an agency without a great portfolio, and many artists believe that you can't get a great portfolio without an agency. You can build a portfolio on your own, and you will have to, if your goal is to be signed by a top agency.

It's not callous, it's just business. The makeup, hair and styling industry is a multi-million-dollar business. With that many decimal points and commas at stake, the owners are not playing around when it comes to their talent acquisitions (signings). They are looking for tearsheets, talent, credits and a growing social media following that they can market right along with that fabulous portfolio.

The Brass Ring

Competition is stiff among the top agencies, and every agency owner and division head is keeping an eye open for the next Kevin Aucoin, Bobbi Brown, Pat McGrath, Patricia Fields, Deborah Lipmann, Sir John or Oscar James. Sports teams aren't the only organizations looking for the first-round draft pick. Owners are looking for the two or three stars who exude that mysterious "X" factor, and Instagram, "the Mother of all agencies," as NY-based photographer Mike Ruiz put it, has made the task easier than ever. Not only can you see what an artist has to offer creatively, you can friend and follow them right to the club. As an artist who wants to get picked up, you might not want to be holding your dress up over your head while standing on top of that cocktail table if you're hoping to get signed by Bryan Bantry in New York. It's not a good look.

Representing artists who are liked and desired by the hottest photographers, models, clients, and celebrities can propel an agency from obscurity to stardom, and put the agency's name on the lips of every art director, fashion editor, photographer and commercial director within three thousand miles.

Many agency owners feel that the time they once had to groom an aspiring artist has gone the way of conducting business with a simple handshake. Deal memos, invoices, contracts, liability insurance, social media and issues of workers' compensation for freelance artists can fill up many hours of an agency owner's work day, leaving little time to coach and mentor the rising star. It's a matter of economics. You are obligated to keep the workers working, and that leaves little time for pampering and grooming newcomers with potential.

Frank Moore, *Agent, Celestine Agency*

Frank Moore is a top agent at the well-respected Celestine Agency in Los Angeles. For the last 24 years, he has developed and represented some of the industry's best makeup, hair, styling, nails, and set design talent. Having worked first as a model and then an agent, he can easily pinpoint the artists who will rise to the top. Frank shares how he began his career and what he looks for in new artists.

How did you end up becoming an agent at Celestine?

Frank: It's a funny story. When I was in high school, the local mall was holding a casting call for a big fashion show. I wasn't really into it, but my friends insisted that I go and I ended up getting chosen to do the show. Some photographers saw me and asked me to test with them. Elite Model Management ended up seeing my photos and called me in. I really didn't want to do it, but eventually, they persuaded me to come in. I told them that the only way I would do it, is if they would send me to Paris or London within two months. I was in Paris two weeks later.

I modeled for two years but didn't really like it. I started to go to school for physical therapy but stayed in contact with the contacts I had made while in the business. This led to me becoming an assistant for a variety of people in the industry. I assisted stylists, photographers, and did a lot of freelance work. At one point, I wanted to dedicate myself to representing photographers. I ended up getting a job with LA Models as an agent and worked there from 1988 until 1992. Earlier on, I had become good friends

The Agency Search: What To Look For

The relationship between an artist and an agent is a partnership. An artist should therefore look for some of the same qualities in an agent that you find valuable in a friend or partner. Here are three things to consider:

 RESOURCES

Does the agency have resources that you don't? A good partner should have a strong business network, industry connections, a great client list, credentials and expertise that can raise your value and your profile over time.

 ETHICS

Is the agency known for practicing good business ethics? In other words, are they honest, do they pay in a timely manner and will they be forthright with your clients about your availability when one of your clients calls and asks for you specifically? You should enter into a business partnership only with someone you trust. A bad partner with a bad reputation will use you and steal from you.

3 **RESPECT**

Do you respect the agency, its owner and the agents (bookers) who will be handling your business and your career? Never get into bed with someone you don't hold in high regard.

Looking For An Agency: Whose Choice Is It Anyway?

The choice is yours and theirs. The search for an agency should be handled in much the same way you would look for a job. You've got to do your homework, be nosy, talk to artists who are happy at the agency, and find out if there is any movement—are they adding new talent to the roster? Is there talk of anyone leaving? Are there any rumblings that the agency might be looking for new talent?

Notice I said, "Talk to artists who are happy." If there's one thing I learned during my first divorce it is, if you want to stay married, talk to people who have been happily married for 20 or 30 years. They're the only people who can help you with your relationship. In turn, if you're interested in working with a specific agency, be sure to talk to the artists who have been there for 10+ years and are still happy. They will give you the straight skinny, and they don't become insecure every time the agency takes on a new artist.

Take The Meeting

So, you got the interview. Now what? Agents respond better to artists who have taken the time to learn something about the agency, are professional and have some questions of their own. The biggest mistake an artist can make while looking for an agency is to treat it like a crap shoot—happy that someone, anyone will take them.

An interview in person, over the phone or on facetime is a two-way street. The agent is going to ask questions to learn about you, your focus, your motivation, your skills and your dreams—where do you see yourself in five years? You in turn should have some prepared questions ready to ask the agent about the company, the founders, their philosophy, their plans for the future and how they see you fitting in.

NOTES

with Angelica at Celestine, and she kept offering to bring me on board. I finally decided to make a move, and I've been with Celestine as an agent for 24 years!

What do you love about working at Celestine?

Frank: I just really like the artists. I feel an obligation to them and really admire them for dealing with the ups and downs of freelancing in the industry. I know how hard it can be for them.

Have you ever been disappointed in an artist?

Frank: Have you ever been disappointed in a relationship? [laughs] I haven't actually been disappointed by one of my artists. I think everything is relative. I know that I am dealing with adults, not kids, and they are just trying to run a business with my help. We have to respect each other like in a relationship. I can't strong arm them. They are professionals. The only time I get disappointed is when one of my artists doesn't book a job that I know they deserved.

What has been your greatest joy working as an agent?

Frank: I think just looking back and thinking about all of the bookings we've made happen. Being able to achieve all of those successes. I love sitting with a colleague and talking about all of those moments and looking back on them with pride and satisfaction.

What do you think has changed in the past 5-7 years about how you do your job?

Frank: Not that much is different except for the

Following is a list of actions you should take before approaching an agency for representation:

STEP 01
Find out as much as you can about each of the agencies you are interested in signing with. Learn something about their track record, their philosophy, the kind of work they do, and their specific requirements for signing an artist.

STEP 02
Be ready to tell the owner or division head why you would be an asset to the agency, the contribution you can make, and how you see yourself fitting in to their current roster.

STEP 03
Be prepared to talk about the work in your portfolio, the creative choices you've made, and what your creative contribution was to the editorial stories, test photographs and commercial assignments in your book.

STEP 04
Make a list of recent or upcoming paid and unpaid job assignments that will soon produce new tests or tearsheets for your portfolio. Know the names of the photographers, art directors, producers and editors that you have worked with.

STEP 05
Create a résumé of two pages or less. Make sure it lists all of the most notable photographers, directors, celebrities, and recording artists as well as the most current and prestigious magazines, catalogs, e-commerce, print ads, television commercials and music

videos, feature films and television shows you've worked on. Also include your Instagram social media statistics and mention growth if you are experiencing some.

STEP 06
If you have a YouTube channel, teach classes, or get asked to speak at events like The Makeup Show or the International Beauty Show—tell the interviewer. These kinds of activities and commitments demonstrate your drive to succeed and your interest in expanding beyond your day-to-day freelance gigs. It's very sexy.

STEP 07
Don't bother mentioning or showing work that has appeared in publications like The Enquirer, Star, People (in most cases), or Soap Opera Digest. These publications are not highly regarded.

STEP 08
Keep catalog work separate from the rest of your portfolio unless you are showing your book to an agency whose work is primarily catalog and e-commerce based.

STEP 09
Prepare some questions of your own that you would like to ask the agent. Following is some food for thought:

Ask what kind of work you could expect to get from the agency. You want to know what they can offer you, and how they would promote you. Find out who pays for what when it comes to advertising and expenses like the website, and who is responsible for collecting your tearsheets and work for your online reel. Find out how many artists they represent and how many agents are on staff. Be confident but not cocky. Be enthusiastic but not overly eager. Don't slouch. Present a firm, not crushing, handshake.

Look the person in the eye and don't apologize for anything that is in your portfolio. If you have to give disclaimers every time the agent clicks on a page, you're not ready for representation. Let your personality show through so they will know who and what they are going to get. Wear something to the interview that makes you look and feel successful.

While shopping for an agency, keep in mind that it's a buyer's market. There are ten times as many artists as there are agencies, and the competition is stiff. Put your best foot forward and keep it there. If you are serious about being in this industry, learn your craft, execute like a pro, stay ready and take the time to look like you belong. You never know who's watching or referring you for the position of your life!

NOTES

....

....

....

....

....

oversaturation we are seeing. There are more artists and agencies, but the same number of clients. I do think that the market might be correcting itself though. Everyone thinks they can do makeup now and put their work online, but you have to ask yourself if it will hold up in a studio. People who don't have a beauty school background, who haven't really worked hard and invested in their craft will weed themselves out.

Has social media has changed how you do your job?

Frank: Well, I think you have to accept the threat that clients might hire someone off social media to save money, but in the end, they won't be dealing with the same level of talent we have. Sometimes, my artists lose jobs to the Instagram artists, but it's not because of talent. It's a budget issue.

Have you had clients who have chosen to go the cheaper route come back to you for a better artist?

Frank: Yes. A lot of times, clients end up having to retouch so much that the money they saved on the artist they now have to spend on Photoshop, or on overtime. They end up seeing that it's not worth saving money on the front end.

So, what hasn't changed about how you do your job?

Frank: The importance of personal connection, relationship building, and the responsibility I feel towards my artists.

What to Do When You Don't Get Signed

Every agency has its own style, personality and market focus. Each one is looking for something different when it comes to signing artists to its roster. The ideal artist must possess a body of work that can be sold immediately within the agency's existing market. Next, the artist's personality, creativity, work and personal style must mix well with the agency owner's vision of their brand, what the agency represents, and how it is perceived in the marketplace.

Finally, the artist and their work must compliment the agency's existing cadre of talent and fill an existing need, or the looming potential of an upcoming need—perhaps someone is leaving soon, or a recently-won contract is going to require more artistic power in a particular area, for instance e-commerce. That need can be different things at different times.

For instance, if an agency determines that it is missing opportunities in the e-comm market, it may decide to take the following actions:

1	Assess its current roster to determine which of its artists can move into that area so they can generate more bookings and revenue.
2	Do an online review of the books and/or comp cards they have received from artists who have [already] submitted their portfolios (online or in person) and are interested in joining the agency.
3	Put an agency staff person in charge of sourcing talent with e-commerce credentials (work) on Instagram.

If your book had catalog or catalog-like work in it, you may get a call back from an agency whose needs are changing, even though you didn't get signed on the first visit.

Getting signed to the agency of your choice isn't just about having a great book. The large agencies have tons of great people with fabulous portfolios. Don't be discouraged if you aren't signed to the agency on your first meeting. I scheduled appointments with an artist three times before signing them. It's not personal. It's just business.

There can be several reasons why an agency may not take you on at that moment, the least of which is timing. What you should do is ask for constructive criticism about your portfolio, comp card, social media and yourself. The right advice can change everything, and asking will demonstrate to the agent that you are committed to making improvements.

If the agent says they like your work but the timing is bad, or that they are currently carrying another artist whose work is very similar to yours, then accept that answer for now. Be encouraged that the agency is showing interest in your work, and ask if it would be all right for you to follow up in a few months to show your new work and inquire about openings. Be sure to send a handwritten thank-you card within 2-3 days of the meeting, and send an email update every 30 days without fail. And don't stop just because you don't get a response. They're watching!

NOTES

Do you ever look on social media to find new artists?

Frank: Occasionally, but mainly if someone I trust recommends for me to check out an artist. I need to be able to know their background. For example, someone who does nails and posts it online may have talent, but do they also know the technical side of being a manicurist? I think so many of the people on social media are mainly influencers. They may have great pictures, but what happens when they show up on set? Can they work well with others? Do they have good set etiquette? Can they deliver? Not everything you see online transfers over to set.

Do you find that clients are asking for how many Instagram followers your artists have?

Frank: Some do. It's a form of advertising for them to have the artist post on their platforms. Just gives them more eyes on their products. So much advertising is done online too that people aren't buying magazines as much anymore, or watching TV commercials. It's all about those 5-second ads they scroll by on social media.

So, if an artist with a high number of followers gets booked, can they get paid more?

Frank: Yes. If an artist has a lot of followers and the client wants them to post on their platforms, then they are essentially asking for two services. So, they will pay for the makeup, as well as the post. It's a dual service.

How do you prefer to be contacted by artists?

Frank: Email. Just keep it short and simple and include a

If, on the other hand, they don't like your work, ask some open-ended questions:

> What do you like about my book?
>
> What didn't you like about my book?
>
> Where do you suggest I make changes?
>
> What specifically are you looking for?
>
> What about my work does not meet your needs?
>
> How did you feel about my social media presentation?
>
> Is there a required number of followers that I must have in order to be considered for representation?
>
> Can you give me any specific feedback that will help me to grow as an artist?

Answers to these questions will give you a better handle on what agencies are looking for and what the industry standards are that you will need to meet in order to get to the next level with or without an agency.

If in fact the agency seems genuinely interested in your work, but the timing may not be right and you are interested in assisting, ask to be added to their assistant roster.

Angelika, the president of Celestine, told me a great story of how an assistant fashion stylist performed so well on a shoot that the photographer called the agency and booked her to key a job.

If you don't get signed right away, STAY READY! There is always another day. Situations change, people come and go, they move out of state, have babies, get married, or change careers. If the agent likes your work, and you do a great job of staying in touch and keeping them updated, the call to join the agency could come sooner than you think.

COMPENSATION & EXPENSES
How It Works

Agencies are paid twice. Once by the artist, and once by the client. They are paid 20% by the artist and 20% by the client as an agency fee. Modeling agencies work the same way although the commission may be different.

When Do I Get Paid?

Most agencies pay their artists upon receipt of payment from the client. There are a few who pay on performance at the completion of a gig, but those arrangements are few and far between. A "pay on performance" system demands a hefty cash flow and can be extremely demanding of an agency's time and manpower, depending on the size of the talent base the agency maintains. If an agency represents 20 or more artists, stopping to write a check all day every day is a heavy burden on time and resources.

Most agencies write checks once each week. If the agency receives a check for you on Tuesday, your check is written on the upcoming Friday or the next Friday if it hasn't cleared the bank. However, a check that comes in on Thursday more than likely won't get paid until the NEXT Friday.

Agencies who do pay upon performance usually take an additional five percent commission and charge interest or an additional fee for doing so. Why? Because they haven't received the money from the client yet, and maybe never will. I'll leave that story to a live broadcast.

NOTES

link to your website. I want to see a full website. I need to be able to see what you do. A few pictures on Instagram is not going to be enough.

Do you have a preference for how an artist's online portfolio is arranged?

Frank: I want to see quality over quantity. I think artists should take time to look at the websites of the agencies they want to work with. They should gear their portfolios towards the people that they want to have represent them. You need to know what they want.

Do you have any advice for novice artists that are starting out and trying to make connections?

Frank: The number one thing is that they should know what they are capable of doing and what they are passionate about. Don't stop practicing. Know the difference between what you think you can do and what you can actually do. Go to school. Learn your craft. Study the history of it. Understand the products that you are working with. Get your license. Know that talent will only get you so far, that you also need to have a good personality and be easy to work with. Assist artists that you admire and really specialize in your craft. That way, you won't need to worry about any job that you walk in to.

Do you maintain a list of assistants for your bigger jobs?

Frank: Yes, but it a list of assistants that have been referred to us by our key artists.

When The Client Pays

Each industry has its own pay schedule. The following chart shows how most clients pay agencies and independent contractors. This list will assist you in creating your own personal accounts receivables calendar.

Accounts Receivable Schedule

CLIENT	PAY SCHEDULE
Record Companies	30 - 60 days
Advertising Agencies	45 - 60 days
Magazines - National	45 - 90 days
Magazines - International	90 - 120 days
Catalogs	30 - 45 days
Department Stores	30 - 45 days
E-Commerce	30 - 45 days
Production Companies Commercials	15 - 30 days
Production Companies Music Videos	15 - 45 days
Television	Weekly through payroll
Feature Film	Weekly through payroll

What Happened to My Check?

Artists spend a lot of time complaining about the money that is deducted from their checks. They often forget that while representing themselves, they shouldered these very same expenses. The bottom line—in addition to the commission, it isn't free to be in business and your agent isn't your employer. If the agency spends money on your behalf, they are going to deduct it from your check.

Breakdown of an Artist's Check

DESCRIPTION	ARTIST RECEIVES	AGENCY RECEIVES
MAKEUP ARTISTS FEE	$ 850.00	
20% Agency Commission (Artist)	-$ 170.00	-$ 170.00
20% Agency Commission (Client)	-$ 170.00	
SUB-TOTAL	$ 680.00	
Website Expense	-$ 25.00	
TOTAL AMOUNT DUE	**$ 655.00**	**$ 340.00**

Following is a list of monthly, bi-monthly or annual expenses that may be deducted from your check:

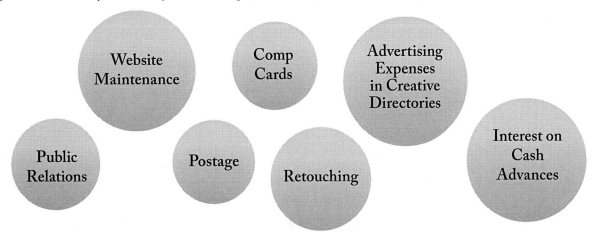

Website Maintenance

Comp Cards

Advertising Expenses in Creative Directories

Public Relations

Postage

Retouching

Interest on Cash Advances

What have been the top client complaints you've heard about an artist?

Frank: Not being attentive on set. That's really it.

What are your 3 top professional turn-offs from a freelance artist?

Frank: Being too pushy, too cocky, and ungrateful.

Is there anything else you want to say that could help empower a new freelance artist?

Frank: It takes more than talent to get you to the top. Learn to work through fear because one of the toughest things that keep people from succeeding is the fear of success. It leads to self-sabotage. It can take hold of your mindset and your personality. So, you need not lose sight of what you have; be grateful for it, and keep moving forward.

 celestineagency

 www.celestineagency.com

Money

There are up and down sides to agency affiliation. When you start asking around about the various agencies, you'll get mixed reviews depending on whom you ask. I have heard horror stories from artists who claim to have been ripped off financially by an agency, while others swear that their portfolios didn't get circulated enough. Buyer beware. There are three sides to every story—what the artist is saying, what the agency is saying and what really happened.

For every artist who claims to have been duped by an agency, there are a dozen very happy and successful artists thriving at the same agency. Artists blab on and on about how their agency didn't pay them, all the while leaving out the important details apparent in the story that follows:

> *One of the makeup artists I represented at Crystal Agency is still quite popular and well known. During the time that I represented her, she rarely took the time to record any of the paychecks we mailed to her. Consequently, she would call the agency week after week swearing that she hadn't been paid for something that we already had a cancelled check for. I got so fed up with the behavior and harassment of my bookkeeper that I had my booker schedule an office meeting wherein we presented her with all of her cancelled checks. Her mouth remained open so long I nearly had to pull a fly out of it. She just couldn't believe that she was unable to account for all of the money that she was spending faster than we put it in her hands.*

All the while, she was going around town blabbing to everyone she could tell that we were not paying her.

I'm sure you can see how this kind of loose-lipped badmouthing can be disastrous for a small agency attempting to sign new artists. You will surely meet a few of these on your way to agency representation. Beware of the one artist out of 20 who doth protest too much.

Many financially challenging situations are out of the agency's control. One agency owner shared a story about how, without paying its bill, a production company closed its doors and filed bankruptcy. The agency couldn't pay out what it didn't collect. The makeup artist was so angry after having worked on the television commercial for three days, she sent a messenger over to retrieve her portfolio. A year and a half later, the same makeup artist called and asked if the agency would take her back.

Just Plain Crazy

I once had an artist who would come by the agency and remove her books every couple of months and return them in a few days. It was always a drama. After the second time this happened, I realized that this is the way it was going to be and our entire staff would just ignore her.

She was a lovely high-strung British woman whom I loved representing until she lost her mind. When she came to me from the U.K. her book was absolutely beautiful but lacked

diversity. She said to me, "I want to do black gurlz. I want to put some black gurlz in my book."

At the time, we were doing covers, fashion and beauty for Essence magazine. While I did have to get on my knees once in the fashion department and beg the editor to hire her— after that, my artist was regularly booked to work on Essence projects.

It seemed that the more work we secured for her and the more money she made, the crazier she became. Early on she would call and praise me and the staff for all of the jobs we were getting for her and ALL of the great money she was making. In fact, on more than one occasion she would call me and say, "Crystal, no one has ever made me this much money." However, all at once one day we were on her s*!t list. We simply couldn't do anything right.

We soon parted company and the next thing I heard, she was going around Los Angeles telling everyone that I hadn't made her any money. I did what any smart business woman would do: I called my attorney. He sent her a cease and desist letter and all of that talk stopped.

The moral of this story: There are some things worth balling your fists up about, and someone trying to sabotage your ability to make money and sign new talent is one of them.

The Hair Makeup & Fashion Styling Career Guide

Monae Everett
Hair & Makeup Artist
New York, NY
www.MonaeEverett.com
Focus: Lifestyle, On Camera
IG: MonaeArtistry

ADVICE

I began in Washington, DC as a hair stylist and developed a love for makeup. I thought I would only be an artist while in college, but after graduation, I realized that there was a world of opportunity outside of the salon. Awesome because working in a salon was never my passion. So I made a plan, and worked it.

I lived off my tips in the salon and banked the rest. I took every client or photo shoot (paid or unpaid) that came my way. I also worked for a haircare company and became an educator for their product line. Working for a corporation was challenging, and taught me that I wanted to work for myself. During a corporate restructure, I decided to take my show on the road, and I move to New York alone.

That bank of tips I saved made it possible for me to live on my own in NY and work with agencies. I've worked on magazine editorials and with celebrities that I only dreamed of meeting. I also combined my communications degree with my love of beauty and created a beauty blog and YouTube channel.

I will leave you with this; iIIf you want it bad enough, you will sacrifice, plan, and work to make it happen.

Taxes & The IRS

Ah yes, the Internal Revenue Service. The two forms that you should become familiar with are the W-9 and 1099-MISC forms. As business entities, agencies are required to file form 1099-MISC for each person to whom it has paid at least $600.00 in income during a calendar year. Income is reported in Box #7 (non-employee compensation) of the 1099 form. Box #7 indicates to the IRS that the recipient (that's you) is subject to self-employment tax.

Most agencies will have you fill out a W-9 form the moment you sign with them. The W-9 form is a request for your taxpayer identification number and certification. The tax identification number (Tax I.D. #) in the case of most artists is usually their social security number. The purpose of the W-9 form is to certify that:

1. the Tax I.D. number you are giving is correct

2. you are not subject to backup withholding.

Freelancers are independent contractors, and not employees of the agencies who represent them. As independent contractors, you are responsible for paying your own taxes. When you receive your check from the agency, none of the taxes will be taken out.

Buyer beware. Get a good accountant and pay your taxes.

NOTES

ARTIST CLIENT RELATIONS
The Client Come-On

A common situation encountered by artists after signing with an agency is what I call the "Client Come On." Symptoms include, but are not limited to, clients who initiate the following activities and conversations with artists:

- The client insists on calling you at home to find out your availability for a job after you've told them repeatedly to contact your agency directly.

- The client suggests that since they have a really small budget on this job, it would be helpful if they could bypass the agency just this once.

- The client drags the artist into a hallway or separate room before, during or after concept meetings and insists that your agency is going to ruin your career if they continue to charge these exorbitant day rates for your services.

- The client suggests that they could pay you more, and hire you more often, if they didn't have to pay that pesky 20% agency fee.

And the list goes on. Throughout your career you will be forced to listen to a host of decision-makers complain about paying the agency's 20% commission on top of your fee, even though they learned about and hired you through your agency.

It's a test of your character and your will. Young children try their parents in much the same way. They push and push to see just how much pressure you can take before you give in. This can be a difficult aspect of agency life until you become skilled at dealing with the "Client Come-On."

NOTES

The process often leads to uncertainty in the mind of the artist, internal upheaval, and short-term memory, better known as the "What has my agency done for me lately?" syndrome. In my Win Now Mentorship Program, celebrity makeup artist Renny Vasquez and I discuss a concept we call, "Trick or Treat," that helps an artist discern whether they are about to treat themselves with an opportunity, or trick themselves out of one. Trust me, falling prey to the client's advances when your real relationship is with your agency is definitely a trick. Don't fall for it! Artists often justify their actions by thinking:

- Well, I'm only going to do it this once.

- My agency will never miss the booking, it's only $500.00.

- They have fifteen other artists, they won't miss this little bit of money.

- Who's going to find out anyway?

- I give them all my other bookings, what harm will it do?

The choice is, and always will be, yours. Succumb, and you run the risk of getting caught, being in violation of a written or verbal agreement with your agency, and being summarily dismissed from the roster. Is it worth it? Probably not. Either way, you won't be the first or the last artist forced to take a stand with or against his or her agency. It is both a legal and moral decision. Consider this:

I was introduced to a hair stylist. At the time, he was working in a trendy West Los Angeles hair salon and had never been with an agency, nor had he ever done any commercial work.

He had begun to do a little testing with some model friends of his. Most of the pictures he had taken himself.

We exchanged phone numbers and a couple of days later he visited me at the agency. I reviewed his portfolio which at that time had about eight test shots in it. His talent was apparent. We spent over an hour at the agency discussing how the agency worked, what was expected of him, and what I could do for him. We agreed to begin pursuing a professional artist/agency relationship.

On the day we met, he was making $46.00 per head for a shampoo and blow dry. Within three months I was getting him $700.00 - $850.00 per day. During this time, he met another artist whom he allowed to influence him regarding his career. Sometime around the fourth and fifth months, he became so full of himself that his behavior became unbearable to me and my staff. He became very mean-spirited and started ordering everyone at the agency around. Unfortunately, this transformation came along with his new stardom and the star company he began to keep.

One day I received a phone call from a well-known publicist who represented a celebrity whose hair my artist had allegedly just done—without my knowledge. The publicist was outraged by the amount of the bill, $1,050.00 for three hours work.

We had worked with this PR firm before and the publicist had always known us to be fair and honest, so he called me. Since I had no idea what the publicist was talking about, I asked him to email me a copy of the bill. I was shocked to find that not only had the artist circumvented the agency by accepting the booking without our knowledge, he had tacked on a 20 % billing fee.

I contacted the artist immediately and requested his presence in my office where untold amounts of drama, denial and then arrogance ensued.

The client refused to pay the artist without us. I sent the client a new bill from the agency, collected our commission and, once paid, instructed the artist to pick up his portfolios.

Was it worth it? You would have to ask him.

NOTES

....

....

....

....

Tania Russell

Makeup Artist
Los Angeles
www.MakeupWerks.com
Focus: Commercial Beauty & Lifestyle
IG: tdrussellmua

ADVICE

I remember getting my first copy of the Career Guide like it was yesterday. I loved reading the interviews of working makeup and hair stylists, and photographers. Part of me was excited at the new opportunities, but the other – larger – part was apprehensive and a bit scared; all of these people's stories were so different from my own. They all seemed to know right from jump street exactly what they were meant to do, and they all (seemingly) got to the top in a straight line of success. My own story was nothing like that.

My advice is to be and stay true to yourself. Be who you are because there is room for all of us. There is no certain way you have to be, and no one path you have to follow to be successful. Your personality will guide you to the areas of this profession that are right for you.

I am born and raised in Los Angeles, California—the Entertainment Capital of the world. Early in my career I tried my best to "fit in" with the celebrity crowd and for real—that's just not me. I also do not care for working on films. What's a makeup artist to do? It took a few stops and starts and twists and turns but I DID find my niche—beauty-commercial-lifestyle. Once I did, everything fell into place. I have a successful career that feels like me."

TO BE OR NOT TO BE
Commitment

The decision to join an agency is the first step towards commitment with a business entity that will represent you, and handle your money. Once an artist says, "I do", so to speak, they have made a conscious choice to put in their time, tough out the rough spots, and work out the inevitable disagreements with the agency for at least the term of the agreement which may be one, two or three years.

Most agents are very good about sitting down with an artist and explaining how the agency works, what is expected of you upon joining the agency, and all the terms and conditions that apply once you sign on. In turn, this kind of meeting provides the artist with the same opportunity to get their questions answered.

Financial Considerations

The financial commitment for an artist (giving up 20%) can be the most difficult aspect of joining an agency. This of course depends on where you are in your career. A new artist usually has little or no concern about handing over the 20% commission to his or her new agency because 20% of their jobs seems a small price to pay for the benefits of joining an agency that will also get them work.

On the other hand, the established artist with a portfolio full of Vogue and Elle tearsheets, high-paying advertising clients and a five-figure beauty contract has some very different issues.

Artists often wonder how much work the agency will generate for them, whether or not the agency will give their established clients to other artists, if the agency will take 20% of their existing clients and bring nothing more to their bottom line, and how their existing clients will respond to working with the agent after having dealt directly with the artist for years? These are genuine concerns that must be weighed carefully against the benefits of agency representation. A well-established artist may want to discuss what should and should not go through the agency. The artists' arguments usually include topics such as:

- People the artist knew and clients they had before joining the agency.

- Whether or not jobs that pay small amounts should go through the agency.

- A possible reduction in agency commission for the clients they are bringing to the agency.

- Commission rates for different segments of the industry.

When you join an agency, you enter into a partnership. Like in any partnership there is give and take, and rules governing the relationship. In return for bringing your existing clients and relationships to the agency, you will receive a manager, negotiator, career advisor, collection agency, more work, better work, the prestige of being signed to a reputable agency, and, in many instances, more money from your existing clients.

Getting together with an agency will not come without its up and downs. Like any other relationship, there are stages.

NOTES

Reesa Mallen
Creative Director
www.theinkedjewess.com
Focus: Fashion
IG: the_inked_jewess

ADVICE

Once you have the technical skills down, be pleasant and positive. People like me (photographers, producers, fashion editors, video directors, and art directors) who hire people like you, have to like you. Nobody wants to spend 8-18 hours a day with a whiner. This is, after all, show business, folks! Bring a good attitude, be a team player and know your job. And no matter how negative the director, model, or artist working next to you becomes hour after hour, don't let them get to you!

Don't count anyone out. The guy standing at the craft services table all day munching on the fat- free pretzels and red vines may be the one who chose you for the job you're working on, and he may be checking you out and trying to decide if he wants to book you for Beyoncé's next music video.

Test. Test. Test. Believe in yourself. If you have confidence in yourself, we will too!

Stages of a Professional Relationship

1	**DATING** To meet	I like you.
2	**COMMITMENT** A pledge, engagement or contract	I am bound.
3	**CONVERSATION** To talk; exchange thoughts and feelings	We are speaking to each other.
4	**MISCOMMUNICATION** To misunderstand	It's what I said, but it's not what I meant.
5	**DISAPPOINTMENT** To frustrate; fail to satisfy	I don't feel satisfied.
6	**COMMUNICATION** Readily and clearly understood	I feel connected.
7	**UNDERSTANDING** Perceive; comprehend; know; grasp	I know what you mean.
8	**PARTNERSHIP** A contract	We're in this thing together.

Personally, in my boutique agency, I could ill-afford to have everyone playing by different rules, with different deals and different commission structures. It would have spelled disaster for me. Eventually, one artist finds out that their buddy at the agency is only paying a 10% commission and they are paying 20%. The rumors start to fly, everyone becomes dissatisfied and, the next thing you know, your booker is opening up her own agency and taking all of the artists with her because she promised everyone that that would never happen at Kramer & Kramer.

I bring this up because I want you to understand that in order for the agency to work for everyone, everyone must play by the same rules. It's best when everyone gets to complain about the same 20%.

In the spirit of most things being negotiable, what an artist can do is suggest a trial period of six months wherein if the new partnership isn't working for all parties concerned, everyone walks away with whatever they brought to the relationship. No harm. No foul.

THE ASSISTANTS LIST

While most agencies don't publicize this fact, some create, keep and make available to their artists lists of possible assistants. The key to getting on the assistant list is to be persistent without being a stalker. Contact once a month is all most agents can take. Initiate contact in the following manner:

STEP 01	Once each month, contact the agency by email and include links to your website and comp card and résumé or growing list of credits. In your email, be specific about who you would like to assist and why. No one can wrap their head around, "I just want to assist anyone."
STEP 02	Within 2-3 days after sending the email, follow up with a telephone call and leave a pleasant message even if you don't speak with anyone. This will give the agent an opportunity to connect with your voice.
STEP 03	Repeat the process by sending a monthly update until you get added to the list.

The key to making it in this or any business is perseverance. You will hear NO from time to time. Remember that NO spelled backwards is ON. So, keep ON keeping ON. Besides, NO is not personal, and usually has nothing to do with you. If an agent is having a particularly hectic day, NO can sound like NO! It just means call back tomorrow. Acknowledge that today may not be such a good day, verbalize that you will call again, and when you do, open your conversation with a little light fare such as: "You sounded really busy the other day, have things calmed down a bit for you?"

Nicole Jay

Makeup Artist
New York
nicolejay.com
Focus: Fashion & Beauty
IG: nicolejaybeauty

ADVICE

When I began my journey after years of working as a physical therapist, I didn't know where to start or how to go about building a career as a makeup artist. I had a vision of what I wanted to do but really didn't know how to go about getting there.

Starting seemed overwhelming until Crystal helped me to break down and navigate the steps needed to build my portfolio, develop an online presence, and grow my freelance business.

It's important to realize that building your career is a PROCESS. It is not something that happens overnight. There are no real days off. Each day, you have to put in some work that will benefit your future. That might be sending emails, making follow-up calls, networking, studying products, planning for your next job or reaching out to more experienced artists for assisting opportunities.

Your portfolio will change and grow as you grow. It can be scary reaching out of your comfort zone to make connections for new opportunities, but putting yourself out there is the only way for people to get to know who you are, what your work is like, and what you're like to work with. I reached out to an artist for five months before getting the opportunity to assist her on a photoshoot. It's a PROCESS. Each time you check something off on your goal list, it is so worth it!

What's In A Name?

And finally, the agency you are signed to can either help or hinder your progress and advancement in the business. Being with the right agency can get you in a door that appears locked to many of your peers. Make a wise and informed choice about representation, and, in most cases, you will find yourself up to bat more often and with more work than you can handle. The phrase, "What's in a Name?" was never truer than with the selection of an agency.

Locating agencies that represent makeup artists, hair stylists, fashion stylists and manicurists is much easier than it used to be. Type a few key words like: makeup agency, makeup agencies, hair and makeup agencies, or styling agency into the Google search engine and voila! you will arrive at tons of listings. To get more targeted results, just add a city or state.

You can use Models.com as a starting point to help you with your research:

•   Models.com

        models.com/agencies/Makeup

        models.com/agencies/Hair

        models.com/agencies/StylistRep

        models.com/agencies/haircolorists-agency

        models.com/agencies/groomers-agency

You can also download a complete listing of United States and International agencies from my website.

NOTES

"*Part of the reason I'm still here and successful is that I let everything go that was weighing me down. I don't have baggage, if I do have baggage I inventory it and get rid of it.*"

—Sir John

Celebrity Makeup Artist

6

Makeup & Hair

W ith so many choices (Print, Video, Film, TV, Runway and Bridal), the best place to begin is by asking yourself "What am I passionate about?" Do you get all gooey when you see Jeff Goldblum peeling his skin off in a movie like The Fly, or do you have to sit down and admire the lipstick every time a Cover Girl commercial appears on your TV screen? Do you have a stack of fashion magazines piling up in your living room because you can't bear to throw away the issue in which that Noir nail polish by Chanel first appeared in Vogue, or do you salivate at the thought of working on a period film?

Since I am a firm believer in the old adage, 'Do what you love and the money will come.', I caution you against making a

Uzmee Krakovszki

Celebrity Makeup Artist

Microblading Specialist

choice to become a makeup artist because you heard that some politician's makeup artist was paid $20K to do makeup over a two week period. While that breaks out to a handy $1,429 a day, if you ask the makeup artist, you will probably learn that she was working 12-hour days, had to be up at the crack of dawn, and was on call 24/7 for emergency eyebrow-tweezing.

My point is this, there is a lot more work involved in becoming a successful freelance artist than there are times you will see or hear your name mentioned in the national news. So, decide to do it because in the deepest recesses of your heart you can't see yourself doing anything else.

People call me and ask, "Is it hard to become a makeup artist?" My first question is "Does it matter?" Because if it does, and my telling you that it is going to require hard work, dedication and sacrifice is enough to send you scurrying for the nearest IT job, you don't really want a career in makeup or anything else creative.

Doing BIG things requires a singularly focused mindset that others simply don't have. It's hard getting coffee for your boss at the bank if you would rather be at the beach. That's why it's so important to do what you love. Because when you love it, hard never enters into your mind. Choose wisely.

Before I break it down, I asked a seasoned veteran, who worked her way up from bank teller to celebrity makeup artist to give you some words of advice. Monifa Mortis took my Packaging Your Portfolio Workshop over a decade ago. She is a successful working makeup artist and her clients include Queen Latifah, Common, Heather Headley, Essence magazine and more. What she has to say about building a freelance career, I could not have said better myself.

CAREER BUILDING BLOCKS
In the campaign for success, what road choose you?
By Monifa Mortis, Celebrity Makeup Artist

Images courtesy of Honey Magazine

The Hair Makeup & Fashion Styling Career Guide

On the road to success there can be many twists and turns. Some turns lead you down the right path and some run right smack into a dead end. Upon reflection, my road to success was not smooth and direct, but rather a zig-zag of indecision, miseducation and downright ignorance. However, all was not in vain, thanks to God, my mother, supportive friends and generous mentors. Without them, I would not have made it through the tough times.

Know Thyself

The path I took, rocky and frustrating as it was, led me exactly to where I wanted to be—a well-respected, well paid, sought-after celebrity makeup artist. But hindsight is 20/20 vision, and, in the midst of it, I was a woman on the verge of a New York breakdown.

I never knew if what I was doing was right, wrong or insane. But it all came down to what felt right and what made me happy. If it didn't feel right, I would quickly cease the activity, analyze where I went wrong and correct it.

Uzmee Krakovszki is a freelance makeup artist and microblading expert in Los Angeles, California. Her work and positive energy brings out the best in her clients and has led to her working with celebrities like Jeannie Mai, Kelsey Grammar, Matt Lanter, and Jaimie Alexander, as well as cosmetic brands; Too Faced and wet n wild.

Originally from Mongolia in East Asia, Uzmee's is a truly inspiring story about finding the courage to change careers from business to makeup artistry, and crossing a continent to start over in America where she could not even speak the language.

What path led you to becoming a makeup artist and moving to the U.S.?

Uzmee: I never really thought about becoming a makeup artist when I was growing up, but I was always fascinated by faces. When it was time for me to go to college, my parents insisted that I attend business school in Germany. I hated it. I have always been a visual and creative person, and business school was the opposite of that. While in school, I met my future husband who also had a similar story. He was a musician, but his parents insisted that he study engineering. He noticed that I always had a new manicure and my makeup was done, and he encouraged me to try beauty school. So, that is what I did! His support, and being so far away from my parents gave me the courage to do it.

After I graduated from beauty school, I was hired to teach there and did that for 2 ½ years. Then, my husband

Rolling the dice, I stumbled and groped along the dark maze of the makeup business. Driven, and sometimes carried, by my faith in God and my love of makeup.

Whether your pursuit of makeup or hair is in editorial, advertising, entertainment, movies, television or high fashion, you need a sense of direction to prevail in any of these industries. You don't have to know what exact industry you want to work in, but you do have to know what your likes, dislikes, strengths and weaknesses are in order to find your niche. Each area has very distinct nuances that can either make your choice feel like a cozy robe, or a prison-issued straitjacket.

Looking over my career, I can clearly see what helped me become the artist that I am today. Check out the diagram illustrating the "Career Building Blocks" (on page 223) that led to my calling as a celebrity makeup artist. Keep in mind that I didn't know what direction I was headed in until I was well into the game. Reflect on your own "Career Building Blocks" by listing all of the various types of makeup work you have done. Then identify what skills or information you learned from each job and how you incorporated it into your career.

I've summarized some personal tools of inspiration that I have lived by throughout my life and career. These can be great weapons to combat the ugly demons of confusion, doubt and despair. I hope they will help you as they have helped me.

Socrates had it right when he said, "The unexamined life is not worth living." He understood that your inner truth must be discovered before success and happiness can be had. People run into problems because they do not fully comprehend their abilities or limitations, or the full knowledge of their personalities. Do you know yourself?

Some of you are in touch with your persona and know what you want,. while some of us late bloomers, by trial and error, and, sometimes, trial by fire, discover along the way what we want. What should you do first?

Starting today:

STEP 01	Identify your makeup or hair style—your beauty vision—and embrace it fully. Pursue your "authentic self", inside and outside of the makeup arena.
STEP 02	Make a wish list of what your ideal career would be, pessimism aside, and truthfully examine if you have the personality and characteristics that match that dream.

William Shakespeare's inspiring mantra from the tragic epic, Hamlet, was, "To thine own self be true." And, if you don't follow this key point, tragic will your epic be! In other words, don't sell out if you can possibly help it. I know how hard it gets out there and I understand 'ya gotta do whatcha gotta do' to make ends meet.

> *To thine own self be true*

Let me break it down for you: Sometimes you take those "whack" jobs because Mr. Car Note doesn't really care about your artistic integrity. Fine, we can all relate to that; however, don't be fooled. If you keep taking jobs solely on the basis of money, you will short-change your career.

Don't allow your money fears to be your agent. You will look up one day and realize that you are light years away from where you planned to be, because you have built a résumé with

B-movies and beauty pageants. I can promise you this: If you consistently stick to your makeup guns, you will not regret it down the road. You may be broke now, but you'll be fabulous [and fulfilled] later.

Sometimes we get locked into an idea of how our makeup career is supposed to be and can't let go, even when we are obviously mistaken. Mistaken on how a career should develop, and deluded on how we have developed as artists.

So, you're not the next great Kevyn Aucoin—who is? There is no shame in that. Keep in mind, Kevyn was a 20-year vet in his heyday, so give yourself a break. There is work out there at every level of makeup skill and style.

Avoid dismissing anyone or anything as not being useful to your career. You won't realize how small the business is until you start running into the folks you laughed at back in the day. Today's nobody can be tomorrow's somebody—big time! Be open to everything and everyone—at least once, in order to maximize every opportunity. Think Shonda Rhimes, The Year of Yes!" Everybody needs at least one.

I know you. You read countless magazines, buy up every lipstick, go to all the fashion shows, and have attended three makeup schools. You have done everything "right," right? Wrong! There are some things that can only be gained with time—for instance, reputation, experience and understanding. There is a very methodical progression to being a successful artist:

—Someone gives you a chance,

—you prove yourself worthy,

—you get called back, and

—you get another chance.

won the green card lottery, and we made plans to move to the US. Initially, I didn't want to come to America. I didn't speak the language or know anyone here, but everyone encouraged me to go. So, we moved, and when we got to California, I signed up at Cinema Makeup School in LA and took a 4-month course that allowed me to experiment with all sorts of classes from beauty to prosthetics. I wanted to see what else I could be good at. I also started going to language classes to learn English. After I graduated from the course, I asked, "How can I get a job?" I was advised to answer all of the Craigslist ads, and that's how I met you, Crystal and became part of the agency. I answered an ad for a charity fashion show, and I began assisting your artist, Laly Zambrana. Then I started getting more freelance jobs and more than ten years later I'm working in TV and I own my own microblading studio.

Yes, you just opened your own microblading studio. How did that come about?

Uzmee: I knew I wanted to do something more. I wanted to be more creative, and I wanted to help people. I started learning about microblading, and it really interested me. So, I went to three of the top schools that were teaching it and learned all of the techniques. Then I started practicing on models and became very good at it.

I think what really made me decide to finally pursue this career change was the fact that my mother passed away last January and I realized how short life could be. I decided that I couldn't let this dream and opportunity

That is the work cycle of an artist. You can't get around it, go over it, or bust through it. The cycle repeats itself over and over again, and then it splits. After you prove yourself worthy, three people will call you back and you get three additional chances to prove yourself worthy and so on. Just when you thought the world was sleeping on your skills and overlooking you as the new Charlotte Tilbury, you come across some pictures of your early work and realize how bad it really was. So, don't embarrass yourself protesting and being impatient with your career. I have seen it, and I have lived it. The difference between juice and wine is time. You can't cheat the process.

Remember, the love of makeup is the fundamental power of the makeup artist. And it's true for hair stylists, fashion stylists and manicurists. Money and glamour is not what keeps you going, especially through the lean years. I repeat—The LOVE of makeup is the power behind a makeup artist. Be content with making a few coins doing what you love, rather than possibly making big dollars and being miserable. Stop being naïve and be happy for those rinky-dink jobs you've been turning your nose up at (I know how you kids get, 'cause I do it, too). Mark my words, the minute you become ungrateful, a dozen artists are circling around those gigs just waiting for a chance to get on. Stay strong and remain faithful.

Now, go forth and paint!

NOTES

....

....

....

MONIFA's
CAREER BUILDING BLOCKS

Student at NYC Fashion College	Assistant Manager in a Retail Store 9-5	Temping as a Bank Telemarketer 6AM - Midnight	Working as a Limo Driver and doing overnights at a 24hr Grocery Store	Makeup Artist at Bobbi Brown Essentuals Saks Fifth Avenue	FULL TIME FREELANCE PROFESSIONAL MAKEUP ARTIST
					Directed FOCUS of my career toward being a celebrity Makeup Artist.
				Started getting hired to work on hair salon books and hair magazine shoots. Created 1st business card. Consistent call backs.	Found an Agent. More Celebrities calling me for jobs!
		1st paid test with a professional photographer. Fired by same photographer.	Started getting hired to work on hair salon books & hair magazine shoots. Created 1st business card. Consistent call backs.	Landed my 1st big Celebrity job with Stevie Wonder. Referred by a hair photographer.	Purchased the Hair Makeup & Styling Career Guide. Attended Crystal's Packaging Your Portfolio Workshop.
	Makeovers for friends. Makeup for weddings. Discover I can make a living at this.	Put fliers in photo labs. Networked with modeling agencies.	1st job with Soap Opera magazine. Worked with 1st Celebrity.	Developed key relationships with Hair Magazines. Start getting tearsheets. Invest in my 1st portfolio.	Shopped for an agent. Rejected 5 times by 4 different agencies. One turned me down twice.
	Selling Mary Kay Cosmetics				
Product junkie and magazine addict	Compliments on my own Makeup Application	Hooked up with a modeling agency through a girl friend	Getting booked for paid and free testing gigs. Get my 1st set of pictures, —they're bad.	Continued testing. Worked on small projects and odd Makeup jobs.	Stopped commuting from the suburbs. Moved to NYC.
Student at NYC Fashion College	**Assistant Manager in a Retail Store 9-5**	**Temping as a Bank Telemarketer 6AM - Midnight**	**Working as a Limo Driver and doing overnights at a 24hr Grocery Store**	**Makeup Artist at Bobbi Brown Essentuals Saks Fifth Avenue**	**FULL TIME FREELANCE PROFESSIONAL MAKEUP ARTIST**

pass me by, and I wanted to stop feeling empty. I wanted to do something more meaningful, and that is what microblading has done for me.

Are you currently represented by an agency?

Uzmee: No, I'm not. To be honest, I learned so much when I was working with you and developed such a strong platform that I felt confident to go out on my own. Things like negotiating can be difficult, but I use that as a learning experience.

What have been some of your favorite jobs?

Uzmee: I love working for wet n wild and Too Faced doing their ad campaigns. I also really love test shoots. I have so much fun on those because I get to be really creative and play and do whatever I want. Testing lets you have freedom, whereas jobs are more structured with guidelines.

You hire assistants. What personal and professional traits do you look for before you hire someone?

Uzmee: I look for someone that has a similar style to me. Someone that is professional and always on time.

> I want to work with an assistant who is focused and doesn't over-talk. I'm loyal. If I like you, I stick with you.

I also need to see their kit before I hire them. I really need the kit to be clean and organized.

BREAKING IT DOWN

How TV & Film Differ From Print

Film and TV is about creating characters. Most print, video, television commercials and runway are focused on creating a look for today—what's happening now and in the very near future. For this kind of work, keeping up with the latest fashion trends is an asset. In film and television, however, historical research is often part of the job. TV shows like Peaky Blinders and The Queen are set in a time long since past, and require lots of research to bring authenticity to the screen and thus the characters.

A print-focused fashionista might get bored working on a contemporary TV show where the characters' makeup and hair rarely changes from year to year. Actress Ellen Pompeo's character Meredith Gray on the night time drama "Gray's Anatomy" is a good example. Rarely is she seen dressed in anything but a white doctors coat or scrubs. As a fashionista, you might think you can walk onto the set one morning after pouring over the latest issue of Vogue and give Meredith a makeover—think again. The shows interest is in maintaining the continuity of Meredith's look and the relationship she has with her loyal fans.

On the other hand, the Vogue magazine research and all the time a fashionista spends keeping up with the trends will come in handy on music videos, for magazine shoots and even television commercials, where staying on the cutting edge is a prerequisite for job success. Recording artists are made notable by their makeup, hair, clothing and nails. Magazines such as InStyle and US Weekly portray celebrities as confident beauty experts. They ramble on in interviews about the lipstick they are wearing and the products that make their hair shine, all the while inquiring of their glam squad, "What lipstick is this, or what did you say you put on my hair?"

In filmmaking, the scenes are shot out of sequence, requiring immaculate attention to detail, known as continuity. The actor better be wearing the same mustache in scene 20 that he had on in scene 17, which was shot 3 weeks ago, or you're in trouble. Re-shooting that scene could cost hundreds of thousands of dollars.

Unlike film and television, print is pliable and stationary. Discovering an actress' unsightly blemish or fly-away hair is easily fixed in retouching for $150. By contrast, if you made up Brad Pitt a week ago with a scar on his face, and less than one week later on screen, the scar is miraculously healed because you didn't check the script supervisor's report, that can mean a costly reshoot.

Concepts like continuity, script breakdown, bald caps, lace front wigs and shooting in sequence don't mean anything to the print-focused artist who works on projects that typically last one to three days at a time. Worrying about whether some guy's faux tattoo was on his right or left hand in a scene will rarely be the concern of a makeup artist who primarily works in the print industry, on music videos and on TV commercials, but it will be yours if you've decided that working in film and television is for you.

Furthermore, if television and film are going to be your focus, getting into the union should be one of your long-term goals, since the majority of films made on American soil are done with union crews. So, let's start with what you need to know to succeed in television and film.

TAKE 01 — THE UNION

by TOBI BRITTON, Makeup Artist | Educator

Whether a makeup artist or a hair stylist for film and television, some of the skills that are commonly required, and must be mastered, include but are not limited to cuts, bruises, and bald caps. These skills are also valuable for print because you never know when you may be asked to do a bruise or a cut. The more you know, the more you will work! Education is never wasted. Be a sponge and soak up as much as you can!

To be accepted into the union you must begin by accumulating a minimum of 180 days on actual productions over a three-year period. This is commonly referred to as 60-60-60. You may have heard about the rigors and requirements of getting into the union. Don't let those negative thoughts take root. There are plenty of non-union jobs produced each year, and the days worked on those projects (television commercials and independent films) will count toward getting into the union. This is how many artists make their way into the makeup and hair union.

Small-budget, non-union projects are a blessing to the makeup artist and hair stylist who are working to amass the days they need to apply for union membership. That's exactly how it happened for makeup artist-turned-entrepreneur Eva Marie Denst, owner of online makeup emporium MakeupMania. com. "I knew if I got on the right film I could probably go union," she says. "A film called 'Boogie Nights' came up and I took it. It was a lot of extra work. I came in whenever we had big calls, and there were a lot because Boogie Nights had

Your first and second assistant have been with you for a few years. What's the secret?

Uzmee: I think it's important to communicate with your assistants. Tell them what you expect and what you want. That can help to avoid problems.

How do you prefer a potential assistant to reach out to you?

Uzmee: It's really difficult to always respond to the phone or texts, so I prefer email. Just something simple with their information and website.

How much is too much when an assistant is contacting you?

Uzmee: If they are polite and a real go-getter, then I don't think there's such a thing as too much.

What etiquette do you notice is missing from artists today?

Uzmee: I notice that the younger artists aren't interested in improving past what they already know how to do. They want to just jump to the top without going through all of the steps that will help them really improve. I also notice the trend that so many are doing the same repetitive makeup on everyone. Everyone looks like Kim Kardashian! I think because of social media, these new artists believe they have it easier and don't have to work as hard or take it as seriously as we did. Another thing I see is that they are accepting meager rates. They don't realize how bad that is for their careers as well as other artists in the industry. There is a sense that everyone is in it just for themselves.

so many club and big party scenes. I finally got my required days and was able to join Local 706. I signed up as soon as the film wrapped."

In the beginning you should take every job that comes your way in order to gain valuable experience. As time goes on, you will learn under what conditions you do or do not want to work. Non-union jobs will help you qualify for the union.

The trick is to:

1	Keep track of the days that you work.
2	Scrutinize your time cards and check stubs.
3	Confirm that you are always listed on the call sheet as doing makeup, hair, or both.
4	Check and keep your call sheets.

Used together, these four actions can be used to verify your position and attendance on non-union projects which will help you to get into the union local of your choice. It can also happen that a celebrity insists on having you work with them on a union project. This is referred to as a 'Star Request'. When a celebrity request happens to be a non-union artist, the producer must explain why the non-union artist is being hired—hence, the Taft-Hartley Rule comes into play. Check out paragraph 3 in the gray box that follows.

The Taft-Hartley Act

The Taft-Hartley Act is federal legislation that is designed to limit union power and outlaw closed shops. Fondly called the Taft-Hartley Rule, it is best known for getting non-union actors/artists onto a unionized film shoot.

Essentially, the Taft-Hartley Rule says that a non-union artist can be hired for a certain number of days as long as that artist joins the union and pays the same amount that union members are paying to the union. After 30 days, the non-union artist must join the union if they want to continue working on that project.

The producer must explain why the non-union artist is being hired. Under "Reason for Hire", the makeup or hair person is usually listed as having a "special skill".

When they have been requested by a celebrity, this is the way some artists have made their way into the union, gaining access to higher-paying, more prestigious work.

However, even for this stroke of good luck you must be ready. And, as Crystal says, "If You Stay Ready, You Won't Have to Get Ready". Start now putting away your pennies to join the union. If an actor requests you, and you don't have the money to join, it could be years before that stroke of good luck presents itself again.

Tate Holland, Founder and President of Makeup Designory makeup school in New York and Burbank, California says, "for a professional makeup artist developing a career in film and television, the question of joining the Makeup Artist & Hair Stylist Union may become a major consideration. It is only necessary to join the union if you have an interest, the intention or the opportunity to work on productions that are under union contract."

Typically, union contracts are limited to the major broadcast networks for television, certain live theatrical productions, and large multi-million-dollar film productions. The majority of cable television, music videos and infomercials, and a vast majority of low-budget independent films, are non-union productions.

Print advertising, editorial, and runway work is non-union.

NOTES

What advice do you have for new artists trying to break into the industry?

Uzmee: Take a character makeup class. This is the class that I felt really taught me to understand features and completely change a face without using prosthetics. Instead of taking a bunch of random classes, this is the one I would recommend.

Then I would say test, test, and test! It is the best way to experiment and put into practice what you have already learned. I also think young artists need to remember to reinvent themselves. They need to always work on getting better and making themselves irreplaceable. Don't get too comfortable. Keep being your own competition.

Have you ever been hired on Instagram?

Uzmee: Yes, many times! I've had people message me saying they have seen my work and loved it. The actress, Bianca Lawson, found me on Instagram and I've been working with her for the past couple of years. I've also booked weddings and other events. Instagram has been good for me.

Was it easy for you to find your voice on social media?

Uzmee: No, it wasn't! I was always questioning myself if I was doing it right. It stressed me, and I was always comparing myself to other accounts.

Then someone just told me one day that it was my platform and I should do whatever I want on it.

If your dream is to spend a lifetime working in film and TV, there is no question that being a union member should be one of your goals. Start now by visiting the website of your local union so that you are clear about the specific qualifications for joining the union local in your region. Once you apply, your application must go through contract services, and it's a process. Union membership will enable to you to submit yourself to films in pre-production all over the world. That's a WRAP.

MAKEUP & HAIR UNION FACTS

The makeup, hair and costumer's unions are controlled by the International Alliance of Theatrical Stage Employees, known as I.A.T.S.E. Each local has its own set of rules and regulations for applying for membership, dues, initiation fees, etc. Local 798 in New York has an open period for submitting applications, but Local 706 in Los Angeles does not.

What is pretty standard is that in order to be eligible to submit an application, you must provide verifiable proof (via pay stubs, 1099's, call sheets, etc.) that you have worked on professional (moving media) sets for no less than a total of 180 days. An individual is eligible upon the completion of 60 days of work experience in each of three (3) years, within the last five (5) years. No exceptions. There is no gray area here. Miss the mark and you will be starting over. Additionally, upon becoming a member you must choose to do either hair or makeup but not both, so keep that in mind when submitting your documents.

N.A.B.E.T. stands for the National Association of Broadcast Employees and Technicians and is based in Toronto, Canada. They also represent makeup artists, hair stylists and wardrobe stylists.

The Union: What Have You Done For Me Lately

The purpose of the union, is to improve the social and economic conditions of workers identified with the motion picture, television, theatrical and videotape industries of the United States and Canada. The union endeavors to ensure the maintenance of a fair rate for all members in these industries and secure benefits for its members, and pledges to manage the financial aspects of its members' affairs as they relate to wages and working conditions.

Joining the union, however, does not come without a price. How high, you ask? That depends on your personal and professional goals. A financial commitment is relative to the value of its desired result as compared to one's goals. For those of you who intend to dabble in film and television, the price—somewhere between a $3,000 and $5,000 initiation fee—may be too high. For those who see their future in film, television and movies like Logan or Wonder Woman, the price may be a small one to pay to fulfill such a big dream.

One of the greatest benefits of union membership is the unions' influence and power over unscrupulous characters and companies who would have you working into the wee hours of the morning and night for little or no pay. The watchful eye of the union forces production companies to strictly adhere to certain rules and regulations that govern an artist's pay and working conditions. Those items include but are not limited to:

- How much and when you should be paid
- The time and length of break periods and appropriate meal times
- The amount of overtime and accrual time
- The driving distance to and from a location before the production company will begin compensation
- Safe working conditions
- Reimbursement for expenses (also known as a kit fee)

Union membership has its benefits, but there are two important things it does NOT do:

1	Get you work
2	Recommend you for jobs.

Many artists spend years working to get into the union, thinking that the union is going to get them work. It does not. Getting hired for work is something you must undertake on your own. Yes, you will have to be your own agent and advocate for yourself.

Unlike with print-focused artists who have an agency that assists in securing and booking jobs for them, the union does

Uzmee Krakovszki, *Celebrity Makeup Artist*

So, that is what I did, and I started getting all of my loyal followers.

Who is on your bucket list to work with?

Uzmee: Beyoncé. She is such a great role model. She has so much influence and fame, but she sets a good example. I really admire her as a human being and as a celebrity.

Going forward, what do you see changing in how you do your work?

Uzmee: I want to focus on education and passing down the knowledge that I have learned. I want to share advice and inspire other artists. Perhaps by sharing quick tips on video. I'm not quite sure how I want to do this yet, perhaps with social media, but that is my goal for the New Year.

IN HER KIT: 3 THINGS UZMEE CAN'T LIVE WITHOUT

- A really good face and body foundation
- The Too Faced highlighter in Candlelight Warm Glow,
- My Say me makeup brushes from Japan.

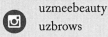
uzmeebeauty
uzbrows

www.uzmeekrakovszki.com
www.uzbrows.com

not provide this service. Once you become a union member, your name will be placed on the member roster. If a production company calls the union to request a list of its eligible members, your name will be on that list as long as you pay your dues on time and don't violate any rules or regulations.

You may be saying to yourself, "Well, why join the union if they are not going to get me work?" Because many of the biggest movies and television shows are produced under union contracts. Being in the union makes it possible for you to work on those projects. However, it is up to YOU to get the work. This means finding out which company is producing a show, who the producers (decision-makers) are, when the show goes into production, and other related information.

For the rest of our conversation on joining the union, I have enlisted the help of Los Angeles-based makeup artist, educator and writer Michael Mosher. This makeup veteran just finished wrapping the last episode of the Originals in December 2017, and really knows what it takes to succeed in television and film.

NOTES

....

....

....

....

....

TAKE 02 — THE UNION

by MICHAEL MOSHER, Makeup Artist | Educator

In considering joining any union, be sure to visit its web site to bone up on their specific rules and procedures. A word of caution: if they have step-by-step instructions, follow them to the letter. They are famous for disallowing your membership over a technicality.

While each union may have slightly different requirements—I'm a member of I.A.T.S.E Local 706 in Los Angeles—any of the I.A.T.S.E locals has pretty rigorous entrance requirements. There is no longer an exam, However, mastering everything that you would have been required to execute during the exam is an excellent mastery of your craft for any makeup and hair stylist.

GETTING STARTED: KNOWLEDGE

The first step to success is knowledge. Knowledge in this case is meant to mean that you have the skills, aptitude and experience to apply makeup in various settings—for instance, Beauty, Period, Fashion, Horror and Science Fiction. There are several paths that you can take. One is the path of gathering the knowledge you need through reading books, watching videos, practicing on others and assisting those who can teach you. Another might be working at a makeup counter or salon and using your clients as your experimental canvas. Another way is through a formal education from a school like Makeup Designory, Empire Academy of Makeup or any of the many schools that exist throughout the US and abroad, but make sure you do your research before you spend your money.

Like many successful makeup artists who work in film and television I went to school. The benefits of school are not just the skills that you gain, but the opportunity to work with and meet other artists that share your interests and career choices. A school may also send work your way!

In addition, a good school can also open doors for you through their placement program. Most importantly, classes can teach you proper techniques and on-set etiquette that you won't learn from working at a counter or salon.

Television and film sets operate differently than photo studios for print or runway shows for fashion. You will need to know how to break down a script, put together a budget, negotiate rates and hours, etc. Whether you choose to do it on your own or get a formal education, here's what you'll need to know:

Daven Mayeda

Beauty Director

Splashlight Studios

- Natural Beauty, Corrective Makeup and Blowstyling. These activities will represent the bulk of your work.

- Fashion Makeup, Hairstyling, Updo's.

- Bald Caps, Wigs, Prosthetics, Blood Effects. These skills come up, but not that often. But you will need to know the skill set.

Study

If you are passionate about film, know the history of film, directors, actors, etc., get a list of required textbooks for college film courses, or enroll in film school! You will definitely make connections there. Hey, you may wind up working for a future Steven Spielberg! Stage makeup books are very helpful in learning how to breakdown a character. Richard Corson's STAGE MAKEUP was the first book that I learned makeup from, and it is still known throughout the industry as "The Makeup Bible". Get to know your sandbox (industry). Things like sitting in as a member of a television studio audience are a great way to see first-hand how a show is taped. It's not enough just to know how to do GREAT makeup.

Invest In A Kit!

Whether you are a makeup artist, hair stylist or wardrobe stylist, in order to work—even for free—you must have a kit! I know that building a kit can be expensive, but you will find it awfully tough to complete a job if you don't have one!

Makeup & Hair

The makeup and hair union covers all persons engaged in applying facial and or body makeup, prosthetics, or cosmetics of any description, as well as those involved in styling hair, both human and synthetic, in every phase of television, video, film, and theatre.

Membership in the makeup and hair locals is composed of four separate groupings:

1	Facial Makeup Artists
2	Body Makeup Artists
3	Hair stylists
4	Wigmakers

In contrast to the familiar, beautiful faces created by print makeup artists, a union makeup artist's skills must go far beyond beauty, as they may be called to do that and much more depending on the project. For example: aging a 70-year-old man 50 years with the use of prosthetics or special effects makeup, as was the case in The Curious Case of Benjamin Button with Brad Pitt, is not an unusual request.

The term prosthetics is used to describe the act of changing or altering the structure of the body or face. If you remember the movie Batman Returns, where Danny DeVito was turned into the Penguin, then you are aware of the impact that prosthetics accompanied with special makeup effects can have on turning an individual into a character. Other examples of prosthetic makeup include creating a bulbous nose, a scar or bruise.

If you are a wig maker, you may be asked to pull together hairstyles for a period film where the characters require elaborate hair designs—for example, The Tudors, The Other Boleyn Girl, Dangerous Liaisons or Gone with the Wind. Even recreating a rock star's look of long, flowing, tangled tresses from the 70's would be considered working on a period piece.

Procedures

Both New York (Local 798) and California (Local 706) have done away with their exams. However, knowing the procedures and requirements for live television and motion picture makeup and hairstyling will help you to prepare yourself for any task on the set of a real project. Remember, KNOWLEDGE is POWER.

That's A Wrap

Following is a list of essential skills every makeup artist or hair stylist should possess and be able to execute in less than an hour to be considered a competent film and television professional..

NOTES

....

....

....

....

Daven Mayeda is the Beauty Director at Splashlight Studios in New York City. His finely tuned eye for aesthetics has made him a strong , talented artist. Some of the celebrities he has worked with include Adele, Shay Mitchell, Niki Minaj, and Mariah Carey. Daven has also been published in Vogue, Cosmo, Flaunt, and Nylon. He shares his story about how he took his passion and turned it into a highly successful career.

Describe your path from freelance hairstylist to beauty director?

Daven: I thought I was going to do graphic design when my dad suggested that I look into hairstyling. He planted the seed which grew into my life. I think I blocked the thought of being a hair and makeup artist because I struggled with being gay and didn't want to embrace my love for fashion.

Looking back, I used to make scrapbooks of all the little editorial cut-outs of the InStyle Magazine beauty editorials with photos of some of my favorite celebrities and beauty products. I was 16, not realizing that being a Beauty Director, makeup artist, or hairstylist were actual viable careers.

In beauty school I was learning to do hair and really didn't care for it. That's when I fell in love with makeup. I was always into color and painting. I decided, "Okay, I'm going to study makeup while I'm in school for hair and really take advantage of this experience." I did makeup on my clients in school while their hair color was processing. Many of my classmates thought that I was crazy and really didn't quite understand my overachiever

Makeup Artist Essentials: Skills For Live Television & Motion Pictures

 ## CORRECTIVE BEAUTY

You should be able to produce a natural-looking makeup worn by an actress appearing in feature film or television soap opera. No high fashion model or runway looks. The colors should be natural and no single element of makeup should call attention to itself. All elements should be balanced and well-blended.

 ## OLD AGE STIPPLE APPLICATION & COLORATION

You should be able to produce an old age stipple application from hairline to collarbone with natural coloring.

 ## LACE SIDEBURNS APPLICATION

You should be able to trip the lace properly so that it lays flat and is easily glued. The sideburns should have a natural appearance.

4 OLD BROKEN NOSE

You should be able to produce this look using soft modeling materials that have been sculpted, blended, sealed and textured realistically, and the skin color should blend to model's.

5 BLACK EYE

You should be able to produce a 2-4-day old bruise. Dimension should be created with subtle use of color.

6 FRESH CUT

You should be able to produce an incision or laceration that is 1 to 2-1/2 inches long on the face or neck using soft modeling material, a prosthetic piece or a combination of materials.

7 OLD SCAR

You should be able to produce a naturally appearing healed injury such as a keloid scar on the face or neck, using a prosthetic piece, collodion, soft modeling material or a combination of materials.

8 BALD CAP

You should be able to produce a non-airbrushed bald cap using Pax, and finish with a shaved head stipple.

9 HAND LAID BEARD

Using a Marcelle iron heated in an oven, you should be able to produce a beard using yack or human hair that blends up to the sideburns.

10 BEARD STUBBLE & FATIGUE

Using chopped hair, you should be able to produce natural-looking beard stubble that resembles a man who has not slept or shaved in at least 24 hours, without the use of a flocking gun. The coloration should appear natural, and you should establish a realistic growth pattern that is neither spotty nor uneven.

HAIR STYLIST ESSENTIAL SKILLS FOR LIVE TELEVISION & MOTION PICTURES

1 WIG BAND

You should be able to prepare the subject's head for a wig band and apply the band.

2 HAIR LACE FRONT PERIOD WIG

You should be able to apply and comb out a lace front wig after it has been applied to the head.

3 FALL APPLICATION

You should be able to create a one-half and three-quarters fall.

4 CROQUINOLE

You should be able to croquinole an actress' hair.

mentality. Eventually I fell in love with styling hair and the rest is history.

What did you do once you were out of school?

Daven: I assisted Joslyn Basilio, one of the most important mentors of my life. She was very technical, precise, organized, and disciplined. It was incredibly hard learning how to navigate as an assistant but I learned so many valuable tools on how to be a quick thinker, trouble shooter, and efficient asset. I love it when the comb has to be a certain way, the scissors have to be positioned in a certain way, and everything is organized from large to small. I figured out that 1% of people did session work, fashion shows, commercials, etc., and I really wanted to do that. I moved back home with my mom and started contacting random photographers to do test shoots.

**So you started testing and building your portfolio…..
What was the next important thing that happened in your journey?**

Daven: Well, to be honest, I had to deal with some things on my journey before I could really take a big step careerwise. I struggled with alcohol and drug abuse for quite some time. I have been sober for many years now and that part of my life is behind me. I wanted to make something of myself so badly, I didn't know how to deal with the fear of failure or success.

It was a cycle of self-hatred that pushed my body and mind so hard that it manifested into sickness. My health started to deteriorate and I knew I had to make serious changes if i wanted to grow into a successful artist.

5 | PERIOD HAIRSTYLE

You should be able to comb out the croquinole, and create a period hairstyle.

6 | CLEAN ENTIRE HAIR LACE

In 20 minutes, you should be able to clean an entire hair lace by only blocking one side.

Now you know, and knowing what is required of you is a priceless piece of information. Use it.

My advice for being successful in film and television: take your time, develop your skills, compete only with yourself, be open to getting help from others, give back along the way and enjoy the process. Before you know it, you won't have to look for work; work will come looking for you.

Joining the Union should be a long-term goal that you plan. Start SAVING your union dues now while you are gaining valuable experience. It will be easier to start saving now and for the next three years than to have to come up with $2,000 or more within 30-days of being approved.

U.S. And Canadian Makeup & Hair Unions

MAKEUP ARTISTS & HAIR STYLISTS			
CITIES	UNION LOCAL	PHONE	WEBSITE
USA			
Chicago, IL	I.A.T.S.E. LOCAL 476	(312) 775 - 5300	www.iatse476.org
Honolulu, HI	I.A.T.S.E. LOCAL 665	(808) 596 - 0227	www.iatse665.org
Los Angeles, CA	I.A.T.S.E. LOCAL 706	(213) 877 - 2776	www.local706.org
New York, NY	I.A.T.S.E. LOCAL 798	(212) 627 - 0660	www.local798.net
Seattle, WA	I.A.T.S.E. LOCAL 488	(206) 448 - 0668	www.iatse488.com
CANADA			
Toronto	N.A.B.E.T. LOCAL 700	(416) 536 - 4827	www.nabet700.com
Toronto	I.A.T.S.E LOCAL 873	(416) 368 - 1873	www.iatse873.com

NOTES

....

....

....

....

....

Ironically, those super tough times led me to some of the most beautiful places and moments of my life. Now I understand why people say that it is only through the darkness that we see the light.

When did you know that you were ready to be signed to an agency?

Daven: I tried really hard to perfect my craft before trying to get jobs. I read books and watched Youtube videos. I learned how to do sew-in weaves and cornrows. I learned how to work every texture of hair I could find and it was then that I really got serious about testing. I had already been studying fashion and editorials and I tried to just shoot what I saw was published in magazines. Not long after I met an artist who was represented by an agency. He hired me for a job as an assistant. I later sat next to another artist signed to the same agency at a MAC master class and ended up assisting her as well. Before I knew it I was assisting an array of artists from that agency, which really got my foot in the door.

What do you think made you such a great assistant?

Daven: Hard work. I had mannequin heads. I had makeup muses. I relentlessly practiced day and night and made sure I could do all of the things that I saw in magazines. I had been so conditioned professionally by working in a salon. When I worked with agency artists they would go to set and come back to their stations and it would be clean and reset without even asking me. There was never a time when I stood there waiting for them to tell me what to do. I made sure their job was easy as possible so that all they had to do was entertain their

WHO'S WHO ON SET

This list of job titles and descriptions will help you avoid the embarrassment of asking the caterer if they know which scene is up!

Art Director	The person who designs or selects the sets and decor of a picture.
Agency	A collective term used on commercials to describe the group of people from the advertising agency hired for the commercial.
Client	A collective term for the person or group of people representing the company for which the commercial is being shot.
Best boy	Also, first assistant electrician. The gaffer's principal assistant. The key grip's principal assistant is the best boy grip.
Cameraman	**1** The Director of Photography, also called the "first cameraman". see "cinematographer".
	2 A camera operator or camera assistant of either sex. The camera operator, who runs the camera, is the "second cameraman". the focus puller is the "first assistant cameraman" or the "first camera assistant" first ac. the clapper/loader is the "second assistant cameraman" or the "second camera assistant."

Cast

1 All of the performers in a movie or show.

2 To select an actor for a role.

Caterer

The person/company responsible for preparing, setting up and serving the crew meals.

Craft Service

The food table that sits near the set all day long to keep us happy.

Cinematographer

Also, Director of Photography, abbreviated D.P., and lighting cameraman. The head of the camera crew, responsible for supervising the lighting of the set and all details relating to the camera. The DP's job is to determine how the set is to be lit, and is responsible for maintaining the "Optimum photographic quality of the production."

Director

The captain and creative coordinator of the production team, responsible for the most effective use of production materials and personnel and often for the creative integration of camerawork, performance, and editing.

1st AD

First Assistant Director is directly responsible to the director, works in close cooperation with the UPM and is also responsible for maintaining coordination between the crew and actors so that the production stays on schedule.

2nd AD

Assists the 1st AD in production duties such as getting actors on set in a timely fashion, filling out contracts and releases, background action coordination.

Gaffer

Also, key electrician. The chief electrician on the set.

Grip

A stagehand attached to the camera crew.

Independent Producer

1 Someone who produces a film and arranges for its distribution without studio support.

2 Someone who produces a film autonomously but has a financing or distribution deal with a studio.

Key

1 Principal.

2 Supervisory.

Key grip

The head of the grip category.

Line Producer

Is directly responsible for supervising a production."

Principals

Actors who play the most significant speaking roles in a film.

clients. I tried really hard to make myself an asset rather than just an assistant.

The agency eventually threw me a little LA Times job that didn't pay much. They didn't have any other artists available that day to take it and asked me to be the key hair stylist. The makeup artist was already signed and It was such a thrill to be working on a job alongside someone who was already signed with an agency.

So how did you transition from that little LA Times job to working with celebrities?

Daven: A stylist I knew was friends with one of my idols—James Vincent. I told him I was dying to assist him. He put in a call to James who happened to be in LA at the time and the next thing I knew I was on set cleaning his brushes. He ended up recommending me to assist makeup artist Linda Cantello. I did American Vogue with Blake Lively and Jessica Biel. Later I ended up assisting on campaigns for Dolce and Gahanna, Stefan and Revlon with the great Mario Testino.

It was on those shoots that I met Oribe. He was the key hairstylist and I used to watch him from the corner of my eye. I asked Linda if it would be ok to ask him if I could assist and she gave me her blessing. He called me one day out of the blue and said he needed an extra pair of hands for a job. I met his good friend Roque Jimenez and asked to assist him as well. Roque called me the following week to come on the set of a music video he was doing. I didn't ask for who, for what, or how much. I just showed up.

WHO'S WHO ON SET

Producer — The head and supervisor of a filmmaking enterprise; the person who hires and provides funds for the filmmaking team and who often owns and licenses the finished product. See "executive producer," "independent producer," and "line producer."

Production Designer — An art director who designs the overall look of a movie, coordinating and integrating its sets, costumes, props, and color schemes.

Production Assistant — "PA" entry level position which helps all departments and is directly responsible to the UPM or whoever he is assigned to. Production Associate (For TV &Video only) Directly responsible to producer and production manager, maintaining the efficient flow of communication as well as taking production notes.

Production Manager — The below-the-line producer, who approves production costs, handles the payroll, and reports to the line producer. Sometimes an executive who delegates these responsibilities to one or more unit production managers.

Script Supervisor	Keeps track of what was actually shot and reconciles that with what was originally planned to be shot. She also times the takes to make sure they are not too long or short. Script is also in charge of the overall continuity and flow.
Talent	The performers.
Wardrobe	The Costume designer designs and selects the outfits for the film. During the production, the Key Wardrobe person is responsible for the care, maintenance and storage of the costumes, as well as supervising the costumer or asst. wardrobe and the dressers.
Unit Production Manager	Also unit manager. An on-the-set production manager in charge of the day-to-day functioing of a first, second, or insert unit and sometimes of an entire production.

NOTES

Daven Mayeda, *Beauty Director*

I walked into the trailer and he was working on Mariah Carey. The only word I said to her the entire shoot was "Hello". The next day, he asked me if I had a passport. I was confused and asked him why. He told me Mariah wanted to use me for her North American Tour doing her hair and that they were leaving in a few days for the first show. This is such an important story because I learned its not about what you say or how loud or fabulous you are. It is your energy that gets you noticed and hired. That was my big break, and it took me many years of hard work and barely any pay to get that opportunity.

Now that you've been in the industry for so long, what would you say are the top professional turn offs from freelance artists?

Daven: Not being present when you are working. I understand that we have lives, families, and other things that need to be handled, but if you are working with a new client, you need to put everything else aside for that day. Check your phone at lunch or when the talent isn't present. It is so important to be focused and free of distraction. I think my second pet-peeve is relying on the circumstances that you are provided in order you to do your job.

What do you mean by that?

Daven: If you are someone who is gluten free, needs to eat breakfast, needs a half an hour nap in the afternoon, or if you have things that you need to do on a daily basis in order to excel, you need to make sure that you take care of your own needs before you get to the job. Bring your own gluten free lunch, eat breakfast before you come to

NOTES

IN YOUR KIT
Professional Makeup Artist Kit Checklist for Film & Television

- ___ Professional Makeup Case
  (a must for film, TV and print)
- ___ Range of Foundations
- ___ Neutralizers and Concealers
- ___ Range of Contour and Accent Colors
- ___ Dermablend Pallet
- ___ Translucent Face Powder
- ___ Setting Powder
- ___ Pancake Makeup
- ___ Dual Powder Foundation
- ___ Creme Rouge
- ___ Powder Blush
- ___ Lip Conditioner
- ___ Super Matte Antishine (dark and light)
- ___ Duo Waterproof Eyelash Adhesive
- ___ Eye Pencils
- ___ Lip Pencils
- ___ Brow Color
- ___ Rouge Stick
- ___ Scissors
- ___ New Skin
- ___ Breath Spray
- ___ Eyelash Curler

- ___ Brow and Lash Comb/Brush
- ___ Tweezers
- ___ Pencil Sharpeners
- ___ Variety Stipple Sponges
- ___ Visine
- ___ Mascara
- ___ Current Lip Colors
- ___ Current Eye Colors
- ___ Basic Manicure Supplies
- ___ Synthetic Mu Sponges
- ___ Sea Sponges (gradated)
- ___ Large Puffs
- ___ Natural 100% Cotton
- ___ Q-Tips
- ___ Disposable Mascara Brushes
- ___ Disposable Lip Brushes
- ___ Alcohol
- ___ Brush Cleaner
- ___ Pallet for Mixing
- ___ Hand Sanitizer
- ___ Kleenex (tissues)
- ___ Hand Mirror

set, sleep extra well the night before. Do not expect the clients or team to shuffle their schedules to accommodate you. Take extra good care of yourself and think of anything you might need in advance so you can focus and really do your best.

Under what circumstances would you never rehire an assistant?

Daven: It is important to come dressed appropriately for the job. I've had assistants come to set in heels and expensive clothes, when previously told that we would be hiking on rocks, in the sand, and going in and out of the ocean. I really had to carry their weight those days because they just weren't prepared to do that type of job and it was very difficult as key artist to need to pick up my assistants weight. Its also important to try to leave your personal issues at the door and keep them to yourself as much as possible. Jobs are stressful enough and bringing things to work as an assistant makes them more complicated than they need to be for the key artist.

What would you say to artists who want to book jobs with decision makers like yourself?

Daven: Broken people make broken artists. Do the personal work to find out where your fear, insecurity, and problem areas are. You have to navigate within this industry being completely grounded or else your work and energy will reflect that. I meditate, exercise, eat healthy, dance, paint, and have plenty of alone time. Do the these things that feed your soul and mend your heartache so you become a strong person. It's only then that all the pieces connect. Also, never stop learning and don't limit yourself to one skill set. I knew early on that the industry

IN YOUR KIT

Additional makeup artist supplies that you should have on hand and know how to use!

Acetone:	For blending bald cap edges and cleaning lace.
Adhesives:	Spirit Gum, Duo Surgical Adhesive, Water Soluble Spirit gum, Prosaide, Telesis Adhesive.
70%-99% Alcohol:	For cleaning, sanitizing, and removing spirit gum from utensils.
Baby Wipes:	For washing hands, cleaning counters and your kit and removing stains, etc. Huggies Huggies Original is my favorite brand.
Blood:	Liquid, squirt, dark and light, coagulated, dried, etc.
Castor Oil:	To mix with RMG to thin out.
Clown White:	Cake, grease or liquid, water soluble or oil based.
Collodion:	Flexible (sealer), Non-Flexible (Scar material)
Dermacolor:	Paramedical camouflage from Kryolan that comes in a great little palette. Used to conceal any kind of blemish, discoloration, undereye circles etc. Excellent for covering men's beard shadows when turning them into women. Waterproof and sweatproof when applied properly.
Naturo Plasto:	Mortician's wax is used to fabricate quick injuries, cuts, and other fun stuff. Great for one time fast effects, but hard to maintain continuity for extended periods of time.

Hair:	Crepe wool, natural hair crepe
Yak:	Used to create beards, moustaches and other small hair pieces for the face and body. Yak may be ventilated onto lace or glued to the face. Crepe is applied directly to the face.
Eyedrops:	Sterile single use tubes are preferable.
Eyewash:	Sterile eyewash is important incase the eye has to be flushed out.
Eye Lashes:	Strip, clump and individual.
Nu Skin:	A spray-on bandage to seal cold sores or other "weeping or bleeding" things on actor's faces so you can conceal them properly.
Glycerine:	For tears, and sweat. (Do not get it in the eyes!!)
Hairdryer:	To dry adhesives, stipple and other things just in case.
Sunblock:	An SPF 30 to put on actor's faces, necks, ears and other exposed areas when shooting outside. If you don't, you will have an actor who gets progressively redder as the day goes on and will never match in the edit.
PS:	It is the makeup dept's job to tend to all exposed areas of skin on the talent's body. Have a good one for the face that does not shine too much- try Yonka's Ultra-Protection SPF 25 or MD Formulations SPF 30. Have a cheaper version on hand for the crew!
Electric Razor:	Shaves actor's faces w/o water or nicking, and can be used over a finished makeup! Great for fixing that 5 o'clock shadow after lunch! Remember, cordless & rechargeable!

Lip Balm:	Used with a tissue to wipe away dead skin. Put it on the most horribly chapped lips before you start the makeup. By the time you are ready for lipstick, wipe away with the tissue and the rest will lie flat for you. Carmex is my favorite.
Hair Trimmer:	To clean up men's side burns and neck lines. (Fondly called, Buzzer)
Makeup Cape:	Don't leave home without it!
Moustache Wax:	You will probably never use it, but when you need it there is no substitute. You can also use it to help tame eyebrows.
Polaroid Camera:	A must for continuity. Even on commercials. Polaroid Spectra is a good one, move in really close and take the picture vertically. You can also use a digital camera, but always have a polaroid back up.
Removers:	You must have the proper removers for any adhesives that you carry.
Tooth Enamel:	Black, stain, white.
Trauma Colors:	Bruise wheel, burn wheel, old age wheel.
Topstick:	Toupee tape.
Tuplast:	Scar material by Kryolan.
Latex	
Tweezers	
Water	

was going to start combining hair with makeup and I really did put in the leg work to learn two skills. I'm so glad I did that because it led me to where I am today.

IN HIS KIT: 3 THINGS DAVEN CAN'T LIVE WITHOUT

- 3/4 inch curling iron. That's the magical size
- A Comb
- Le Maquillage Pro Palette

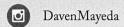 DavenMayeda

honey-artists.com/div/hair/artists/daven-mayeda

IN YOUR KIT
Professional Hair Stylist Kit Checklist For Film And Television

____ Brushes: 3 different sized round brushes and flat brushes

____ Water Bottle

____ Combs: Rat tail, wide tooth, regular, teasing, cutting

____ Cape

____ Blow Dryer

____ Clips and Pins: Long clips, roller clips, hair pins, bobby pins (3-colors: golden brown, black and silver)

____ Rechargeable Clippers

____ Rechargeable Trimmers

____ Rollers: Velcro, hot rollers

____ Products: Leave-in conditioner, gel, spray, pump and aerosol (laminate "cuticle smoother"), pomade

____ Scissors and/or Razor

____ Hair Accessories: Comb, clips, rubber bands (variety-leather, ribbon)

____ Curling Irons: Small, medium, large sizes

____ Marcel Irons (3-4 sizes)

____ Heating Oven

____ Spray Gel

____ Laminates Spray

Options: Hair pieces, wigs, falls, extension hair, braids

IN YOUR KIT

Additional hair stylist supplies that you should have on hand and know how to use!

Sunblock: An SPF 30 to put on actor's faces, necks, ears and other exposed areas when shooting outside. If you don't, you will have an actor who gets progressively redder as the day goes on and will never match in the edit.

PS: It is the makeup department's job to tend to all exposed areas of skin on the talent's body. Have a good one for the face that does not shine too much, try Yonka's Ultra- Protection SPF 25 or MD Formulations SPF 30. Make sure to have a cheaper version on hand for the crew!

Electric Razor: Shaves actor's faces without water or nicking, and can be used over a finished makeup! Great for fixing that 5 o'clock shadow after lunch! Remember, cordless & rechargeable!

Lip Balm: Used with a tissue to wipe away dead skin. Put it on the most horribly chapped lips before you start the makeup. By the time you are ready for lipstick, wipe away with the tissue and the rest will lie flat for you. Carmex is my favorite.

Hair Trimmer: To clean up men's side burns and neck lines. (Fondly called, Buzzer)

Makeup Cape: Don't leave home without it!

Moustache Wax: You will probably never use it, but when you need it there is no substitute. You can also use it to help tame eyebrows.

Polaroid Camera: A must for continuity. Even on commercials. Polaroid Spectra is a good one, move in really close and take the picture vertically. You can also use a digital camera, but always have a polaroid back up.

Removers: You must have the proper removers for any adhesives that you carry.

Tooth Enamel: Black, stain, white.

Trauma Colors: Bruise wheel, burn wheel, old age wheel.

Topstick: Toupee tape.

Tuplast: Scar material by Kryolan.

Latex

Tweezers

Water

NOTES

....

....

....

....

....

....

....

....

....

....

....

....

....

....

....

....

....

IN YOUR KIT
Basic Special Effects Kit Checklist
For Film And Television

___ Professional Makeup Case (small)

___ Prosthetic Makeup

___ Beard Block

___ Artificial Blood

___ Blood Capsules

___ Chinese Eyelids

___ Variety Crepe Hair

___ Plasto

___ Curling Iron

___ Duo Surgical Adhesive

___ Glycerine

___ Tubplast

___ RCMA Scar Material

___ Matte Adhesive

___ Eyebags

___ Assorted Appliance Pieces

___ Ben Nye Greases

___ Fresh Scab

___ Ben Nye Bruise Wheels

___ Fuller Earth

___ Clown White

___ Blasco Death Gray

___ AF Powder

___ Ben Nye Neutral Set

___ Various Liners

___ Lip Colors

___ Shading/Contour Shadows

___ Chopped Hair

___ Menthol Blower

___ Datex

___ Clear Sealer

___ Collodion

___ Prosaide (Prosthetic Adhesive B)

___ Allergy Relief Visine

___ Spirit Gum

___ Old Age Stipple

___ Latex

___ Mineral Oil

___ Medical Adhesive

___ Reel Creations Tattoo Colors

___ Hair Whitener

___ New Skin

___ Tooth Enamel

___ Assorted Black Stipple Sponges

___ Roux Mascara

___ Acgua Colors

___ Mascara

NOTES

....

....

....

....

....

....

....

....

....

....

....

....

....

The Hair Makeup & Fashion Styling Career Guide

*You can't get
the jobs you don't
apply for.*

—Melissa Mangrum

7

Freelancing

The word "freelance" is used to describe a lot of different folks doing a variety of different things. Webster's dictionary defines a "freelancer" as any artist who sells his or her services to employers without a long-term commitment to any one of them, without the benefit of an agency. Simply put, it means that YOU do everything to get your name out there, your book seen, and your money collected. While the dictionary says, 'without the benefit of an agency,' I'm here to tell you that even if you do get an agency, you will still be a freelancer because your agency is NOT your employer.

Now lets turn to the next page to find out what everything consists of.

10 TIPS

FOR ESTABLISHING A BETTER RELATIONSHIP WITH YOUR ASSISTANT

Often what goes wrong between a key and an assistant could be avoided if everyone were upfront. The problems that arise with an assistant are not unlike those that arise between friends or lovers when expectations are not discussed in advance. We assume that our girlfriends know not to wear our favorite piece of jewelry, and we get angry when it's missing from our jewelry box. In the same vein, we neglect to tell an assistant that it is inappropriate to show their book to a client on our shoot, and we're aghast when they do. We want people to be business-like on the job, but we haven't told them what business-like behavior means when they are working with us. One would think that a person should know what is good and bad behavior. However, it is hard to know what you have never been taught.

STEP BY STEP

Prospecting

- Contacting people by email, telephone and/or written correspondence.
- Scheduling appointments.
- Emailing links and meeting with people to show your book.
- Following up by telephone, email, and written correspondence.

Negotiating

- Discussing and handling all specifics and logistics regarding the terms, conditions and financial arrangements under which you will accept and proceed with the job assignment.

Facilitating

- Arranging for pick-up, deposit, and verification of funds available on advance checks, electronic funds transfer, money orders and cashier's checks.
- Hiring assistants to work with you.
- Proper budgeting of your personal finances in the face of irregular income and the demands of updating your portfolio and social media regularly.

Collections

- Following up on the payment of your invoices.

Schmoozing

- Remembering the birthdays, anniversaries, and other special occasions of clients by sending greeting cards, making phone calls, sending small gifts at times, and picking up the tab for meals and other entertainment-related activities.

Networking

- Showing up at social events properly attired with marketing materials such as business and comp cards, a firm—but not crushing—handshake, a smile and the ability to listen more than you talk.

- Never leaving home unless you have a clear purpose for what you intend to achieve when you arrive at an event, job or meeting.

Sounds like a lot of work, right? It is. These are just a few of the reasons that artists seek out representation. The 20% an artist pays an agency is seen as a bargain when compared to the amount of time, legwork, and paperwork an artist can spend getting, negotiating and facilitating their own jobs. The process of landing those highly coveted beauty, fashion & entertainment job assignments should be put into motion long before you ever get that first job. It begins with a working knowledge and understanding of how beauty, fashion, photography, and the makeup, hair & styling industries work together to create images, each element dependent on the other to get to the next level.

On The Job Training

Success, in this business, is comprised of a few simple rules and activities. Follow them, and, if you are talented, you will be successful. Don't follow them, and you can flounder around for years wondering why you never achieved the kind of professional and financial success you dreamed of.

NOTES

The Hair Makeup & Fashion Styling Career Guide

10 TIPS FOR ESTABLISHING A BETTER RELATIONSHIP WITH YOUR ASSISTANT

1 Discuss your needs and expectations openly before hiring an assistant to work with you. Write them down and present them to the assistant in advance, giving them an opportunity to think about what you expect of them.

2 Ask yourself if you are willing to help an assistant get ahead. Try to put yourself in the shoes of someone who is where you once were. Figure out what you are willing to do for the assistant and communicate it to them. No one will work for you forever without wanting something in return, i.e., tearsheets, referrals, pass-along work.

3 Ask yourself what kind of performance you expect from an assistant before they can gain your support. Then communicate those expectations verbally and on paper.

4 Give some thought to your tearsheet policy. Is it okay for an assistant to share the spoils, if you gave them faces to paint, heads to style or bodies to dress? Let them know. Be fair, if you want them to stick around.

Consistency

Believe it or not, you only have to implement these three actions to be successful as a freelance artist. Where people fall short is in the consistency of their actions. These are not things you can only do once or twice. They have to be repeated month after month.

As you read through these 3 actions, remember that magazines come out every month. You will have to send out links to share your updated materials every month. You will have to be on time all the time not some of the time. And you will have to be the one to extend your hand to build new relationships.

You are in business, and these actions are how you fulfill your career aspirations.

3 Actions You Should Take Throughout Your Career

1 Do your homework. Keep up with what's going on in beauty, fashion, entertainment & photography by reading the beauty, fashion and entertainment magazines of New York, Los Angeles, and Europe. Curate Pinterest and Instagram to ensure that you are looking at and keeping up with the classics, the trends and the trendsetters.

Take stock of magazine credits to keep abreast of who the hot photographers, fashion designers and stylists are. Learn to spot the subtle differences between competing magazines and how changes in key staff members affect the look and feel of the magazine. Watch the latest fashion segments on television.

Send links to your book and reel to the right decision-makers. Get to your interviews on time. Be positive. Meet and greet others with genuine enthusiasm and interest. Have good things to say about your peers, or say nothing at all.

Collect and take action on what inspires you. In other words, DO SOMETHING!

2 Meet and introduce yourself to decision-makers and crew members. Mingle. Be seen. Be visible. Be a good listener. Hire skilled and reliable assistants who will follow your direction. Work with vendors you can depend on, and trust. Show up early to your jobs. Give 150%. Be a team player. Be a leader. Stand your ground with grace and style.

3 Always send thank-you cards to decision-makers who hire and refer you for jobs and give you career advice. Keep your promises to vendors. Follow up with new and existing decision-makers. Close the deal on opportunities by asking for the work. Stay top of mind by mailing comp cards as reminders. Follow up on and collect your tearsheets, videos and commercials. Circulate your online portfoli and reel to decision-makers. Make the effort to follow up with peers that you got along well with on a job. Make time to take the first step towards forming new alliances and professional relationships.

Networking

In Chapter 3, Marketing Yourself, I stressed the importance of networking and its significance as a cornerstone of a complete marketing campaign. With this in mind you should agree that every job provides the consummate networking opportunity.

As the key artist you need to be seen. Don't make the mistake of being invisible on the job. Too often an artist cloisters him or herself away in a location trailer or dressing room, only to be forgotten at the end of the day by the people who are giving out work tomorrow, next week, next month, and next year.

Let everyone, especially the decision-makers see your lovely face. If you don't, the next time a project comes up, and the discussions about who to use for makeup, hair or fashion styling ensues, your name will be absent. You don't want the conversation between a producer and director after they've been awarded a new job to sound like this:

PRODUCER:	Do you have anyone in particular you'd like to use on this video?
DIRECTOR:	Um, let me think. The makeup was nice on that last video we did for Atlantic Records. Who did that?
PRODUCER:	Yeah, you're right. It was clean. Very high fashion. But I can't for the life of me remember who the makeup artist was. What was her name?
DIRECTOR:	Denise...Karen... oh, I don't know. Just call a few agencies and get some books for me to look at.

10 TIPS FOR ESTABLISHING A BETTER RELATIONSHIP WITH YOUR ASSISTANT

5 Define what loyalty is to you. Communicate it to the assistant along with a description of the prize for that loyalty.

6 Be business-like with your assistant. Don't begin your relationship by treating them like a friend. It can give the impression that anything goes.

7 Discuss the positive and negative aspects of previous relationships with assistants to your new assistant?

8 Tell an assistant what you want. Don't expect them to be a mind reader.

9 Present a prospective assistant with your list of what a good assistant means to you.

10 Don't wait 'til the last minute to hire an assistant whose references you haven't had an opportunity to check out.

No artist wants a conversation like this one to end without their name being mentioned and their phone number being dialed. If you did a great job on the video, commercial, or photo session, the key people should and must remember your name and have your comp card and/or business card close at hand. BE VISIBLE. Especially after you've left the job.

On a music video or television commercial (at the production company level), there are several people who can create future work for you. The producer, director, production coordinator and production manager are key people you should get to know. Each of these people is a decision-maker. They can and do make and influence the choices of others when it comes to whom is selected to work as part of the crew. Confused? Let me make it a little clearer.

Think about your own life for a moment. You make choices about your friendships and acquaintances. Try to think of the when's and if's that you and your immediate friends impose on others before you let them into your circle, or clique. Those same when's and if's apply on a job. Everyone is sizing you up to see if you fit in.

Have you done your part? Are you friendly? Do you introduce yourself to others? Do you take the first step? Do you get involved and pitch in? Are you a team player?

A lot of your success is dependent upon how you fit in. How you mesh with the rest of the people (crew) on the set. Many of the crew people you will work with on your first jobs have been working together for years. They know each other and they know what to expect. You will be tested. You will be challenged. You may be snubbed. No matter what, you must do your best and maintain a positive attitude. It's the only thing that will be good enough.

The Book Review Process

The book review process is what happens when your online portfolio gets selected for review, often unbeknownst to you. In the past, the book review process at entertainment companies was a closed-door session often held by one person, the art director. The art director would make his or her selections, inform the management of their choices for makeup, hair, fashion styling, and photography and the shoot was on. That kind of autonomy rarely exists any longer. The process has become much more democratic as key players (recording artists & managers) demand to be made a part of the process from the very beginning. This new trend is most often apparent in the entertainment industry.

Recording artists, celebrities, and their management companies insist on reviewing portfolios personally. In a twist of events, management often requests that the art director email a link to the book preferences to them or the artist for consideration. Once a decision is reached, the art director is notified, and asked to contact and book their choices for makeup, hair, fashion styling, nails and photography. Powerful artists like Taylor Swift, Rhianna, Adele, Britney Spears and Justin Bieber will not tolerate being told whom to use on a photo session, music video or feature film.

As this new hierarchy in decision-making is now the norm, your opportunities as an artist increase. Now, in addition to emailing your book and comp cards to a single art director at a record label, you can forward those same materials to the appropriate people at the management and public relations firms. The secret of success in this environment is to be upbeat, on time, professional and master your craft. All of these qualities will give decision-makers more than enough reasons to remember you and want you back on their next project.

A touchy subject with makeup, hair, fashion stylists and manicurists is dealing with the frustration they experience while attempting to get the photographers they long to work for to look at their books in person or online. Artists spend countless hours emailing and on the phone cold-calling to set up appointments with photographers. Many times they are turned away by a rude studio manager or photographer who may or may not have even looked at their work.

The egos of some photographers, their reps, and their studio managers (who live vicariously through the stature of the photographers they work for) means that early on in your career you may find it difficult to get an opportunity to show the photographer of your dreams your portfolio. That is unless your resume can show that you just completed work on the latest GAP campaign with a photographer the caliber of Annie Liebovitz or Michael Thompson.

Guess what? There is a better way. A seemingly nobody photographer can be tomorrow's star just by being in the right place at the right time, and by being talented of course. I wasted the first couple of years as an agency owner trying to get huge photographers to notice my artists at my boutique agency.

Only after I hired my first agent—Reesa—did we surmise that it would be easier to get something going on with hot new photographers who were talented but not well known. It paid off when we focused on the value of building relationships with photographers we could grow with, and we did. One of those

THE LAST WORD: ACTRESS & SINGER VANESSA WILLIAMS

I once represented a "very" French photographer. His portfolio was requested by Vanessa Williams from a referral by her hair stylist, Roberto Leon. It was thought that he might be right person to shoot her upcoming CD. Prior to our meeting with Vanessa and her manager, I had a conversation with the photographer about the subtle differences between shooting fashion photography with models who do what they're told, and shooting a multi-platinum recording artists with opinions and marketing plans that existed before he arrived on the scene.

In his French-ness was wouldn't hear of it. He was sure he could persuade Ms. Williams to see his vision, his way. He was determined to use 'this' person to do her makeup, 'that' person to do her hair and someone else to do her styling (even though it was her hair stylist who had recommended him for the job—so much for loyalty). No matter how I tried to convince him that she would get another photographer before she would abandon her glam squad, he persisted.

During the meeting in her manager's office, he went into detail explaining why he needed specific artists to work with him on her project. She listened politely and said "no". He continued. Still polite, and a little more sternly, she said "no". He was relentless and insistent with his argument. This time, however, Ms. Williams raised her voice, glanced over at her manager, looked back at the photographer and said "NO!" one final time. The photographer finally got the message, gave up, and got the job.

photographers was an as-of-yet undiscovered genius by the name of Mike Ruiz. He and I collaborated on an editorial shoot with Tyra Banks which helped to launch the careers of celebrity hair stylist Neeko Abriol and fashion stylist Lisa Michelle.

NOTES

A Time And A Place

My grandmother always said, "there's a time and a place for everything." This statement is true of workplace etiquette and ethics. As an artist, you may be privy to conversations and information involving well-known persons in entertainment and industry. A word of caution—keep what you see and hear to yourself. Sharing private and sensitive information will get you canned, and quick! If you learn that a well-known actor or actress is wearing a toupee or a weave, keep it to yourself. Sharing it will get you D-Listed in the industry.

There was a time when I would have said, "If you are just dying to tell someone about your latest celebrity secret, confide in your best high school buddy who lives and works in a small cave at least 2,000 miles away." However, even the hills of South Dakota aren't far enough away from Instagram, Facebook and Twitter. Take my word for it. Mums the word. I know a fashion stylist who got canned while working for Janet Jackson after being overheard in a trendy LA clothing store discussing Ms. Jackson's weight. Don't—gossip.

Be on time! A lot of people, places and things are affected negatively when a crew person (YOU) is tardy getting to the set. If you are 30 minutes late and the production goes 15 minutes overtime, the producer may have to pay 10 to 20 or more people time and a half for that 15 minutes. Think you'll ever get hired again? Think again, and don't be late!

Don't put a decision-maker on the spot by asking questions about your fees and expenses in the presence of other crew members. Everyone may not be making the same amount of money. If you have questions or concerns about your rate, overtime, or expenses, ask the person in charge for a private meeting to discuss the issues. Don't discuss your fees with peers. Everyone cuts a different deal.

If you learn that you are making less money than someone whom you feel is your equal, don't make a big fuss on the set. It's unprofessional. Cut a better deal the next time you negotiate with that producer.

MONEY MATTERS

1 SETTING A DAY RATE

As a freelancer, you will be setting your own day rate (fee). While you can and should charge whatever the market will bear, getting it is quite another matter and requires experience, skill, demand (desire for your services and expertise), an impressive book, reel or résumé, and the audacity to ask for what you want. For a better gage on how to price your services, check out the 'Show Me The Money' chart on page 233.

Talk to others in and around your field. Makeup artists and hair stylists tend to get about the same day rate and a bit more when they do makeup and hair. As an example, if you are doing makeup on a national commercial in Chicago, and you're making $700 for the day, the hair stylist is probably making $700 as well. A fashion stylists' day rate tends to be a bit less per day, but they generally work a minimum of three days at a time (prep, shoot, wrap) and quite often a lot more.

These rate rules go right out the window when an artist works with a celebrity. One day you can be making $850 doing makeup on a Coca-Cola print ad, and the next day you're getting $2,500 to do makeup on Rhianna.

REESA'S FYI: ON THE JOB TIPS

PERSONAL HYGIENE: Remember how physically close you are to the people you are working on, and make sure your breath is minty fresh. Mints are always a better idea than gum, which, if chewed like a farm animal or a cracking fool, can make one lose one's mind. Check your teeth to make sure you don't have evidence of your last meal in your teeth. Be aware of your finger nails. Chipped polish, dirt under the nails, and six inch-long neon green dragon lady claws with hoops through the tips won't get you far in this business. Deodorant, please! Nobody is going to tell you that you stink; they just won't ever hire you again.

SANITATION: Make sure your kit and brushes are squeaky clean. Sanitize your tools. Don't wear dirty clothes or wipe your makeup on the clean ones you are wearing, and take an extra ten minutes to iron the creases out of the shirt you wore last night if you are going to wear it to today's shoot.

TARDINESS: Never be late. The production can be four hours behind, you can't! If you get into an accident on the way to a shoot, and you're not dead, call the production to tell them what happened, and then call your mother.

DRAMA: Check your personal baggage (problems) at the door. Yes, it will be hard to have a sunny disposition if your boyfriend or girlfriend just walked out on you, but act, and act well. Never bring a friend or unconfirmed assistant to the shoot with you. If you feel like you need help with an assignment, tell your agent so they can negotiate it into the budget, or tell the client if you are handling your business transactions.

Gravitas

Gravitas may be translated to mean weight, seriousness, and importance. It connotes substance and depth. Each time you add a new tearsheet to your portfolio or a new credit to your resume, you are adding substance. The more published work you garner, the more credibility you gain, and the more professional you appear. With that and excellence you are positioning yourself to be able to command better rates as well as working conditions. Remember to collect your tearsheets and update your resume. They add value.

Raising Your Day Rate

My suggestion is to raise your day rate every 6 months. A good way to keep the bookings coming in is to only raise your rate on new clients. When the new client bookings start taking over, you will be unavailable for your old clients without alienating them. You are simply unavailable. If you have an assistant that you love and are ready to promote, this is a great opportunity to pass work onto them or a trusted colleague.

Through my one-on-one coaching practice, I've even helped some artists with a large clientele to create an agency of their own which they use to book other artists and themselves out on those jobs and gain a new revenue stream.

NOTES

....

....

....

SHOW ME THE MONEY

	MAKEUP	HAIR	FASHION STYLING	MAKEUP & HAIR	NAILS
ADVERTISING					
Print Ads	$500-2500	$500-2500	$500-2500	$750-3500	$500-750
Commercials - Non-Union	$500-2000	$500-2000	$500-2000	$750-2500	
Commercials - Union	21-62/hr	21-62/hr	N/A	N/A	
Catalogue	$450-1250	$450-1250	$450-1250	$650-1500	
Movie Posters	$500-2000	$500-2000	$500-2000	$750-2500	
CD COVERS	$500-2500	$500-2500	$500-2500	$750-2500	
ECOMMERCE:					
Lifestyle	$400-850	$400-850	$400-850	$600-1200	$250-400
Luxury	$850-1500	$850-1500	$850-1500	$1000-2000	$500
EDITORIAL:					
Magazines	$150-350	$150-350	$150-350	$250-350	$120-200
LIVE ACTION					
Runway	$250	$250	$250	$250	$150-350
Award Shows	$500-2500	$500-2500	$700-2500	$700-3000	$250-350
Theatre - Off Broadway	$500-900	$500-900	_____	$600-1000	
Theatre - On Broadway	$1000-1800	$1000-1800	_____	$1100-1900	_____
LOOKBOOKS	$300-500	$300-500	N/A	$300-500	$500
MUSIC VIDEO					
Non-Union	$300-2500	$300-2500	$500-2500	$500-3000	$250-1000
Union	21-62/hr	21-62/hr	21-35/hr	N/A	N/A
PUBLICITY					
Press Junkets	$500-2500	$500-2500	$500-2500	$750-3500	
Publicity	$500-2500	$500-2500	$500-2500	$750-3500	$300
TELEVISION					
Sitcom/Drama - Non-Union	$300-500	$300-500	$300-500	$300-500	
Sitcom/Drama - Union	21-62/hr	21-62/hr	21-35/hr	N/A	
Film/Mini-Series - Non-Union	$200-400	$200-400	$300-500	$300-500	$350
Film/Mini-Series - Union	21-62/hr	21-62/hr	21-35/hr	N/A	
TV Talk - Non-Union	$550-700	$550-700	$550-700	$650-850	$300
TV Talk - Union	$700-1000	$700-1000	$700-1000	$700-1250	
Reality - Non-Union	$250-400	$250-400	$250-400	$250-400	
Reality - Union	25-32/hr	25-32/hr	21-35/hr	N/A	
WEDDINGS/EVENTS	$150-2000	$150-2000	N/A	$150-2000	$150-350

REESA'S FYI: ON THE JOB TIPS

PERSONAL SPACE: Never look through the director's or photographer's camera without asking permission first. I have heard many times from photographers how annoyed they became when an artist just walked up to the camera and started fussing around. It's like asking a stranger if you can hold their baby. As a makeup, hair, fashion stylist or manicurist, wouldn't you be offended if the photographer came up to the model and started rearranging her hair, changing her lipstick color, rummaging through your racks of clothing or removing the nail polish with an acetone soaked piece of cotton? Think about it.

HUMAN RESOURCES: Having a problem with another artist who will not get out of your mix? Be subtle about your objections. DO NOT yell at them or throw a tantrum. Pull the person aside quietly and work diligently to have an adult and professional discussion. Remember, you are being paid to work. Even when the other person is wrong, it doesn't look good to be involved in a brawl. If, after you speak with the individual, the situation in question cannot be resolved, take your issues to the next level. Quietly, of course.

RESPONSE TIME: Bookings come and go in a matter of minutes. If you're stuck on the freeway when you get a text, and you can access your cell phone without driving into a Mack truck, then call back ASAP. When clients call to check availability, they usually put in more than one call to more than one artist or agency. If it's a last-minute booking, the client will usually hire whoever returns the call first.

2 GETTING PAID

What a concept. For many of you, this is the toughest part of the job. Most artists dislike the part of being a freelancer that requires them to discuss, arrange for, pick up or collect money from clients. Paychecks are fine. It's just the discussion leading up to the paycheck that can be a little unnerving.

While you are on your own (without an agency), you'll probably be doing what I call the money dance: Negotiating your fees & expenses, preparing deal memos to ensure that the terms and conditions of your work assignment are met, invoicing for payment and collecting the money that is owed to you.

If you were to talk to an established artist, I'm sure he or she would be able to recount the times they didn't get paid, or got paid less than the amount that was agreed upon over the telephone, because the terms and conditions of the job were not confirmed on paper. I wish I could tell you that a handshake or a verbal ok is enough. IT ISN'T. The paper work will protect you and removes all ambiguity regarding what was agreed to. In the event that small claims court becomes a necessity to get paid, all of your bases are covered.

I have taken two clients to court. One was a small record company and the other was a former Miss USA. I won both times because I showed up to court with all of the authorized (signed) paperwork.

In the case against Crystal Agency vs the former Miss USA, she was proudly displaying the images styled by my hair stylist Beth Carter on her website. The judged looked askance at the defendant when I produced screen shots of the images that Miss USA swore she hated and found in our favor.

A paper trail replete with signatures is the only way to insure you will get paid what was agreed upon…consistently.

Discussing money does get easier with practice. It's just the first ten or fifteen conversations that make you sweat. The trick is not to panic. The phone call from an art director or fashion editor excites you but the negotiation makes you sick. With practice, it all gets easier.

PETTY CASH AND LARGER AMOUNTS OF MONEY

Petty cash has to be accounted for even when receipts aren't given if you intend to be reimbursed by a company or the IRS in the form of a write-off. For instance, when you use meters for parking. You can throw small amounts ($50-$100) in your purse, but it's not prudent to do that with several thousand. Artists have been robbed or have left their purses in studio services or at a professional beauty supply store, only to have to spend their own money.

A great way to handle large amounts of cash is to deposit it into your business or personal [interest- bearing] checking or savings account and then use your debit card to pay for the purchases. Another good system is to cash the check. Deposit it into your bank. Pay your creit card bill immediately and use a point-driven credit card to make purchases. What a great way to get your clients to pay for your vacation.

Benefits of using your credit or debit card for production expenses:

- You can use the points for vacation travel or to accept a cool job with a client that doesn't have enough of a budget to put you up in a hotel or pay for your airfare.

- Credit card companies offer insurance for most things that are lost or stolen. Now you can stop worrying your makeup kit or the $500 latex swimsuit in the trunk of your car.

COMMITMENTS

Here's a trick question. You accept a job for less money than you want as a fee, and less money than you need for expenses, what do you do now? Answer: A great job! Nothing is more dishonorable than someone who accepts a job that they don't want to do, and then they do less than their best. A minimum of 100% is what every client deserves once you have accepted the job. If you don't like the pay or the job conditions, don't accept the assignment, and if you didn't know what you were getting yourself into, you should have asked more questions before you said yes.

5 NEGOTIATION

Whether you are with an agency or not, you will be responsible for negotiating with and asking your clients for large and small amounts of money to cover clothing, accessories, props, wigs and hair pieces, special FX makeup, per diem, mileage, kit fees, and more.

While the need for this kind of negotiation happens daily with fashion stylists, costume designers, and prop stylists who can't do their job without spending money, hair and makeup

REESA'S FYI: ON THE JOB TIPS

BE PREPARED: Don't turn into a whiner when a shoot you're on goes longer than expected.

1 Wear comfortable shoes to all of your shoots.

2 Pack snacks that are high in protein for a boost of energy when your blood sugar slips. Power bars or protein shakes are good.

3 Pack and stash personal hygiene products in your kit for "that time of the month". Leaving a shoot because you "forgot" something is unacceptable, even when said with a cute little embarrassing giggle.

EDUCATION: Gain an extra skill, and you can open yourself up to much more work. It increases your marketability. If you're a barber and you take a basic makeup course, you then become a men's groomer. If you're a makeup artist and you take a hair styling course, now you can offer yourself as a hair and makeup artist, which is called for on certain kinds of jobs.

TESTING: You're never too hot to test. Testing should be a never-ending activity. It keeps your work fresh and your mind ticking with creativity. It also gives you an opportunity to experiment with new ideas and trends without the risk of being thrown off a job for not doing what the client wants.

TOO MUCH FUN: Drugs and alcohol are a touchy subject. If the client who hired you is drinking wine near the end of the shoot, and offers you some, you should probably refuse—politely, of course. If everybody is doing it and they keep asking you over and over to take a glass of wine, well, all I say is use your best judgement. Whatever you do, do not consume enough to make you drunk or high and then start acting foolish.

artists who become the heads of their departments in film and television will be responsible for managing the budgets of their departments, and that means money.

Your agency can and will negotiate your fees, per diem, travel expenses, assistant rates and overtime. However, as the artist, only you will be able to determine how many assistants you will need, and estimate the costs of the supplies necessary to successfully complete an assignment.

As an agency owner and negotiator, I often found myself redirecting a conversation that begins as a discussion about my artist's day rate and mysteriously leads into how much I think my stylist will need for clothing, right back to my artist. Here's my typical response to "Well, how much do you think your stylist will need for clothes?":

"Mr. Art Director, without up-to-the-minute knowledge of what's in the marketplace (clothing stores) and a thorough understanding of the clothing needs for this job assignment, I couldn't possibly tell you how much my stylist is going to need for clothing. However, if you're going to be in your office for a little while, I'll have my stylist give you a call, and the two of you can hammer out the details and the numbers. After the two of you have spoken and agreed on a figure for expenses, I will plug the numbers into my estimate and email over a deal memo for your signature."

The keys to getting the budget you need are:

* Not to commit to a figure until you have gathered all the facts about the job.

- Be ready, willing and able to justify (in writing, if necessary) why you need the dollars you say you do to complete the assignment.

- Be prepared to walk away from a job when you are confident that you can't complete it successfully within the budget.

- Stand by your convictions, that's what they're paying you for.

 AGENT TIP:

Here's a trick I have used to successfully negotiate for my artists for years. Once you have all of the numbers written down on paper and the client still insists that you can do the job for less money than what you are requesting—email them the budget and suggest that they cut out anything they feel is unnecessary for the job. Faced with being responsible for cutting something out that might compromise the quality of the production, they often back down and cut the check!

A decision-maker will throw out a figure that the company would like to spend. You don't have to feel tied to that number. Later on in this chapter, I provide a scenario so you can examine the dialogue between a stylist and an art director. By asking lots of questions and fine-tuning your listening skills, you'll soon learn the important questions to ask any decision-maker and how to buy yourself a little time before you blurt out a number that you have to live with.

Now, I haven't forgotten that, in the beginning, artists sometimes have to work miracles and call in a lot of favors from vendors to get the job done. Just be very careful about where you spend your favors. Not everyone needs them, even when it looks that way on the surface. Become a detective when it comes to getting the facts. Don't be afraid to dig a little deeper. Listen very carefully to what people say and even closer to the details they leave out.

Everything is negotiable. Negotiation is intended to produce an agreement about courses of action, or to craft an outcome that will satisfy all parties. You can negotiate your prep, shoot and wrap rate, your assistant's rate, how many assistants you have, the kit fee, the mileage rate, the clothing budget and even how much money you get for petty cash. Everything is negotiable.

If you asked for $800/day to key a job, and you are offered $700/day, and the producer tells you that you can have $300/day for your assistants, ask the producer if you can juggle the money around as long as you accomplish his goals. When he says yes, offer each of your assistants $250/day, and give yourself a raise to $800.

You And The Crew

Every negotiation should begin with you knowing your top—the rate you believe you deserve—and your bottom—the rate below which you will not go. Now, a certain amount of realism must be injected. Everybody wants to make $3,500 a day. But just like the asking price for a house that has been renovated and over-built for the neighborhood, asking for an amount that isn't realistic for your market, the client or your level of experience won't get you anywhere.

Oscar James

Celebrity Hair Stylist

Take a look at our [Show Me the Money] rate chart on page 259. These are pretty standard for the industry as a starting point. For example, CD cover fees start at around $500, and go as high as $2,500. Here's how those numbers roll out regionally:

	Atlanta	Chicago	Los Angeles	New York
CD Covers	$ 500	$ 500	$ 850	$ 1,000
Commercials	$ 500	$ 600	$ 750	$ 900
Press Junket	$ 850	$ 850	$ 1,500	$ 1,500
Print Ad	$ 650	$ 700	$ 850	$ 1,000
Music Video	$ 500	$ 500	$ 600	$ 1,000
Catalog	$ 650	$ 650	$ 700	$ 750

Certain variables that can affect these base numbers upward or downward include:

1 **Your relationship with the decision-maker**

- Has the decision-maker already paid you more money on a previous job? If so, you can begin by asking for the last amount you received for an assignment, as you have established a precedent with that client.

- Has the decision-maker paid you less and wants to keep you there? If so, you'll probably have to fight for every penny you get. Just keep asking for more. You may be able to inch him along.

- Is this a long-time client? If so, he may feel like he gave you your start, and you ought to be grateful. It's unlikely that you'll be able to get this client to step up to too much more money until the tears in your book show him that you really are a star.

2 **Tearsheets**

- If you have several tears in your book that establish you as a player, the decision-maker will already expect you to ask for more money. Do it!

3 **Your relationship with the artist, celebrity, Manager and publicist**

- This is where you're really in the cat bird seat, and it matters little what production says they have in their budget. If the celebrity or their management are insisting that you are the only one who can work on one of their clients, ask for the moon!

4 **Budget**

- They really can't afford to go any higher.

Quite often when you start out, you're not getting the rates you are asking for, but because you want to work, you accept less than you think you deserve. This is okay, everyone does it in the beginning. You have to start somewhere. But, remember, it's hard to get a $500-a-day client to pay you $1,000 once they've gotten used to paying you $500. And what's worse, if you accept too low a rate for the promise of future jobs with better pay, when the client gets more money and can spend a couple thousand dollars a day, they often won't hire you, because you're the $500-a-day artist. With them you've established your rate. But not with a new client. Ask for the money. ABC.

Sometimes you just have to accept it, or stop working for that client. Pick whom you lower your rate for carefully, because some people are short-sighted, and will never see you as more than that. Also, it's important to be able to read people. Some

people just like to argue, and if your rate is $850, and you're dealing with someone who always wants a deal, then you'll have to start at $1,000 and back down to $850 so they feel like they got a deal, and you'll feel like you're being paid what you're worth.

Assistants

You will have to ask for assistants when you need them. Better yet, you'll need to make it known that you have an assistant (or two), and that you require their assistance on whatever job you are being booked for. When discussing your rate with a potential client, talk about your assistant very matter-of-factly. Assume that you will be given a budget for an assistant and talk as though it has already been approved.

Examples:

- Well, Don, I think my assistant and I can knock this out in about three days; let me email over a deal memo for your signature.

- Well honestly, Cliff, my assistant will actually save you money. With her help I can prep this job in two days instead of three.

ABC – Always Be Closing

Remember, at some point, you have to ask for the order. The business. The job assignment. In sales, there are closing questions. For instance, if I thought I had answered all of a client's questions, or objections about purchasing a particular copier, I would go in to close the deal by saying something like, "Mr. Customer, would you like us to install the copier on Monday or Tuesday?" That's called an either or close. You're giving the customer a choice. As a makeup artist, you might say "Would you like to meet with me on Monday or Tuesday to go over the makeup color choices for your wedding?" Or, after

Oscar James is an Emmy Award- winning hairstylist based out of New York. His natural ability to create beautiful hairstyles has afforded him the opportunity to work on beauty campaigns for Revlon, L'Oreal, and Pantene. His editorial work has appeared on the pages of Vogue, Elle, Essence, Cosmo, Vanity Fair, InStyle and his celebrity clients are among the top actresses, models, and singers known today. Tyra Banks, Iman, Vanessa Williams, Halle Berry, and Jennifer Hudson, all have one thing in common, and that is Oscar James. In this interview, Oscar discusses his career trajectory and offers heartfelt advice for artists who are about to strike out on the path of the freelance beauty professional.

Can you tell me how you ended up becoming a hair stylist? Was it something you always wanted to do?

Oscar: I really never thought about hair as a career. As a kid, I loved art, and was always fascinated by colors and making art projects. When I was in the 7th grade, we moved to New York, and I started winning awards in school for my artwork. In the 9th grade, I was able to attend a specialized arts & music high school and got a really great start to my education in the art world.

After 9th grade, my mom moved us back to South Carolina. I remember one day she took me to a beauty salon and something just clicked. I knew it was something I wanted to do. Mind you;, I had been doing my mom and grandma's hair as a kid. I would set their hair at night and comb it out in the morning. I would do my friend's hair too. It just wasn't something I thought of as a career, but something I loved doing. When I was at the salon, I realized it could be a career. I started

talking with a producer about the budget, [even though you may know that he is talking to other stylists], you could say "What's the best time for me to pick up a check for the clothes, 3 or 4 this afternoon?" ABC. Always be closing.

The following pages of dialogue illustrate a typical situation and conversation between an art director and an experienced fashion stylist. You hear the phone ring.

THE KEYS TO NEGOTIATION

1 Listen carefully, and read between the lines.

2 Ask questions.

3 Take notes.

4 Think before you speak.

5 Take your time. Don't feel pressured to answer right away.

6 A-B-C. Always be closing. In other words, ask for what you want.

DENISE: Hello.

DON: Hello, may I speak with Denise.

DENISE: This is Denise.

DON: Hi, Denise, this is Don Drisdale from Artful Records. I looked at your online portfolio today and I think you might be right for a job I've got coming up this Friday. It's a CD cover for a new group, so we don't have a big budget on this one. What's your availability on Friday?

He's asked what appears to be one question, but it's really three.

1	Do you want the job?
2	Are you available to prep Thursday, shoot Friday and wrap on Saturday?
3	Can you work within our budget?

Here's the place most stylists get into trouble. They're so excited about getting the job, they forget to gather enough details about the job to determine whether it's worth their time, effort, resources and, sometimes the favors they will have to call in to get the job done. This is also often a danger zone where the stylist commits to everything and anything, just to get the job. STOP! Be smart! Before you say yes, buy yourself about thirty seconds, take a deep breath, then respond (notice I didn't say answer).

DENISE: It sounds interesting, I'd like to hear more about it. Can you hold on a moment while I grab a pen and my calendar?

DON: Sure, no problem.

Locate a pencil, legal pad and calendar to confirm the dates. Sit poised in a comfortable chair, pick up the phone and ask lots of relevant (leading) questions that will help you to determine how much money, time and manpower it will take to complete the job the clients complete satisfaction.

DENISE: Hi Don, I'm back. Thanks so much for waiting. So, tell me a little bit about the group?

DON: Well, it's a three-guy group. They're pop. We're thinking along the lines of a Rag and Bone sort of vibe. We plan on shooting in the studio and on location.

Hold it! How much information you can glean from the AD's answer to the stylist's last question? Time to ask more questions.

DENISE: What kind of locations have you selected, and how will we be moving from the studio to the location (and back).

DON: We're going to shoot the guys in three locations. One's an old warehouse downtown, the other is a museum in Pasadena, and we'll spend half a day in a studio downtown not far from the warehouse location. The photographer is renting a mobile home for transportation.

Whoa! The art director said there was a small budget on this job. Three locations and a mobile home, locations fees, permits and security are expensive. He may have more money than he is letting on. We're getting some really good information. However, there is one big question that hasn't been asked.

DENISE: By the way Don, who is the photographer?

DON: Kwaku Alston.

As an artist, you should know who's in your sandbox. If CD covers are something you get calls for regularly, it means that you work in the entertainment genre and as such should know who the top shooters are.

The name Kwaku Alston should conjur up images of celebrity portraits, recording artists and advertising campaigns. Alston has shot some of Hollywoods most famous faces and therefore he isn't cheap. Knowing this about the photographer will help

The Hair Makeup & Fashion Styling Career Guide

working at the salon every day after school and taking cosmetology classes at the local vocational school in the evenings. When I graduated from high school, I had both my diploma and my cosmetology license!

Once you graduated, what was your next step?

Oscar: I started working full-time at the salon. I started off shampooing clients' hair. I would sometimes work on 20 people in a day. But I just wanted to be there and learn everything. I was insatiable. I knew it was my passion, and that I could make money at it. I stayed in South Carolina for another three years, but it felt too small. I loved it in New York and felt like that was where I was meant to be, so I moved back. I slept on my friend's living room floor for two2 years, but I was where I needed to be.

I remember seeing a really glam salon down the street that I would pass by every day. I would look up at it and know that I wanted to work there. But I had to wait for my license to transfer to NY. Once that happened, I went in and applied and got hired. They worked me hard, and I stayed for 2 years making $200 a week. The salon owned another location down the street that I wanted to work in, but it required the hair stylists to have a large client base. So, I kept working until I had the clientele, and then just moved on up. But the training I got from that first salon experience was invaluable, and some of it I use to this day.

What did you learn in those early days at the salon?

Oscar: I learned every aspect of doing hair. I just wanted to create really beautiful hair, and that's what I did. My

you to determine whether you will get your day rate when you ask for it and what the clothing budget should be for a recording group that can afford to hire Kwaku Alston to shoot their cover.

DENISE: It sounds great, Don. I really like Kwaku's work. I was working on a job for Sony last week, and got a chance to see some photos he took of a girl group. What's your clothing budget for this act?

DON: Well, I think we have about $2,000 - $3,000.

DENISE: How many changes?

DON: Four.

DENISE: Oh, a rental budget. I'll need to speak with them about bringing their own shoes and accessories?

DON: You don't think we can get clothing and shoes for $3,000?

DENISE: Not really, if you're talking about Rag and Bone, it's kinda' pricey.

DON: We really wanted them to keep the clothes for their upcoming video shoot. How much more do you think we would have to spend if we want to keep the clothes and shoes?

DENISE: To keep the clothes and add shoes? Why don't you let me do a little research and play around with some numbers. I would like to make a few phone calls and see what's out there. I can call you back tomorrow. Would you like me to put together a budget that includes the clothing, my fee plus my assistant?

DON: Yeah…that sounds great.

DENISE: I'll call you in the morning and email it over. Bye.

DON: Bye.

WHAT YOU HEARD	WHAT IT MEANT
1 There are 3 men in the group.	You are going to need an assistant. There is a lot of work involved in styling three people.
2 The music format is pop.	Labels always have money for a 3-boy pop group.
3 The clothing direction is Rag & Bone.	You will need plenty of cash. Rag & Bone clothing is pricey.
4 There are at least two locations.	You will be moving clothing and bodies from one place to another.
5 There are 3 locations, not 2 as mentioned. They is a warehouse downtown, a museum in Pasadena and a photo studio.	There's a budget for security, a mobile home, locations & studio rental.
6 The photographer is well known, working, accomplished.	He's probably getting a reasonable day rate, between $5,000 - $7,500 per day.

NOTES

....

....

....

....

....

client base grew because these women had never had their hair look so good. It was my passion, and I did what I had to do to perfect it. I ended up with so many clients that I was able to negotiate a higher commission at the salon and was booked solid. I had no room for new clients.

Did you need an assistant at that time to help with all of the work?

Oscar: I did. She was one of my favorites. This girl worked so hard, was so professional, and I could tell she really wanted to be there. She was quiet and got work done. That made me really appreciate her.

What made you go from working at a salon to working on celebrities?

Oscar: I needed a change. I wanted to be inspired. I ended up leaving the salon and moving over to one that was very high profile. While there, I met Sam Fine and he saw my work. He recommended me to Kimora Lee Simmons, then Tyra Banks, and Vanessa Williams. It just went from there. Tyra wanted me to do her hair for her jobs, but I didn't have a name for myself yet, so her clients wouldn't hire me. Instead, she would just have me come to her house the night before a booking so I could do her hair. In 1997, I decided to just take a leap of faith and go completely freelance.

Did you sign with an agency?

Oscar: Yes, I did, but I got a lot of work via word-of-mouth. Essence Magazine also introduced me to so many people that really helped build up my career up.

Quite a few things went on during this conversation. For one, the Art Director, Don, asked a buying question: How much more do you think we would have to spend? This is an indication that he has more money, and that he probably knew he was going to have to spend more to get the look he wants. Other issues that might need to be addressed in order for the stylist to complete this job successfully include:

— **Prep days:** How many will be needed for shopping, fittings and meetings with the group?

— **Assistant:** You will probably need your assistant for each day. What kind of day rate can you get for him/her?

— **Clothing budget:** You may need MORE money. The look is contemporary. You won't be able to rent anything for them. You'll be shopping from department and specialty stores, and they DON'T rent clothes.

— Take the budget that the Art Director (AD) has offered ($3,000) and divide it by the number of guys in the group (3) and then divide that number by the number of looks (4) that the AD wants. You can determine whether or not $3,000 will meet the goals of the AD for the kind of look he wants for this group. $250 per look seems quite low for authentic Rag and Bone where a single pair of pants cost $250. However you can create a Rag and Bone look by mixing and matching some other less expensive brands if necessary.

I hope this exercise helped to get you thinking about the realities of doing a job of this magnitude and each person's role in the success of the shoot. I can't stress enough the importance of understanding who's in your sandbox, cultivating your resources, knowing your value and taking your time during these kinds of negotiations.

Now that you know what to say, let's take a look at the kind of fees you can expect for each segment of the market place, i.e., editorial, music videos, advertising, commercials, runway, etc.

Editorial

Magazines have what the industry calls an editorial rate. It's a fee schedule that usually ranges from $100.00 to $350.00 per day. Many of you will be surprised to find out that Allure pays a makeup artist $150.00 per day regardless of whether it's a cover, inside spread or a tiny 2X2 photo of an author in the New Books section.

Check out the RESOURCES section in the back of the book for a list of magazines that you may want to approach once you have started working on your portfolio. The editors of Vogue know (and so should you) that one of their pages in your portfolio or on your website can take you from obscurity to stardom as a makeup, hair, or fashion stylist or manicurist in the blink of an eye.

Donna Karan tells a story about her early days as a designer. In a TV interview, she tells of how no one was buying her dresses. One day she received a review from the fashion editor of Vogue and moved thousands of dresses in a single day.

The exception to the editorial rules is that 'the bigger the magazine, the smaller the rate'. They don't have to pay more than $150. Everyone wants to work for them. When small magazines do pay, they sometimes pay MORE to get good people. However, often with small publications, you work for credit only.

Runway

Aaah, the lure of the glamorous runway shows with all that back-stage action and fun in exciting cities like New York, Paris and Milan. The reality is more like $250 per show. Not bad, actually. You can do more than one in a day and the hours—just a few—aren't bad either.

Catalogue

Catalogue is the assembly line of the fashion industry. The idea is to crank it out. It's not at all like editorial where you might do 4-6 looks or less in a day. On a catalogue shoot, you may have 10-15 looks in one day. Of course, there's the cool catalogue like Victoria's Secret, J. Crew and Banana Republic, but there are also the factory catalogues like Sears and JC Penney. The beauty of catalogue is the number of days in a row that you typically work on a single project. The rates start at about $450 a day and can go as high as $850. Not bad when you're working for 5 days at a time.

CD Covers

In the music business, day rates aren't set in stone like those in the editorial market. Getting well paid on a CD cover usually depends on 1) Whether the artist is new or established, 2) Whether you are new or established, and 3) Whether the artist or their management has clout.

An artist with clout usually means that the powers at the record label from the president to the publicist believe the artist could be the next Ed Sheeran or Beyoncé Knowles. The company is pulling out all the stops and sparing no expense on

Are you still focusing on celebrities, or are you working in different avenues now?

Oscar: I do still work with celebrities, but want to move into doing more hair for TV and film. When I did Top Model, I had to join the union. I realized that through the union, I could get a pension and health insurance. I have a financial planner, and I'am good with my money, but having that extra benefit for when I retire is something I love. So, I really want to focus on more union work. I would advise young artists to start working in TV & film early and join the union. That way, they can start accumulating a good pension for their future.

How often do you hire assistants?

Oscar: Not often. Maybe once a year. Most of the work I do now is on a one-on-one basis, so I don't need the extra help. I also have trust issues when it comes to bringing someone new on board. Young people these days are just so different. You see them on set with their phones taking pictures, and going "live" on social media. You just need to be quiet and do your work!

What advice would you give to someone that wanted to be an assistant?

Oscar: Be of service. This is not all about you. Be giving. A great assistant can look and see what needs to be done without being asked. Pay attention and be there to help.

What are your favorite types of jobs outside of TV and film?

Oscar: I love jobs that are just pleasant. For example, I

the accoutrements necessary to propel the artist to STARDOM! I have witnessed makeup, hair and fashion stylists being flown in from faraway cities to style and groom the likes of a perceived new star. The artist without clout, on the other hand, can mean that even though the deal is signed, the record label is not expecting huge numbers of record sales, so they aren't coming out of pocket with big dollars for glam. The objective for the label in this scenario is to get the pictures taken and the CD released with the least amount of expense possible.

After speaking with quite a few art directors in Los Angeles and New York, where most of the music business is centered, we found that the rates listed in the chart on page 233 applied across the board. We also learned that most record companies were accustomed to paying an additional twenty (20) percent agency commission.

It's worth noting that a lot has changed in the music business in the last 10 years, since downloads became the norm. Not nearly as much money is spent on artists until they start to show real promise as money-makers. Still, the numbers aren't bad and the music business can be a lot of fun.

Print Advertising & Commercials

The rates for print advertising depend upon who's being marketed to. "General market advertising campaigns market to the wealthiest and as well as the most populous segment of the United States and therefore spend the greatest amounts of money producing print advertising and commercials for that segment.

Multicultural advertising is broken down into African American, Asian, Latin American, etc., and Urban is often used to refer to inner city youth. Less money is expected to be returned from marketing to these groups and thus the rates paid for glam can be less.

Our research showed that an average day rate for an artist on a general market ad campaign was $750 per day and could go as high as $2,500 per day if a celebrity was involved. African American and Hispanic day rates started at around $500 per day and went as high as $2,500, again if a celebrity was included. Asian campaign day rates were stable at about $750 to $850 per day. The Latin market has become very important to America and you can expect to see those numbers rise over the next few years.

Music Videos: How They Work

While the pay for working on music videos isn't what it used to be, record companies and musicians still do them occasionally. The record company queries 2-3 directors about working on a new or established recording artist's upcoming music video. The music for the recording artist's new song is given to the directors who then write what's called a treatment (one-three-page storyline). The treatments are read and the director who wrote the best treatment gets the gig. At this point the production company, as well as the recording artist and his/her manager, begin looking at glam portfolios—separately.

If the recording artist worked with people that he or she really liked on the CD cover, they typically request those people for the music video—which is often not the same people that the director wants to work with on the project. At this point, a few things can happen—and do.

The Hair Makeup & Fashion Styling Career Guide

1 The producer may request that the recording artist's portfolio picks be emailed over, so that they can be evaluated by the director.

2 The director may look through them, say they're fine and tell the producer to go ahead and book them.

3 The director may look at them, not like them, and communicate this to the recording artist, at which point the recording artist may defer to the director.

4 The director may look at them, not like them, and communicate this to the recording artist, at which point the recording artist does not defer to the director, and a test of wills ensues wherein the director gets some of what he or she wants and the recording artist get some of their choices as well.

5 Or, in the most drastic of cases, the director does not like the recording artist's picks, and instructs the producer to pretend to book the requested glam squad. The recording artist and management are told that the glam artists that they requested were unavailable. Usually the artist doesn't find out that their glam squad wasn't booked until the day of the video.

love when I get called to work with Vanessa Williams. I'll have a normal call time and can drive to her house where she'll shoot. She makes nice food;, it's a relaxed atmosphere, and we wrap early. Those are my favorite types of jobs!

What do you think of social media?

Oscar: I love it. It's so much fun! I think it can be helpful if used correctly. I use my platforms to uplift people and give them a glimpse into my life in a real way.

Who's on your bucket list?

Oscar: The icons! I would love to do hair for Oprah, Diana Ross, J. Lo, and Dionne Warwick.

What has changed in the way you do your work in the past 5-7 years?

Oscar: Social media is something new, but it hasn't affected me or my work. It does help you reach more people and give you a voice, but you need to be careful not to get caught up comparing yourself to others. You need to be mindful of how much you absorb, and use it to motivate and inspire.

What hasn't changed in how you do your work?

Oscar: Nothing. I've always been "first come first serve" with my clients. I stick to my commitments. I'm prompt, courteous, pay attention, and do what's right.

 TIP: If you have a close relationship with an artist and their management, be sure to stay connected. If you are told about an upcoming project and don't get a call to book you for it, be sure to let the artist know that you are available and haven't heard from or been booked by the production company,

Working on most music videos is not going to make you rich. Tired—yes. Rich—no. No one thinks they are making enough money on a music video. Not the director, or the producer, and certainly not the glam squad. Music videos come with long hours. It's not uncommon for one to shoot for 16 hours.

Music Videos: How Much They Pay

Music video budgets are low for everyone except artists like Beyoncé, Janet Jackson, Sam Smith, Taylor Swift, Meghan Trainor, Adele and Rhianna who still get million-dollar video budgets. Everyone else gets a $40,000 to $100,000 budget and a request for miracles, please!

Makeup artists and hair stylists on these low budget projects get between $350 to $650 per day, unless the recording artist is demanding their presence on the video. When the artist is represented by an agent, the twenty percent agency commission is squeezed out of a nearby rock. The poor fashion stylist is lucky to get one prep day to style a four-girl group and ten extras for $500 per day. Requesting overtime can get you the proverbial dial tone quicker than you can say "Hello, are you there?" Music video budgets have been slashed so much these days that producers think flat rate is a new line item on their budget sheet. Is it that bad? Sometimes, however, don't ever let that stop you from asking for what you deserve—and that includes overtime.

Television And Film

Television and film rates depend on several variables:

1	Whether the project is union or non-union.
2	The overall budget.
3	What position classification you are hired for (Department Head, Key, 1st, 2nd, etc.).
4	How much the producers want you.
5	Your level of experience (How long have you been in the business?) and expertise.
6	Your résumé (How many TV/Film credits do you have?).
7	If you have special skills (Are you known for producing excellence in a specific area?).

If you are just starting out on non-union projects, you will not be taking home the big paycheck. So, chalk it up to paying your dues and getting all the experience you can. We discovered that the lowest printed hourly rate was about $20 per hour, and the highest printed hourly rate for a makeup department head was about $33 per hour.

NOTES

The Hair Makeup & Fashion Styling Career Guide

Do you have any advice for novice hairstylists starting out in the industry?

Oscar: Don't give up when things get tough. Keep working hard. I've dealt with losing everything I owned and had to reinvent myself and start over. Make peace with everything and take tough times as a lesson.

Focus and find out who you want to be. You need something to ground you and remind you of who you are. Focus on the kind of stylist that you want to be and don't let anyone "should-you." ". You just do you.

Last question.....what are the three things in your kit that you cannot live without?

Oscar: A good holding spray, an edge control product, and brow gel.

IN HIS KIT: 3 THINGS OSCAR CAN'T LIVE WITHOUT

- A good holding spray.
- An edge control product.
- Brow gel.

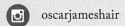 oscarjameshair

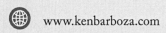 www.kenbarboza.com

PAPERWORK

Handle your business! Once everything is agreed to, the paperwork mill starts to grind, and never more loudly than it does with freelance artists. Makeup and hair stylists generally use three simple forms: **Deal Memo, Invoice** and **Credit Sheet,** and occasionally the Request for Advance. However, for a fashion stylist, we add the **Stylist's Letter, Request for Advance, Clothing Addendum,** and **Stylist's Worksheet.** On the next pages, we'll share some of them with you (in the order that they are typically used, explain what they're for, and even fill some of them out for you, so you'll know how to do it yourself.

Deal Memo

The DEAL MEMO spells out the terms and conditions, day days, dates and rates rates under which the artist will work on a project. It can be adapted for use in all industries. At Crystal Agency, we used it to confirm every job our artists worked on, including those where only a written credit was being given in lieu of payment. The deal memo provides the creative decision-maker with a clear and concise description of the deal (your rate, overtime, kit fee, mileage, etc.). It is a legally binding document. Fulfill your part of the bargain and, if a client refuses to pay you, a document like this one with a signature from the powers that be will assist you in your quest for payment in small claims court. You can also add and/or delete words or paragraphs as needed. The vital information contained in a deal memo includes:

1 A JOB DESCRIPTION. Spells out who you are, what you do, the job you are working on, whom you are working on (celebrity/recording artist) and whether or not you will have people (assistants) working with you.

2 A DAY RATE. Spells out how much you are getting paid for the first "X" number of hours (Rate Base) in a specific day before overtime begins to accrue.

3 The OVERTIME RATE. The rate of pay for two-hour increments of Time that begin to accrue over the rate base hours called Time and One Half, Double-Time and Golden Time (Triple Time).

4 A FLAT RATE. A flat dollar figure you agree to work for without overtime, regardless of how many hours the shoot goes on.

5 The agreed-upon number of days you work be on the job.

6 The number of approved assistants and their rates.

7 The clothing, makeup, hair or nails budget.

8 When the artist is to be paid.

9 What happens if something is damaged.

10 When you are to be reimbursed for damaged items.

11 What should happen to the remaining items at the end of the shoot.

RESET SAVE
PRINT SUBMIT

DEAL MEMO

This deal memo confirms that _____ will work on

CLIENT: _____	CLIENT JOB NO: _____
CLIENT JOB NAME: _____	CLIENT PO NO: _____
JOB NO: _____ PHOTOGRAPHER/DIRECTOR: _____	
CONTACT PERSON: _____	JOB TITLE: _____

PREP DAYS: 0 ____ DATES: _____
TRAVEL DAYS: 0 ____ DATES: _____
SHOOT DAYS: 0 ____ DATES: _____
WRAP DAYS: 0 ____ DATES: _____
WEATHER DAYS: 0 ____ DATES: _____
ASSISTANT DAYS: 0 ____ DATES: _____
TOTAL DAYS: 0 ____ NOTES: _____

RATES • TERMS • CONDITIONS

DAY RATE/FEE: ____ 0.00 PER ____ FULL OR ____ HALF DAY UP TO ____ HRS
STRAIGHT TIME FEE @ 1.0 X THE RATE/FEE: ____ 0.00 PER HOUR FOR EACH HOUR IN EXCESS OF ____ HRS
OVERTIME FEE @ 1.5 X THE RATE/FEE: ____ 0.00 PER HOUR FOR EACH HOUR IN EXCESS OF ____ HRS
OVERTIME FEE @ 2.0 X THE RATE/FEE: ____ 0.00 PER HOUR FOR EACH HOUR IN EXCESS OF ____ HRS
PREP RATE/FEE: ____ 0.00 PER ____ FULL OR ____ HALF DAY UP TO ____ HRS
TRAVEL RATE/FEE: ____ 0.00 PER ____ FULL OR ____ HALF DAY UP TO ____ HRS
WRAP (RETURN) RATE/FEE: ____ 0.00 PER ____ FULL OR ____ HALF DAY UP TO ____ HRS
ASSISTANT RATE/FEE: ____ 0.00 PER ____ FULL OR ____ HALF DAY UP TO ____ HRS
OVERTIME FEE @ 1.5 X THE RATE: ____ 0.00 PER HOUR FOR EACH HOUR IN EXCESS OF ____ HRS
EXPENSES: ____ 0.00 FOR _____
0% AGENCY COMMISSION: ____ 0.00 _____
MINIMUM BOOKING: ____ 0.00

CANCELLATIONS & POSTPONEMENTS
IF NOTICE OF CANCELLATION OR POSTPONEMENT IS GIVEN LESS THAN THREE (3) BUSINESS DAYS BEFORE THE SCHEDULED SHOOT DATE, THE CLIENT WILL BE CHARGED 100% OF THE FEE.

INVOICE PAYMENT
The invoice associated with this job assignment is due and payable no later than _____. If payment has not been received by that date, a new invoice will be generated with a 2% late fee per month due on the unpaid balance. To avoid this charge, please pay your invoice promptly. If you will be paying by credit card, please initial here: _____, and complete the additional paperwork titled Credit Card Authorization.

AUTHORIZATION
Your signature, working title and today's date is required below, and will serve as confirmation and agreement of the number of days and dates booked, and agreed upon fee/rate. Once signed, you have agreed to the terms and conditions as they are stated above. Please email a signed copy to me at _____ by ____:00 ___ on _____.

NAME: _____ TITLE: _____ DATE: _____
       SIGNATURE

NOTES

....

....

....

....

The Hair Makeup & Fashion Styling Career Guide

NOTES

Items 9, 10 and 11 are very important, because you don't want to get strung out with several hundred or thousands of dollars sitting on your credit cards, while you wait for someone to approve reimbursements for clothing that was damaged on the shoot. This sometimes requires that an additional clause be added to the confirmation. At Crystal Agency, when necessary, we always added a clause after "Total Minimum Fees" and before "Cancellation & Postponements". Here's an example:

Sample Clause

Production Company agrees to accept financial responsibility for damage to clothing, accessories, shoes, etc....that occurs during the music video shoot as a result of wearing by the artists, extras and/or principals. Monies due for damage to clothing, accessories, shoes, etc.... that cause fashion stylist Stylist Name to go over her $7,000.00 budget must be reimbursed to Stylist Name within 12 hours of damage assessment given to Production Company by Stylist Name. Upon verbal and/or written damage assessment, Production Company will provide Stylist Name with a check for overages which she will use to pay her vendors.

NOTES

NOTES

Many years ago, one of my fashion stylists; Lisa Michelle, was doing work for a small record label in LA. Everything was going along nicely until' we sent in the invoice. Thirty days, 45 days, 90 days later, we still hadn't been paid. I called numerous times, and as a last resort, I filed our case in small claims court.

The president of the company—who was named in my complaint didn't show up, and so the judge found in our favor.

The next day, I sent a letter stating that we had won, and that he was required to send me a check for the balance due, plus the additional fees that the judge had tacked on. Still I got no word. Luckily—Now this is the 'Being Organized Part'—since this was a styling job, we had collected a check from the record label for the clothing advance.

I went to the folder, and there it was, a copy of the check. I promptly took a copy of the check to the sheriff's office, and they promptly took $5,000 dollars out of the record label's bank account. If money is important to you...Get Organized!

Sample Deal Memo
The Request For Advance

This form is a special invoice that permits a client to release funds to an artist for expenses such as clothing, accessories, props, wigs, makeup, etc. It gives the client a record of your social security number, as well as a description of what and/or whom the funds will be used for.

An artist was confused about why a record company would send her a 1099 tax form at the end of the year for monies they had given her. "I spent all the money on their artist," she said. True enough. She had spent all the money on the artist, and, further, she had dutifully given the record label all of the receipts. But, artists, here's the deal. It is your responsibility to make copies of all receipts and keep them on file to show your accountant at the end of the year. As a matter of fact, you should maintain a file drawer with duplicate folders complete with your own set of job numbers for each assignment. In it, you should catalogue every piece of paper collected by you or your assistants in the execution and completion of a job assignment. A single manila folder with all of the paper you have gathered for a job will keep you from having a big IRS headache down the line. Following is a general list of contents you should keep in each of your job folders:

NOTES

1. A contact sheet with the names, addresses, phone and email addresses of every creative decision-maker you come in contact with on the job.

2. An ENVELOPE for your receipts.

3. Two credit sheets. One for your professional credit and one for the clothing or product credits.

4. The DEAL MEMO that you got signed by a decision-maker prior to the job.

5. An ADVANCE REQUEST form if you submitted one prior to the job and received funds for expenses (ie. clothing, props, accessories, makeup, hair, wigs, etc.)

6. A copy of the CHECK or bank transfer paperwork you received for expenses.

7. The INVOICE you submitted upon completion of the job.

8. An EXPENSE Sheet which is used to record expenses for which you have no receipts such as mileage, parking meter use, tipping valet's and sky caps at airports, etc.

Sample Request for Advance

REQUEST FOR ADVANCE

INVOICE

DATE | INVOICE NO.

BILL TO:

ARTIST JOB NO: _____
SOCIAL SECURITY NO: _____
CLIENT JOB NAME: _____
CLIENT JOB NUMBER: _____
KEY CONTACT PERSON: _____
PURPOSE FOR ADVANCE: _____
MEDIUM: _____

This invoice is for _____ . The scheduled shoot date is: _____ .
CLOTHING, PROPS, KIT EXPENSES, ETC.
It is imperative that I receive the advance by: _____ .

EXPENSES:

1. _____ $ _____
2. _____ $ _____
3. _____ $ _____
4. _____ $ _____
5. _____ $ _____

EXPENSES TOTAL: $ _____

NOTES:
_____
_____
_____

PLEASE MAKE YOUR CHECK PAYABLE TO:

_____
_____
_____

© MOTIVATIONAL MEDIA PRODUCTIONS dba CRYSTAL WRIGHT ENT. 2011

The Hair Makeup & Fashion Styling Career Guide

15 ACTIONS
YOU CAN TAKE TO GET REHIRED AND REFERRED
By Susan Cabral-Ebert

1 You are a reflection of your work. Come to work dressed and groomed as a professional, and you will be given respect. Leggings and a t-shirt or shorts are inappropriate for work on the set. This is not your hobby.

2 Be on time.

3 Remember that the camera sees everything. Never think "the camera will never see it."

4 Be sure your equipment is neat and clean and that your station looks organized.

5 Treat everyone with kindness and respect. Everyone on set serves a vital function that is necessary to the successful completion of the project.

6 Check your ego at the door.

7 Listen carefully and cultivate the ability to translate as well as create.

Advance Check

The advance check is given to artists for the purpose of renting and/or purchasing clothing, accessories, and props if you're a fashion/wardrobe stylist, and supplies such as prosthetics, wigs or other makeups that may not be regular items in a kit.

Without that advance check, I have witnessed artists get burned by large and small companies alike. The client insists that the budget will be "X" amount, and directs the artist to GO AHEAD and get started shopping on their own cash and credit cards. The result is usually a clothing budget and stylist's fee that are cut in half two days later, leaving the stylist hanging out to dry with a bunch of returns, restocking fees and an invoice from an assistant for two days of work. Paperwork first. Remember I said it.

THE RULE IS THIS: Unless you are working with a longtime client you trust or have worked with before, or you have a signed deal memo describing the terms, conditions, fees, and expenses connected with the job, STOP! Keep your credit cards in your pocket, your cash in the bank, save your contacts for the gig that has been confirmed on paper, and let your assistant work for another stylist today. You are about to get Screwed!

Authorizations: Who Can Sign

If the person who booked you isn't around to sign the deal memo or addendum and/or they can't be tracked down so that you can email it over for signature, think again about the PA who says, "Oh, I can sign it!" A lesser person's signature might not be enough to get you paid or reimbursed for overages on the job. You might just want to sit tight until a person of authority (producer, production manager, director, art director, photographer, etc.) shows up.

Who Should Sign Your Paperwork?

TO SIGN	NOT TO SIGN
Print Advertising: • Creative Director • Art Director • Corporate Publicist	• Someone's Assistance
Print Advertising: • Creative Director • Art Director • In House Publicist (works for the Corporate)	• Someone's Assistance • Artist Managers (when you are billing the label for the Job) • Independent Publicists • Recording Artists
TV Commercials/Video • Executive Producer • Line Producer • Production Manager • Production Coordinator	• PA (Production Assistant)

NOTES

....

....

....

The Hair Makeup & Fashion Styling Career Guide

15 ACTIONS YOU CAN TAKE TO GET REHIRED AND REFERRED
By Susan Cabral-Ebert

8 Be willing to learn from others and never feel that your way is the only way. Colleagues have knowledge that is valuable to you and for you. What you learn can shorten your learning curve and serve you for years to come.

9 Stay clear of company politics and gossip as much as possible. Listen but don't repeat.

10 Be prepared. Do your homework and don't assume anything. If you have questions or are unsure of something—ASK! People are usually willing to help and asking will save you the embarrassment of being wrong.

11 Make everyone who enters your room, trailer or space feel welcome.

12 Be honest with your UPM (Unit Production Manager) and AD (Assistant Director) about time and money. Actors are fickle, but UPMs and ADs never forget.

13 If you accept an assistant position, embrace it. Even though you key and department head your own shows, it's an honor to assist someone who needs your help and trusts your abilities.

Invoice

Professional people have professional invoices. Prepare one IMMEDIATELY when you get home at the end of the job, and send it in along with a signed copy of the deal memo that was signed when you accepted the job. ALWAYS include vitals such as: PO Numbers, Job Numbers, Job Dates, etc. on your invoice. It will expedite the processing of your invoice and make it easier for the accounting department to pay you on time.

There are two invoicing services that you should look into: Freshbooks.com and Zoho.com. Freshbooks is a little pricier but totally reliable. I've been using Zoho for 2 years now after switching from Freshbooks and I love it. It has more capability and it's a lot less expensive.

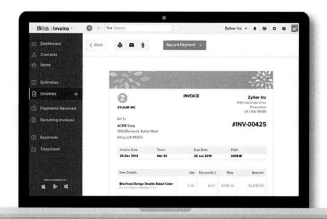

Credit Sheet

The credit sheet is sent to the editorial department of a magazine to ensure that the artists are credited properly in the publication. Following is an example.

FIRST & LAST NAME

JOB TITLE

CREDIT SHEET

Client:	SONY MUSIC
Job Name and/or Number:	SM41776
Project Title:	OVER THE MOON
Artist/Subject:	CELINE DION
Editorial Section & Issue:	N/A &
Photo Session Date:	MAY 22, 2013
Art Director:	KELLY GLEASON
Photo Editor:	N/A
Fashion Editor:	N/A
Sittings Editor:	N/A
Photographer:	DAVID ROTH

CREDITS SHOULD READ AS FOLLOWS:

Makeup by:	CARRY STYLEWISE
Makeup & Hair by:	
Mens Grooming by:	
Hair by:	
Fashion Styling by:	
Hair, Makeup & Styling by:	
Set Decoration by:	
Prop Styling by:	
Manicure by:	
Art Direction by:	
_____ by:	
_____ by:	

Should you have any questions regarding this information
Please call FIRST NAME LAST NAME @ (323) 555-1212
or email us at FirstName@FirstLast.com

FIRST NAME LAST NAME
WWW.FIRSTNAMELASTNAME.COM
FIRSTNAME@FIRSTNAMELASTNAME.COM

If you are represented by an agency, they will take care of this detail. However, if not, you will need to do it yourself.

When emailing over your credit, it's important to remember that editors and art directors are working on lots of different projects, and while your one-credit line in the magazine is important to you, you may have to provide them with a little more information than just MAKEUP BY MARY COLETTI to ensure that it is printed accurately in an upcoming issue.

The credit sheet pictured here will give you an idea of the kind of information a credits editor or art director will need in order to put your name beside the right photo(s).

A purchase order is often referred to as a PO. Pronounced Pee-Oh. It is an official document issued by a buyer (record label, clothing company, production company, etc.) to a seller (fashion stylist, wardrobe stylist, costume designer, etc.), indicating the type, quantities and agreed upon prices for products or services the seller will provide to the buyer.

It's a legal offer to purchase products or services at agreed-upon prices (your day rate for a specific amount of time).

Acceptance of a PO by a seller (that's you) usually forms a once-off contract between the buyer and seller. Other important information on a purchase order can include how merchandise is to be returned to the client plus how and when the invoice is going to be paid (15 days, 30 days), etc.

15 ACTIONS YOU CAN TAKE TO GET REHIRED AND REFERRED
By Susan Cabral-Ebert

14 Learn and practice the complexities of your craft.

15 Familiarize yourself with protocol on a film set.

Susan Cabral-Ebert is President and Assistant Business Representative of IATSE Local 706 Union for Makeup Artists & Hair Stylists. She is a member of the Academy of Motion Picture Arts And Sciences and the Academy of Television Artists And Sciences. She has been nominated for 4 Emmys.

You should always ask for a PO#, and add it to your invoice when you send it in. It confirms that you were authorized to provide the services, and ensures that you will get paid.

ASSISTING

Assisting is a great way to learn and experience set life without being responsible for the outcome of a project. You will learn set etiquette, politics, tips, and techniques from the best in the business. All without getting in too much trouble if you make a mistake here and there. But there are some mistakes that can get you canned forever. Tobi Britton explains:

THE ART AND ETIQUETTE OF ASSISTING
by Tobi Britton

There is no doubt that assisting an established artist is a fabulous way to learn the craft of freelance hair, makeup or fashion styling. It can be challenging to inspire a key artist to bring you on, and being an assistant doesn't always guarantee that the diva artist you are working for will, in turn, share their pearls of wisdom, thus making life easier for you. I would like to suggest that you should welcome the more difficult road, for, in the long run, you will be a better prepared and more solid artist than those who found an easy way.

When I decided to become a makeup artist, I figured that as soon as someone important saw my natural talent, they would hire me immediately. I looked at other artists' work in magazines and thought—I could do that, it's no big deal. Fortunately, I never said that to anyone. I was a bit obnoxious, but, at the time, I just thought I was extremely motivated!

Let's take a look at the industry. Ours is a most unnerving of art forms. We are the only artists that have our canvas talk back to us and tell us whether they like it or not! If that isn't bad enough, we then have art directors, photographers, directors, and editors waiting to let us know if they like it, too. There are also times when the director loves it, and the actress hates it and vice versa. Successful artists need a pretty strong sense of self, a heaping tablespoon of talent and a truckload of people skills.

Just remember this:

- The world owes you nothing.
- Be grateful for any help you receive along the way.
- Stay open.
- Be loyal and give credit to those who help you.
- Your time will come—be patient.

So, what is assisting? Assisting is a form of the old 'give and get'. What you actually do on set depends on the key artist's needs.

- What You Give:
- Make another artist shine.
- Keep all of the supplies, tools and the table organized.
- Set up and pack the artist's kit.
- Clean and sanitize tools and products.
- Run errands.
- Watch the set like a hawk.
- Create makeup and hair applications and touchups when requested.
- Have your key's back.

What You Get:

- An opportunity to see and experience a shoot.
- An opportunity to see how a pro handles the set, organizes and problem-solves.
- An opportunity to see how a pro talks to and negotiates with the key players on set.
- An opportunity to learn on the set, without responsibility for the outcome.
- An opportunity to learn new techniques.
- An opportunity to be referred for jobs.
- An opportunity to add the key artists name to your résumé and someone who can vouch for you.
- Credibility with other artists who are looking for a trustworthy assistant.

NOTES

_____
_____
_____
_____
_____
_____
_____
_____
_____
_____
_____

What Assisting is Not:

- A networking opportunity.

- Your opportunity to hand out all of your marketing materials and share your online website with the decision-makers, .

- Your opportunity to become besties with the decision-makers or talent.

- Your opportunity to outshine the key.

- Your opportunity to demonstrate how much more you know than the key artist.

- The time to ask tons of questions.

- A good time to return all of your phone calls because there is a lull in the work flow.

- Your opportunity to let those in charge know how YOU would have done the work differently.

So why all of the rules? What's the big deal if you hand out a few cards? Think of working as an assistant as being invited to the home of your best friend and her fiancé's. Your best friend is the artist who hired you. Her fiancé is anyone you may feel like networking with. Would you approach her fiancé and tell him that you would make a better girlfriend than she, or that you would cost a lot less to live with?! Would you give him your number? What if he asked you for yours? Would you give it to him then?

Be worthy of another's trust. It will benefit you many times over, and much more than handing out your card inappropriately. Not only will it build character and good karma, the artist that you are assisting will probably recommend you for other jobs in the future. If your ego won't allow you to work for another artist, or you feel jealousy toward other artists, then DO NOT accept assisting jobs. If you are really serious about assisting, here are some things to do:

1	Don't give up! It may appear that doors are being slammed in your face but if you are consistent, persistent, and nice, something will open up. Just don't be surprised if it takes four to six months of contacting the same person.
2	Maintain a list of five to ten key artists that you are reaching out to at all times. You will have to throw some stuff up against the wall to see what sticks.
3	Be specific about why you want to work with a particular artist. They are going to want to hear more than, "I like your work." Everyone likes their work.
4	Don't give in because some artists are being downright rude to you when you ask to assist. Unfortunately, people sometimes mirror and then project (unwittingly) their own bad experiences onto others
5	If someone asks you for your card, refer them to your key. Many times, the key will tell you it is all right to give your card. This says a lot about your character and professionalism, to the key and others.

When you get an opportunity to assist, remember that your place is one of a support person. Make the person who hired you shine. Following these simple guidelines will help you tremendously with your career.

Agency Assistants Lists

We receive calls from people daily asking if they can assist our artists. While we only have a small roster of artists who maintain a list of 1 or 2 assistants each, the bigger agencies, like Celestine, Cloutier Remix, Bryan Bantry and The Wall Group, have much larger rosters of artists who need assistants.

Every agency has an assistants list whether they own up to it or not. The best way to get on the list is by doing your homework. Gather information about five to ten artists you would like to assist, the kinds of projects they work on and the agencies who represent them. This approach is more impressive than, "Hi, I'm a makeup artist and I want to work with your artists." Some agencies represent 20 makeup artists. Be specific so they can help you.

Agencies receive résumés and cleverly put-together cover letters from freelancers wanting to work with their artists all the time. The agency photocopies the résumé and forwards it to the artist. However, very few of artists even bother to follow-up, because they are so busy. The need for an assistant materializes when there is a big job with lots of principals and extras that need dressing, grooming or makeup. That's the moment when our artists begin frantically trying to find more assistants to help them out. Often it's the agency that fielded those calls in the first place that does the searching and booking of assistants, so don't give up.

The Hair Makeup & Fashion Styling Career Guide

NOTES

I often hear artists say, "Well I called them but they didn't get back to me." And guess what, they probably won't. The person who needs to follow up is YOU! The squeaky wheel gets the grease. After you have made the initial introduction via email or phone, be sure to follow up with an email update and then a phone call once every 30 days. You'll have a much better chance of getting work, because agencies remember those artists who continue to follow-up, and follow-thru with a smile. Also, if you have even a single picture of your work—send it. It will give the agency something to keep on file and reference.

TV and film hair stylist Susan Lipson of On Set Motion Picture Hair Academy suggests that you go to the set and introduce yourself. Ask for the makeup or wardrobe department if it's a TV show, or the costume department on a feature film. People bond with people and voices, rarely paper [résumés].

Lastly, follow directions. If you meet or speak with a person who says call me on Monday at 12PM, call on Monday at 12PM.

BUILDING THE STORY

In her book Mastering Fashion Styling former fashion stylist Jo Dingemans said, "A fashion story begins with an editor's choice of trends, direction and seasonal musts for that month." What follows is a way to think about and include a magazine editor's thought process into your own when building a story for a test.

In creating your own fashion or beauty stories for testing, take a moment to think beyond the pages of your favorite magazine for inspiration.

Think, as the top editors must, about world affairs, art, celebrity, pop culture and politics and how they impact a designers' work or an emerging brand. What's big news? Is it a particular color? Or is there a political or social theme that permeated the runways this season? Is there an artistic or cultural renaissance emerging?

Like a magazine editor, the team (glam squad and photographer) must decide what they will work on, and then how to interpret the story through fashion, beauty, photography and the environment (location) that you are going to shoot in.

Perhaps the editor noticed that the designer showed a preponderance of gray on the runways in response to the world's own military build-up in a particular war. How would you interpret that build-up in your own story? How might you or your team interpret the dot com demise of 1997 – 2001 through testing? The enormous excesses and internet gains of the time gave way to huge personal losses in 2002 right along with the waning of the fur stigma in 2000. The stark contrast of people losing their fortunes in a single day on the internet when compared to a resurgence in American women's love of fur could make for an interesting story—don't you think?

Think of it. A shot of a model lying on the floor in the kitchen of her fabulous home. Empty. She is dressed only in Blackgama mink laying amongst broken DVD software in one shot. Next, she lays poolside in another Blackgama mink with a martini, but the pool is empty—except the leaves and a computer. What images come to mind? Let your imagination go wild. A story can be as elaborate and as staged as this, or as simple as a girl shopping for the season's best strappy shoes in Beverly Hills. What would the story look like on paper—with pictures? Think of it like a storyboard, the way commercials are scripted out. And this isn't just about fashion. A beauty story from the chest up could be called dark beauty and show a single model in four different shots showcasing four different smokey eyes with alternating lips.

Ask yourself these questions:

About Logistics

How many pages will the story have? 4? 6? 8? (Remember, one picture does not a story make). How many different locations will we shoot in?

About The Story

What would a girl who was going shopping all day do—from morning 'til night Where would she go? What would she eat? Where would she eat? How would she get to Beverly Hills? On a bus? In her Car? How would she get home? What if the car wouldn't start? Who would she interact with throughout the day? Would she window shop—or not? And in every shot, the shoes are the focal point.

About The Looks

What will she wear in each shot? What will you do with her hair, and the makeup? Will there be drastic or subtle changes in makeup and hair? Here's a little exercise.

What you'll need to collect:

1 Copy of this week's Newsweek

1 Copy of the current issue of Vogue, W or Elle.

Post-It Notes

Yellow Hi-liter

NOTES

....

....

....

....

....

....

....

....

....

....

....

....

What to do with the items you collected:

First, flip through the copy of Newsweek and use post-it notes to identify three world events that interest you. They can be anything. Business. Politics. News. Life. Death. Art. Sports. Hip-Hop.

Next, flip through a copy of one or more of those three fashion magazines. Use the post-it notes and hi-liter to identify one trend, one direction, and one season must-have.

Now, find the trend, direction or season must-have that inspires you and match it to one of the world events.

Then, work on the details. The who, what, where, why, and when.

Using the storyboard squares provided, write in your storyline as if they were pages in a magazine. If you can draw (which I can't), fill in the story with pictures, and write the storyline in the spaces provided.

Lastly, go to the back 1/3rd of your favorite fashion or beauty magazines and look at the STORIES. That's what they are—stories. Ask yourself, "What is the story that they're telling in this editorial.

Now construct your own using the magazines, post-it notes, and hi-liter. The Storytelling is what pre-production meetings are all about.

Name of Project:_____ Group Members:_____

> *Don't be afraid to start from the bottom and prove your way up.*
>
> —Mary Delgado
> *Makeup Artist*

8

Fashion Styling

There's a rumor going around that being a fashion stylist is a glamorous job, replete with invitations to parties with celebrities, first-class round-trip airline tickets to exotic locales where you shop endlessly with credit cards and loads of cash given to you by huge record labels, and film companies to style A-List celebrities who can't possibly live without you. Sounds amazing, doesn't it? However, there is another side, and it starts with the fact that fashion styling is one big, multi-faceted priority requiring tremendous concentration, creativity, an eye for detail, tact, diplomacy, discipline, the ability to delegate, manage money and think on your feet.

Mary Delgado

Makeup Artist & Executive Manager

Art Naturals

I've always been intrigued by the job of a fashion stylist, because I love a challenge and thrive on seeing all the pieces come together in perfect harmony. But ask any stylist who has been working in the business for a few years and they will tell you, "Sometimes that perfect harmony is being held together with top stick and safety pins."

That said—a good fashion stylist is a joy to watch. Poetry in motion. I have had the pleasure of representing some extremely talented stylists, including but not limited to Lisa Michelle, Melinda Tarbell, and Hollie Williamson. Talented visionaries who got almost everything right. However, there have been a few others who rarely got a call back because they were always late, couldn't get their paperwork in on time, didn't know how to talk to the client, were always name-dropping, treated their assistants badly, or were just plain unpleasant to be around.

Beyond the pulling of clothes, there is a lot of other stuff that you have to get right in order to get booked repeatedly. Not every stylist is going to work on Pink's new CD cover; however, if you are dependable, and can be counted on to see every project through to its natural conclusion—i.e., down to the paperwork and petty cash envelopes balancing—you will work. And, if you market yourself properly, you will work consistently. Follow me while I attempt to articulate the qualities of those stylists who consistently rise to the top!

NOTES

....

....

....

WHAT IT TAKES: QUALITIES OF A GOOD FASHION STYLIST

STORYTELLER	Always thinking in story form. As the direction is being given by the Creative (art director, producer, photographer, etc.), the stylist is putting the action together in their head like an editorial (magazine) layout or a storyboard.
RELATIONSHIP BUILDER	Maintains and enhances business relationships with clients, vendors and assistants through trust (doing what you say you will do) and a commitment to excellence.
COMMUNICATOR	Exercises good listening skills. Able to visually interpret the client's needs and use language to demonstrate understanding. Able to communicate with clients and production, vendors, talent and crew.
LOGISTICS SPECIALIST	An expert at planning, implementation and coordinating the details of the wardrobe department. Accessing what it will take to accomplish a good shoot.
LEADER	The one who guides and directs the team. Determines how much money and manpower it will take to get the job done, and then asks for and justifies it.
ORGANIZER	Organizing and/or schedules the tasks of the team. Figures out how to do the job when you don't get the requested money and manpower.
DELEGATES	Assigns tasks to the team in a way that maximizes their strengths.
FLEXIBLE	Able to adapt to the changing nature of print, video, film and TV production, and maintain a positive attitude.
BOOKKEEPER	Keeping systematic records of money transactions.

Mary Delgado is a makeup artist and Executive Manager at Art Naturals. She has experience in all aspects of media makeup including fashion, beauty, and advertising. She prides herself on providing her clients with a detail oriented and multi-faceted approach to makeup that shows in every aspect of her work. Mary has provided a little insight into her world as a freelance artist and what she's done to grow her career into what it is now.

What first inspired you to start a career in makeup artistry?

Mary: In high school, a friend decided that I needed to get my makeup done for the Winter Formal. She set up an appointment for me at Merle Norman at the mall and that was it. I didn't know what to expect, but when I saw myself I was amazed. I realized I could be pretty and feel pretty. I needed to know what I had to do to become this artist that can make people feel so pretty. That just really stuck in my head and when I graduated high school I decided to pursue a career in beauty.

A few years later I enrolled in the Napoleon Perdis Makeup Academy in Hollywood. I was interested in everything that they taught us. I went home and read it, analyzed it and practiced it. At the end of the course, the directors chose a student and awarded them with an opportunity to assist at an industry event. I got that award!

What was that first job like?

Mary: It was a high profile wedding for the daughter of an airline CEO. I drove to the event with the director of

FASHION STYLING DEFINED

Fashion stylists get paid to make people look sexy, beautiful, comfortable and real in environments that do, or have been manipulated to, mirror a lifestyle or the dream of a lifestyle that the consumer can aspire to. The beautiful girl wearing a Dolce & Gabbana dress and Manolo Blahnik 4-inch heels walking toward

the Richard Gere look-a-like, who is leaning up against a yacht in the Isle of Capri, is more dream than reality. A stylist is part of the team who creates that. The entire creative team is there to make this scene look real.

There are different disciplines inside the world of styling: Wardrobe styling, fashion styling, prop styling, set styling, and food styling. Within the styling world, the way a stylist is referred to tells you what kind of styling he/she does. And, sometimes, they (regularly) do more than one type. Fashion and Prop Styling, for example, or Prop and Food Styling.

FASHION STYLING refers to work done on magazines, fashion and beauty advertising campaigns, work with celebrities and recording artists, music videos, and the runway. They all want fashion stylists, not wardrobe stylists, because a fah'-shun stylist sounds much cooler, don't cha' think?

EDITORIAL STYLING refers to work done by fashion stylists and fashion editors on magazines and newspapers. Big magazines like Vogue, Elle, and Glamour have lots of editors on staff who pull the clothes and accessories for photo shoots. They are really fashion stylists with full time jobs and their titles are Fashion Director, Fashion Editor, Associate Fashion Editor, and Assistant Fashion Editor. The fashion editor reports to the fashion director, who sets direction for the department. The fashion editor often has a staff of associate and assistant fashion editors that report to him/her.

Smaller magazines rarely have staff stylists—it's too expensive. Instead, they book freelance fashion stylists to pull the clothes and accessories for shoots, and pay them a day rate. Sometimes, they even write articles for the magazines.

Big newspapers like the New York Times, the LA Times, and the Chicago Tribune have fashion editors and other staffers as well, but you won't find those big staffs on smaller regional papers. They too will hire freelancers.

When styling for magazines (editorial clients), one has to remember that magazines work three-four months in advance. Stylists must pull from designer showrooms and fashion PR houses instead of department stores, because the clothing won't still be in the store when the issue hits the news stand. Luckily, designers present their collections months in advance, so when the magazine comes out, the goods are in the stores.

With online publications and newspaper, however, you can pull from department and specialty retail stores, PR offices, and showrooms, because you may only be working a couple of weeks in advance of the publication date. Either way, no one wants to have to tell a consumer that an item is not available in the store. Editorial clients are Vogue, Elle, Essence, Glamour, Allure, Paper, etc.

WARDROBE STYLING is thought of as more commercial, and refers to work done on television commercials, lifestyle print ads, and stock photography—things that are considered more commercial in nature than fashion. Styling for this genre is marketing-driven, and the stylist's job is to ensure that the looks they pull represent the audience (consumer) that the advertiser is trying to reach. It just wouldn't do to have a fah'-shun stylist working on something as serious as a Tide commercial—now would it?

NOTES

the academy. I told her how excited I was to start working. At the wedding, I made sure to work hard. I barely did any makeup but I made sure that I kept busy, paid attention and showed them that I was a team player. The academy director took note and a month later called and asked me to take over the academy coordinator position. Of course I said yes! In time they let me become more involved with changing the curriculum modules and teaching. I was there for two years.

After that, I knew I wanted to gain more industry experience on my own and work on events, so I left the academy and started to freelance.

How did you get things started after the academy?

Mary: I ended up doing a lot of random little jobs. I had a day job, but kept trying to make connections and doing little makeup parties. I met a woman whose boyfriend worked in fragrances. He and his partner wanted to start their own business selling holistic, organic beauty products. They had all of these ideas and understood the marketing and selling side, but I knew I could help them with the presentation and reaching the correct audience.

They brought me on board and I felt like all of the little random jobs I had done had led me to being able to do what I needed to do with Art Naturals. The company kept growing and I became Executive Manager.

CATALOG STYLING refers to work done on direct mail (things that come to your house) catalogs. Like lifestyle advertising, the goal is to sell products. This kind of work is not always terribly creative. Clothing must be shown clearly so that the consumer can see and purchase items they see themselves in. Quite often, a single catalog is broken into sections and shot by several different creative teams (photographer, makeup, hair and stylist) of people at the same time.

Spring and Summer catalogs are shot in the first months of winter (Jan/Feb).

Fall and Winter catalogs are shot in the heat of summer (July/Aug).

Clients for catalog styling are companies like Gap, Banana Republic, Lands' End, Nordstrom, Victoria's Secret, etc.

E-COMMERCE STYLING refers to work produced for online retailers, which now-a-days is just about everyone. A lot of this work resembles the work done on catalogs. Lots of models. Some with heads some without. Others with only the bottom of their faces showing from the nose or lips down.

OFF-FIGURE STYLING refers to styling clothing that is not worn—those sweaters sitting on a rock in the middle of nowhere, or the dresses hung perfectly on hangers suspended from a water pipe in the middle of the New York subway, or the pants folded and stacked so neatly on a stool in a store. All of this is off-figure. Clients for off-figure styling include catalog, magazines and e-comm.

PROP/PRODUCT STYLING refers to the person who shops for portable objects such as dishes, lamps, chairs, beauty products, etc., for a variety of shoots. On shoots that require an abundance of prop styling, the client will hire a prop stylist. However, in many cases, when there are just a few things to pick up, the wardrobe stylist is asked to do the prop styling as well, and often for NO extra money. In smaller markets, like Cincinnati, a stylist may be EXPECTED to wear both (styling) hats, regardless of how much work there is to be done. Potential prop styling clients would include companies like Crate & Barrel, Pottery Barn, ZGallerie, and Restoration Hardware.

SET STYLING, a.k.a. set decorating, refers to the person who is responsible for dressing the set with furniture, draperies, carpet, etc. Clients for set styling would also include prop styling clients, as well as architectural publications such as Architectural Digest, Elle Decor, film and TV sets, etc.

Storytelling: Who Rises To The Top

Really good stylists think in story form. The thought process is similar to the way an illustrator sketches (storyboards) out a scene in a movie or a television commercial. There's a beginning, a middle and an end. Remember, we discussed it in Chapter 7: Freelancing: Building a Fashion Story.

The average stylist shops for an outfit. A really good stylist shops the story in all its complexity, variations and possibilities, keeping in mind the location that the story is being shot in and the time of year that the story will appear or the ad will be released into the market. A good stylist is like an actor, always needing to know his or her motivation—the who, what, where, why and when.

A good stylist can be a great help to a photographer who is searching for an idea or a new twist on an old subject. On jobs they are looked at as an integral part of a production, and, within the recording industry, are often called upon to suggest photographers for photo shoots.

While hair and makeup artists are often booked as late as two-three days before the shoot, a fashion stylist can be invited to participate weeks or months ahead if there are imaging challenges, or a full makeover is required. At the least, they are invited to sit in on meetings to discuss concept and begin prepping four to five days prior to the actual shoot.

Stylists are sometimes asked to offer suggestions for hair and makeup direction, since those elements have to work with the clothes, and make recommendations for the hair and makeup artists who are ultimately selected to work on the shoot. It's a big job, with a lot of pressure, responsibility and an enormous amount of risk. It seems simple, doesn't it? The stylist's job is to Shop! How hard can it be?

The Glamourous Life

I field plenty of calls from young people who think they want to be fashion stylists. What they really want is the glamorous life of 'the fashion stylist' that they see and hear about on television. However, unlike Rachel Zoe most stylists will not get their own TV show, just like most kids who play basketball will not become one of the 360 players in the NBA. However, there are a lot more stylists all over the world than there are NBA players, so, even if you don't get your own TV show or ever get to style Charlize Theron, you can still have a really fun, fabulous and creative life that pays very, very well.

What advice could you give someone who discovers their aptitude for leadership but doesn't have a clue about where to begin to locate corporate jobs in the beauty industry?

Mary: I would give them the same advice that I gave myself. Don't be afraid to start at the bottom and prove your way up. Don't be afraid to take jobs that you think are beneath you. It doesn't matter because once you are in there, you have your foot in the door. From there you can show people that you are capable of much more.

What has changed over the last 5-7 years about the way you do your job?

Mary: Everything is a lot faster. Everybody is using text messaging and group chats, as well as emails and apps. Everything is instant. People want a response right away. And because we're so connected with the world, I get phone calls and emails and text messages from China and all over the world.

We also always need to be very up to date when it comes to social media as well as hosting our own blogs or just sending product to different bloggers and social media influencers to get their feedback.

And what hasn't changed over the last few years?

Mary: I would say the fact that everybody is still demanding for you to be organized and involved and be willing to sacrifice anything for the benefit of the company. Everybody wants to be a priority in your life. They don't really care if you're sick, if your kid is sick, if you ran out of gas. They just want you to get it done.

The Real Deal

Ask any successful stylist, and they'll recount a story about someone who begged to be their assistant, and, when finally given the chance, was completely overwhelmed with ALL the WORK involved in making a shoot happen. None of which had anything to do with being glamorous, says Atlanta-based wardrobe stylist Camille Morrison, who as a stylist for the last 15 years can tell you that styling is many things—but glamorous is rarely one of them.

For Music Lovers
The Typical Music Shoot

So what's it like to get hired to work on a CD cover for a recording artist? There are prep meetings with the art director, the artist's manager, the publicist and the artist. There are fittings and sometimes shopping with the artists as well, not to mention all the shopping you have to do after you've wasted a full day with an artist who wants to stop and potty every 2 hours, and have lunch and snacks in-between.

There is getting up three hours before the shoot so you can pack up your car, and showing up to the shoot an hour before everyone else so you can set up and steam all the stuff that got wrinkled on the way to the shoot.

Oh, and two hours of deliberation about what the artist is going to wear for the first shot, and sending your assistant back to the stores to get the stuff that the art director and photographer said they didn't want—just yesterday. You, of course, are the last person to leave the shoot because you now don't have an assistant, though you paid one for half a day—out of your own pocket, to help you prep.

And now, the day is over, and you're exhausted. But you still you have to pack up everything and lug it down two flights of stairs to your car. Tonight, you will stay up 'til 2AM retagging everything for tomorrow's returns, praying the entire time that the stores don't notice which items have been worn and are being returned because the clients budget wasn't large enough to purchase everything.

With that all done, there are four more hours of organizing receipts and balancing the budget that you were given, so you can get your paperwork to production before they wrap today at tomorrow at 3PM.

Sound like fun? Read on. If you watch reality TV, you undoubtedly think that ALL stylists get large sums of money and unlimited budgets each time they head out to New York's famous Fifth Avenue to shop. The truth is that not everyone styles celebrities and recording artists.

You see, being fabulous is the thing you get to do after you've hired all the assistants, stayed up all night pinning and packing, had numerous meetings with the production staff about the direction of the project, and spent hours at the all-night tailor making sure that the pants will fit the talent who (you just found out) gained 35 pounds while on vacation.

JOB CHRONOLOGY: HOW THINGS WORK

In every styling job there is a way and an order in which things happen. From the moment you pick up the phone and hear the decision-maker or your agent offering you a job, all the way through to handing in that last bunch of receipts, there are a series of things that will most certainly occur (for the most part) each time you do a job.

You can and must plan for them in order to be successful—long term. Planning ahead will help you to meet objections and challenges along the way. Following is a list, and a discussion of each subject:

1. Creative Conversation
2. Presentation, Options and The Client
3. Paperwork: Request for Advance, Purchase Order, Stylist's Pull Letter, Petty Cash
4. Pre-Production: Meetings with Creatives, Managers, Artists and Models
5. Shopping: Boutiques, Studio Services & Designer Showrooms
6. Fittings & Alterations
7. The Shoot
8. More Paperwork: Addendums, Wardrobe & Credit Worksheets
9. Returns & Reconciliation

Mary Delgado, *Makeup Artist*

How do you find artists for your photoshoots?

Mary: I always go to my past students first and offer them the opportunity if they're available. If they are not available, then I post on social media asking for submissions. I look at their Instagram and Facebook accounts, but I always refer back to their websites because I like to go straight to work that somebody has photographed with a real camera. I want to see what they can do in its purest form without all the extras and filters.

I would give them the same advice that I gave myself. Don't be afraid to start at the bottom and prove your way up.

If you're hiring for a photoshoot, you kind of need more information, don't you?

Mary: Exactly. I use Instagram and Facebook to kind of gauge an artist's personality and what they're like. Especially for us because our brand is natural, green, and organic. I go for artists who have a little bit more of a natural green lifestyle versus somebody who is a partier and doing all the dark liners with the blue eyeshadow. I want them to be able to connect and relate with the brand.

1 CREATIVE CONVERSATION

In the first conversation between the client and you, the stylist (if you have an agency, the client should have already spoken with them and discussed your day rate), the client, usually an art director (on CD covers), a production manager (on music videos and TV commercials), or a print producer (on advertisements and catalogs), describes the creative aspect of the project and its direction, spells out the budget, and answers any other questions you might have about the project, logistics, crew (photographer, makeup artist, hair stylist, manicurist, prop stylist), etc.

A list of questions that you will need answers to can be found at the end of this chapter. While not every single question is included, these are a great jumping off place! One question typically leads right into another. It is natural to have small hiccups along the way.

Whether or not an assignment progresses to the next level can hinge on many factors. During the creative conversation, you should seek answers to your list of questions that will help you to decide whether or not this is a good project for you to work on. During this phase, it is important to get answers and clarification on important questions that will help you do your job. In the end, you need to know:

1 If the BUDGET you are being offered is adequate enough to produce the results that the client expects to achieve. Remember, the client has an expectation that you will be able to deliver the quality of work that they see in your portfolio, and nothing less. If a client tells you that the

clothing budget is $3,500 and you don't think this amount is sufficient to meet the client's goals for four looks on three guys, you have several options:

- NEGOTIATE FOR MORE MONEY

- LET THE JOB GO

- DO A MEDIOCRE JOB (because there was not enough money)

- DO A GREAT JOB & RUIN YOUR VENDOR RELATIONSHIPS IN THE PROCESS

2 If you can hire the MANPOWER necessary to accomplish the task at hand.

Manpower = Assistants, Seamstresses, Dressers, etc.

3 If you have enough of the right RELATIONSHIPS set up with vendors to be able to pull off a great shoot. Vendors: Accounts with studio services, boutiques, showrooms, costume rental houses, etc.

4 If you are truly interested in and excited about the project? Does this project sound like something you can sink your teeth into, or are you just doing it for the money? Be clear about your motivation and know that, even if it is just for the money, and/or you are bored, you still owe the client 100% at all times.

At this point, if you are somewhat interested, share your interest with the decision-maker, and tell him/her that you need a little time (perhaps an hour) to think about how you will approach the project. If the budget seems adequate, cool. However, if you're feeling that the job will require more cash, express some initial concern about the budget, and request a good time to get back to the decision-maker. The purpose of this strategy is to:

- Keep you from agreeing to a situation or an amount without giving it the proper thought.

- Give you some time to do a little number-crunching and compare the client's goals with the clothing budget.

- Help you to come up with what you will need to get and do to accomplish the job.

Wondering what I mean by client's goals? Simply this: If the client says, "We want the group in cutting-edge, upscale designer threads," to you that might mean Dolce & Gabbana and Marc Jacobs. The client has said that the budget is $3,500, and that he wants three looks for the band. Ask yourself if that is realistic based upon the kind of look that the client has requested. Your conversation with the decision-maker may be that he needs to revisit his goals, or come up with more money.

Here's a simple way to break down an uncomplicated budget:

$3,500 / 3 guys = $1,167 each

$1,167 / 3 looks = $ 389 each

Now ask yourself? "Can I do Dolce, shoes, accessories and dry cleaning for $389.00 per person?" I think not! Maybe you can do Donna….Johnson, but you'll be hard pressed to do Dolce anything for $389 per look. Unless they make cufflinks.

Mary Delgado, *Makeup Artist*

You are busy, and get lots of emails and phone calls. What should an artist place in the subject line to capture your attention?

Mary: I like things to be very simple. Just say, makeup artist, that's it. It doesn't have to be anything fancy, nothing elaborate. Just tell me who you are and what you do. That's it. And send me a link to your website.

Would you want anything physical that you could hold on to or put into a folder if somebody sent you a comp card, would you keep it or would you throw it away?

Mary: I love comp cards. Anything that's printed and pretty. I have a binder with clear pockets. Whether it's a pretty ad, or a pretty card, I always store it in there and I organize it by color and by theme and what they do. And I always refer back to it later on. I think, wow, they took the time to get this printed and to send it to me.

So, my main piece of advice to anybody is, if you reach out to a company, try to make it as personal as you can. Don't make me have to figure out what your phone number is, where your website is. Attach in your email a couple of images of work that you've done that will resonate with us. Natural and earthy.

What advice would you give an artist who's in the process of building his or her portfolio to attract somebody like you?

Mary: I would say focus on creating clean and beautiful images. And one of the tips that I remember from your class was making sure that the whole entire image is

Because that's about all the DKNY you'll be able to pick up for under $400. Well, I'm kidding—sort of!

But, honestly, asking the creative if you can crunch some numbers is an opportunity for you to figure out what you'll really need.

A good stylist should know what's in the stores (at all times), how much (these) clothes and accessories will cost to purchase, the restocking fees on items that will be returned, and the estimated charges for items that typically have to be dry cleaned, re-tagged and returned.

Here are some rules of thumb when talking with a creative about the details of the job. Getting answers to these questions will help set up the negotiation phase of the exchange.

 A. B. C. Always Be Closing (ABC). Assume the Sale.

Words are very powerful. A "What is" question is always better than an "Is there" question. Here's why.

What Is

"What is" says to the decision-maker, I already know that you have the thing I'm asking about. I am just trying to figure out how much of it I can get for myself and my team.

"What is," is confident and is known as an either-or question. It gives the decision-maker an option, and puts you in position to negotiate.

"What is" says, "I know there is money for X in the budget.

Is There

"Is there," says to the decision-maker, I'm not sure if you have the thing I'm asking about, so I'm prepared to do without it and my team and I will just do our best to get by.

"Is there" is passive and insecure and puts you in a position to receive a YES or NO.

There is nowhere to go once you get the NO.

For example, which would you rather ask?

1. What is the budget for per diem, $75 or $100 per day?

2. Is there a budget for per diem?

Number 1 of course!

---

2   **Always sell the benefits.**

People don't buy features, and producers don't spend money on additional manpower when it is positioned as something that is only going to help YOU.

For example, which of these would sound better to the producer?

> *Well, Tom, I need an assistant because this is too much work for one person. The last time we did a production, I ended up doing everything myself.*

> *or*

> *Well, Tom, the last time we did a similar shoot, we ended up going 45 minutes overtime. I can eliminate the overtime in my department by adding a second assistant for $200 instead of the $1,500 in overtime spent on the last job.*

---

3   **Never agree to anything** until you have had an opportunity to review all of the information that you have gathered.

All producers are not created equal, but in certain situations they can be expected to act alike. I have found that the best producers to work with are on the print side of the business, probably because they have the best budgets and are used to paying good rates for makeup, hair, and fashion stylists and manicurists. Producers who work on TV commercials are a little tighter, but the music video producer is the tightest of all, and doesn't think twice about asking any member of the glam squad to work for peanuts on a 14-hour day.

A good negotiation is what happens when preparation meets opportunity. Many people never get comfortable with negotiating because they don't do their homework. Once you learn that most clients object to and challenge you about the same thing—why you need so much money—negotiating gets easier because you know what to expect. You can practice your answers, and be prepared to meet each of their objections with a solid benefit.

Mary Delgado, *Makeup Artist*

telling a story. It's not just about the makeup but also giving your input and making sure that the wardrobe and the hair and everything tells that story.

What are your expectations from an artist that works with you?

Mary: I expect them to come in prepared and to have all the tools.

Generally, before I schedule a shoot, I'll send them a basic description of what I'm looking for and I'll send them pictures of the models and give them all the basic information. I expect them to come in prepared for that. Come with clean brushes. Come with a clean white towel. Don't come in with your kit all in shambles like it just rolled out the back of your car and you just kind of threw it back together. Come in looking professional and ready to go. It doesn't matter if it's a huge shoot or if we're just doing a quick little lifestyle one.

in www.linkedin.com/in/mary-delgado-5b3815118

A little fact-finding and preparation before the call back goes a long way towards alleviating the gnawing feeling in the pit of your stomach that reminds you of how you dislike talking about money. What follows is a list of things that clients like to challenge you about:

Money For

Clothes:	Why do you need so much?
Assistants:	Why do you need so many?
Prep days:	Why does it take you so long to do the job?
Wrap days:	Why can't you get it all done on the day of the shoot?
Prep days:	Why can't you prep for 1/2 your day rate?
Wrap days:	Why can't you wrap for 1/2 your day rate?
Prep days:	Why can't your assistant do it?
Wrap days:	Why can't your assistant do it?
YOU to do returns:	Why can't your $150/day assistant do it?
Overages:	Why can't we just have it dry-cleaned?
Travel:	Why can't you drive?

You:	Why is your rate so high?
Your agent:	Why can't we just call you at home to book you?
Messengers:	Why can't you drop it off?
FedEx:	Why can't we use UPS?
The time it takes you to prep:	Why do you need three days, can't you do it in two?
The time it takes you to wrap:	Why do you need two days, can't you do it in one?
Hiring you again:	We'd hire you more if we didn't have to pay an agency fee.
Clothes:	Can't we get them cheaper?
Clothes:	Where can we get them cheaper?
Clothes:	Why can't we get them cheaper?

After a few encounters with a client who says, "Do you really need two assistants on the shoot days?", you will know how to sell the benefits of the second assistant.

NOTES

Reesa Mallen

Photography Director

After you have been offered the job, confirmed your rate, or gained agreement from the decision-maker to redistribute the dollars for you and your team, comes the hour or so that you will need to put pencil to paper. Here are three must-haves:

1	A Strategy
2	Resolve
3	A Bottom Line

A Strategy

With strategy, you must consider two things:

a. Your Approach

Your opening statement should be positive. It should set the tone for the decision-maker to agree with you.

> Example Opening Statement:
>
> *Tom, I'm really excited to work with you on this project. I've taken time to sit down and go over the notes from our conversation earlier today, and I think I've come up with something that everyone will be happy with.*

b. Your Overall Plan.

This is the body of your presentation and it includes all of the points that you intend to bring up on the call or in a face-to-face meeting.

It doesn't have to be written out, although I do suggest it. A few bullet points on a sheet of paper serve as a great reminder, and go a long way toward keeping you focused and on point.

Following is a list of items you will want to [be prepared] to discuss during your conversation:

- The clothing you plan to dress the artists in.

- The designers you plan to use.

- The approximate cost to dress the artists in three looks.

- The approximate cost to dress the artists in two looks

Following are some things you'll need to consider in the event that the art director says, "Well, what if we only do two looks?" Always estimate a little OVER, or you'll have nowhere to go.

- How much of the clothing has to be kept (purchased)?

- Which items of clothing the artist will and won't be able to keep.

- What can (more than likely) be returned to the stores?

- What items of clothing will the artists need to bring with them from their own closets to the shoot if the budget cannot be adjusted (i.e., shoes, jewelry, etc.)?

- What will have to give up (perhaps a look) if the budget cannot be adjusted?

Why you are the right person for the job.

c. Your Closing Statement

The final element of your presentation should include:

- Your vision and the reasons (benefits) why the group should have the clothing you are suggesting.

- Spending justifications for your clothing suggestions.

- Why you are the best person for the job.

Resolve

Remember, you are good at what you do, and you are the best person for the job. You know your craft, and you are bringing a wealth of information, experience, taste, expertise and enthusiasm with you to this and every job assignment.

The dictionary defines resolve as:

firmly decided on a course of action

firm determination to do something

I think it's safe to say that a person with resolve is confident and self-assured. Decision-makers love working with people like this. It makes them feel safe and secure that this person will do their job, thereby leaving the decision-maker free to focus on other important things.

Reesa Mallen, *Photography Director*

In her roles as creative, art and photography director, Reesa Mallen has been responsible for creating, overseeing and art-directing seasonal campaigns for print advertising, digital content, video, social media, and catalogs. She hired and managed large freelance photo crews and glam squad artists for location and studio shoots for companies such as Lands' End, Chico's, Forever 21, Victoria's Secret, and Disney Publishing. Her creative vision, passion for photography and attention to detail made her a sought-after hire by these top brands. Here, Reesa talks a little about her experiences in the industry and offers advice to glam squad artists looking for a way in.

Can you tell me a little about your path to becoming a photo editor at TEEN Magazine?

Reesa: Sure! You know, back then, it was different when you started out to establish your career. Everything was face-to-face. There wasn't this technology that there is now. We had to go out and meet people, and bring our portfolios. And we had to use our phones to follow up.

I started off working with you at the Crystal Agency, and TEEN Magazine began using us to book their hair and makeup artists regularly. After a while, the style director at the magazine contacted me and offered me a position at TEEN as a bookings editor. That led to my becoming the photo editor and then the director of photography before the magazine closed shop.

After the magazine folded, I was hired to work as an agent at Ford Models. I learned a lot about that side of

A Bottom Line

Stand for something or you'll fall for anything the old saying goes. Everyone needs a bottom. And it's okay if your bottom moves with different kinds of opportunities.

I do it with my speaking engagements. I may insist that a large corporation pay me $7,500 to speak for an hour while I am happy to speak to aspiring makeup artists at a makeup school for $500. I have my corporate bottom and my educational bottom. I will also go speak to a group of high school kids for nothing if there is a need that my expertise and experience can add value. I believe that everything simply cannot be about money if you are to lead a happy and fulfilled life.

Some things for you to consider in establishing your bottom include:

- The lowest amount you will accept for your fee
- The lowest amount you will accept as a budget for clothing.
- The number of days you need to do the job.
- The number of assistants you need to do the job.
- How much those assistants must be paid

This exercise will help to keep your thoughts in order, and give you a way to attack the client's objections should they come up.

 TIP! It's a good idea to create a simple low, medium and high grid to show the art director, what you could do if? Many times, a client will say yes to a bump in the wardrobe budget if you can show them the "benefits" they will gain by choosing path A over B.

3 PAPERWORK

And you thought fashion styling was all about shopping? Not so. At least 40% of what you do as a fashion stylist is paperwork. Every piece of clothing that you remove from a store, showroom or costume house has to be accounted for—paperwork. Every piece of clothing that you return has to be accounted for—paperwork.

And, on the really good days, every piece of clothing that is purchased and kept by the client or the talent makes you look like a rock star to the retailers because you are spending money. However, there is still paperwork. Drop the ball on the paperwork and you could end up owning that size-zero Narcisco Rodriguez gown that neither you or any of your girlfriends can fit into. Stylists have more paperwork and liability than everyone else. That is why every job should start with the all-important DEAL MEMO.

Request For Advance

The Request for Advance (a.k.a. pro forma invoice) is simply an invoice requesting that the client provide you with money up front to shop and pull clothing for the job. Once filled out, the client should release funds to you for expenses such as clothing, accessories, props, etc.

You should fill it out and email it to the client immediately after you have been awarded the job and the client has agreed to the clothing and/or prop budget.

You will notice that the Advance Request has a space for your social security number, thus making you accountable for the funds and what they will be used for.

In most cases, the client will provide you with a check that you can deposit into your bank account. However, don't be surprised if they want to wire you the money, give you cash, or provide you with their company credit card. All of the above are fine.

FYI: Unless you have worked with a client several times, and are familiar with how they pay their bills, and their level of solvency, I wouldn't start shopping without the money in hand. As 2008 has shown us, even Bed Bath & Beyond can file bankruptcy.

A stylist was miffed about why a record company would send her a 1099 tax form at the end of the year, for monies they had given her. "I spent all the money on their artist" she said. True enough. She had spent all the money on the artist, and, further, she had dutifully given the record label all of the receipts. But, artists, here's the deal. It is your responsibility to make copies of all receipts and keep them on file to show your accountant at the end of the year. As a matter of fact, you should maintain a file drawer with duplicate folders complete with your own set of job numbers for each assignment. In it, you should catalog every piece of paper collected by you or your assistants in the execution and completion of a job assignment. A single manila folder with all of the paper you have gathered for a job will keep you from having a big IRS headache down the line. For a general list of contents, you should keep in each of your job folders, see page 7.28.

the industry, marketing models and photographers rather than hiring them. It was interesting, and I was grateful, but I knew I wanted to be doing something more creative. I knew that I wanted to work for a magazine again. However, in LA, there just weren't many magazines being published. I knew I would have to expand my market. I ended up applying to Disney Publishing and moved to the East Coast to work for them as the senior photography editor. Then they shut down. A lot of my friends suffered the same fate because print was fizzling out. Magazines were shutting down left and right. I had to think of something else to do.

I moved back to LA and got hired by Forever 21. After a while there, I got a call from a recruiter at Lands' End who told me a bit about a job description and asked me to submit my book. I didn't really expect much from it but got called the next day for an interview. I got the job and moved to Madison, Wisconsin. After a few years, the company ended up with a new president and layed off a bunch of people. So, I found myself without a job again. I decided to go to New York and worked freelance for a year, mostly for Victoria's Secret, until I got hired to work as an art director for Chico's.

What industry changes did you notice while you were working for Lands' End and Chico's?

Reesa: I noticed that the companies started to pull back and make less printed catalogs. They were starting to promote more on the website and doing lookbooks that you could click through online. So, print was being trimmed down, and social media and the web were

Advance Check

The advance check is given to artists for the purpose of renting and/or purchasing clothing, accessories and props. Without that check, I have witnessed artists get burned by large and small companies alike. The client insists that the budget will be "X" amount and directs the stylist to GO AHEAD and get started shopping on their own cash and credit cards. The result is usually a clothing budget and stylist's fee that are cut in half two days later, leaving the stylist hanging out to dry with a bunch of returns, restocking fees and an invoice from an assistant for two days of work.

THE RULE IS THIS: Unless you are working with a long-time client you trust or have worked with before, OR you have a signed deal memo describing the terms, conditions, fees, and expenses connected with the job, STOP! Keep your credit cards in your pocket, your cash in the bank, save your contacts for the gig that has been confirmed on paper, and let your assistant work for another stylist today. You are about to get Screwed!

The Stylist's Pull Letter

A stylist's letter is just about the most valuable tool there is when it comes to working with magazines. It's a letter given to the stylist by a magazine that allows the stylist to pull clothes from PR (public relations) houses and stores with little or no risk to the stylist, because the client assumes financial responsibility for any clothing that is damaged during the execution of the shoot.

Once you've been given an assignment by a photographer or the magazine, call the contact person at the magazine and ask for a stylist's [pull] letter. It's that simple. Also, if the magazine's editorial department doesn't have one, you can read them the verbiage in this one , or type it up and email it to them. They can drop it onto a sheet of letterhead and email it to you. Print it out, and carry it with you. You can also email it to your blackberry or your online email account where you can get to it easily. Just make sure you get it or you could be stuck with some very expensive clothing if anything goes wrong.

Petty Cash Envelope/Voucher

A petty cash envelope/voucher is used for the reimbursement of expenses of $300 or less. It enables you to track how you spent production monies that were advanced to you. Petty cash vouchers bypass the reporting mechanism to the IRS. As a result, accounts payable does not send a report to IRS. If a production is audited, however, and these services are not reported, the production can be heavily fined, or at least get in trouble, which is why it's so important to keep every receipt, and turn your paperwork in on time.

Always write the job particulars on the envelope. If you're a smart stylist, you'll write the job number and the PO# (Purchase Order Number given to you by the client) on each receipt.

Petty cash envelopes really help when you are working on more than one job at a time and have more than one assistant on board. Without them, and a system for keeping track of which receipts go with what job, production will NOT reimburse you for monies that you have spent.

NOTES

The Hair Makeup & Fashion Styling Career Guide

expanding. That is the direction everything has continued to go in. They still need to hire models, hair and makeup artists, and stylists, but the photographers need to almost be digitechs. They need to know how to do all the digital stuff, not just have a great eye.

There are also these huge new studios in New York that major retailers are using to shoot their web stuff, and these places do hundreds of shoots, so they need to hire freelance artists and stylists. Instead of reaching out to the brands directly, artists should contact the studios for work.

What hasn't changed?

Reesa: You still need hair and makeup for sure, and models. You also need someone to style no matter what. Tons of shoots are going on. These are one-stop shops. Likewise, certain clients do shoot on location, so there is always the opportunity to travel a lot. Companies are still doing seasonal shoots. That has stayed the same.

What advice would you give to an artist that wants to work for companies like Lands' End, H&M, Forever 21?

Reesa: They need to do their homework and find out who the contacts are. Go onto LinkedIn, search around. Find out the titles of the decision makers. Find out who the Photo Producer is, the art producer, etc. and where their corporate offices are. Actually, look for the work. You have to become like a detective. Just dig around and find out who you need to talk to. I had to look in the Yellow Pages when I was starting out. Now, people have the Internet. Things couldn't be easier!

4 | PRE-PRODUCTION MEETINGS

The most important part of a pre-production meeting is being prepared. Preparedness in this case means having done your research, showing up with a list of questions (see facing page) that will enable you to carry out your part of the assignment, taking notes on those aspects of production that will impact your job, and gathering information about purchase order numbers and job numbers that will appear on your invoice so that you and your team can get paid.

It's quite normal for the stylist to meet with a recording artist prior to a shoot. Everyone wants you to get a look at the person that you're shopping for. Production, management, and creative are pretty good about facilitating that kind of encounter.

If the person is not available for a meeting, because they are out of town or busy with show dates, then you should request a phone meeting wherein you will both have an opportunity to get to know one another, and you can ascertain if they are being forthright about their size and weight, among other things. It's important to remember that only women who are a size 6-8 don't lie about their size—they're proud of it. Everyone else wants to be a size 6-8, so you should shop accordingly. Better too big than too small. Clothes pins can fix too big. Only scissors can fix too small. Celebrities are just too busy for meetings with stylists, at least in the beginning of the relationship. Once they get to know you, you'll find yourself shopping for them for all kinds of events. Meetings with models are rare. You may request to be at the casting for a look-see, but, most of the time, you will shop based upon a comp card and a phone meeting when necessary.

Pre-Production Meeting Phone Call Questions

CD Covers & Music Videos

___ What are the shoot date(s)?

___ What is the name of the group?

___ How many members are in the group?

___ Will there be extras?

___ Are they men, women or both?

___ Do you have pictures of the group?

___ How old are each of the members?

___ Are they similar in weight and height?

___ Who has all of their sizes?

___ What is the music like?

___ Can I see the music video treatment?

___ What's their demographic?

___ Do you have music that I can listen to?

___ What's the title of the CD?

___ Can I meet with the group?

___ What kind of look do you have in mind?

___ How many looks do you want?

___ What is the budget for clothing?

___ Who is the photographer/director?

___ When will the CD or video be released?

___ Have they released any other CD's/Videos?

Advertising & Commercials

___ What are the shoot date(s)?

___ Who is the client?

___ How many ads/commercials will we be shooting?

___ When can I get layouts?

___ How many talents will I be dressing?

___ How many are principals?

___ How many are extras?

___ What is the talent mix?

___ How many are men?

___ How many are women?

___ Are there any animals in the shots?

___ What is the budget for wardrobe?

___ What is the budget for props?

___ How many assistants, besides my first, are budgeted for wardrobe?

When people are trying to contact you…how much is too much before it gets annoying?

Reesa: Well, email is always my preference. Sometimes, it gets too crazy to be able to pick up or respond to phone calls. I would say that if you're going to follow up, once a month or once every 3 ½ weeks is good. Every two weeks is too much.

Do you use social media when you were sourcing for artists?

Reesa: Only at my last job. The client had such a low budget that they couldn't pay the modeling agency fee. So, I found that I could hire models off Instagram. I'd look at their work there and request digitals, and we saved time on having to do castings that way too. Now, I feel like if someone doesn't have an Instagram account, they are out of the loop!

If you were hiring for an important job, is Instagram enough or would you also want to see their body of work on a website?

Reesa: It depends on the budget, but if it were a big budget, I'd need to see both. What I do have to say about websites, is that people need to keep them simple. So many of them have a ton of tabs with a hundred pictures under each one, and no one has time to go through all of that. Just have maybe 4 tabs and 30 pictures in each.

When hiring artists, do you care if they had an agency or not?

Reesa: No, I didn't care. What mattered to me was what their work and vibe looked like. If I'm really stuck in

Pre-Production Meeting
Phone Call Questions

Questions

____ When can I get the layouts?

____ Has a PO been issued for wardrobe yet?

____ Will there be a separate PO for props?

____ How much petty cash will I get for incidentals?

____ What is production's FedEx Number?

____ Are we shooting in studio or on location?

____ Are we traveling out of town?

____ Are we staying overnight?

____ What would you like me to do with the clothing and accessories after I wrap the job?

____ Are we shooting locally?

____ Who should I speak to about the check for wardrobe?

____ What local courier do you use?

____ When is the model casting?

Pre-Production Meeting
Phone Call Questions

Money Questions:

___ What is the PO Number for Wardrobe?

___ What is the Job Number?

___ How long will it take me to be reimbursed for an approved overage?

___ How will you be handling overages on the day we wrap? Cash or Credit?

___ How do you prefer the shipping and handling of the clothing to be handled?

___ Shall I ship in advance with FedEx?

___ Shall I bring the trunks with me on the plane?

___ Who will be handling my car rental?

___ If we are in a trailer, will I have dedicated power for my steamer and iron?

___ Are there any special parking or loading and unloading instructions?

NOTES

finding someone, I would go to an agency just because if I'm hiring someone I don't know, the agency could keep them accountable.

What are your expectations of artists on set?

Reesa: I'm lucky that I've worked with such a high caliber of artists and there hasn't been really any drama, but I've heard crazy stories. I think it's important to have a good, pleasant vibe. Be easy to work with. Keep your problems at home and be a part of the team. If you don't know a lot of people on set, don't sit by yourself at lunch. Try and mingle with people; get to know them. You want to have good energy because people can detect if you have a darker vibe. Another thing that I can't have on set is gossiping. That's just a no-no.

Do you have any tips for an artist setting up their portfolio?

Reesa: Like I said, keep it simple. Something like 4 tabs and your bio, and contact info. Make sure that you are up to speed. You don't want to have a slow website, so upgrade it as necessary. Likewise, you don't want your images to take too long to load. Ensure your work is current. You would want to avoid presenting images that are dated. Run your work by friends in the know, and get opinions.

Is there anything else you would like to share?

Reesa: Never stop learning. Even if you are at the highest level, keep up with everything that is going on in hair, fashion, and styling. The main thing is to believe in yourself 110%. Even if you have to do another job to make

5 | SHOPPING

Artists ask me about shopping all the time. How the heck they are supposed to get clothes? Well, there are three types of shopping:

1 Shopping for a commercial project (print advertising, catalog, TV commercial, CD cover, music video, feature film, television show, webisode, with e-commerce, etc.) with a budget and petty cash in your pocket.

2 Shopping for an editorial assignment (magazine) with a stylist's letter.

3 Shopping for a test with hope, and a prayer.

Shopping for a commercial project is easy. You have a budget—cash or a credit card, petty cash—money for incidentals—and a purchase order—a document from the production company that confirms that the vendors who give you clothes are going to get paid.

Shopping for an editorial project, ahhh, sometimes easy, sometimes not. But doable with a stylist's pull letter that inspires showrooms, boutiques and PR departments in department stores to give you what you need, because the lines that they carry will be credited in the magazine which will drive consumers to the stores to buy the items that they see.

But shopping for a test, now that's what separates the men from the boys. Testing is the thing stylists cut their teeth on. The

InStyle

Time, Inc.

InStyle
Time & Life Building
Rockefeller Center
New York, NY 10020-1393

212-522-1212

To Whom It May Concern:

This is to confirm that Denise Davenport is working as a stylist for a photo session with Gloria Reuben that Jerry Avenaim is shooting for InStyle on April 29. In Style will be responsible for all items borrowed, and will credit those items used in published photos.

Sincerely,

Carolyn Swindell

Carolyn Swindell
Deputy Photo Editor

XXX-XXX-XXXX (phone)
XXX-XXX-XXXX (fax)

question I hear time and time again: "But how do I get clothes, Crystal?" My response, "Any which way you can." The would-be stylists who don't figure that out won't be styling for long. Stylists need clothes. To get them, begin by assessing your available resources of retail, boutique, specialty, and vintage clothing, shoe and accessory stores.

Shopping for tests requires a combination of these resources. People do not have to give you clothes so that you can get pictures for your book. You won't be able to borrow from boutiques all the time, but, when you do, it will be because you have developed a reciprocal relationship of mutual respect, trust and benefit. In other words, you have proven to the vendor that you will return the clothing when you say you will,

in saleable condition, and the store will benefit in some way (pictures, credits, mentions in social media, etc.) from loaning clothing to you for your shoots. The most basic expectation is that when you have real commercial and editorial clients and a budget, or an opportunity to provide on-page credit, that you will come back to shop and spend money at their store, and/or ensure the appropriate credit is given in magazines, and on television.

However, from time to time, you will have to purchase things from department and thrift stores, as well as pick up items from costume rental shops. This is why good credit is so important. Before you know it, the money you spent on those pantyhose, shoes, and vintage earrings that couldn't be returned start to add up, and they do so way before you begin to make a living from styling.

Studio Services

Studio Services is used by fashion stylists and individuals in the wardrobe and costuming fields such as costumers, costume supervisors, wardrobe stylists and costume designers. Studio services departments permit the removal of clothing from their stores for review, use, exposure, and ultimately sale of the merchandise. Each department varies slightly in its policies and procedures, but the basic premise is that by loaning (for a nominal rental or restocking fee) the working stylist clothing for a day or two at little or no charge, something will be purchased, possibly seen in the media on a well-known celebrity, and, with any luck, credited in writing for consumers everywhere to see.

The expectation is that you, the fashion stylist, while working on various projects, will borrow items from the stores, and that out of those items you will purchase some.

Reesa Mallen, *Photography Director*

ends meet, keep your dream in the front of your mind. Do whatever you need to do, like put a vision board in your room or your favorite fashion photo as the lock screen image on your phone. Also, keep a good attitude.

 the_inked_jewess

 www.reesamallen.com

Anyone with good credit or one or two existing credit cards in good standing can open up a studio services account. You simply go to the studio services department, request an application, and, in some cases, can be approved in 48 hours or less. Your credit limit will depend upon your credit report, so if you have not been a good steward in regard to how you manage your credit, NOW is an excellent time to get it in order. It's fairly difficult to be a good fashion stylist without a decent credit rating or established credit cards.

Terms, Conditions & Worksheets

A studio services worksheet and contract are given to stylists who want to pull clothes for review and use for projects. It's the means by which the store keeps track of what you have pulled and will take out on loan. It will also help you keep track of the items you have pulled from stores. This type of agreement is used whenever you take clothing from stores like Barney's, Saks, Nordstrom, Neiman Marcus, Banana Republic, etc. They are all just about the same.

Rental

Rental. Now there's a misnomer. Aside from costume houses that rent clothing, there is no such thing as renting clothes. The term is much overused in the fashion styling business. Department stores, boutiques, and shoe stores do not rent anything. However, as this was a word that clients understood, stylists began substituting it for its true term, restocking fee. Most decision-makers outside of the editorial world use the word rental, and assume that fashion stylists can take any garment or accessory out of a department or specialty store and return it for little more than a thank you. Not true at all. In fact, any clothing that is photographed, put on video tape or filmed is considered owned.

Restocking Fee

The restocking fee is an amount that stores charge the fashion stylist for the privilege of taking the clothing out for approval. The fee usually ranges from twenty to thirty percent of the clothing, or the stylist is required to purchase a certain percentage of the entire pull.

Shoes

Shoes, the curse of the stylist. While clothing can usually be dry cleaned and retagged to look like new, this is not ordinarily the case with shoes. So delicate and easily marred are the soles of shoes, that most experienced stylists warn their clients in advance "if the shoes are damaged, or unacceptable to the stores in any way, you will have to pay for them." PERIOD!

A ruined Manolo Blahnik shoe can cost between $350 and $1,000. This sometimes equals half of a fashion stylist's clothing budget on a small job. And know this, the department stores have heard it all. They are not the least bit interested in why or how the shoes got that tiny little scratch. If the shoes are ruined, you or the client must buy them! Murphy's Law. What can go wrong will go wrong, and it always does with shoes. Do yourself a favor and ask the models, celebrities and anyone else you know to bring their own shoes.

Designer Showrooms

Designer showrooms are an East Coast phenomenon, while studio services is a West Coast thing. There are a few designer showrooms in the merchandise marts throughout the country in places like Los Angeles, Dallas and Miami, but nothing like the showrooms of New York, Milan, London and Japan.

Designer showrooms and magazines are inexplicably tied to one another. Showrooms loan clothing to fashion stylists who are doing work for high-profile fashion or entertainment magazines. The magazines include: Vogue, Elle, Bazaar, Marie Claire, L'Uomo, Vogue, GQ, Details, Vibe, Entertainment Weekly, Essence and InStyle, to name a few.

The secret to working with designer showrooms is knowing that the only good reason for them to loan you a $2,000 dress is that there is a high probability that the dress will be seen by hundreds of thousands of consumers, some of which can and will buy the darn thing. The fact that only a small percentage of the world population can afford a two thousand-dollar dress tells you something else you should know about the kind of exposure a designer is seeking. Okay, let me spell it out for you. Narciso Rodriguez is not going to loan you his $2,000 dress to put on some unknown model for a magazine that neither he nor anyone else has ever heard of.

NOTES

Titilayo Bankole

Global Manicurist

Here are a few rules of thumb to employ when working with designer showrooms.

1 Don't waste their time. Have your facts together, and know whom you want to speak with before you pick up the telephone. Sometimes, that means going on a fishing expedition the day before the real sock-it-to-me phone call to get the scoop on who you need to talk to.

2 Know the collection. It's best not to call Dolce and Gabbana about sending you all of their brights if they didn't do any for the collection you are requesting clothes from. I once called the ad agency that represented Absolute Vodka to try and secure an ad for 1stHOLD. When the account executive asked me what our demographic was, I said "18-34". He then said, "We don't sell alcohol to minors". That was the end of that. From then on, I made sure I did my homework ahead of time so I didn't look like an idiot. I had one chance, and I blew it.

3 Be nice to everyone. The receptionist can be just as important as the showroom supervisor. The receptionist may be the only person who knows where the supervisor is at a given point in time.

4 Be ready to email, fax or hand over a copy of the stylist's letter from the magazine that names and authorizes you to pull clothing for a particular story.

5 Always include the magazine's express mail carrier (usually Federal Express) number on all correspondence to the showroom. Most showrooms will want an account number before they send you clothes.

6 Make sure that there will be someone available to accept the clothing at the location where you are having the merchandise shipped.

7 Be aware that some designers will want to know what other designers you are using in your story before they will loan out clothing.

Stylists spend countless hours on the phone attempting to convince the New York showrooms that they have the next great photo session going on day after tomorrow, and must have some items in their newest collections. For the right magazine, editorial spread, model or celebrity, you can get just about anything if it's available, and if the clothing used will be credited to the design house.

NOTES

Titilayo Bankole, *Global Manicurist*

Titilayo Bankole is a global manicurist. Her client list includes Uma Thurman, Liv Tyler, Iman; Elle, Vanity Fair, Vogue, Cosmo; Puma, Clairol, Revlon, and Coca-Cola as just a small example. Her ability to scale the most natural nail to a creatively stylized one has made her a coveted artist in the industry. Titi, as she is called by clients and friends, discusses her career and reveals helpful career tips to aspiring nail artists.

What inspired you to become a manicurist?

Titilayo: I actually went to college to study computer science, but found that I was really bored. My mom owned a salon at the time, and I remember one day getting my nails done and thinking someone should be doing that at my mom's salon. I had her take me to a beauty supply store and bought what I needed to do nails. I saw that the manicurist that did my nails worked so effortlessly, so I figured I could do it too. I got to my mom's salon and realized it was actually hard work! I've been doing this for 25 years now, and it's still not as easy as it looks!

It's not easy in what ways?

Titilayo: It's not as simple as people think it is. After 25 years, I continue to take classes and sharpen my skills. Techniques and products change too, so you need to stay sharp.

Did you attend cosmetology school when you started out?

Titilayo: No. In the beginning, I did nails without a license. Then I realized I needed to get serious because it

6 | FITTINGS & ALTERATIONS

The purpose of a fitting is to see how things look on an artist or model as much as how they fit. Fittings work best when they occur two to three days prior to a shoot day, giving the stylist time to return items that don't fit or fail to work for some other reason. It is usually attended by more than just the stylist and subject. Quite often, the manager, creative decision-maker, publicist, and boy or girlfriend shows up. As you can imagine, that's way too many chefs and not enough room in the kitchen. Often, every one of those people has an opinion about what the subject (actor, actress, recording artist or model) is supposed to look like in the clothing, and you, Ms. or Mr. Stylist, will be the therapist that nudges them into the right direction.

Once a decision has been made about what to keep, the stylist can drop clothing off at the tailor for final alterations while she continues to shop for last-minute items and make returns.

NOTES

....

....

....

....

....

is a financial investment. I also knew that I was working with people's nails and needed to learn more about anatomy, and skin disorders. I had to understand the chemistry of everything that I put my hands on, so I went back to school.

Would you recommend assisting for established manicurists who want to get in this business?

Titilayo: Assisting shouldn't be a taboo for anyone. I believe it should be a platform for seasoned artists and novices to come together and help each other. Assisting will help you understand how to handle tasks on a job in a variety of situations. It allows you to learn and ask questions so that you can be better equipped once you start booking your own jobs.

What are the professional and personal qualities you look for in an assistant that you would want to work with?

Titilayo: I look for someone that is ambitious, pleasant, and polite. Someone that wants to learn, that wants to be there and is willing to take advice and put it to use.

What kind of personal or physical tools do you expect an artist to have in order to work with you?

Titilayo: I actually would like to hire someone who has read your book and taken your class. That way, I know I have someone that knows how to work. I want someone that's invested.

7 | THE SHOOT

Today the stylist should be prepared for anything, including being sent back out to shop because everyone has changed their minds about what they want. There was never a better case for the additional expense of an assistant than the shoot day, when inevitably some piece of clothing gets left behind, or the actor decides that he does like those pants that he told you to take back just days ago. Cool heads must prevail. It's all in a day' s work. On the day of the shoot, you're only as good as the team of people that you have surrounded yourself with.

Stylist Assistant

The assistants that you bring on the set to work with you are an extension of you. While every key artist is different, there are some universal expectations that every stylist has for their assistant. Fashion stylist Tiffani Rae has some very specific requirements when it comes to hiring an assistant. Do these things and you will probably get hired back as an assistant often. An assistant must:

Have their own kit, if only a small one, with at least the following items: Safety pins, seam ripper, needles and thread (travel packs are fine), scissors, top stick and a lint roller, a fanny pack or a workman's belt (Home Depot).

1	Unload the car.
2	Set up the steamer.
3	Unbag everything.
4	Ask what needs to be steamed.
5	Step out of the way when I (the stylist) am being spoken to by the client.
6	Always look busy. Organize something. Everything.
7	Wear good walking shoes.
8	Not wear a tank top, because bending over should not cause an earthquake.
9	Be comfortable in a pair of jeans or cargo pants; they have great pockets for holding stuff.
10	Not wear spandex or high heels to a shoot.
11	If it feels like you are a slave...it's because you are.

NOTES

Do you ever use social media as a tool for finding assistants?

Titilayo: I never use social media. I go to my network and ask because at the end of the day, with social media, you don't know who you are bringing in. Social media, for most people, is a platform to create an illusion. This industry is not about an illusion when it comes to product and brand.

When you get a referral, what is your hiring process?

Titilayo: I think it's important to have a conversation with the person. You can pick up a lot from their tone of voice. I like to meet with someone face-to-face, but if I can't, I would consider Skype or FaceTime.

Do you have any assistant horror stories you can share?

Titilayo: I had an assistant leave me hanging on a magazine shoot once. She never showed up, and I was left to do several manicures by myself. Thank God I knew I could work fast and I had worked with the photographer before. But I think the lack of consideration that she never even called to say she couldn't come was painful. In the end, I had to tell her that I would NEVER be able to hire her again.

How do you like potential assistants to contact you, and how much is too much?

Titilayo: Phone or email, either is fine. I personally like to be the one to contact them. So, I would say one phone call and a follow-up email is enough. If they don't hear from

8 MORE PAPERWORK

Clothing Addendum

A clothing addendum is a form that can be used during a shoot to get additional purchases or rentals (over and above the original budget) approved by a decision-maker on the spot.

A good stylist always over-pulls; however, that doesn't mean that the client can afford to use all of the clothes the stylist brought to the shoot. They sometimes forget that the extras are for selection. If the client has a $5,000 budget and wants four looks, a good stylist may pull $10,000 worth of clothes—enough for seven or eight looks (just in case). Here's what often happens: Somewhere on location, a shoot is taking place in the middle of Chicago. It begins to rain. A conversation between the art director and the stylist ensues:

Art Director:	"I want the model to wear that silver metallic leather jacket."
Stylist:	"Well, Sir, that's what I had planned for her to wear, but it's raining now and if the jacket gets wet, I can't return it."
Art Director:	"So what?"
Stylist:	"Well, Sir, this jacket is $1,600 and will put us $1,732 over budget. We're already $132 over."
Art Director:	"I don't care; it's perfect for the shot."
Stylist:	"Okay, if I can just get you to sign my addendum (guaranteeing payment within 24 hours) for the additional overages, then we're good to go."

A savvy stylist with an addendum helps an enthusiastic art director put creativity back into business perspective. Sure, that jacket rocks! And the recording artist would look good in it, but unless the art director is willing to sign the addendum, the money isn't there, and you could end up trying to sell that jacket to one of your girl friends for a fraction of what it costs. The decision-maker must put up, shut up, or wait until it stops raining. Don't get stuck with a $1,600 jacket that you cannot fit or afford because you were afraid to speak up. Remember Cuba Gooding, Jr. in the film Jerry McGuire: "Show Me the Money".

Wardrobe Credit Sheet

The wardrobe credit sheet—not to be confused with the credit sheet in Chapter 7—is turned into the magazine at the end of a shoot so that the editor can properly credit the clothing for the vendors who loaned you the clothes. Following is an example of what the editor should get. You may make up your own, or ask the editor at the magazine for their internal form.

You can download this wardrobe credit worksheet from my website.

NOTES

FASHION STYLIST: _____
PHONE: _____ FAX:_____

WARDROBE CREDIT SHEET

Client Name: _____
Phone Number: _____
Project: _____
Artist/Subject: _____
Editorial Section & Issue: _____
Art Director: _____
Photo Editor: _____
Fashion Editor: _____
Photographer: _____
Photo Session Date: _____

Item	Garment Description	Clothing Designer	Price
			$
			$
			$
			$
			$
			$
			$
			$
			$
			$
			$
			$
			$
			$
			$
			$
			$
			$
			$
			$
			$

me, then maybe give it a couple of weeks and follow-up again.

In your early days, were you ever released from a job early? If so, what did you learn from it?

Titilayo: Yes. I remember one fashion week I worked for an elite team and the designer was one of my favorites, so I decided to go ahead and watch the show. When the key artist saw me, she really launched into me. I had never felt so bad in my life. I didn't know that I couldn't watch the show. No one stopped me. I didn't get fired, but I had to work the rest of the shows with the team not wanting to be around me, and I didn't get hired back the next season.

What I learned from it is that I needed to understand the dos and donts. I also learned that when you are on a team, and you see someone new struggling or about to do something wrong, you should nudge them in the right direction.

Do you use social media to market yourself, and if so, which platforms do you use most regularly and why?

Titilayo: I use Instagram regularly for my global manicurist material. Facebook is more of my personal stuff.

Was it easy for you to find your voice on social media? Do you have a plan for how and when you post?

Titilayo: Sometimes, I have to plan my posts because I don't want things to become redundant. I'll think about what to share and what audience I want to target. It's

Wardrobe Worksheet

The stylist's worksheet is a post-production form that I designed for our stylists at Crystal Agency to help them organize their receipts and balance the budget prior to turning all of the documentation in to their client. The worksheet is usually stapled to the top of the pile of receipts, fastened inside a manila folder or taped to the front of the receipt envelope.

You can download this wardrobe worksheet from my website.

FASHION STYLIST: _____
PHONE: _____ FAX:_____

WARDROBE WORKSHEET

Client Name: _____
Phone Number: _____
Project: _____
Artist/Subject: _____
Editorial Section & Issue: _____
Art Director: _____
Photo Editor: _____
Fashion Editor: _____
Photographer: _____
Photo Session Date: _____

Item	Garment Description	Clothing Designer	Price
	Amount if any carried forward from previous page		$
			$
			$
			$
			$
			$
			$
			$
			$
			$
			$
			$
			$
			$
	Sub-Total Clothing Purchase and/or Rental		$ 3,217.00
	Monies Advanced to Stylist by Client		$ 3,000.00
	Sub-Total		$ 217.00
	Other Expenses: _____		$ 54.00
	Monies Due ___ Client or _X_ Stylist		$ 271.00

NOTES

also important to see how your clients feel about sharing. Recently, I worked on a commercial for a big client, and the director posted a video on Instagram. After he did that, I reposted it with the brand hashtag, and the producer contacted me and asked me to take it down. I took it down and didn't argue about it because my relationship with the director and producer is more important.

What jobs are you most proud of?

Titilayo: There are so many, but I am so proud of the job I did with Iman for Italian Vanity Fair with:Coca-Cola, Nestle Water, and P&G.

I've always told artists that they may come with skills, but the battlefield is in the mind. Have you had any mental battlefields?

Titilayo: I think getting unstuck is a challenging job. I had to break out of the mindset of thinking too small, of self-doubt. Instead of thinking that I wouldn't be able to land a certain job, I had to let myself know that I could do it.

Now that everything seems to be going online, how do you feel about having a physical portfolio?

Titilayo: I think having a physical portfolio gives you more confidence. I didn't realize the importance of having one until I got my pictures printed. I got to see the detail of my work, and it also helps you improve your work to see it in print. You don't want to rely on Photoshop for everything.

What changes have you seen in the last 5-7 years?

Titilayo: I have to say it's the way people in the industry

9 | RETURNS & RECONCILIATION

That's A Wrap - The Perfect Return

Every styling job has a beginning, a middle and an end. The beginning is called Prep. The middle is the actual shoot or performance, and the end is known as Wrapping. Wrapping is often referred to as doing returns, because taking the clothing, accessories, shoes and jewelry back to the stores, costume design houses, and showrooms that they came from is such a big part of the job.

Returns should be handled quickly, and immediately following the shoot. Without the final tally, production finds it difficult to close out a job and move on. It's important to remember that the photographer, producer, and director that you will be working with are freelancers just like you. They cannot get paid and move on to their next gig until everything is wrapped up, and neither can you.

Wrapping is the toughest part of any styling job. And for some reason—usually because they have never had to do it—clients think that they should pay less for it than they do the prep or shoot days. Clients are known to offer up one of their PA's (production assistants) to do the returns for you in an effort to cut costs. They'll say just about anything to keep from paying a full day rate for the wrap/return day(s).

Right after you say my rate is $850/day, and my assistant is $300, some producer says, "Well, what if I give you a PA (production assistant) to do the returns for you? Can we let the assistant go?" My answer to that scenario is typically NO. A PA doesn't know what your relationship is with the stores or other vendors that you pulled from. Nor are they privy to the tall tale you had to spin to get the items the director wanted in the first place, all so that the talent could look like a million dollars while carrying a bottle of Heineken in the red-carpet scene of that Super Bowl commercial.

Also, returns are only part of your job, is the PA going to retag all of the clothes and put the Neiman Marcus tags in the right sleeve of the clothing, while the garments you pulled from Saks Fifth Avenue require the tags to go in the left? And what about the petty cash?

Furthermore, it's a bad precedent to set. A day rate is a day rate. The best habit to get into is one where you calmly and logically explain to the producer why you should get your day rate, not why you should accept less than you are worth for doing the job that they hired you for.

Now, I don't want to make it sound like I have never cut an artist's rate to get a job; I have. But I don't make it a habit, I only ever did it for clients whom had paid the artists rate more than once, and I never gave up without a fight. You shouldn't, either. Favors are for people who have already treated you fairly.

Something like "Well, Tom, I can see how on the surface it might look like using your PA is a better idea than paying me and my assistant to do returns, but let me tell you why I think hiring us is a better use of your client's money". And then you give him/her all the benefits.

Wrapping out a job consists of the following:

— Organizing and returning clothing, jewelry, accessories, and shoes to the stores where they were purchased, rented and/or borrowed, and/or to the client who commissioned the job.

— Reattaching price tags to the clothing.

— Keeping track of which sleeves and/or necks that the price tags must go back into before they can be returned to the store.

— Dry Cleaning.

— Removing tape from the bottoms of shoes.

— Organizing receipts, handling and accounting for petty cash.

— Removing personal items from clothing pockets.

— Packing & Shipping items back to vendors by local messenger and/or overnight courier.

— Removing random safety pins.

— Keeping track of mileage or gas, parking and tolls.

— Mending.

Depending on how chaotic a shoot is, a stylist may try to start wrapping out the job (by getting things organized and back into their respective boxes or bags) as the day draws to a close. It's like your mom used to say about Thanksgiving dinner: "If you clean up as you go along, it won't take nearly as long to clean up the mess."

Flawless paperwork is the last step to professionally wrapping out a job. Every single item and every penny must be accounted

Titilayo Bankole, *Global Manicurist*

interact. People seem to have their guard up more now.

What are things that haven't changed?

Titilayo: What hasn't changed is how production seeks out talent. They have to create an environment for their client, and they will build a team that can do that. That's why it's so important to treat your work as a business and be respectful.

What is some advice that you would give newcomers?

Titilayo: Really enjoy what you do. Learn everything you need to learn to evolve into the artist that you want to become. Be pleasant and thoughtful with everyone you work with. Send thank you cards, and holiday cards, and really let the people you work with and want to work with know that you are thinking of them. That makes an impact. And always be kind.

IN HER KIT: 3 THINGS TITILAYO CAN'T LIVE WITHOUT

- My Cindy Nourishing Remover
- DeborahLippman hand cream,
- My Mehaz implements.

---

 www.titilayobankole.com

for on paper. Either way, the Wardrobe Worksheet should have at least four columns. Check out two examples below:

Date	Vendor	Item	Price
10/19	Barney's NY	Navy Men's Pants	$ 275.00

Description	Designer	Vendor	Price
Navy Men's Pants	Dolce	Barney's NY	$ 275.00

There should also be spaces at the top of the form for your contact information as well as specific job information:

Name: Cynthia Jones   Client: Kontent Partners
Phone: (323) 555-1212   Job Name: Keds
Email: CynthiaJ@gmail.com   Job Number: KP-101177

And, if you hope to be reimbursed for automobile expenses such as mileage and parking, you will have to keep decent records that include at least the following basic information. Mileage is on the honor system; however, for most parking you will have to include receipts unless you parked at a meter, in which case your paperwork needs to include a legend (see beneath table).

Date	Miles	Rate	Amount	Parking
10/19	74	0.052	$ 38.48	$ 4.75 R
10/20	25	0.052	$ 13.00	$ 2.00 M

R = Receipt Included

M = Metered Parking

Reimburseables

To know what is reimbursable besides mileage and parking, ask the client. Typically, they will allow you to expense a certain amount each day beyond what it given to you as petty cash, or for what would be given to you as petty cash. It may only be $20 a day, but it's better than paying for it yourself.

Petty Cash

Petty cash is money that is given to an artist for miscellaneous small expenses such as taxis, bellhop tips, parking at meters, water, and production-covered meals.

Invoicing

An invoice is required at the end of every single job, regardless of whether you are the key on the job or an assistant to someone else. Include the job numbers and PO numbers I've talked about in this chapter; including them on your invoice will make the difference between getting paid in 10 days or 10 months. No one will be able to pay your invoice in a timely manner if your job name is: Shoot in Las Vegas in the Desert. That is not recognizable to the accounting department. If you're assisting, you should ask the person who booked you whom you should submit your invoice to. Send it in, and follow up!

There are online companies like Zoho.com and Freshbooks.com who offer invoicing as a service, and, for $10-24/month, you can subscribe to the service and email professionally prepared invoices to your clients.

NOTES

The Hair Makeup & Fashion Styling Career Guide

Ca-Trece Mas'Sey
Costume Designer
Focus: Film & Television
IG: bluecollarsquad

What made you want to become a fashion stylist?

Honestly, someone else saw my potential. A former boss of mine, called me in his office, began talking to me about a career in fashion styling, and gave me some suggestions on how to pursue it.

How would you describe the job of a fashion stylist?

We really determine the next trend because we are responsible for picking out the clothing worn in photo shoots and music videos, on TV commercials, television shows, for concert performances, and many other public appearances made by celebrities, and other public figures.

We purchase, rent, borrow and have clothing custom made for our clients. We consult with the client, photographer, director, hair stylist and makeup artist to put together looks for a specific project.

We spend so much time with the client, it's not unusual to become a friend and confidant. The important thing is learning to listen while allowing what you hear to go in one ear and go out the other. You cannot get involved in the rumors or gossip that follow your celebrity clients.

What is the most difficult aspect of fashion styling?

The factors you have no control over like trying to get people—especially celebrities—to believe in the vision that you have for them. There are always several voices in the room outside of the talent. The publicist, best friend, homeboy, manager, product manager, and label or studio executives all have very different opinions about the direction of the talent.

ODDS & ENDS: A FEW MORE THINGS TO KNOW & DO

The Entrepreneur In You

The great thing about setting up your own company is that you can sell, rent or lease your own products and services to production.

Items that you have been collecting for years, that are just taking up space in your second bedroom, can now become part of your inventory, and a new source of income. All those shoes, hats, pants, skirts and jewelry that couldn't be returned to the store can be rented to the production companies that you work for.

And there will be many things that you will be able to rent as the years go by and you amass a great library of reusable items that you have purchased and/or been given by production companies and clients who have no interest in keeping the leftover merchandise from shoots.

So, how do you know what to do with the clothing that is purchased and cannot be returned to the stores? You simply ask the client that has hired you for the job. There are at least eight possible answers to the question, "What would you like me to do with the items that cannot be returned to the stores?"

1	Return them to the Client.
2	Return them to the Agency.
3	Return them to the Showrooms.

4	Return them to the Costume Houses.
5	Give them to the Production Company.
6	I'll take them.
7	Give them to the actors or models.
8	You can have them.

Vendors

Vendors are like water—you can't live without them, so treat them well. Fashion stylists have been known to promise a vendor the world in order to get them to loan out the clothing, accessories and jewelry needed to complete a test or a job.

The promises usually take the form of pictures the stylist swears they will give the vendor, credits that are supposed to appear in this or that magazine, a shout out on social media, the CD cover the stylist vows to bring the vendor once it's released, or the merchandise that will be returned by a specific date and time. Unfortunately, the favors extended by vendors are usually long forgotten by the time the pictures are available or the tearsheets run in a magazine. And, while many stylists have forgotten the small boutiques that came through for them in the beginning, the vendor has not forgotten the stylist who didn't keep his or her word.

Los Angeles, New York and Chicago are littered with stylists who promised vendors the sun and the moon until they got what they wanted. The stylist didn't follow through, and thus, the next stylist may find that vendors want his/her first-born child before so much as a sock can be removed from the premises. Keep your commitments and all will be well. A little honesty goes a long way toward building and growing your relationship with a vendor.

Many years ago, I booked a stylist for a magazine cover shoot. I loved this stylist's work. All she had were tests in her book, but I saw something special in her, and in fact, I had helped her to organize her book during a portfolio review several months earlier. I believed that she would one day be a real force in the industry. So, here's what happened. I offered up two of my interns—also aspiring stylists—as assistants for her. She also had her own assistant. After committing to do the cover, she become aloof and stopped communicating with me. Ursula and Lauren had a terrible time getting in touch with her. She would ask them to do things, and then refuse to return their phone calls and emails, even though she had them calling all over kingdom come for clothing for the eight people who were going to be on the cover. She had to pull two looks. One was very formal, the other—jeans and white t-shirts.

Three days before the shoot I got a call from one of the stores she was trying to pull from. They said, "Under no uncertain terms may Ms. X pull from this store. We have had problems with her in the past, and will NOT work with her." On the day of the shoot when I arrived, I found Ursula, Lauren and the other assistant dragging clothing and accessories out of their trucks and cars, but no Ms. X. When I asked where she was, I was told by her assistant that she had food poisoning, and she wouldn't make it.

As a Stylist, you have to take control of the situation and try and create a "signature look," especially for musicians. And you have to do it within the approved budget, and the [crazy] time constraints that they put on you. Oh, and you better get it right on the 'first attempt' or you might never work with that person again.

What was your first fashion styling gig?

My first styling gig was a video for a rap group. I recruited all my family and friends to help me and it is one of my proudest moments and best work to date… timeless.

What job are you most proud of?

Actually, the one that stands out is my first movie "You Got Served". It made roughly $60 million out the gate and took me from being a freelance fashion stylist to a Union costume designer on a whole new level.

Was there a point that you felt like you had arrived?

I felt a great sense of accomplishment when a client began his acceptance speech at an awards show with a special thank you to me and my assistant Chesney. We were flooded with calls and emails telling us about it.

Tell me about your assistant.

Chesney. She has become my sister—really! I had no desire to train a new person and teach them all the tricks of the trade. I was extremely hard on her and gave her no special treatment. She became the best assistant that I ever had and working a job without her now is like working with only one arm. She has become a great stylist in her own right.

My anger that day was palpable. But, "The Show Must Go On". Ursula was reliable and calm, so I put her in charge. Since that shoot, I have not ever heard from Ms. X. But rest assured, everyone on that shoot knows her name, from the photographer to some of the most powerful makeup, hair and fashion stylists in the industry. One day, her name will come up, and someone will say, "Oh no, you don't want her. Let me tell you what happened…"

What's Tough About Being A Fashion Stylist

A fashion stylist's job is the most physically demanding and financially risky. It has several levels of difficulty, less room for error, and less of an opportunity to fix a mistake if one is made. It's also easier to pay a makeup artist or hair stylist an $850 fee for one day than it is to pay a fashion stylist that same fee for three or four days (prep, shoot, wrap/returns). Consequently, it's always the fashion stylist's fee that has to be justified to the client, and elaborate means taken to show the specifics of how and where money is going to be spent and the stylists time used. Here are some of the obstacles you can expect to encounter as a stylist:

1 Getting paid for the actual time spent preparing for the job.

The stylist is usually required to attend two or three meetings with the client and/or artist, celebrity or model prior to the shoot. The agenda may include fittings, concept discussions, etc.… The stylist often spends numerous hours the night before the shoot untagging, bagging for transportation, taking digital images, and packing in preparation for the next day's shoot.

2 **Getting reimbursed for actual expenses incurred during the shoot.**

- The stylist can put hundreds of miles on an odometer for each job assignment.

- The stylist who works with recording artists often takes them out shopping and incurs meal expenses.

- The stylist can incur substantial miscellaneous non-receipt bearing expenses, such as metered parking, valet and bellman tips.

3 **Getting approval for one more assistant.**

- The stylist almost always requires the help of an assistant.

- Assistants range in price from about $100 to $500 per day.

4 **Client resistance.**

- The client rarely wants to pay the stylist for attending meetings that can take up a substantial portion of a day.

- The client usually wants to pay less for the prep and wrap days which are perceived as less work than shoot days.

5 **Budget Restrictions.**

- The client expects the stylist to work miracles for very little money.

- The client expects the stylist to return used clothing to the stores.

6 **Every job averages three and one-half days (3 1/2).**

- On an average 3.5-day job, the client typically wants the following arrangement regardless of the actual time it takes to do the job: 1 prep, 1 shoot, 1/2 wrap. No assistant.

- The stylist works more days than they are paid for.

Still wanna' be a fashion stylist? Well, in spite of the ups and downs, it is a very exciting and fun field. If you're very good at it, and you stay ahead of what's going on in the fashion world, you will probably spend only a single year dealing with low budget jobs. Great stylists are few and far between and word travels very fast. Once you catch on fire, so does your career and your day rate. From there, you will get the opportunity to pick and choose the jobs you want at the rate you desire, and bring the right number of assistants along with you.

NOTES

....

....

....

....

What made her such a great assistant?

She anticipated my needs. She could read my mind and did things before I asked her to. She took a lot of pressure off me.

When I saw how hard she worked for me, it only made sense for her to work with me.

My advice to aspiring makeup, hair and fashion stylists is to give it your all, because you truly never know who is watching or where that effort can take your career. I also suggest assisting for as many stylists as you can until you find the right one for you. You spend a lot of time with that person, so it's great when you really bond like Chesney and I did.

Everyone who works for me is allowed to have some creative input. It's my intention to groom future stylists, and although I hate to lose them, I always want to see another professional succeed. For me it's enough to know that I have contributed to their success.

You are a costume designer now. When did you decide that you wanted to work in film and television?

When the studio called and offered me a job—ha ha… I never really made a map for my career; I've always let God lead me, because if I made my own map, I would never have gotten this far.

What mistakes have you made and corrected in your career?

1 No matter what, it's always wardrobe fault, so no need to argue.

2 Sometimes it's best just to listen, and bow out gracefully. You can win the argument and never get booked again.

3 You can never be prepared enough. Over prepare, and when you think you have enough wardrobe, accessories, and shoes— prepare some more.

NOTES

On Location

The last question on that list brings me to the next question: Who is watching the remaining items in the car while you're lugging two armloads up to the roof of the building where the shoot is taking place? A stylist must always think about how they are going to get the clothing from point (a) to point (b) safely. It's normal to see an itty-bitty fashion stylist with arms full of clothing walking up two flights of stairs to the set.

You must never leave the clothing unattended in an unsecured environment. That may mean calling the photographer to arrange for his assistant to meet you at the car when you arrive. Once you have spoken with the studio or location manager to determine whether or not they will be able to offer you help, you can, if you need to, call the photographer the night before and let him/her know that you will need the assistant to meet you at the doc/street corner at a specific time (10:15AM) to carry the clothing upstairs, or watch the vehicle while you do.

Studio/Location

When shooting in a studio or on location, it's important to find out how the location you will be shooting in is equipped. Even the best studio dressing rooms can come up short. And assuming anything when it comes to fashion styling will most certainly make...well, you know what they say about assuming.

____ Is there a steamer?

____ Does the steamer work?

____ Is there an iron and ironing board?

____ Is there a rolling rack, and, if so, how many?

____ Is there adequate lighting?

____ Are there hangers? If so, how many?

____ Is the space I'm working in secure?

____ Does it have a lock and will I have access to the key?

____ Will I have my own space, or will I be sharing with Makeup & Hair?

____ Are there plenty of plugs in my room? And if not, are there extension cords?

____ Is there a loading dock?

____ Is there a parking lot, or on-street parking?

____ Can I unload in front of the building?

____ Is there an elevator?

____ Are there stairs, and if so how many?

____ Will I have help unloading?

Would you have done anything differently?

I would have assisted more. I only assisted once and then that client became mine. I would have loved to assist a few stylists to get ideas and resources.

Of all the genre's, which do you enjoy most?

I would say a combo. When I did videos, I could be extra creative because there were really no limits. With television commercials and print advertising, its basic everyday wardrobe, because you are appealing to the masses. For film, you develop characters, so you get to be creative depending on the characters.

What advice do you have for someone who wants to follow in your footsteps from fashion stylist to costume designer?

Anyone who is a stylist should try crossing over into costume design. It broadens your options. If an opportunity arises, take it.

However, getting into the union does not mean you stop hustling. The union is not an agency. They do not find you work, but if a union job becomes available, you can apply for it.

Any last words for someone who wants to venture into fashion styling?

Stay ready. Be prepared. Success in this business demands that old school hustle, and the ability to communicate effectively with a plethora of people who don't always want the same thing even when they work for the same brand. Also, know your fashion. Read magazines, get to know the photographers and be willing to assist, even if it's just for gas money and food. The experience and the connections will help you in the long run.And remember, "Success is what happens when preparation meets opportunity."

Be a step ahead.

ADVICE

FASHION STYLING KIT

- Collapsible Rolling Rack
- Steamer
- Iron
- Good Fabric Scissors
- Big Pair of Scissors (cut up anything)
- Little Scissors for Kit Bag
- Seam Ripper
- Assortment of Needles & Thread
- Lots of Lint Rollers (w/disposable tape heads)
- Tagging Gum
- Variety of Shoe Polishes
- Tons of Safety Pins (all sizes)
- Buttons, Snaps, Velcro
- Spray Starch
- Scotch Guard
- Wrinkle Guard
- Shoe Laces
- Lots and Lots of Top Stick
- Different Color Rit Dyes
- Hanging Tags
- Sewing Machine (optional)
- Fuller's Earth
- Mineral Oil
- Stain Remover

- Calculator
- Shoulder Pads
- Baby Wipes
- Makeup Scarf (to cover face when pulling clothes over the head)
- Tweezers
- Collapsible Mirror
- Notebook & Pre
- Manilla & Plastic Envelopes (to carry receipts)
- Tag Tamer
- Stain Remover
- Static Guard
- Bra Pads/Lit Pads
- Baggies (From the tiniest to the biggest)
- Digital Camera
- Polaroid Camera
- Sewing Kit
- Hem Tape
- Cosmetic Stain Remover
- Clothes Pins
- Heavy Spring Clothing Rack

- Deodorant
- Foot Inserts
- Breath Mints & Gum
- Double Stick Tape
- Chicken Cutlets
- Petals (for covering nipples)

NOTES

....

....

....

....

....

....

....

....

> "You can't get a
> YES without an ASK.
>
> —Suzie Moldavon

Glossary

1ST ASSISTANT: The person who is selected by the key makeup, hair, or fashion stylist as their right hand. This individual has been identified by the key as fully capable of handling some or all aspects of a job. A photographer's main assistant on a shoot. If there are other assistants on set, the 1st assistant helps to manage the team of assistants to achieve the photographer's desires.

ABOVE THE LINE: The creative people, such as producers, directors, actors, and writers.

ACCOUNT EXECUTIVE: A person at an advertising agency or public relations firm who is responsible for management of a brand. On shoots, they are there to insure that the model, photographer and other creatives are achieving the client's goals.

ACCOUNTS PAYABLE DEPARTMENT: The department that handles payment of your invoice.

AGENCY: A firm that handles the booking, billing and business for an artist.

AGENCY FEE: The percentage that an agency charges a client who calls to book you on a job. It is also the percentage that you pay your agency for getting you booked on a job. It is typically 20%. The agency also receives its percentage on your overtime.

AGENCY OF RECORD: The ad agency that is responsible for producing print, point of sale, billboard and commercials for a client.

AGENT: A sales rep for artists. This person works independently or with a larger agency to represent the interests of the artists that are signed to the agency. They field calls and bring in business on behalf of the artists. Their job is to create opportunities, promote the artists and negotiate deals in the best interest of the artist.

ART DIRECTOR: The individual who helps manage the overall aesthetic of a brand, advertisement, or magazine. They are often responsible for selecting the photographer and glam squad for a project. In the entertainment business art directors must consider the requests of the talent, publicists and management.

ARTIST MANAGER: Represents recording artists. Will often request and review the portfolios of freelancers.

ASPIRATIONAL CASTING: If the audience demographic for a product is 60-year-old women, a woman in her late 30's to 40's is cast for the job.

BEAT (MAKEUP): Term used by makeup artists to describe having slayed face.

BEAUTY ADVERTISERS: Brands such as Maybelline, L'Oréal, CoverGirl, Pantene and Joico. Fragrance is part of the beauty category and would include J'Adore, Chanel No5, etc.

BELOW THE LINE: Refers to the pre-, during- and post-production folks on a film who work for day and hourly rates. This includes makeup, hair, wardrobe, nails, grips, lighting, etc.

BID: When a photographer puts together his/her concept, estimate and proposal for shooting a specific job.

BOOK OUT: When artists notify their agency that they are unavailable on a specific day, days, or longer period of time for personal reasons, other jobs, etc.

BOOKER: The person at an agency who manages artist bookings. The liaison between the artist and the client. Helps the artist to manage their schedule, confirms and negotiates rates for jobs, sends out deal memos, etc. (see Agent)

BOOKING: A firm reservation for a job that has been confirmed via email or on paper with a signature from the client.

BTS: Behind-the-scenes (backstage) photos and videos.

BUYOUT: When a client pays for complete use of one or more photographs. Usually organized and negotiated with the photographer and the models agent.

CALL SHEET: Contains the details of the shoot including location, call times, creative team, contact information, schedule of the day and other important details.

CALL TIME: The time you are expected to be set up and ready to goon a shoot. Call times may be different for different members of the creative team.

CAMPAIGN: Short for "advertising campaign." This is a single image or series of images used to promote a specific brand.

CALL TIME: The time talent is required to be at the shoot. A good rule of thumb is to be at least 15 minutes early.

CASTING: A pre-production process for selecting a certain type of model or actor for a particular role or part in a still, video, commercial or motion picture project.

CASTING DIRECTOR: A person hired by a client/photographer to find the ideal model for a shoot.

CLEAN-CLEAN: Indicates that the model should arrive without makeup on or product in their hair.

CLIENT: The person or company who hired you and/or the person or company who is paying you.

COLLECTION: A seasonal production of a fashion line for a particular season.

COMMISSION LETTER: A letter from a magazine indicating that you have been hired to shoot for that publication. This helps you secure your creative team, models and clothing for a shoot.

COMP CARD: A one or two-sided postcard that showcases your work by displaying a selection of images that represent a small sampling of your larger body of work. The card is given away to potential clients to generate business. Also known as a leave behind. It serves as a reminder to a potential client and is kept on file for future reference. It contains contact information that directs clients to your site and social media.

CONCEPT MEETING: A meeting to discuss and plan the outcome opportunities of a project. This includes test photo shoots where multiple people are involved.

CONCEPT BOARDS: A large board full of visual materials (tearsheets, images, etc.) that help to establish a look, a vibe, direction, talent and resources. For example, an art director might point to the board and say, "This is the location I would like to shoot in and these are the models suggest we use."

CONFIRMATION: A familiar voice on the other end of the phone booking you for a job and assuring you that you'll get paid even if the job cancels at the last minute. Not convinced? Me either. I suggest a deal memo that spells out the terms and conditions under which you will work, get paid, travel, etc.

CONTACT SHEET/PROOF: A collection of thumbnail images from a shoot used to analyze and choose final selections for retouching and delivery.

CONTACT: A person with whom you have a business or personal relationship. An individual whose name and telephone number you are privy to. Someone you call on for information or assistance.

CONTENT CREATION: Contributing information to digital media for the purpose of engaging an audience. This includes maintaining and updating your web site, blogging, photography, videography, online commentary, maintaining your social media accounts, editing and distributing the content.

CONTENT CREATOR: Designs visual content. Interacts with their audience regularly and curates content when they have something valuable to add.

CONTINUITY: Keeping track of the physical qualities and specifics of a particular shot or scene for the purpose of duplicating it at a later date. Continuity is important in feature film because movies are often shot out of sequence. Artists use digital cameras to maintain continuity.

CONTRACT/AGREEMENT: A legally binding arrangement between two or more parties.

COSTUME DESIGNER: The person who creates costumes by designing, shopping or facilitating the production of the garments that will be worn on television, in film or on stage (in print, this person is called a fashion stylist).

COUTURE (a.k.a. HAUTE COUTURE): Refers to high-end clothing that is custom or tailor made.

CRAFT SERVICES: Food that is available on set all day.

CREATIVE DIRECTOR: Facilitates the overall creative vision of a specific job or campaign. Often hired by an ad agency to act as liaison between the client and photographer, and help direct the overall goals and aesthetics of a shoot.

CREATIVE TEAM: The people in charge of executing the creative vision of the shoot. This includes the photographer, hair, makeup and wardrobe. It may also include the set designer, manicurist or other artists that contribute to the execution and development of the concept.

CREATIVE: Refers to decision-makers who work in art departments, advertising agencies, magazines, etc. An art director is called a creative. Also refers to materials, imagery or collateral produced in the midst of the creative process.

CREDITS: The lines of type on a tearsheet that include a person's name, what they did (makeup, hair, styling or photography) and who represents them.

CREW: Anyone who is involved in the production of moving or still images on set. This includes everyone from the assistants, to glam squad artists, to the set designer, producers and more.

CROP: The act of adjusting or trimming a photograph or print before printing or publishing.

CYC (a.k.a. INFINITY WALL, a.k.a. CYCLORAMA): A curved wall used as a background to create corner-less joints at the floor and edges. Typically white/painted for green screen.

DEAL MEMO: (see also Confirmation): A binding agreement that confirms the terms and conditions, days, dates and rates under you will work on a project (i.e., rate, overtime, per diem, mileage, etc.).

DECISION-MAKER: A person with the authority to hire talent and authorize payment. Includes photographers, producers, production managers, art directors, fashion editors, directors of creative services, etc.

DIGITAL TECH: The person who manages the communication and the computer, the tethering, and the image display and image backup. Helps the photographer check critical focus and exposure, and is solely responsible for backing up images.

DIRECTOR OF A&R: The person responsible for signing new acts to a record label, matching existing artists up with producers and writers and facilitating the completion of a CD project. Can be hands-on with their artists and sometimes get involved in, hiring photographers and glam squad.

DIRECTOR: The person with the artistic vision who is responsible for all the creative decisions on a production. The director makes the script or treatment a reality.

DOUBLETRUCK: A pair of facing pages in a magazine where the content extends over two pages. Often referred to as a double-page spread.

DUPED: A thing that happens to fashion stylists who listen to the recording artists and celebrities instead of the client who hired them to shop. Also known being hoodwinked, bamboozled and led astray.

EDITORIAL(s): Stories and features produced for a magazine. Covers, features and spreads are considered editorial.

EDITORIAL/STORY(s): A series of images based upon a specific concept that run together as a story in a magazine.

EMBARGO: Images that can only be used exclusively by a publication for a specific period of time. After that, the images may be used elsewhere.

END USER: The decision-maker to whom and for whom you are focusing your marketing efforts and creating an experience.

ENTRY-LEVEL: Job(s) you that provide you with an opportunity for advancement in your field, such as tests, student and independent films.

ESTIMATE: An overview of the likely costs for an entire shoot, including production costs (hair, makeup, wardrobe, location, models) and any other fees, like licensing/usage fees.

EXECUTIVE PRODUCER: The person who is responsible for financing and overseeing a video, commercial, television or film project. The executive producer also hires the producer and is not involved in the day-to-day production.

EXPENDABLES: Items such as facial tissue, sponges, safety pins, Q-Tips, etc. that will be used up during a production.

EXPENSES: Monies provided for items necessary to complete your job in glam. Expenses include things like mileage, wigs, special effects makeup, clothing, props, etc.

EYEBALLS (a.k.a. IMPRESSIONS): The way web advertisers measure the number of times an ad has been viewed.

FASHION EDITOR: The person at a magazine who manages the style and fashion department of that publication, takes what the fashion director has dictated and translates it into the market. Large publications hire full-time fashion editors.

Smaller magazines often hire freelance fashion stylists.

FASHION EDITORIAL: A series of images based upon a theme and published in a magazine or online publication. A fashion editorial usually consists of a minimum of four images, and can be paid or unpaid depending on the publication.

FASHION | WARDROBE STYLIST: The person who acquires and styles the clothing and accessories for a photo shoot, music video or television commercial; keeps track of and inventories the clothing; manages and records the credits; pulls and returns wardrobe for shoots; and makes sure the clothing fits all models correctly.

FAUX: Fake, or similar to.

HOLD | FIRST HOLD: A request to reserve your time for a specific date. If you receive another job offer during that same time period, you should check with the client to see if they want to confirm (officially lock in) that date with a deal memo.

Example: A client might call an agency and say, "Can I get a first hold on Neeko to do hair for Teen Magazine on May 17th?"

FIT MODEL: Used by designers to size and measure clothing. These models must have very consistent measurements that conform to "sample sizes".

FITTING: Attended by models or talent prior to a shoot so that clothing can be fitted, altered and tailored for a shoot.

FITTING: The time a fashion stylist/costumer/costume designer uses to try clothing on models, artists, celebrities, etc.

FLAT RATE: The amount that talent agrees to work for, regardless of the number of hours they will have to work during the day. All-inclusive. Usually inclusive of the talent's fee, overtime (OT), and agency fee.

FREELANCER: Any artist who sells his or her services to employers without a long-term commitment to any one of them, without the benefit of an agency.

GAFFER: The head electrician who manages the execution of the lighting design.

GAFFER'S TAPE: A special type of tape used in theater, photography and film production due to its useful qualities. It is heat-resistant (better for working with lights), and removes easily without damaging surfaces or leaving residue behind. Preferred over duct tape on set.

GATEFOLD: A magazine cover that folds out.

GENRE: A specific class or category. Action films are a genre of movie-making. Lifestyle, beauty and fashion are genre's.

GO-SEE: When a model goes to meet with the creative team, agency, photographer or other potential client in person to be evaluated as suitable for a role.

GOLDEN TIME: An overtime (OT) rate that is triple the normal hourly rate.

GRIP: Lighting and rigging specialists on still, video, commercial and film shoots. They ensure that the camera and lighting equipment are setup and working properly.

GROOMING: Managing hair and makeup for male models and actors. This includes styling and trimming facial hair on a shoot.

GUTTER: The seam or crease that runs down the center of a double-page magazine spread. When shooting landscape images for a magazine, avoid placing a key part of the face into the seam.

HAIR AND MAKEUP READY: If you ask a model to come "hair and makeup ready," they should arrive with their hair and makeup done and ready for the camera.

HAIR STYLIST: Responsible for styling hair on shoot, bringing all necessary hair products, extensions and tools to achieve the desired looks during the shoot.

HOUSE ACCOUNT: Those clients artists wish to retain as their own after signing with an agent. When agreed to by the agency, these accounts are non-commissionable to the agency for the 20%agency fee usually paid by the artist.

I.A.T.S.E.: The International Association of Theatrical Stage Employees. In Los Angeles, LOCAL 706 (Make-Up Artists & Hair Stylists Guild) is composed of makeup artists and hair stylists that work in the production of film, television, network broadcasting television, commercials, legitimate theater and any place of amusement where Local706 has a contract.

KEY: Used to describe the person in charge of the makeup, hair or styling department on a film, television or commercial production.

KILL FEE: (a.k.a. cancellation fee): Serves to assure payment to you in the event that a client cancels at the last minute.

KIT FEE (a.k.a. KIT RENTAL): Ranges from $75 - $150 a day and is given to makeup, hair, wardrobe and manicurists to replenish the supplies (expendables) being used up in their kit.

LEAVE BEHIND: Self-promotional materials such as comp cards that are given out to people you want to engage with, work with and work for. Can be mailed, handed out or emailed. Anything you use to grab someone's attention, such as a postcard, t-shirt, book or other memorable piece.

LIFESTYLE: Images that represent typical American family situations. Mom, dad, kids, dog, apple pie, baseball, going out to dinner together, watching television, washing clothes, attending a picnic, etc.

LIGHT BOX: Used online to gather images together that you want to view as a group or review later.

LINE PRODUCER: The person in charge of hiring glam artists, negotiating rates and signing on the dotted line to authorize the payment of your invoice.

LISTINGS: A written description of who you are, what you do—along with images—and a resume that speaks to your expertise in the field of makeup, hair, wardrobe or nails. Creative directories and productions guides offer free and paid listings. Examples: productionhub.com and models.com.

LOCATION: The site where the job will take place. The words "on location"are often used to describe any place outside a studio.

LOGO: A unique symbol or design used by an individual or business. Used on business cards, promotional pieces, etc.

LOOK BOOK: A series of photos created to show the designer's collection for the current season.

LOR: Letter of Responsibility. When borrowing clothing for a shoot, a publication insures the clothes for you in case of loss or damage. Designers and showrooms are more willing to lend clothing if you have a LOR.

MAKEUP ARTIST: The person responsible for transforming, improving and correcting imperfections in and on the faces of actors, actresses and models on set.

MAKE-UP DESIGNORY: A prominent makeup school with campuses in California and New York.

MASTHEAD: The pages in a magazine that list the names and titles of the decision-makers (beauty, fashion, photography, sittings and bookings editors) who work at the magazine.

MOOD BOARDS: A collection of images that express the overall direction and inspiration for a shoot. Can contain images for the desired type of hair, makeup, wardrobe and even lighting on a shoot. A mood board helps express a photographer's vision of the shoot to the entire team. (see also CONCEPT BOARDS).

MORGUE: A collection of photographs used by makeup artists when sketching or sculpting a character.

MUA: Short for Makeup Artist

N.A.B.E.T: National Alliance of Broadcast Engineers and Technicians. N.A.B.E.T. is a union organization. Like I.A.T.S.E it is composed of makeup artists and hair stylists that work in the production of film, television, network broadcasting television, commercials, legitimate theater, and any place of amusement where N.A.B.E.T has a contract.

NEPOTISM: Favoritism shown to a relative or close friend for an available position on a production.

NEW FACES: Women and men at a modeling agency who are developing their portfolios and are in need of new images. They often need updated pictures.

NOTICE OF CANCELLATION: Clients have from 24-48 hours prior to a job to cancel the assignment without penalty. The penalty ranges from 50 to 100 percent of the original fee, depending on the time notice of cancellation is given.

OFF FIGURE: Preparing and styling clothing for photography without the benefit of a live model. Techniques include: Lay-downs, stacks, hanging, wall and mannequin.

ON FIGURE: Placing and styling clothing on real models.

OUTDOOR: Advertising that is displayed outdoors, including billboards (EX: Times Square), bus benches, interiors and exteriors of buses, taxis and business vehicles, and buildings.

OVERTIME: The span of time which exceeds the regular hours talent agrees to work for a specific amount of money.

PA (Production Assistant): Helps to ensure that the day runs smoothly and coordinates scheduling, locations, permits, food and other elements of the shoot.

PER DIEM: Money paid to an artist to cover the cost of meals and incidental expenses when shooting on location during overnight shoots.

PERIOD PIECE: A movie, television show or photo shoot that is set in a specific period in time. A shoot set in the 1950's should have clothes, props, makeup and hair reflective of that time period. **Example:** The Crown on Netflix.

PERIPHERAL VISION: The ability to see things from every angle. Can be applied both literally and figuratively.

PERKS: hotel + first class flight + parking + car service

PHOTO EDITOR: The person at a magazine who hires photographers and decides which photographs will be used in stories.

PIXEL: A grid of small squares that come together to form a picture. Used in retouching photographs.

PORT (a.k.a. PORTFOLIO, a.k.a. BOOK): A collection of images and tearsheets that are uploaded onto a website to showcase your work toa potential client who can book you on jobs. You may have more than one portfolio to appeal to different types of clients. This is often the case when an artist wants to separate commercial work (ad campaigns, catalogs, etc.) from bridal and special events work.

POST-PRODUCTION: The span of time after the shooting of a production, when the fashion stylist, makeup artist, hair stylist, costume designers, prop people, etc. turn in their receipts, return unused items to stores and complete and send in their invoices.

PREP: Work days used to prepare for and shop prior to the actual shoot. Prep days are usually billed at one half of an artist's day rate all the way up to their full day rate.

PRET-A-PORTE: Ready-to-Wear.

PRINT: Includes but is not limited to magazines, advertising layouts, CD covers, catalogues, book covers, etc. For example, you might hear someone say, "I just got a great print assignment". They could mean a CD cover, a job with a magazine, an advertising campaign or a Victoria's Secret catalogue.

PRODUCER: The person who is typically responsible for hiring the crew on a video, commercial, television or film project. Often called the Line Producer.

PRODUCTION ASSISTANT: (see PA)

PRODUCTION COORDINATOR: Maintains contact with and gives direction (per the producer) to the crew on a video, commercial, television or film project.

PRODUCTION MANAGER: Manages all aspects and all departments on a production.

PROP: An item such as a chair, candlestick, or book that becomes part of the shot on a still photograph, video, commercial, television or film production.

PROPOSAL: A plan, estimate or suggestion presented for approval.

PROSPECT: A potential client.

PUBLICIST: Generates media coverage for clients in order to promote them to the public through media placements in newspapers, magazines, on television, radio, the internet, etc. Publicists often work hand-in-hand with the talent (celebrities and recording artists) to assist them in making decisions about who to use for photo sessions, videos, live appearances, etc.

PULL LETTER: A letter from a magazine, written on behalf of a fashion or wardrobe stylist, to encourage designers and showrooms to lend them clothing for editorial (magazine) shoots.

PULL: A word used by fashion stylists and costume designers to describe clothing, accessories, shoes and props taken from one or more stores.

PURCHASE ORDER NUMBER (PO#): A number that authorizes payment and insures that you will be paid what was agreed upon in a timely fashion once the job is completed and your invoice is submitted. Proof that a job assignment is legitimate.

PYP: The brand name of Crystal Wright's 4-day Packaging Your Portfolio: Marketing Yourself as a Freelance Makeup Artist, Hair Stylist, Fashion Stylist or Manicurist program.

RATE: The agreed-upon amount that an artist is being paid on a specific project.

READY-TO-WEAR: This is the opposite of couture. Off the rack. Not custom-made or bespoke.

REEL: A compilation of your work that has been set to music and loaded up on your website for distribution and viewing by decision-makers or burned to DVD and mailed out.

REP (a.k.a. Agent): Someone who solicits and secures work for talent at an agency or independently for a commission.

RESTOCKING FEE: An amount charged to fashion and wardrobe stylists, costumers and costume designers by department and specialty stores for the privilege of removing clothing from the store on approval for an agreed-upon period of time (24 hours). This practice gives the stylist an opportunity to take the clothing out for fittings and review by the client.

RETOUCHER: Someone who can remove flaws or enhance a person's features in a photograph.

RETURNS: Prop and clothing items that are returned to stores by a stylist or their assistant at the completion of production.

REVIEW: The process of having your portfolio looked at by art directors, artist managers, photographers and/or designers for specific jobs or critique.

RIGHT OF FIRST PUBLICATION: When your work is accepted to be published by a magazine or online publication, they reserve the right to be the first to share these images online or in print. In other words, do not share your images from these shoots on social media, your website or any other outlet until AFTER they have been published.

RUNWAY: A live show used by designers to present their collections to fashion directors and editors and the public.

SAMPLE: A designer creates a one-off item of clothing for models to wear on the runway, for presentations or for use in fashion shoots.

SAMPLE SIZE: A single "standard" size that designers use to create their pieces. A standard clothing size (model sample size), that fits most runway and editorial models.

SEAMLESS (a.k.a. SEAMLESS PAPER, a.k.a. SEAMLESS BACKGROUND): Paper backgrounds used in photo and video shoots to create a smooth background without a seam. Available in a wide range of colors.

SECOND HOLD: A second hold is a reservation of your time for an upcoming job when you are already on hold for another job. The client is in effect saying, "If the first client who has you on hold cancels, I want you!"

SHOOT CHECKLIST: A check list of prep, shoot and post activities for a photo shoot.

SHOOT DAY: The day(s) the action takes place.

SHOT: The best images chosen from a photo session.

SHOWROOM: Represents different designers who lend their clothes to stylists for publication. Stylists develop relationships with showrooms to facilitate the use of clothing for shoots.

SIGNATORY COSTUME HOUSE: A costume house that is affiliated with the union.

SPEC JOB: A job that a photographer or director takes on (without pay or for very minimal pay) in an effort to further their career by building their book or reel.

SPEC SHOOT: Also known as "shooting on spec"; everyone shoots for free in hopes of selling or publishing the images or grabbing the attention of a brand to hire you to create imagery for their company or magazine.

STILL LIFE PHOTOGRAPHY: Photography of inanimate objects. Often referred to as Product photography.

STORY BOARD: A series of illustrations or images displayed for the purpose of visualizing a concept or project.

STUDIO SERVICES: The department in a clothing stores that makes clothing available to stylists for photo shoots, television and film projects.

STUDIO SERVICES ACCOUNT: A business or corporate credit account at a clothing store that allows fashion stylists, costumers, wardrobe stylists and costume designers to pull clothing for use in print and moving media projects.

STUDIO: Refers to a photography studio. Can be rented. A place where still photography and moving shoots take place.

STYLIST: The person in charge of managing and styling the wardrobe on a shoot. A shoot stylist may also be in charge of managing the overall direction of the hair and makeup, though not actually doing the hair and makeup.

SWIPE: An image gallery that allows you to present and display web content, images, videos in an eye-catching way that tells a story. (Instagram/Pinterest)

TEARSHEET (a.k.a. TEARS): An editorial or advertisement in a publication that you worked on. Tearsheets can be physical (print) or digital (online). To get imagery for their portfolios, artists often work in exchange for credits and "tearsheets". Tearsheets can be sent to an artist in the form of a PDF file. Any job that results in work being published in a magazine, on a billboard, box or a book cover is considered a tearsheet. Even a TV commercial, show or video is your tearsheet. Examples include magazine or advertising pages CD covers, mobiles, point of sale and point of purchase displays, inserts, etc.

TESTING: Testing is collaboration between a team of creatives such as photographer, makeup artist, hair stylist, fashion stylist, manicurist and a model who all come together with a story idea and the objective of creating images that they can each individually add to their online portfolios to share with other creative professionals to: 1) Secure more and better testing opportunities, and 2) paid work assignments.

TETHER: Your images are automatically displayed on a monitor or screen during the shoot so that the client can view the images in real-time.

TFP (a.k.a. Trade for Photos): Artists receive digital images for their portfolios instead of monetary compensation. There is no pay; it is a trade for services and portfolio building. Images are distributed by file transfer programs such as Dropbox.

TRAVEL TIME/DAY: The time and distance between point "A" and point "B". The time it takes to get from one location to another.

TREATMENT: A loosely written story line or concept used to pitch an idea for a music video.

TYPEFACE (FONT): A style of type. Can be used to create a logo.

UNION: A labor organization that sets standard minimum rates for pay, work conditions and benefits for its members.

USAGE FEES: The fee a photographer charges a client to use one or more images for a period of time. The fee includes considerations of where the image is used (online, magazine, billboard), geography (locally, nationally, internationally) and length of time the image will be used (months, years, buyout).

VMA's: Video Music Awards.

WARDROBE CREDIT SHEET: A descriptive sheet with details of the clothing designers, clothing items, accessories and shoes used on a shoot.

WARDROBE STYLIST: (see FASHION STYLIST)

WARDROBE/MAKEUP/HAIR CREDITS: A list of the brands, products, and tools used in the production of a shoot.

WRAP: (see RETURNS)

WRAP TIME: The projected time that you will need to complete the shoot.

NOTES

VISIT

www.crystalwrightliveacademies.com/p/ careerguideexclusives:

- Sign up for our mailing list
- Receive notices of updates to this book and events Crystal is hosting
- Link to and download FREE resources
- Subscribe to Crystal's Freelance Friendly Tip Advisor
- Join the exclusive PYP freelance artist community
- Register for PYP 2018 and beyond

www.YouTube.com/CrystalWrightLive to:

- Get more help with your business through Crystal's awesome videos

www.GigSalad.com/crystal_wright_live to:

- Book Crystal for your next live or online event

www.WinNowMentorshipProgram.com to:

- Register for Crystal's 10-Week Online Mentorship Program

GET IN TOUCH

To learn about Crystal's courses, consulting and training by:

- Emailing Assistant2Crystal@CrystalWrightLive.com
- Calling the office at (323) 299-0500

CONNECT

To become part of the conversation online at:

- crystal.wright
- CrystalAWright
- crystalwrightlive